SOCIOLOGY
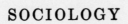

THE MACMILLAN COMPANY
NEW YORK · BOSTON · CHICAGO · DALLAS
ATLANTA · SAN FRANCISCO

MACMILLAN & CO., LIMITED
LONDON · BOMBAY · CALCUTTA
MELBOURNE

THE MACMILLAN COMPANY
OF CANADA, LIMITED
TORONTO

SOCIOLOGY

BY

EMORY S. BOGARDUS

Professor of Sociology
University of Southern California

THE MACMILLAN COMPANY

NEW YORK   1935

Dedicated to
the memory of my Father and Mother
Henry B. and Eliza M. Bogardus

PREFACE

In preparing this new book liberal use has been made of the material in the five editions appearing under the title of *Introduction to Sociology* which have preceded the publication of this work. The first edition appeared in 1913 and the basic theme has been carried over into the present volume.

The volume centers attention on sociology as a study of social groups and particularly of the groups of which students themselves are members. In this way the reader will find sociology to be not an arm-chair philosophy or a subject far above his head but a science for daily application. He learns why and how persons act differently under similar circumstances and why and how they act alike under dissimilar conditions. In the pages of this book he catches a glimpse of the predictive nature of sociology.

The volume begins with the daily experiences of students and moves logically to a consideration of the basic processes of group behavior. It brings the findings of latest scientific research in sociology into language designed to be inviting to the beginning student. It runs the gamut from the concrete and actual experiences of everyday life to the latest and most fundamental concepts concerning human relations.

EMORY S. BOGARDUS

LOS ANGELES, CALIF.
March, 1934

CONTENTS

PART ONE
GROUP APPROACHES

CHAPTER I

SOCIAL GROUPS

Sociology is the study of social groups. Every person begins the day as a participating member of a social group, usually, of the family group. Ordinarily he renews this relationship at the evening meal. Each member comes home and reports his day's contacts at the common evening meal. An exchange of experiences occurs and all who take part enjoy new glimpses of life.

In the course of a day a college student makes contacts in several different social groups. In fact, he spends his day largely in going from one group to another. To the extent that he fills the day with contacts in different groups interested in different constructive activities and values does he find life stimulating and does his personality acquire breadth and depth.

A good starting point for the beginning student of sociology is to think of the various human groups of which he is a member, of how he became a member of each, of the nature of the personal contacts that he enjoys or dislikes in each, of the attitudes of life that his associates in each group hold, of the differences in the social organization and operation of these groups, and of some of the main problems each group is facing. He may also consider the different ways by which each of his groups is molding his personality.

The student will engage in an illuminating exercise if he will prepare a chart of the different social groups in which he participates to some degree in the course of each day of a representative week. A normal day has four major subdivisions: (1) sleep and rest, (2) bathing, dressing, eating, (3) individual activity, and (4) group participation. If the latter item is analyzed in terms of a college student's daily experiences it will be found to involve a variety of groups, such as: (1) family group,

3

(2) class groups (recitation and lecture), (3) social groups (formal fraternal organization, informal friendship groups), (4) literary groups, (5) athletic, recreational, amusement groups, (6) work groups (if the student is paying his own way in part or wholly), and (7) religious groups. If the student would go further he might keep a record of his group participation in time units (minutes or hours). By dividing the time spent in a week in a given group by the total amount that he spends in all groups in the given week he will discover what percentage of his time he gives to each of his groups.[1] In a preliminary study of groups, one will raise a number of questions: What is a group? What is a social group? What are the different types of social groups? What is the nature of group activity? How do groups influence their members, and non-members? How do groups affect personality?

TYPES OF GROUPS

A *group* is any number of units of anything in close proximity to each other. A *social group* is any number of living beings in interaction. A number of houses in the same city block, derricks in an oil field, chimneys on an apartment house, illustrate groups. A forest is a group of trees, but a number of human beings in interaction constitutes a social group.

Social groups vary in *size*. The smallest include only two persons, such as a wedded couple, or two chums. The largest social group would be the whole human race with numbers approximating two thousand million persons, providing each could be brought into an awareness of all the others. However, most of us function most of the time in small social groups. Even an active college fraternity group of fifty members tends to break up into smaller groups as far as genuine friendships go. Most of us are consciously aware of only a small proportion of the persons in our city or even in our neighborhood, not to mention the state, nation, or the world.

---

[1] These percentages may be thought of in terms of *group quotients*. See the writer's *Fundamentals of Social Psychology* (The Century Company, New York, 1931), pp. 305, 306.

Social groups vary in *time-length*. Some are temporary, even fleeting, as in the case of the casual conversational group. Some last only a few months, as a college class in sociology. Other groups are relatively permanent, such as a family or a university or a nation. In these instances it is the generalized group that possesses permanency, for individual members come and go.

Social groups may be *genetic* or *congregate*.[1] The genetic group is the one into which a person is born; the congregate group is the one which a person joins by chance or invitation or force. A person is born into his family group and his racial group, and in a real sense can never get out of either. He may repudiate both but he is still a blood-relationship member of both. Of course one's family or race may be repudiated by adopting the culture patterns of an entirely different family or race. From all other groups into which he is born, such as an economic class, a city, or a nation, he may escape.

The congregate group is the one which a person moves into, or joins, or is sent into. A person may move from one city to another; he may accept membership in a church or a fraternal group; or he may be sent to jail. He may even organize and originate a congregate group and invite other persons into it.

In relation to other groups a group may be *unsocial, pseudo-social, anti-social,* or *pro-social*.[2] An unsocial group is one that lives to itself alone, such as an isolated village or even a private bridge club. A pseudo-social group is one that takes part in the larger group life, but for the sake of its own livelihood. Instead of standing on its own merits it lives off of the larger community. Many organizations, business and social, are social parasites. The anti-social group acts against the welfare of society. A group of "gangsters" of the underworld or of racketeers of the "upper" world illustrate the type. The pro-social group is actively engaged in building up the larger society of which it is a part. It is constructive; it creates human values.

[1] See F. H. Giddings, *Principles of Sociology* (The Macmillan Company, New York, 1896), pp. 89ff.

[2] Modification of analyses by Georg Hansen (*Die drei Bevölkerungsstufen*, Munich, 1889), and F. H. Giddings *Principles of Sociology*, pp. 124ff.

There are degrees of pro-social activity, with the highest degree worthy to bear the label of socialized. A socialized group would be one acting on the basis of rational sympathy in behalf of the common welfare.

Groups may be either *primary* or *secondary*.[1] Primary groups are those which exert the most direct and often lasting influence upon the origin and growth of a person's attitudes and ideals of life. Cooley called them "face-to-face groups," because the members live in the physical presence of each other. As a result of this physical presence of others, we are as a rule more definitely influenced by them than if they were miles away. We can see their immediate personal responses to our acts and thus we are likely to be very suggestible. The family group, the play group, and usually the school group, the work group, and the neighborhood group are of the primary order. It is in the family, play, and school groups that one makes most of his significant contacts in the early years of life.

A primary group may have three characteristics: (1) face-to-face association, (2) precedence in point of time over the influence of other groups, and (3) a "we" feeling.[2] It has been pointed out, however, that a face-to-face group does not always exert a primary influence over its members.[3] Persons living in the same household, for example, do not necessarily cast a magic spell over each other. Moreover, some of our most primary or fundamental influences come upon us from unseen sources, and not all are limited to the early years of family and play experiences. However, these cases are doubtless in the minority, and the main contention that face-to-face relationships are of primary importance stands. We can all testify how much easier it is to say "no" by letter than face to face, and how much greater is the joy accompanying personal achieve-

---

[1] It was Charles H. Cooley who was the first to develop the importance of primary groups. See his *Social Organization* (Charles Scribner's Sons, New York, 1909), Ch. II, "Primary Groups."

[2] See Ellsworth Faris, "The Primary Group: Essence and Accident," *American Journal of Sociology*, XXXVIII: 41–50.

[3] *Ibid.*, p. 42.

ment when we can tell someone face to face rather than write about it in a letter.

The main criterion of a primary group is its generation of a "we feeling." [1] It is this "we feeling," functional and emotional, which puts us in the "in group" and separates us from the "out group." [2] The important thing to keep in mind is that if we share a "we feeling" with a number of persons we are very responsive to the attitudes and actions of those persons.

It is startling but true that "human nature may be said to be created in primary group relations." [3]

Groups which exert no primary influence upon a person are secondary to him. He is aware of them and functions in them in a general way. He takes cognizance of them but does feel that his welfare is intimately tied up with them. As a rule they do not affect his attitudes or his repertoire of values except by external coercion. Such groups are secondary, as far as directly influencing his behavior is concerned.

Groups are either *disjunctive* or *overlapping*. A man in college may belong to only one social fraternity at a time, but later he may become a member of several of the larger fraternal brotherhoods of the country. He may be a citizen of only one national group at a time but he may be a member of several language groups simultaneously. He may have but one wife at a given time, but be a member of several business firms simultaneously.

GROUP PRIORITY

Group priority means that groups exist prior to the individual. It also signifies that groups are well organized with customs and traditions behind them, while the individual when he first contacts most groups is helpless and unorganized. [4] When an individual is born into a family, a race, and a nation he is an in-

[1] See E. A. Ross' discussion of the "we feeling" in his *Principles of Sociology* (The Century Company, New York, 1920), pp. 106–107.

[2] To use terms given extensive emphasis by William G. Sumner in his *Folkways* (Ginn and Company, Boston, 1907).

[3] Faris, *op. cit.*, p. 46.

[4] This point was first developed by the writer as "The Principle of Group Priority," *Journal of Applied Sociology*, VII: 84–87 (1922).

choate mass of impulses, reflexes, and of potentially responsive protoplasm. He is physically, psychically, and socially helpless. Without aid he could not survive more than a few days. Not being able to creep or walk, to talk, or to care for himself, he is a classic illustration of helplessness. As an individual organism, however, he is several months old at birth, but when considered as a prenatal being his helplessness reaches the lowest thinkable level.

On the other hand let us look at the group environment into which a child is brought at birth. For example, there is his parental group with its established language, its developed beliefs and fixed rules of conduct, its mores, its religious traditions. These all-powerful parental forces are made up out of community, national, racial, and cultural heritages millenia old. They are permeated by deep-seated beliefs and interpretations of life that have been passed on from generation to generation and that possess all the force of the ages. Compare the hoary age and the tremendous power of these group forces with the weak naïveté of the new-born babe. Such is the principle of *group priority*.

Then, when we consider the individual as a human organism we find him to be largely a product of *group survival*. Parents, grandparents, great grandparents, generation before generation, were reared in groups, lived only as members of groups, and were subject to the laws of group control and survival. An infant could have no hereditary equipment and hence no life, had there not been group priority for one, five, twenty-five generations before his own life began.

Assuming that an infant could by some means or other succeed in living outside of groups, how far would he develop mentally, socially, and personally, under non-group conditions? Suppose that from birth he could live as it is alleged Caspar Hauser lived, namely, by himself, with food being left for him by someone whom he never saw and with whom he did not communicate in any way.[1] What would this individual, growing up remote

[1] See Maurice H. Small, "On Some Psychical Relations of Society and Solitude," *Pedagogical Seminary*, VII: 32–36.

from social group life, resemble at the age of twenty or forty years? What language would he speak, if any? Would he have learned to cook food? What kind of a house, if any, would he build? If he had associated only with four-footed animals, would he also have run about on all fours? What kind of thoughts would he think? About what, for instance?

A partial answer to these questions is found in the studies of individuals reared in isolation. Of Caspar Hauser it is reported that when he was brought at the age of sixteen years into human company, he paid little heed to what went on about him and recognized no social customs, that he burned his hand in the first fire that he saw, that he had no fear of being struck with a sword, but that the sound of a drum threw him into convulsive fear. He reacted to pictures and statuary as though they were alive, and was delighted by whistles and bright objects. Experts pronounced him idle, stupid, and vain; and post-mortem examination revealed a small, undeveloped, but otherwise normal brain. In other words, outside of group life, the individual organism atrophies.

Take away the medium of group transmission, and the infant of today would have to begin life without any of the equipment represented by civilization—without a modern language, without any literature or history, without any of the inventions of the past thousands of years. He would have to meet life in a far more simple, cruder way than the Neanderthal man began. Without the priority expressed in the group transmission of civilization, the modern infant would be defenseless against animal life, even insect life. Without the advantages of group transmission of civilized defenses, he would not have much of a chance against the engulfing primitive conditions that would obtain.

The ability which the human organism possesses of responding to social stimuli is another evidence of group priority. The child is built to respond to stimuli of all types that come from other social beings. As he grows older, he becomes frantic, insane, if he believes that he is cut off never again to see any other human being.

Darwin was one of the first thinkers to point out the omni-present tendency of higher organisms to respond to social stim-uli and thus to support the principle that the group nature of man is as vital as the self-centered nature. The evidence has accumulated to the effect that animals which respond to group stimuli have an advantage over those who roam alone. Thus, the law of the survival of the fittest is often the law of the survival of the social. If out of group origins the human race has emerged the principle of group priority is sustained.

GROUP-MADE PERSONALITY

Personality is the integrated totality of an individual's re-actions to his social groups. *Individuality* is comprised of the distinguishing reactions. *Sociality* includes one's reactions which identify him with other persons. Thus personality is composed of individuality plus sociality.

Since personality emerges from within groups, it possesses a group coloration. It is composed of group selves. It may be a hilarious self in a play group; a sober self in a Sunday morn-ing church group; a scheming self in a business group.

Personality presents different fronts as social situations change, and expresses itself in a variety of *situation selves*.[1] The situation self is the personality being expressed in a given social situation. Within a given social group, such as a college group, personality may vary with the changes hour by hour in the social situations.

Group life is composed of one significant social situation after another. When analyzed college life becomes a series of social situations. Every social group stages a series of situations pecul-iar to itself daily. A person's daily life, therefore, consists in moving from one social situation to another not only within a particular group but also within a half dozen or a dozen or more different groups. To chart the path of one's daily movement from social situation to social situation on a time chart is both fascinating and illuminating.

---

[1] This term has been suggested by Earle E. Eubank, *Concepts in Sociology* (D. C. Heath and Company, Boston, 1932), pp. 106–10.

A social situation involves a number of persons meeting or attempting to meet a want or need. As soon as the want or need is met, the temporary grouping is dissolved and the members soon regroup themselves in other situations. A social situation usually involves some kind of a conflict. When the conflict is met in one way or another, the situation is dissolved. The phrase, *defining a situation*, refers to the way that any person in the situation interprets and reacts to the conflict. Sociology is the study of the social situations that arise in groups.[1]

Man is overwhelmingly attuned to catch group stimuli. He quickly develops habitual responses known as gregariousness, parental activities, play attitudes, loyalty, and patriotism. Only as he sets himself off from other individuals does he become aware of a self and does he develop self-consciousness.

He who proclaims himself "self-made," is naïvely taking a narrow and egocentric view. He is neglecting the group fact which shows that after all he is a mere pigmy, snatching at perhaps a few material trifles on the vast billowing waves of civilization. He is far more *group-made* than self-made, having been given the advantages of language, literatures, inventions, cultures, that have taken ages to make and that have been preserved and transmitted through group continuity. He is parental-group made, play-group made, school-group made, culture-group made, far more than self-made. This realization need not discourage him but spur him on to be more "of an integer and less of a cipher," "more of an initiator and less of a parrot," "more of a voice and less of an echo," more of a group and social benefactor and less of an individual seeker after material and self-centered power.

A person cannot be understood, and he cannot even understand himself unless group life first be fathomed and interpreted. All the groups of which a person is a member are continually bombarding him with a never-ending variety of

[1] It was Thomas and Znaniecki who first called attention to the importance of social situations and to the significance of the ways in which a social situation is defined by the participants. See Thomas and Znaniecki, *The Polish Peasant in Europe and America* (Alfred A. Knopf, New York, 1927), I: 68ff.

stimuli, sometimes in quiet, indirect, and unsuspected ways, and then again, in brazen fashion; sometimes they operate helpfully, and again with relentless fury.

Sometimes group life is nothing but a dull stagnation; group stimulation is at the zero mark. At another time group life may be throbbing with energy and stimuli. Under the latter conditions a normal growing youth is stimulated beyond measure—perhaps to lead in athletics, in debating, in scholarship, in social life. In a business group young men are sometimes stimulated to take great financial risks. In an Alpine club, the members are constrained to undertake new and difficult mountain-climbing feats. In an athletic club group, the members grow desirous to become champion boxers; in a church group, to alleviate human suffering and to render service to mankind. At every step personality is being made, unmade, or remade by group stimuli.

To study a social group is to see persons emerging here and there and taking charge of group activities. Group priority is paralleled therefore by *personality emergence* and *leadership*.

Sometimes personality emergence is sudden and short-lived. When a class of college freshmen is organized there may be a meteoric rise of certain former high school luminaries, but such dominance may be little more than a temporary flash. Again, there will be other persons who will work quietly but in outstanding ways. You will hear about them long before you see them. Their emergence will be slow, sure, and well grounded. Ultimately they will come into positions of leadership.

When the individual is recognized as somebody in his groups he acquires standing or *status* and becomes a person.[1] It is by this group-conferred status that the group makes or mars persons. One's status is continually shifting up and down. Moreover it is rarely the same in two different social groups. A person will fight to maintain or to increase his status and hence he is especially subject to group influence.

[1] Park and Burgess, *Introduction to the Science of Sociology* (University of Chicago Press, 1921), p. 55.

The individual is not made of putty. He is not a mere blank sheet to be written upon. He is not a nobody. He has self-centered, anarchistic ways as well as a socially-centered nature. Although he accepts and responds to many group stimuli he objects to some. The acceptances are largely traceable to countless indirect stimuli; the objections are usually due to direct demands upon him. By their nature the countless acceptances receive little attention, while a few objections command much attention. Thus, objections are often falsely credited with outnumbering the acceptances.

An individual cannot respond to all social stimuli. There are too many. If a person did so respond, he would "blow up" or "break down." He must discriminate. Moreover it is not his nature to accept the first stimuli only. He objects here and there to demands upon him, reserving some favorable responses for possible later stimuli. It is in this discriminating process and this objecting process that he develops a distinctive personality, or an *individuality*, that he becomes a "somebody," that his judgments become sought after, that he rises to leadership.

As a result of the give-and-take processes that occur between a group and its individual members, between groups, between persons in the same group, and between persons in different groups, personality expands or shrinks, and its quality becomes richer or poorer. Out of intersocial stimulation personality and group life alike grow wholesome or decay. Not only does the group influence its personal units, but the latter remake groups.

As biological inheritance varies, the rôle of the person in the group shifts. A strong or weak biological strain makes a difference. A Mozart or a Mendelssohn play special rôles in group life, while an imbecile counts for little. The percentages of both the highly talented and the mentally deficient are low, while the great mass of a given population possess potential ability sufficient to guarantee to each person a useful and honored career in group life. After all it is this rank and file that furnishes the backbone of all group activities.

GROUP SOCIOLOGY

Sociology as a study of personal interaction within social groups is an old subject, but scientific methods in sociology have developed only within recent years. Therefore, sociology as a scientific study is relatively new in college curricula. It has had to fight its way up for recognition, or status, from the bottom against already overcrowded curricula. Its growth, however, has been rapid. The belief is now becoming widespread that no person is well educated or wholly cultured who is unversed in a knowledge of social processes. Any person who would be well educated must know the operation of group life, and understand the processes by which group members develop socialized personalities.

Sociology is not a propagandist study. Its aim is to discover social facts, or better still, the meanings of social facts in terms of human attitudes. It searches everywhere for all the important social data. It presents and interprets these materials to the student in as unbiased a manner as possible. It strives to be inductive and scientific. It is a scientific study of human groups as exhibited in social situations, in personal attitudes and group values, in group institutions and problems. Sociology deals with the most practical and concrete phases of life, and at the same time with the broadest and deepest social processes.

A person usually finds that the normal result of studying sociology is a more human point of view, an increasing dislike for narrow, prejudiced attitudes, and some advance in the socialization of behavior. Sociology makes possible the building of a just, harmonious, and coöperative society.

The student of sociology can never get outside his laboratory. While at work or play, or while performing in social situations, he is experimenting in his laboratory. By blundering along with his eyes set chiefly on his own gain, he lives and dies, his praises are unheralded or else are sung in a questionable way, without returning to society the talents which he developed through intersocial stimulation. By building up socialized behavior patterns he may serve his fellows helpfully and in so doing develop into a full-orbed personality of the first magnitude in the societary firmament.

Sociology is the study of the social processes revealed in the continuity of social situations. Within social situations are tremendous forces at work, represented by human needs, wants,[1] urges, wishes, desires, instinctive and acquired tendencies. These urges (innate) and attitudes (acquired) combined seem to operate in accordance with deep-seated processes. A *process* may be represented by any connected series of events; and a *social process*, by a connected series of human events. Within group life individuals are subject to social processes and develop complicated personalities. The processes by which personalities are developed within group circles constitute the most advanced subject matter of sociology. In its deepest sense sociology is the study of the social processes of group life.

PROBLEMS

1. What is the purpose of problems for discussion such as these?
2. Why do many students "sit clam-like" in class?
3. To how many social groups do you at present belong?
4. In how many of these groups did you become a member by choice?
5. What is there about any one of your social groups that you like most?
6. What do you dislike most about any of the social groups to which you belong?
7. Are you a member of any group from which you would like to withdraw?
8. What choices do you make that are more important than choosing persons with whom to associate?
9. In what ways are you group-made?
10. In what ways self-made?
11. Can you mention any idea or object that you have originated?
12. Why have you begun the study of sociology?
13. Will this study make you a more successful individual?
14. Why is there a rapidly growing interest in sociology?
15. What is sociology?

---

[1] A need is what a person requires for his sustenance or development; a want is what he thinks that he needs.

READINGS

BEACH, W. G., *An Introduction to Sociology and Social Problems* (Houghton Mifflin Company, Boston, 1925).

BUSHEE, F. A., *Principles of Sociology* (Henry Holt and Company, New York, 1923).

CASE, CLARENCE M., *Outlines of Introductory Sociology* (Harcourt, Brace and Company, New York, 1924).

COOLEY, C. H., *Human Nature and the Social Order* (Charles Scribner's Sons, New York, 1922).

DAVIS, JEROME, and H. E. BARNES, *Introduction to Sociology* (D. C. Heath and Company, Boston, 1927).

GILLIN, J. L., and F. W. BLACKMAR, *Outlines of Sociology* (The Macmillan Company, New York, 1930).

GROVES, ERNEST R., *An Introduction to Sociology* (Longmans, Green and Company, New York, 1932).

HANKINS, F. H., *An Introduction to the Study of Society* (The Macmillan Company, New York, 1928).

HART, HORNELL, *The Science of Human Relations* (Henry Holt and Company, New York, 1927).

HAYES, EDWARD C., *Sociology* (D. Appleton and Company, New York, 1930).

HILLER, E. T., *Principles of Sociology* (Harper and Brothers, New York, 1933).

LUMLEY, FREDERICK E., *Principles of Sociology* (McGraw-Hill Book Company, Inc., New York, 1928).

MacIVER, R. M., *Society* (Ray Long and Richard R. Smith, Inc., New York, 1931).

ODUM, HOWARD W., *Man's Quest for Social Guidance* (Henry Holt and Company, New York, 1927).

OSBORN, L. D., and M. H. NEUMEYER, *Community and Society* (American Book Company, New York, 1933).

PARK, R. E., and E. W. BURGESS, *Introduction to the Science of Sociology* (University of Chicago Press, 1921).

REINHARDT, J. M., and G. R. DAVIES, *Principles and Methods of Sociology* (Prentice-Hall, Inc., New York, 1932).

ROSS, EDWARD A., *Principles of Sociology* (The Century Company, New York, 1930).

WALLIS, WILSON D., *An Introduction to Sociology* (Alfred A. Knopf, New York, 1927).

CHAPTER II

ECOLOGICAL APPROACH

Human ecology may be explained as the study of the nature and effect of the spatial relationships of people. These spatial relationships vary from sparse to dense. Human history may be written in terms of the changing spatial relationships of persons and of the ways in which these changes have affected group life.

The location and development of human groups have been conditioned by natural factors such as hills and mountains; and by physical resources, such as soil fertility, rivers, oceans, heat, cold, and rainfall. They have been conditioned by artificial factors such as highways, boulevards, means of transportation, railroad yards, industrial districts, parks. Certain areas, whether natural or artificial, have developed distinctive characteristics which in turn have separated people widely or brought them together. Moreover, studies of spatial relationships and of their influences have revealed significant uniformities or laws.

Spatial relationships help to determine a person's attitudes, values, and his status. Sparseness permits the growth of independent attitudes, self-reliance, and hinders coöperative activities. Notice how slowly the American farmer has responded to large-scale organization. Likewise the Russian rural peasant takes to collective farming with great reluctance.

On the other hand spatial nearness, or density, forces a certain amount of coöperative action and invites organization. It makes possible powerful corporations, large-scale enterprises, and stimulates some persons to take advantage of the masses. Spatial nearness brings opposite interests into fierce conflicts as well as stimulates socialized tendencies.

17

Location and position are key-words to ecology. Position
changes while location generally remains stationary. Position
is the relation of one location to another. "Changing spatial
distance, as measured by time and cost, is perhaps the most
important factor in human affairs today." [1] Spatial distance
may be measured not only in miles or kilometers but also in
the time and the cost involved in moving economic goods from
one location to another. [2]

Before proceeding further into the strictly ecological aspects
of group life, we may consider some of the wider environmental
approaches to ecology. There is a certain balance between climate and soil on one hand, and population and social development on the other. While this balance varies according to inventions and to culture development there are limits beyond
which man cannot go.

> Man and the wider environment, indeed, have evolved together
> through mutual influences. Land, water, tree, and man are by no
> means separate and independent factors, for by reciprocal influence
> they form a natural equilibrium, parts of which can be understood
> only in terms of the other. Such an understanding of regional inter-
> relation helps us better to delineate social causation. . . . [3]

A person lives in an interesting place in the universe. He is
in direct contact with six spheres. The first is the lithosphere
or the rock layer that encloses the earth. The second is the
hydosphere that covers three-fourths of the lithosphere. The
third is the atmosphere which covers the lithosphere and
the hydosphere to a height of several miles. The fourth is the
stratosphere or the top layer of the atmosphere which man only
in recent years has penetrated through the use of specially con-
structed balloons. The fifth is the biosphere or the world of
life that thrives on the lithosphere and in the hydosphere and

---

[1] Roderick D. McKenzie, "Spatial Distance," *Sociology and Social Research*,
XIII: 536.

[2] Under present facilities of transport a unit of land space is about one-half
the time distance but twelve times the cost distance of a unit of water space.
(McKenzie, *op. cit.*, p. 537.)

[3] Radhakamal Mukerjee, "The Broken Balance of Man and Region," *Sociology and Social Research*, XVII: 405 (May–June, 1933).

atmosphere. The sixth is the homosphere or the world of persons, characterized by culture and living in contact with all the other spheres.[1]

The earth as the home of human groups underwent "a long series of changes" before man appeared thereon. After the advent of man there came the long struggle between various species of animal life in prehistoric epochs. These contests finally ended in human survival, although the outcome was dubious for a long time, because human groups were small, scattered, and without instruments for defense or tools for production. Behind all the struggles, however, was a "world embracing process by which the once uninhabitable globe has come to be man's well-appointed home."[2]

In the first three sections that follow the major attention will be given to physical and geographic backgrounds of the ecological approach in sociology. In the fourth section selected ecological principles underlying group life will be presented.

NATURAL AREAS

A *natural area* is a region where people can associate freely, unhampered by any special physical or artificial factors. A mountain valley is often a natural area. A city district of several blocks located between main streets on four sides is another type of natural area.

Early human groups developed in those areas where food could be easily obtained. The first large population centers arose in the valleys of the Euphrates, the Ganges, the Yangtse-Kiang, and the Nile. "The first dense massing of human population was in that wonderful valley, six hundred miles long, with an average breadth of seven miles, over which every summer from immemorial time the Nile has spread the black

[1] Cf. Ray H. Whitbeck and Olive J. Thomas, *The Geographic Factor* (The Century Company, New York, 1932), p. 59.
[2] W. H. Norton, *Elements of Geology* (Ginn and Company, Boston, 1905), p. 449.

silt of the Abysinian hills." [1] Today the largest groupings of people are located not only in the valleys already mentioned, but also in the valleys of the Po, the Seine, the Rhine, the Thames, the Hudson, and the Mississippi.

Human beings increase most rapidly in river valleys. Here population becomes crowded because of soil fertility and of the resultant ease of securing a cheap food supply. The Amazon river valley, the most fertile area in the world perhaps, is an outstanding exception. Even with the aid of modern invention human groups are weak and helpless in comparison with the power of nature. The rainfall is so high, insects so numerous, pathogenic bacteria so virile, nature so flourishing, that human beings have been unable to make much headway.

The soil is the greatest natural resource and the original determinant of natural areas. A large population must have a rich hinterland. The soil is a source of all life. From it comes food and materials for shelter and clothing. Soil plays a basic rôle in determining the general spatial relationships of the human race. [2]

A river and its branches often set the limits of a natural area. A river system serves as a natural medium of communication. A river is "the common servant" of the life of a valley. Rivers unite people. They are poor dividing lines because the people living on either side of the main current have similar life conditions. [3] They tend to act and think alike. [4]

[1] Franklin H. Giddings, *Principles of Sociology* (The Macmillan Company, New York, 1896), p. 85.

[2] The discovery of mineral resources, such as gold, has brought about sudden migrations of population with accompanying changes in location. If oil is discovered in a city, residences are torn down, a sightly living area becomes an unsightly hive of industry, and a few people who become wealthy, acquire new status in society. In the United States there has been a tremendous exploitation of natural resources with large numbers of people changing their social positions. Natural resources have been used up recklessly, but social control is developing and with it more standardized relationships of people.

[3] Ellen C. Semple, *Influences of the Geographic Environment* (Henry Holt and Company, New York, 1911), Ch. XI.

[4] People living near the mouths of rivers enjoy special advantages. They have opportunity to develop inland trade and ocean commerce, and on the other hand, they tend to become cosmopolitan. They can imprison politically and economically those who live upstream. (Semple, *op. cit.*, Ch. XI.)

Groups of people living in small areas differ in thought-life from those occupying large territories. While islands, peninsulas, and river valleys have been described as bars to expansion, it is also true that close relationships are developed by their inhabitants. Their citizens are handicapped by numerical weakness and lack of a great variety of social organizations. Moreover, they have status through the tacit agreement of large and powerful neighbors. Although Belgium, Holland, and Denmark are near the center of the European danger zone, and are without adequate natural or other defenses, yet they exist as distinct nations on sufferance of the large powers.

The people who live in large areas are likely to be markedly individualistic, and are in danger of overestimating their size and importance. In a small area, the people tend to measure distance with a yardstick.[1] Broad-minded but living in a small-area environment, Plato conceived of an ideal democracy as limiting its free citizens to about 5,000 heads of families, all living within easy reach of the market place.[2] The Mexican Indian in the remote villages of his country lives in a very circumscribed area and hence thinks in small terms:

The Mexican Indian is parochial. His universe is exceedingly limited; the mountains that circumscribe his horizon define his intellectual and spiritual world. The gods he worships are the local gods. The saint is the saint of the village. . . . The gods are local. . . . The notion of an organized church, of a universal Catholic Church, is beyond the experience of the isolated primitive communities. The priest, if he does not reside in the community, is an honored visitor who performs useful services, but who really does not participate in the essential religious life of the village.[3]

The larger the area, the more certain is the guarantee of group permanence, because there are more natural resources, more occupational opportunities, more chances for personal achievement. The larger the area under one political control, the greater

[1] *Ibid.*, p. 195.
[2] Plato, *De Legibus*, Book 5.
[3] Frank Tannenbaum, *Peace by Revolution* (Columbia University Press, New York, 1933), p. 61.

the economic and political independence. A large nation can
put up tariff walls to better advantage than can a small country.
The immense area of Russia has been called the military ally
on which she can most surely count; the length of the road to
Moscow was undoubtedly a leading factor in turning Napoleon's
victorious march into a debacle.[1] China's great area and large
population are powerful defense factors.

A people who occupy a large area are sooner or later likely to
have many contacts with other peoples, easy access to ocean
highways, and opportunities to establish international relationships. A large area gives individuals ultimately a wide
outlook on life and a continental urge.[2]

A natural area may be bounded by *artificial factors*, such as
a factory, several railroad tracks lying together in parallel
lines, a wide and heavily travelled thoroughfare. A natural area
is usually circumscribed by both physical and artificial barriers.
Every large city, for instance, is divided into natural areas,
or areas in which people can engage easily in daily interaction.
A natural area in a city rarely coincides with political or
administrative districts. Politics, or more particularly, gerry-
mandering, often makes queer-looking boundaries.

Social base maps are useful in delineating natural areas.
A social base map of a city, for example, indicates the natural
areas and shows both the physical and artificial boundaries
which separate urban citizens from each other. A social base
map also shows the relation of types of social behavior, such
as delinquency, to the physical and artificial elements of a
natural area.[3]

Area cannot be separated from *location*. Area is important
according to its location, whether isolated or situated on highways of travel and traffic. The location of the Phoenicians
enabled them to become the middlemen between the Orient

[1] Semple, *op. cit.*, p. 194.
[2] *Ibid.*, p. 193.
[3] See Erle F. Young, "The Social Base Map," *Journal of Applied Sociology*,
IX: 202–206; also Earle E. Eubank, "Uses of Base Maps," *Social Forces*, VI:
604–605.

and the Occident. The location of Holland at the mouth of the Rhine waterway helped that nation to maintain a maritime supremacy of the world. The out-of-the-way location of the Isle of Man prevented the inhabitants from coming in contact with new and progressive ideas.[1]

In a stricter sense, location means distribution of a population socially, for example, according to class distinctions. Some people are located high or low on the social scale; some are moving up; others are slipping down. Some live on high spots in a city and rank high socially; others live "beyond the tracks" or in a low marshy spot, and have little status.

Location in the social sense is related to *status*. Location is usually changed when status is lowered. A person grows unhappy and "moves" when his status in a given neighborhood is undermined. When one's social placement becomes unsatisfactory, he generally seeks a new and different spatial placement.

There is evident a relationship between locus or spatial placement, and status or social placement. Locus is interpreted in contiguity, in terms of nearness of spatial relations, and in terms of temporal relations of permanency and transiency. Status is interpreted in terms of social distance. It defines the relative social position of persons in a group and is a potent factor motivating behavior. When status is threatened, locus is apt to be changed; when status is made secure or raised by residence in a district, locus tends to remain stable. Since status indicates the relative positions of persons in association, and since it is both subjective and objective, *i.e.*, involves a psychological reaction or emotional appraisal of position, and behavior in accordance therewith, it must be considered as an important and even necessary phase of social organization. Its function is the adjustment of social relationships and the stabilizing of the social order.[2]

In modern cities people are rated socially according to the topographical location of their homes. Those who do the manual work generally occupy the lowest geographical levels. They are crowded into the "draft streets," that is, where the

[1] Semple, *op. cit.*, Ch. V.
[2] Bessie A. McClenahan, *The Changing Urban Neighborhood* (University of Southern California, Los Angeles, 1929), p. 77.

winds drive through in drafts, or into "dead pockets," where wind rarely reaches. The heights and the commanding spots are occupied by the people with wealth, irrespective of the social value of their lives. Between these extremes the middle classes shift restlessly back and forth. An American novelist has made much of the point that one's social rating depends in part upon the altitude in a city at which he is able to house his family. As one acquires a competence, he moves up topographically and refuses to live down topographically. Thus, locus and status are interrelated.

CLIMATIC AREAS

Climate fixes the location of human groups. Arctic latitudes, high altitudes, and arid regions draw the dead-line for all life. A certain range of temperature and of moisture is essential to the survival of human groups. Temperature, humidity, rainfall fix the boundaries to human effort.

A mean annual temperature of approximately fifty degrees Fahrenheit seems to be best for human progress; seventy degrees or more is enervating; thirty degrees or less gives man too many obstacles to overcome. The greater density of population is found where the average mean annual temperature ranges from forty-five to fifty-five degrees. On either side of these limits the population rapidly diminishes. Less than one-third of the inhabitants live in areas where the mean annual temperature is over fifty-five degrees, and only one-hundredth of the population live where the average temperature is seventy degrees or over.[1] Ellsworth Huntington estimates that an average temperature of forty degrees in winter and of about sixty-five in summer is best for human stimulation.

Thirty to fifty inches of annual rainfall is necessary for the growth of vegetable life upon which domesticated animals and man live. No important groups of people have developed where the rainfall is ten inches or less a year except in the Nile

[1] Ellsworth Huntington, *Civilization and Climate* (Yale University Press, 1915), Ch. V.

Valley, unless extensive irrigation is utilized. A hundred inches or more of rainfall give a growth of vegetable life too luxuriant for mankind to control with ease.

Humidity, or the amount of moisture in the air in proportion to the amount which the air at any particular temperature is capable of holding, influences population activity.[1] A high humidity and high temperature are enervating; a low humidity increases nervousness and lowers vitality.[2]

A combination of proper temperature, humidity, rainfall, and weather variability is difficult to find. According to Huntington's map of climatic energy, northeastern, north central, and middle western portions of the United States, England and Ireland, France, Belgium, Holland, Denmark, southern Scandinavia, Switzerland, northern Italy, Austria, portions of Germany, Czechoslovakia lie within the area of most favorable climatic conditions in the world.[3] It is interesting to compare Huntington's map of climatic energy with his map showing where civilization has actually developed, noticing how closely one map parallels the other.[4]

In general there is a correspondence between the climate of a region and the temperament of the peoples living therein. The northern peoples of Europe are energetic, provident, and thoughtful, rather than emotional; cautious rather than impulsive. On the other hand, the southern peoples of the subtropical Mediterranean basin are easy-going, gay, emotional, and imaginative. In the colder habitats mankind is more domestic than in the warmer. With the southerners of the

[1] *Ibid.*, pp. 121ff.

[2] Another important factor is climatic variability. A long succession of sunshine days or of rainy days is equally monotonous and upsetting. Since human beings are partly products of change, unchanging weather conditions are irritating. Days of sunshine alternating with days of cloudiness and rain is a desirable climatic condition.

[3] *Ibid.*, p. 200.

[4] Climate basically limits what crops shall be raised. It affects radically the size of the harvest, and determines as a rule what herds of animals shall be kept, whether reindeer, camels, llamas, horses, or cattle. It influences extensively the nature and amount of man's food and clothing and the type of his dwelling. (Semple, *ibid.*, p. 609.)

Tropics, the prevailing rule is: Easy come, easy go.[1] They therefore feast, and then famine. A cold climate "puts a steadying hand upon the human heart and brain," and paints life with "an autumn tinge." [2]

The migration of people from cold to tropical areas is followed by an enervation of the individual and a loss of group efficiency. These results are partly due to debilitating heat, and partly to easier conditions of living. Germans, for example, who colonized portions of Brazil, have shown deterioration.

Where human groups have gone into the Tropics "they have suffered arrested development." To the extent that the Tropics was man's nursery, "it has kept him a child." If the subtropics was "the cradle of humanity," then the temperate regions have been "the cradle of civilization." [3] It was chiefly when human groups pushed out within the Temperate Zone that they progressed. In other words, the Temperate Zone provides about enough stimuli and enough obstacles for the maximum development of humanity.

It is partly true that the earth "has mothered man, has fed him, has set him tasks, has directed his thoughts, and has confronted him with difficulties that have strengthened his body and developed his mental outlook.[4] It is true that the physical factors in the long history of human development "have been operating strongly and operating persistently." They have been relatively stable forces; they have rarely slept.[5]

It is also true that man has been "so noisy about the way that he has conquered Nature" and that "Nature has been so silent in her persistent influence over man," that the influences of nature in group life are easily overlooked.[6] In the early days of the race the physical factors dominated. During the centuries

---

[1] Ellen C. Semple, *op. cit.*, p. 620.

[2] *Ibid.*, p. 621. It may be added here that tropical and temperate zones are complementary trade areas. The hot belt of the earth produces numerous useful forms of life that cannot survive in colder countries. A much shorter list of products, however, with greater human activity and efficiency, is found in the Temperate Zone.

[3] *Ibid.*, p. 635.

[4] *Ibid.*, p. 1.

[5] *Ibid.*, p. 2.

[6] *Loc. cit.*

that followed, human groups gained mastery here and there. Today human dependence on nature is unquestioned, but is far less conspicuous and arbitrary than in early times. Urban groups today are not as subject to the caprices of nature as were preliterate peoples centuries ago.

Out of different physical environments have come different social groups and cultures—all combining to form "a great sociological puzzle." The give-and-take between man and his environment has produced changes in spatial relationships and likewise in social values. The processes are complex, for different social groups have responded differently to similar environments. The particular adjustments of a people to a particular environment have often been "influenced as much by circumstances wholly outside of the region as by those within." [1] In other words the culture patterns and the values that a migrating people bring with them may be as influential as the environmental factors. Moreover, the degree of knowledge, the type of inventions, the system of communication, the degree of wealth that a people possess help to explain the utilization that they make of the physical opportunities in a given area.[2] The importance of the physical environment among primitive peoples tends to give way to the rôle of spatial relationships among the more civilized, especially among those who live in large numbers in small areas.

NATURAL BARRIERS

Desert regions are natural barriers to the growth of human groups. In regions where the soil is non-fertile, or where lack of rainfall has created barren, boundless, arid plains, there population is sparse, and "restless, rootless" people are found. As Ellen C. Semple has said, migration alone is permanent; and although the people are continually moving, progress stands still.[3] The habit of migrating on the part of primitive groups does not permit the accumulation of wealth except that "which

[1] Ray H. Whitbeck and Olive J. Thomas, *The Geographic Factor*, p. 398.
[2] *Ibid.*, p. 399.
[3] Semple, *op. cit.*, p. 483.

can move itself," such as flocks and herds. The supply of clothing and equipment is scanty; the use of much furniture in tents is slight; the opportunity to develop large-scale social organization is lacking.

In desert areas marauding groups have the best chance of survival, and hence the term, robber, "becomes a title of honor." The harsh conditions of desert regions make the Arab the hardiest and bravest of human beings.[1] A desert environment encourages the growth of independent attitudes, but hinders the rise of large social groups. Desert people defy conquest. They are among "the hardiest people on earth"; they are protected by their "death-dealing environment." They represent a survival of the fittest whom the fittest of fertile regions cannot easily overcome.

Desert conditions are reflected in the customs of the people. J. L. Burchhart, a Bedouin authority, asserts, for example, that an ordinary American dinner would make six meals for an Arab.[2] Culture traits remain unchanged for centuries. Modes of living or believing remain stable, while fashion suggestion rarely gets a hearing. There is no competition in consumption of economic goods, for the latter are so meager.

The so-called desert-born tendencies for religion may be explained in part by the fact that the desert induces some persons to reflect long and hard on life, and encourages the longing for a hereafter that will compensate for the rigors of this present life. It has been pointed out that the human mind, finding little of variety, finding life a dull monotony, finding one day pretty much like another with no regular work, no books, no opportunities for invention, "develops an impression of unity" and a tendency toward monotheistic reflection. The deserts of Syria and Arabia have played a significant part in the origin of each of the three leading monotheistic religions of the world—Mohammedanism, Judaism, and Christianity.[3]

---

[1] *Ibid.*, pp. 490, 493.
[2] *Notes on the Bedouins and Wahabys* (London, 1831), pp. 57ff.
[3] Semple, *op. cit.*, p. 511.

Mountains constitute another powerful natural barrier to the growth of human groups. They usually stand as "majestic but inert masses," separating growing populations. Mountain passes alone have been used, although the airplane is now beginning to conquer continental divides. Mountain passes are "nature-made thoroughfares," used for travel, migration, military expeditions; they are traversed alike by preliterate people, "armies bent on conquest," the automobile, and even the airplane "follows their dim outlines."

Mountain areas keep human groups small. Only a small percentage of the world's population lives 5,000 feet or more above sea level. Most of the civilized groups of the world live where the altitude is between 100 feet and 1,000 feet. In the high areas food is scarce, and in the low regions, for example, in those below sea level, health conditions are poor.

Mountain barriers, noted Miss Semple, are rarely impartial.[1] One slope is generally steep; and the other, gentle. The gentler side usually offers a wide zone of food supply. On one side of the Himalayas is the vast population of India, on the other, the scattered nomadic groups of Tibet. The western side of the Rockies is the steeper but it feels the warm air of the Pacific winds; the eastern slope is gentler but it experiences in winter the rigor of a subarctic climate, in summer the heat of the subtropics.[2]

Maintenance of life in high altitudes is always a real struggle for existence, hence frivolous living is unknown. Individual effort builds up an independent type of personality similar to that known in desert areas. The conquest of mountain peoples is always difficult, for an invader has "two enemies to fight, the rough mountain topography and the armed foe." [3]

---

[1] *Ibid.*, Chs. XV, XVI.

[2] *Ibid.*, p. 544. It may be noted that high altitudes with their long winters stimulate industries in the home. Almost everywhere mountain people have reached a special skill in indoor industries. The carving of articles from wood, the pounding out of artistic metal work in silver and copper, the making of the well-known Kashmir shawls, and of the finest violin strings in the world are illustrations of what mountain peoples are stimulated to achieve.

[3] *Ibid.*, p. 589.

Mountain areas hinder social integration. Political unity rarely develops from within; it is forced from without. The Swiss Confederation may be cited as the result, in part, of threatened encroachments from outside groups.

Mountain groups are conservative, for little reaches them from urban people to stimulate them, and their own life is likely to be sterile. Religion remains orthodox, legends abound, and dialects survive. The rigid conditions of life explain the motto: To have and to hold. Mountain areas are "museums of antiquity." [1]

Mountain dwellers possess narrow viewpoints and live in closely limited personal worlds. They easily fall into feuds; their lives are characterized by pronounced hates. They lack cosmopolitan interests. When they visit cities, they quickly grow homesick. They react against the artificialities of civilization, and long to return to their mountain homes. The mountain life develops in them "strong muscles, unjaded nerves, iron purposes, indifference to luxury," [2] and an individualistic outlook.

Oceans were barriers to primitive people, for they could not easily be crossed. Only by accident or through great courage could they be traversed. The terror of storms and the frailness of small boats combined to make oceans almost insuperable barriers.[3]

Oceans are also pathways between natural areas. Proximity to coast lines and oceans arouses unique responses within the human mind. The "flow of stream and ebb of tide have sooner or later, stirred the curiosity of land-born barbarians," and the "eternal unrest of moving waters" has constituted a "continual knocking at the door of human inertia." In timid fashion men have followed ocean currents and trade winds to the ends of the earth.

The ocean has called forth inventions from the mind of man:

[1] *Ibid.*, p. 601. [2] *Ibid.*, p. 599.
[3] Today oceans are still barriers to many people. Oceans separate people with limited means, people who are unaccustomed to long distances, people with narrow outlook, people who are fearful of *mal de mer*.

first, floats and rafts; then devices for securing displacement; and in recent decades floating sea giants and submarines. It has made new and varied occupations possible—seamanship, large-scale fishing, shipbuilding.[1]

ECOLOGICAL PROCESSES

When human beings live far apart from one another and when spatial distances are great the resultant influences upon human attitudes are rather limited. When people live close together, however, and spatial distances are short, then persons are likely to have a great deal of influence upon each other. In one case attitudes will be largely self-generated, while in the other they will be socially made.

In the early days of the United States the people were widely scattered and hence developed deeply ingrained individualistic attitudes. Today the United States has become largely an urban people living close together. To the extent that the present sees a breakdown in social functioning in the United States a real explanation lies in the fact that individualistic attitudes developed by a sparsely settled people are still being used to solve problems arising out of closely settled urban areas. It is not democracy which is failing in the United States so much as it is an anti-social individualism born of an era when spatial distances were extensive.

As spatial distances decrease, a sense of population pressure arises. Population pressure leads to a demand for more territory, and national aggressiveness develops. In Japan, for example, a high birth rate operating in a land of limited natural resources has cut down spatial distances to a point recently where population pressure sent the Japanese armies into Manchuria so that the Japanese people might spread out. Crowded spatial relationships throughout a nation give strength to a military class, encouraging them sometimes to defy world opinion.[2]

---

[1] Semple, *op. cit.*, pp. 295, 296.
[2] See E. A. Ross, *Standing Room Only?* (The Century Company, New York, 1927), for significant materials concerning the ways in which national attitudes are affected by population pressure and by the shrinking of spatial relationships.

If it is proved that spatial relationships do profoundly affect
human attitudes then another question arises: Can the varying
effects of different spatial relationships be measured? If standards of measurement can be set up, their practical value becomes
exceedingly great. While such measurements in commonly accepted units are not yet available, yet experimental social
psychology is at work and may be expected to produce significant results. In the meantime general postulates for examination and testing are being developed. For illustrative
purposes a sample postulate may be stated: (1) The closer
the spatial relationships of a people, the more intense become
the attitudes of good will, of ill will, or of indifference, or of all
three.[1]

Another vital question naturally results: When do spatial
relationships lead to friendly, to unfriendly, and to indifferent
attitudes? While research materials cannot be presented here
in answer to these queries, another postulate may be suggested.
(2) Close spatial relationships lead mutually to friendly attitudes when such relationships advance the welfare and meet
the needs of all concerned. People can live peaceably when
close together if each individual feels that he has a distinct
personal advantage in doing so. They can and do put up with
a great many inconveniences and personally distasteful conditions when each feels that there is a tremendous advantage
to be gained. Moreover, people live close together peaceably
when they have somewhat similar temperaments, likes and
dislikes, and tastes. They live close together amicably when
they have similar culture patterns, such as similar religious
beliefs, similar notions of government, and so on.

In Hawaii there are many races with several different cultures living close together but in the main in friendly ways. The
basic race, the native Hawaiians, are friendly people, and the
other races do not engage in strenuous competitive struggles;
hence despite physical nearness and cultural differences, all

[1] For illustrations from the field of race relations see E. S. Bogardus, *Immigration and Race Attitudes* (D. C. Heath and Company, Boston, 1928).

maintain harmonious relationships, for the most part, some-what after a symbiotic pattern.[1]

(3) Close spatial relationships lead to unfriendly attitudes when such relationships retard group welfare and defeat personal desires. When people are widely different in temperament they are unable to get along together well under the same roof. When they have different tastes, ideals, ambitions, coupled with different culture patterns then conflict is almost certain. In *Main Street*, by Sinclair Lewis, the marriage of an idealistic college woman from the city with a staid, self-satisfied doctor of the town of Gopher Prairie ends in separation because of a double set of differences in both temperament and culture patterns. Hence, the marriage becomes a failure. Today Japanese soldiers living in close proximity to Koreans in Korea are continually engaging in strife with Koreans because of differences, first in culture patterns, and second, in social relationships, with the Japanese in position of authority and the Koreans as active and alert subjects.

In the southern states of the United States white and colored people live close together in peace as long as Negroes "keep in their place," that is, do not try to mix socially with white people. Whenever, however, a Negro steps over social boundaries he gets into trouble and if many do so, ill will against the Negro at once bursts into flames. Likewise in India where a caste system exists, people of different castes get along well living in close proximity to each other as long as a member of one caste does not step out of his caste or invade the prerogatives of a higher caste.

(4) Close spatial relationships eventuate in indifference when individuals can meet their desires in mutually exclusive groups. The modern city is an illustration. People get along well with many of their neighbors simply by not having anything to do with them. Most city people do not know by name all the other people in the same city block or in the same large apartment

---

[1] See R. D. McKenzie, "Cultural and Racial Differences as Bases of Human Symbiosis," in K. Young, *Social Attitudes* (Henry Holt and Company, New York, 1931), Ch. VI.

house. Each person in the city has a few friends and is a member of a few social groups, but passes by all the other people in the city whom he meets from day to day. As long as a person can meet his needs in association with a few people and is not bothered or disturbed by other people, he views with indifference the many although they reside near him. It was not so in the rural area in which the present writer grew up in the state of Illinois. In that district although people lived a mile or two apart each person knew all the others by name and considerable about the personal affairs of all the others. Although spatial distances were greater than in the city we were not indifferent to each other. When numbers increase, then indifference develops although spatial relationships are closer.[1]

There seems to be an irresistible pull that stimulates most persons to live near other persons. This tendency has been presented as a process called "centralization."[2] The hermit and the pioneer are exceptions that prove the rule. The result of concentration is that many population centers of various sizes have developed over the face of the earth and have manifested endless drawing power. They give position or status and they shape human relationships.

The setting for the location of population centers, already presented in terms of natural areas, climatic areas, and natural barriers, is being modified by the inventive ability of man. Telic or purposeful activity has begun its work only recently. An airplane view of a flattened out earth would show a few gigantic population centers sprawled out amoeba-like; a greater number of good-sized cities, and many more small urban communities, with the largest centers and particularly those next to the largest, growing the fastest, and with the small groupings standing still or shrinking. The general social product is the urbanization of the world.

[1] For illustrative materials see H. W. Zorbaugh, *The Gold Coast and the Slum* (University of Chicago Press, 1929).

[2] See R. D. McKenzie, "The Scope of Human Ecology," *Journal of Applied Sociology*, X:323, for a discussion of "centralization" and of the other ecological processes that are presented in the remainder of this chapter.

Within larger concentrations occur smaller ones. Similar businesses locate in the same vicinity. "People work according to occupational centralizations." "Birds of a feather flock together." Girls of a type join the same sorority. Athletes hobnob together.

The formation of housing and occupational concentrations creates *segregation*. Between concentrations are physical and social spaces or barriers that account for segregation. Segregation, a natural result of concentration, is often accompanied by personal misunderstandings and social conflicts.

Since segregation sets people off from each other, they easily grow jealous of each other. They fold their arms as it were and regard each other Napoleon-like, if they do not make actual grimaces. Segregation often keeps people from seeing each other in the best light. Segregated groups magnify each other's weaknesses; they exalt themselves unduly.

Persons object to segregation when it creates a loss of status. They remonstrate when it is imposed on them. Persons are forever protesting against segregation and forever seeking it. They protest against that which is imposed, for it usually means a decreased status. They seek segregation, for it enables them to assume superior attitudes. Poor people object to being segregated in the lowest, worst parts of a city; wealthy people seek segregation in the heights, building high walls around their domiciles, holding themselves aloof from "the madding crowd."

However, persons are forever invading someone else's segregated area. People do not stay segregated. A group or some of its members grow restless, dissatisfied, and seek to improve their condition. They move to a better location, but in so doing they "invade" an area already occupied. *Invasion* means that someone is entering the residential area, the occupation, or the social level of someone else.

Many social problems arise from invasion. Competition for status is among the worst. Prejudices develop and will not be easily downed. An immigrant is criticized for living in a "slum" area, but if he moves into a better neighborhood, he is viewed as an invader, and is met by prejudice and hatred from the very persons who criticized him for living under low standards. Invasion by large numbers of strangers, especially by strangers of peculiar appearance or with queer customs, or by strangers of relatively low culture traits arouses ill will. Improvement of one's condition may come at the expense of invasion, but invasion is paid for in terms of prejudice.

If a people cannot keep invaders out, they may invade some other area, occupation, or social level, and thus the process of *succession* is inaugurated. In a large city an expansion of a business area means that certain business houses must invade residence property. The "residents" move into another residence area. Fine residences are followed by apartment houses and flats, then by rooming houses, which in turn give way to a business block. An urban community is continually experiencing such a succession of the uses of land. Succession of this type is characterized by a period of social disorganization. During the process, residence property becomes dilapidated and slums are created.

Over a period of decades a particular occupation, such as the clothing industry, may experience a succession of races or classes of people. Domestic service in the United States has undergone a racial succession in the past century. The succession of given persons up through a series of graded occupations may be called vertical occupational mobility. Invasion and succession are both dynamic and disorganizing elements in social life.

In any social group or area one person or one set of persons may be dominant over the others. *Dominance* as a process refers to the ways in which some persons exercise control over other persons, either by "lording it" over them or by stimulating them indirectly to develop fuller, richer personalities.

At one time the medicine man and the magician were dominant; later, the priest; more recently in Western civilization, the business man. In other words there has been a succession of different types of leadership which have been dominant. Once autocracy was dominant, then feudalism and paternalism; more recently, democracy; today, dictatorships of varying degrees. Two hundred years ago rural patterns were dominant in the Western world; today, urban patterns are in the ascendancy.

The struggle for political dominance is illustrated by the life and death conflict that is going on in India between the natives and the British. Manchuria is a focal point of a three-cornered contest for dominance between China, Japan, and Russia. Germany is seeking to dethrone France from political dominance in Western Europe. Many Latin American republics resent the political dominance of the United States in the Western hemisphere.

Between world religions such as Christianity and Mohammedanism there is an indirect struggle for dominance. Within Christianity there is a striving for dominance between Catholicism and Protestantism; within Protestantism, between fundamentalists and modernists. Within a local church one faction may seek dominance at the expense of another. Sometimes the contest is between religion and the enemies of religion.

In the operation of ecological processes changes in human relationships occur, changes in position or status are common, and changes in attitudes are countless. The study of ecological processes is an excellent background for considering the cultural and psycho-social approaches to sociology.

PROBLEMS

1. At what temperature can you study best?
2. Can you work better on a cloudy day or on a clear day?
3. Is it a matter of accident that "the weather is a topic of conversation the world over"?
4. Why is the term, robber, a title of honor in the Arabian deserts?
5. Why do people who live in small areas measure life with a yardstick?
6. Explain the general orthodoxy of farmers in the past.
7. Under what conditions might a large population develop in the Amazon valley?

8. Why are mountaineers conservative?

9. Why are the hates of mountaineers so pronounced?

10. Why are mountaineers independent in attitude?

11. Who are the more independent: mountain peoples or desert peoples?

12. How do you explain the gaiety of open-air peoples?

13. Explain the suggestibility of people who live on monotonous plains.

14. Explain the superstitiousness of sailors.

15. How do you interpret the statement that "the eternal unrest of moving waters has knocked at the door of human inertia"?

16. Explain the statement that "the Tropics is the cradle of humanity."

17. In what sense is the Temperate Zone the cradle and school of civilization?

18. What factors help to determine the location of cities?

19. What factors influenced the location of the city in which or near which you live?

20. Why have people developed natural resources before developing socialized attitudes?

21. What is human ecology?

22. How are geographic and ecological factors related?

23. Why are ecological principles significant in the study of sociology?

24. What accounts for "centralization" even when living conditions are less wholesome in centralized than in non-centralized areas?

25. In what ways is segregation an entirely natural tendency?

26. What are the positive and the negative values in invasion?

27. Cite a concrete case of "succession" that you have personally observed or read about.

28. When is dominance a positive social value and when is it a negative value?

29. How are human attitudes affected by changes in the spatial relationships of persons?

READINGS

ANDERSON, NELS, and E. C. LINDEMAN, *Urban Sociology* (Alfred A. Knopf, New York, 1928), Part I.

BUCKLE, H. T., *History of Civilization in England* (D. Appleton and Company, New York, 1874), Vol. I.

DAVIS, JEROME, and H. E. BARNES, *Introduction to Sociology* (D. C. Heath and Company, New York, 1927), Book II, Part I.

GILLIN, J. L., and F. W. BLACKMAR, *Outlines of Sociology* (The Macmillan Company, New York, 1930), Ch. II.

HANKINS, F. H., *An Introduction to the Study of Society* (The Macmillan Company, New York, 1928), Ch. V.

HUNTINGTON, C. C., and FRED A. CARLSON, *The Geographic Basis of Society* (Prentice-Hall, Inc., New York, 1933).

HUNTINGTON, ELLSWORTH, *Civilization and Climate* (Yale University Press, 1922).

——, *The Pulse of Progress* (Charles Scribner's Sons, New York, 1926).

KELSEY, CARL, *The Physical Basis of Society* (D. Appleton and Company, New York, 1928), Ch. I.

LUMLEY, FREDERICK E., *Principles of Sociology* (McGraw-Hill Book Company, Inc., New York, 1928), Ch. II.

MCKENZIE, R. D., "The Ecological Approach to the Study of the Human Community," *American Journal of Sociology*, XXX: 287–301.

——, "The Scope of Human Ecology," *Journal of Applied Sociology*, X: 316–23.

MUKERJEE, R., *Regional Sociology* (The Century Company, New York, 1926).

ROSS, EDWARD A., *Principles of Sociology* (The Century Company, New York, 1930), Ch. VII.

SEMPLE, ELLEN C., *Influences of Geographic Environment* (Henry Holt and Company, New York, 1911).

THOMAS, FRANKLIN, *The Environmental Basis of Human Society* (The Century Company, New York, 1925).

WHITBECK, RAY H., and OLIVE J. THOMAS, *The Geographic Factor* (The Century Company, New York, 1932).

CHAPTER III

CULTURAL APPROACH

Culture is all the ways of doing and believing of a human group. Culture is "the stock in trade" of a group. It is an antecedent complex of values into which every individual is born. It is an omnipresent medium in which every person lives, moves, and has his being.

Social groups are distinguished from each other by differences in their stocks of culture patterns and values. It is also true that all social groups have basic similarities in their culture systems. By virtue of their culture differences groups may stimulate each other or they may misunderstand each other. Culture differences all too often lead to destructive conflicts. By virtue of similarities in culture patterns groups may co-operate, although these similarities sometimes throw groups into bitter competition.

CULTURE PATTERNS

A *culture pattern* is an objective expression of a way of doing or believing that is common to a number of people. A *culture trait* is the subjective aspect of a culture pattern. A *culture complex* is any combination of culture patterns which belong logically together, such as manufacturing a particular style of shoes with all of its constituent phases from tanning hides to putting the finished product in boxes. A *culture adhesion* is a combination of unnaturally attached culture patterns such as the swagger stick carried by a democratically-minded person.

A *culture area* is the unit region wherein a specific social value may be found. It is the regional base of a way of acting or believing. For example, when you travel across Switzerland you may pass through three different language areas—French,

German, and Italian. Most areas have centers from which a specific trait has emanated or where it is followed more faithfully than in other parts of the area. A *culture center* is the emanating point of a culture pattern. Paris has been the culture center of new styles in woman's dress for the world. New York City is the culture center of new plays for the United States. More particularly, Broadway is the specific center.

Culture area is related to natural area in that culture patterns spread most easily through natural areas. However, a given culture area is not necessarily synonymous with a given natural area, which means that a study of both is essential for understanding social changes and processes.

Special verification of the rôle that culture areas play in human behavior may be observed in the interesting studies of delinquency by Clifford R. Shaw. For example, he has found that delinquent behavior in Chicago varied with the different areas of the city, that it varied inversely in proportion to the distance from the center of the city, and that in certain areas delinquency patterns arise, become socially dominant, and shape personality patterns.[1]

> The first and perhaps most striking finding of the study is that there are marked variations in the rate of school truants, juvenile delinquents, and adult criminals between areas in Chicago. . . . A second major finding is that rates of truancy, delinquency, and adult crime tend to vary inversely in proportion to the distance from the center of the city. . . . Delinquency and criminal patterns arise and are transmitted socially just as any other cultural and social pattern is transmitted. In time these delinquent patterns may become dominant and shape the attitudes and behavior of persons living in the area. Thus the section becomes an area of delinquency.[2]

In groups of size, such as races, each has its family patterns, play patterns, work or occupational patterns, religious patterns, art patterns, social control patterns. The fact that all large racial or national groups have all these types of patterns, each

---

[1] Clifford R. Shaw, *Delinquency Areas* (University of Chicago Press, 1929), pp. 198, 202, 206.
[2] *Loc. cit.*

after its own experiences, indicates the fundamental unity of mankind.

In other words, the human race is characterized by an underlying, universal culture system. Clark Wissler has developed the universal culture concept, pointing how every race has a type of family life, a type of government, a type of religion, and so on.[1] This universal culture theory is supported psychologically, for the members of all human groups are characterized by a similar "inhibition of impulses, power of attention, power of original thought." Franz Boas continues: "The organization of mind is practically identical among all races of men."[2]

All the culture traits and patterns of a people have been called *folkways*.[3] These are all "the ways" of "a folk," and include both *customs* and *traditions*. The former are the ways of *doing* of a folk and the latter, the ways of *believing*. Of course customs and traditions are closely intertwined.

Those folkways which are judged by the members of a group to be necessary to the welfare of that group are called *mores*. These phases of the folkways have the sanction of public opinion and of law behind them. The driving of an automobile on the right hand side of the road in the United States, or on the left in England, is a part of the mores, but whether one shall drive an automobile or not is outside the mores. To wear clothes is a phase of the mores in civilized countries, but usually the particular color that is worn is not regulated by the mores.

The mores are closely related to *morals*.[4] A person often gets his ideas about what is moral or not moral from the mores. Mores are part of the social environment, while morals are a part of the behavior of persons. Mores are based on social experience, while morals often include ideals and goals to be attained. The mores are generally not thought out; morals may

[1] Clark Wissler, *Man and Culture* (Thomas Y. Crowell Company, New York, 1923), Ch. V.

[2] Franz Boas, *The Mind of Primitive Man* (The Macmillan Company, New York, 1911), p. 105.

[3] William G. Sumner, *Folkways* (Ginn and Company, Boston, 1907).

[4] Charles A. Ellwood, "Social Development of Morality," *Sociology and Social Research*, XII: 24–25.

not be thought out either, but often they do include reflection and careful reasoning even to the fine points of conscientious discriminations.

CULTURE HERITAGE

Culture heritage is the sum total of the culture patterns that a person receives from the various social groups of which he is a member. Remove the culture heritage from the life of Thomas A. Edison and which one of his more than one thousand inventions could he have made? Remove the knowledge of the culture patterns of many peoples from the equipment of Shakespeare and which of his magnificent dramas could he have written? Everyone of us is indebted in so many culture ways to preceding generations, that we can scarcely realize how deep is our indebtedness.[1]

Social groups vary greatly in the extent and quality of their culture heritage. One group may have a scanty heritage of primitive culture patterns. Another group may have a replete heritage of complex and carefully thought-out culture patterns, and be striving to improve the scope and quality of these patterns. Still another group may have an unusually wide variety of culture patterns but have become so self-satisfied with its glorious culture that it offers no encouragement to any of its members to develop new patterns. In fact a group may penalize anyone who criticizes the group's traditions or customs. An autocratic class, satisfied with its own influence and affluence, may crush out any attempt to incubate new ideas.

Since culture patterns are largely an accumulation from the past, a careful view may be taken of the cultural past of mankind. Could we picture all human groups past and present we would have a cornucopia, narrow at the bottom but wide at the top, beginning with earliest man and extending to the earth-wide spread of humanity today. Irrespective of what our understanding may be of the origin of man, we are interested socio-

---

[1] One of the first writers to develop extensively this idea was Graham Wallas in his *Social Heritage* (Yale University Press, 1921).

logically in the fact that human groups began life in a very
humble way on earth, without much in the way of traditions
and customs, and that from a simple start they have expanded
and developed until now they envelop the earth with complicated systems of culture.

The picture of utmost simplicity with which human groups
began their career on earth is followed by a complicated development from humble beginnings, and by the present vastness of
numbers and an intricate array of social activities and institutions. Today the human group, composed of nearly 2,000,000,-
000 persons of all ages, can hardly be visualized. If all these
human beings were able-bodied adults and could pass by a
reviewing stand, the procession practically would be endless.
If they came in single file, one every six feet, passing by at the
rapid rate of one a second, sixty a minute, 3,600 an hour,
day and night, the procession would continue for more than half
a century. Moreover, what a load of culture traits each would
carry, even the primitive persons, while the modern civilized
persons would almost be buried from sight beneath their bundles
of culture traits.

Human culture began long before the dawn of history. The
artifacts and the remains of primitive man have been found in a
region extending from Java through India to England. From
this central strip of territory, early human groups seem to have
migrated far and wide. They wandered northeast into Mongolia [1] and adjoining areas, and they migrated southwest into
Africa. It appears that some of their number drifted from Asia
across the Pacific, or travelled by land to America in prehistoric
times when America was connected by land with Asia on the
west, and with Europe on the east.

Earliest culture evidences are tools, or implements, made out
of flint and other imperishable materials. Closely related to
these implements are early monuments, mounds, elementary
works of art crudely etched or drawn on the inside of stone
caves or elsewhere in places where weathering could not

[1] Some authorities consider Mongolia as the cradle of the human race.

efface. The drawings upon ancient walls speak interestingly concerning the nature of primitive culture. Along with the artifacts and other culture elements are the remains of human skeletons. Moreover, the comparative age of primitive culture patterns is often revealed by the nature of the geological strata in which they are located and by the types of associated fauna.

The earliest period of the culture history of groups begins with man, not with animals. It has been contended by Clarence M. Case that animals do not have a culture.[1] Culture is composed of tools and symbols that are accumulative. Animals transmit ways of doing from parent to offspring, but these are behavior patterns. There is no "external storage" that accumulates and that is transmitted. Culture "consists essentially in the external storage, interchange, and transmission of an accumulating fund of personal and social experience by means of tools and symbols."[2] Animals do not follow this procedure. Beavers do not build better "houses" from generation to generation; birds do not improve in nest-building. Culture is the possession distinctly of human groups, and gives a highly important medium for group continuity and for group and personal advancement.[3]

Animal groups thus are social groups, if not culture groups. The pack of wolves, the herd of cattle, the swarm of bees, the covey or flock of birds, the school of fish—these terms indicate the associative nature of animal life. However, the arbitrary and autocratic activities of physically and psychically powerful leaders are paralleled by a blind obedience, and sometimes by a stifling degree of overorganization. In fact, a study of

[1] "Culture as a Distinctive Human Trait," *American Journal of Sociology*, XXXII:905-20.

[2] *Ibid.*, p. 920.

[3] Hart and Pantzer, "Have Subhuman Animals Culture?" *American Journal of Sociology*, XXX:703-709, take a point of view different from that of Dr. Case, claiming that culture consists in behavior patterns transmitted by imitation or tuition, and that hence there is no sharp culture break between man and the lower animals. This interpretation is supported by Read Bain, "Culture of Canines," *Sociology and Social Research*, XIII:545-56.

social life among insects,[1] for instance, indicates that the processes are largely mechanical, and that little of a real social nature takes place. The individuals are largely automatons, operating on a simple stimulus-response basis.

CULTURE HISTORY

The earliest culture period in the history of human groups is sometimes called the Paleolithic or Old Stone Age. At that time metal implements were unknown. While stone was utilized mainly, other materials such as bone, horn, shell, and wood served well in the manufacture of tools and weapons. The implements of the Paleolithic Age were all of the crudest type; they were neither ground nor polished; they were simply roughly chipped. In the Paleolithic period, no animals seem to have been domesticated, and fire was probably unknown. Food consisted chiefly of uncooked vegetables and the raw flesh of fish and animals.

An interesting picture of prehistoric days is given by R. R. Marett, who helped to make an important discovery while excavating in Jersey, one of the islands in the English Channel.[2] A prehistoric hearth was uncovered. There were the big stones that had propped up the fire. There were the ashes. There were the pieces of decayed bone, which proved to be the remains of a woolly rhinoceros, of reindeer, of a strange-appearing horse, in other words, of species of animals which have not lived in that given region for thousands of years, and which indeed have been long extinct.

In the next place the food heap yielded thirteen human teeth—a discovery which prompted the question: Did the beasts eat the man or did the man eat the beasts? This prehistoric sketch is completed by the statement that there were many coarse flint instruments lying about. It takes but little

[1] W. M. Wheeler's *Social Life Among the Insects* (Harcourt, Brace and Company, New York, 1923), deals intensively with the social traits of the bees, ants, beetles, and wasps, and reveals the mechanical nature of much of this type of so-called social life.

[2] *Anthropology* (Henry Holt and Company, New York, 1912), pp. 13ff.

imagination to reconstruct the culture patterns which existed at that time.

After the Paleolithic came the Neolithic, or New Stone, Age. Neolithic implements are distinctly superior to Paleolithic, and represent skill of a higher order. They were made of many kinds of stone besides flint, and were often ground to an edge that was sometimes polished.

Another important distinction between Paleolithic and Neolithic culture is the fact that the latter includes crude pottery. In Neolithic culture fire was used for human purposes; the method of kindling it artificially had been discovered. Cooked food supplemented raw food. The domestication of the horse, sheep, the ox, the goat, the pig, and the dog had taken place, and helped to make civilization possible. Cattle were used to some extent as a measure of value. Monuments indicating the nature of religious rites of primitive groups have revealed the culture of Neolithic groups. Fortifications and burial mounds, especially the latter, are numerous; in Ohio, for instance, there are many of these reminders of Neolithic culture. Around Stonehenge, England, there are 300 of these burial mounds.[1] Wiltshire "boasts of 2000 similar sepulchral mounds."[2] The art of navigation was inaugurated by Neolithic people, and the evidences of a commercial culture are many and varied.

Then came the so-called Bronze Age of human culture. The discovery and use of metals mark a definite step in human advance. It seems that copper in its native condition generally preceded its use in a form mixed with tin or zinc. The compound, bronze, was much harder and tougher, and hence more useful. As a measure of value cattle were supplanted by copper; and copper bars, used as coins, were stamped with the image of the animals which were once standards of value, namely, the cow, sheep, or the dog.

[1] Frank Stevens, *Stonehenge Today and Yesterday* (His Majesty's Stationery Office, London, 1929), pp. 59–90.
[2] *Ibid.*, p. 73.

It is believed that iron was first used about 1000 B.C., at which time the so-called Iron Age may be said to have begun. Implements were now made out of a hard and valuable metal, iron. The Iron Age, however, did not enter upon its main era until the latter part of the eighteenth century A.D. in England, when the use of steam power gave to the world the factory system, made iron and steel of paramount importance, and created an industrial age.

The Iron Age merged into the Steel and Oil Ages with the Carnegies and the Rockefellers coming into industrial prominence. Perhaps the present might be called the Electrical Age, or it may be that this is the Technological Age, that is, the age when technique and its god, the machine, make ordinary labor, or hand labor, on a large scale unnecessary.

During the centuries preceding historic times, the development of tool-making was the outstanding cultural feature. Migration and hence the spread or diffusion of culture was common. Human groups were at first loosely related to the soil, and thus were on the move a great deal of the time. Coöperative behavior was common. Persons worked together in house-building, cause-building, fishing, hunting.

It has been said by O. T. Mason that whatever one's belief concerning the manner, the place, and the time of man's advent upon the earth, a study of prehistoric culture shows that man was at first a houseless, unclothed being, without experience or skill, and that through association in groups he has achieved his present high civilized level.[1] It is partly the possession of a culture that grows more and more complex which distinguishes human beings from the rest of the animal kingdom. It is in the origins of culture, a culture that is ever changing and developing new forms, that sociology has one of its important starting points.

Within historic days, the chief emphasis in human society has been shifting. In addition to the invention of material objects of culture, increasing attention has been given to psychical and social phenomena. Social attitudes and values are now

[1] *Origins of Invention* (Charles Scribner's Sons, New York, 1910), p. 20.

central data. The development of constructively-minded and wholesome personalities in and through group life has become a theme of far-reaching significance.

Outstanding in the history of human groups is cultural growth and advancement. For example: Compare the loose family life of the best peoples among primitive tribes with the developed forms of love and affection that now characterize family life at its best. Put the conjuries of medicine men or the practices of witchcraft alongside the achievements of Pasteur, of Koch, or of the Mayo brothers. Consider cattle and bars of iron in comparison with highly organized credit systems. Think of the advance from government in the hands of a despot to government in the hands of disinterested statesmen. Compare ethical conduct dictated by a thousand years of custom to ethical conduct based on rational processes of socialized thinking. Picture the esthetic effect of a Bushman playing on one string stretched across a gourd, in comparison with a modern rendition of Handel's Messiah including the Hallelujah Chorus. Parallel primitive methods of preserving information through laborious remembering exertions with the twentieth century and lightning-like printing process. Think of the animistic superstitions of early man in connection with the highly rational and broadly social interpretations of the finest current religious life. The simple associational activities of a Fuegian are kindergarten in size and quality when the national and international activities of a President of the United States are considered. These illustrations of cultural change and progress reveal something of the tremendous rôle of culture in group life.

CULTURE DIFFUSION

Culture diffusion is the spreading of a culture pattern from one group of people to another and from one culture area to another. Culture patterns spread in two ways, either *incidentally* or by *direction*. A culture pattern is in itself lifeless and must be "carried" by persons. Whenever a person migrates from one culture area to another, he carries culture patterns with him. If these appeal by their utility or their uniqueness irrespective of utility to many people culture diffusion is likely to occur.

When missionaries are sent from one country to a "heathen" country, then culture diffusion may take place by direction. When a country undertakes to colonize a new area, and imposes its own culture patterns upon the colonized region, then again culture diffusion by direction has occurred.

A pure culture diffusion theory implies that each culture pattern has had but one origin and that from this single origin it has spread to its present stage of distribution. It denies the theory of *independent origins*, which holds that many objects of culture have been invented or discovered in two or more parts of the world and that they have spread from these several culture centers. This theory is accompanied by another, that of *culture parallels*. Here the idea is that a given culture pattern has arisen in two or more widely separated areas and has spread in parallel fashion in these different areas. Another related theory is that of *culture convergence* which holds that two or more different culture patterns originating in different areas may grow to be alike without contact of people, because of similar life conditions in the two areas. Thus, culture pattern similarities in different areas without culture diffusion may occur.

Whatever may have been the situation among preliterate peoples, it appears that today the independent origins theory has less support than formerly. By virtue of current methods of rapid communication, an invention in one part of the earth is quickly heralded among civilized peoples everywhere. Culture diffusion appears to be at present the main process, and independent origins to be supported with but few illustrations in a civilized world.

The culture of a people is a large unwieldy mosaic. The culture of a dynamic people is continually changing. At least parts of it are changing faster than other parts. The latter lag. *Cultural lag* means that some patterns of a people's culture do not change as fast as do other traits.[1] As a result conflicts

[1] See W. F. Ogburn, *Social Change* (Huebsch and Company, New York, 1922), pp. 200ff.

and problems arise. Physical inventions have preceded inventions for social control; destructive instruments of war have advanced ahead of peace machinery and the peace spirit. Moreover, culture traits often outlive their usefulness. Culture traits may persist until they are no longer adapted to new social conditions and needs. By its nature culture cannot easily keep apace of new social conditions; neither can it in all of its phases keep up-to-date evenly. Some parts of it are bound to lag. An analysis of these culture lags at any given time helps to explain conflicts and problems.[1]

Unfortunately there is a strong tendency for ways of doing and believing to operate long after their original meaning, or any real meaning, has been lost, and long after their utility has ended. Note the American veneration oftentimes for a common law which is at variance with current industrial needs. A deference is shown on occasion for certain traditional aspects of the law which exhibit too great concern for powerful interests and too little respect for individuals of the weaker groups. In religion also beliefs often outlive their serviceability.

The undue prolongation of customs and traditions is supported by ecological, psychical, and social barriers. These shut out new stimuli; they prohibit contacts with the advanced ideas and methods of the day. In the isolated areas of civilized countries there survive clannishness, patriarchal authority, narrow religious dogmatism. In immigrant areas in modern cities, traditions and customs rule. In the secluded sections of one's own home many useless objects are preserved, and in the protected side of one's own thinking cobwebs gather on antiquated beliefs.

An old Chinese saying reads: "I approach my elder brother with respect, my father and mother with veneration, my grandfather with awe." To ancestor worship with its emphasis on the past, the phenomenal stability of China is partly due. All human groups, in fact, rely upon culture patterns for stability.

---

[1] The lag in family culture is clearly presented in an article by F. Stuart Chapin, "The Lag of Family Mores," in the *Journal of Applied Sociology*, IX: 243–48.

If it were not for tradition and custom no human group would possess permanence, and yet, where tradition and custom rule, there is danger of overconservatism and group stagnation. Where culture diffusion is blocked, progress is stopped.

On the other hand, the culture patterns of a group at any particular time are an invitation to make new inventions. They constitute a dependable starting point from which to make new sallies into undiscovered realms of knowledge and technique. They are the groundwork of all social stability and the spring-board of all progress.

PROBLEMS

1. What is culture?
2. What makes a cultured person?
3. Give two illustrations of folkways with one representing the mores and the other not.
4. Cite an item that belongs to your traditions and one to your customs.
5. Distinguish by illustration between the mores and the morals of any group of which you are a member.
6. What does the study of culture show regarding the unity of mankind?
7. Although two persons may have the same general cultural heritage, why does the actual heritage that each appropriates vary?
8. Do animals have culture?
9. Compare Paleolithic culture by illustration with Neolithic culture.
10. Cite two or three of the predominating elements in the culture of Western Europe today.
11. How do the predominating phases of the culture today of Western Europe differ from those of Eastern Asia (China and Japan)?
12. In what ways can you say that there has been an advance in culture since Neolithic days?
13. Distinguish between culture pattern and culture trait.
14. Select any culture trait and indicate its culture area boundaries.
15. Distinguish between culture adhesion and culture complex.
16. What is the relation between culture patterns and social problems?
17. Illustrate concretely how some particular culture trait has travelled from one part of the earth to another.
18. Illustrate concretely culture diffusion by direction.

19. How are "independent origins" of culture, "culture parallels," and "culture convergence" related?

20. Give a concrete illustration of "culture lag."

21. When is culture diffusion a positive value and when is it a negative one?

READINGS

BABCOCK, DONALD C., *Man and Social Achievement* (Longmans, Green and Company, New York, 1929).

BLACKMAR, FRANK W., *History of Human Society* (Charles Scribner's Sons, New York, 1926).

BOAS, FRANZ, *Anthropology and Modern Life* (W. W. Norton and Company, Inc., New York, 1928).

DIXON, ROLAND B., *The Building of Cultures* (Charles Scribner's Sons, New York, 1928).

ELLWOOD, CHARLES A., *Cultural Evolution* (The Century Company, New York, 1927).

FOLSOM, J. K., *Culture and Social Progress* (Longmans, Green and Company, New York, 1928).

GOLDENWEISER, A. A., *Early Civilization* (Alfred A. Knopf, New York, 1923).

KROEBER, A. L., *Anthropology* (Harcourt, Brace and Company, New York, 1923).

LOWIE, ROBERT H., *Are We Civilized?* (Harcourt, Brace and Company, New York, 1929).

RADIN, PAUL, *Social Anthropology* (McGraw-Hill Book Company, Inc., New York, 1932).

SMITH, G. ELLIOTT, and others, *Culture* (W. W. Norton and Company, Inc., New York, 1927).

SPENCER, ANNA G., *Woman's Share in Social Culture* (J. B. Lippincott Company, Philadelphia, 1925).

SUMNER, W. G., *Folkways* (Ginn and Company, Boston, 1907).

TYLOR, EDWARD B., *Anthropology* (D. Appleton and Company, New York, 1916).

——, *Primitive Culture* (Brentano's, New York, 1924).

WALLAS, GRAHAM, *Our Social Heritage* (Yale University Press, 1921).

WALLIS, WILSON D., *Culture and Progress* (McGraw-Hill Book Company, Inc., New York, 1930).

WISSLER, CLARK, *An Introduction to Social Anthropology* (Henry Holt and Company, New York, 1929).

——, *Man and Culture* (Thomas Y. Crowell Company, New York, 1923).

CHAPTER IV

PSYCHO-SOCIAL APPROACH

In group life the psycho-social factors are more important perhaps than any others. They are the most subjective and the closest to the dynamic heart of personality. In fact they are the center of personality.

Psycho-social factors function within the limits set by ecological and cultural factors. They give groups their characteristic trends, and they are the keys to all social problems.

Psycho-social nature is composed of instinctive tendencies, feelings, desires, wishes, in short, of impulses to action of all sorts. It is guided by attention, and through repetition becomes habitual. It includes gregariousness and communication. It stimulates invention and suggestion. It reacts to group life in terms of attitudes and values. It is the essence of social processes and social control.

INSTINCTIVE AND FEELING REACTIONS

Every person begins life with *instinctive* impulses, that is, with inborn psychical tendencies biologically transmitted. A specific sensory stimulus releases a definite mode of behavior, which is the same in all members of the species.

Instinctive reactions are ways of behaving which have been the most successful in the past. They are modes of behavior that promote the welfare [1] of the individual through the self-preservation impulses; the continuance of the family and racial groups through the sex impulses; and the welfare of all social groups, through the gregarious impulses. In addition there are inquisitive, acquisitive, combative, play, and creative

[1] As such they bear a definite relation to the *mores*, discussed in a preceding chapter.

tendencies with instinctive bases. Instinctive tendencies, however, are so definitely conditioned or modified by social stimuli that it is impossible to draw any sharp line between them as hereditary and as environmental forces.

Social groups are partly the products of instinctive factors. For example, the family rests upon sex, parental, and gregarious impulses. Occupational groups are products in part of the urges to be active and to satisfy hunger, vanity, and other deep-seated urges. Acquisitiveness explains many business organizations. The play tendencies culminate in a variety of recreational and amusement groups. Gregariousness leads to neighborhood, community, and national group life. Inquisitiveness partially explains not only invention and discovery, but also the nature of school, college, and university groups. Unsatisfied longings regarding the hereafter culminate in religious groups. All the human groups to be studied later in this book are indebted to the instinctive elements in human nature.[1]

The term, instinct, was once used to designate certain complex sets of activities, which taken together very largely determined personal life.[2] It is now thought by most sociologists that the term is too-inclusive, and that an instinct is chiefly an innate tendency emerging in traits that are environmentally stimulated.[3] Instincts as once conceived were too inflexible, readymade, deterministic. The preference today is to keep the idea of instinctive tendencies with a flexible modifiable make-up, but to discard explanations in terms of large-scale, ready-made, inflexible instincts.

The *feelings* represent the tone of the organism and evaluate

[1] An instinctive urge is composed of a drive or mechanism. A specific stimulus will automatically set off or release this mechanism. The mechanism in question is composed of neurones, sensory and motor, coördinated closely, so that a stimulus traverses the combination and emerges in overt action. After the stimulus first releases the mechanism it is difficult for the individual to control the process.

[2] See William McDougall, *Introduction to Social Psychology* (John W. Luce and Company, Boston, 1914), Ch. II.

[3] L. L. Bernard in his volume on *Instinct* (Henry Holt and Company, New York, 1924), shows how the term "instinct" is used in several hundred different senses, and hence has become unusable.

activities on the basis of *past experiences*, either personal or group. Instinctive and all other actions are likely to be accompanied by feeling evaluations. The mention of an activity, such as going to a specific social affair, produces a pleasant feeling or an unpleasant tone of the organism, according to the person's past experiences in that particular. The pleasant feeling is accompanied by an approaching reaction; the unpleasant, by a withdrawal response.[1] A feeling has been defined as the lowest form of consciousness.[2]

Both instinctive and non-instinctive actions are accompanied not only by feeling tones but also by emotional responses. An *emotion* is a complex of feelings and sensations which accompanies a particular set of responses. The blocking of one's urgent desires is often followed by the rise of the emotion of anger. A victory won is followed by an emotion of joy. The realization that a valued possession may be lost is accompanied by the emotion of fear.[3] Certain emotions are energizing, as anger; others are debilitating, as sorrow. Emotions represent a higher form of consciousness than do the feelings.[4]

Sympathetic emotion is a powerful socializing force, that is, it draws people together, and arouses in them a "we feeling." When one has sympathy for another person, he can put himself in the other's social situations and can feel as the other person feels. Such an exercise tends to produce a socialized person and to develop a deep-seated sense of social responsibility. When sympathy operates, for example, between an employer and his employees, problems of capital and labor tend to be solved with relative ease.

[1] The amoeba which approaches and surrounds certain substances, and which withdraws from other substances shows rudimentary reactions similar to those of the child who reaches for candy but pulls back from castor oil, or similar to the person who wants to get better acquainted with the stranger whom he likes at first sight, but who turns away from the stranger whom he suspicions and dislikes.

[2] L. L. Bernard, *An Introduction to Social Psychology* (Henry Holt and Company, New York, 1926), p. 159.

[3] William McDougall coupled a particular emotion with a particular instinct, such as the emotion of anger with the instinct of pugnacity, but this interpretation is doubtless carried too far.

[4] L. L. Bernard, *op. cit.*, p. 160.

Sentiment is a highly developed form of feeling. It is a combination of feelings organized about a definite object, person, or idea. It is more enduring than an emotion or a simple feeling. It is dynamic and colorful. A person is more conscious of his sentiments than of his emotions and feelings. Sentiments are permanent forces in personal relations. In the form of love or hate they assume lasting proportions.

The term, basic urge, or wish, is more satisfactory sociologically than instinct. A *basic urge* has hereditary origins, is dynamic and powerful, requires satisfaction, but it can be satisfied in countlessly different ways. It is not so ready-made by heredity as is an instinct and it does not demand one and only one type of satisfaction. Hence, "basic urges" seem to fit actual human behavior more appropriately than do "instincts."

Lester F. Ward, distinguished American pioneer in sociology, called desires the dynamic agents in human society; and mind, the directive agent.[1] He likened desires to the engines of a ship; and mind, to the directing rudder. Without the rudder the ship flounders along with the current; without the engines, the ship goes in circles. When the rudder is pointed toward a specific goal and held steady, then the engines drive the ship across the waves and tides, as well as through gales and storms.

"Wishes," the term used by W. I. Thomas,[2] has been criticized because it is easily confused with "the Freudian wish." Since Thomas' classification has elements of fundamental worth it may be kept but considered under the title of "basic urges." To his four wishes, a fifth one, namely, to aid, may be added.[3] As a result, we may think of five basic urges which drive people and groups across and along the currents and cross currents of human society.

There is (1) the urge for *new experience*, the craving for adventure, the search for the different. Everyone, "if he be young

[1] L. F. Ward, *Pure Sociology* (Ginn and Company, Boston, 1903), p. 103.
[2] W. I. Thomas, *The Unadjusted Girl* (Little, Brown, and Company, Boston, 1923), Ch. I.
[3] E. S. Bogardus, "The Fifth Wish," *Sociology and Social Research*, XVI: 75–77.

enough, possesses the urge for new experience." Experience often repeated grows dull and non-stimulating; new experience is "the spice of life," is stimulating, and is expansive in its effects on personality.

(2) The urge for *security* is the opposite of the urge for new experience. It holds the latter in check and prevents it from becoming foolhardy. It is accompanied by fear and results in avoidance. It conserves. Were it not for the urge for adventure, it would hold back too much and stagnation would ensue.

(3) The urge for *response* has a social hue. It is the generic force in group life. It seeks company. It fears being alone. Nearly everyone seeks response from other persons daily. To be cut off from all other human beings is a gigantic shock, the worst of punishments, the most disorganizing of experiences.

(4) The urge for *recognition* is found in tendencies to obtain social standing. *Status* is the goal of this urge. Rank, wealth, power are its aims. A person will fight to obtain a coveted status; he will struggle hard to maintain that status. Ideals will often be sacrificed for status. A person may have high status in one group and low status in another at the same time. Everybody wants to be a somebody. However, status is unscientifically awarded. It is based on feelings and opinions, and on values little analyzed or scrutinized. Therefore, a person is continually in a dilemma: he wants to develop a well-rounded personality and yet his urge for recognition may pull him in untoward directions and distort his personality.

(5) The urge to help, to *aid* others in trouble also seems at times to be generic and to operate even in the face of the other four self-building urges. It may lead to sacrificing one's life for the welfare of other persons. It endures great hardships without thought of personal praise or gain. It builds the noblest personalities.

ATTENTIVE AND HABITUAL REACTIONS

The individual begins life equipped with impulses, feelings, urges, but the group environment presents so many problems that the individual must make special efforts to cope with them. Environmental pressures are so numerous and so insistent that the individual must distinguish between them. The result is *attention*. By attentive activity a person can make necessary adjustments to environment.

If you do not give attention in a college class to what the instructor is saying or to the class discussion, you are not present. To pay attention is to be present and to be a potential participant. To the extent that one is thinking of other matters during a class hour, to that degree he is absent.

Attention is more complex than feeling and emotion, for while the latter forces enable one to evaluate the past roughly, attention helps one to evaluate the future as well as the past. Moreover, the evaluation afforded by attention is more accurate. Through usage there comes a development of attentive activity known as *cognition*. In its most developed phases, cognition evaluates life factors that are present "in neither time nor space"; it transforms environmental conditions; it builds new levels of personal and social living. It reaches the heights of pure *reason*, dealing with abstractions and with their meanings.

All the scientific inventions of the past, all the developments of the arts, all the human control over nature are largely the product of reason. At present, man's reason is confronted with mastering his social environment, his anti-social attitudes, his self-centered and powerful private interests. Technocracy has described well the challenge that now faces civilization, namely, the necessity to direct to welfare ends the processes of production and distribution of wealth.

An individual is a somewhat independent center of energy. He is not compelled to respond to every stimulus that he receives. If he were forced to react to all the stimuli which come his way he would soon go to pieces mentally. He is able to be selective.

Selecting is determined by *stereotypes* and *prototypes*. Stereotypes are the "pictures" that a person has in the back of his head and that are generalizations of past experiences.[1] A prototype is the "picture" that one has in the front of his head and that represents the kind of a person he would like to become in one or several particulars.[2] A person's behavior is guided by many stereotypes and prototypes. A prototype includes ideals. The stereotypes and the prototypes may work together or they may create mental conflicts. Where they function harmoniously the selecting process is greatly simplified.

As a result of selecting, a person is not wholly a machine. He is much more. His margin of "choice" varies in different social situations. This margin dwindles when a person's health breaks, when poverty increases, or when vicious and criminal attitudes develop. It is far more difficult for a person who has been reared in extreme want, vice, and crime to live a socially constructive life than it is for one who has responded favorably to love, good will, and group welfare.

Attention leads to new types of behavior. If repeated several times in succession these new behavior activities become habits and attitudes. They are modifications of instinctive reactions or of previously formed habits. When a problem is solved, a new way of acting is discovered and perhaps reduced to a habit, and a person's attention is freed for other problems.

The only reliable person is one who has established "a number of well organized habits."[3] The only person who is honest is he "who is honest by habit." When a person seriously raises the question whether or not he shall be honest, he cannot be trusted; the person who is trustworthy is he who is habitually honest.

Groups are based on well-formed habits in persons. Group life would be impossible if one person could not trust, or depend in any way upon, any other person. As soon as mutual con-

[1] Walter Lippmann, *Public Opinion* (Harcourt, Brace and Company, New York, 1922).
[2] Alfred Adler, *The Science of Living* (Garden City Publishing Company, New York, 1929), pp. 67ff.
[3] John Dewey, *Human Nature and Conduct* (Henry Holt and Company, New York, 1922), Part One, Section I.

fidence breaks, the group goes to pieces. Modern credit transactions break down when a few big financiers are convicted of unreliability or crookedness. The League of Nations contends against the grim fact that nations do not fully trust one another.

Habit is more than standardization; its main function is not to enslave, as in the case of persons whose lives are lost in powerful habits, but to give freedom. Habit frees a person from attending to the countless details of walking, talking, spelling, calculating. It utilizes chains of mechanisms which when released by appropriate stimuli operate automatically. Some persons have relatively few dependable habits and are "wishy-washy." Others are almost completely "habitualized," and have become automatons. The former type of person rarely knows his own mind; the latter hardly knows that he has a mind. Between is a happy medium. Habit comes from *habere*, "to have," but all too often habits have the person instead of the person having helpful, freedom-giving habits.

In some groups nearly every person has similar habits of thought and action, and "nobody thinks at all." There is little interstimulation and little progress. Stagnation rules. Vested interests in any field try to prevent new habits from developing.

In other groups nearly every person has habits that are different from those of his associates. Interstimulation often breeds antagonisms. Intra-group conflicts dissipate group energy. Again, there is a happy medium for group efficiency.

GREGARIOUSNESS AND COMMUNICATION

Human beings often respond similarly to like stimuli, because their basic physical equipment is similar. The fact that human beings react to fundamental social stimuli in similar ways enables them to survive in the struggle for existence. Persons the world around, irrespective of race, respond in similar ways to losses and gains, to loves and hates, to kindness or abuse. Their common nature explains *gregariousness*.

Those groups of animals survive best which respond together against danger. Similarity in responses is necessary for survival.

Such similarities lay the groundwork for social groups, and comprise the essence of gregariousness.

Gregariousness implies none of the higher attributes of mind. Among animals it manifests itself in a strong uneasiness in isolation and a sense of satisfaction in being one of a group. The classic illustration is that of the ox which shows no affection for his fellows so long as he is among them, but when the herd becomes separated from him he displays extreme distress until he is able to rejoin the group.[1]

Gregariousness is usually confirmed by habitual reactions. Since individuals are born in a group and grow up in groups the strength of the gregarious tendency is accentuated. Since every person is partly group-made, it is torture to him to be forced to be entirely alone for any length of time. Hence solitary punishment is regarded by many as a mode of torture too cruel and unnatural to be longer practiced.

For everyone except a few highly educated persons, the primary condition for amusement is to be a member of a crowd.[2] For every person who goes to the mountains to enjoy a vacation there are hundreds who frequent Coney Island. The normal daily occupation of hundreds if not thousands of Milanese is that of walking up and down the streets and in the Gallerio Vittorio, where thousands regularly gather. Gregariousness unites, but it also segregates. It affords the boundaries for groups and of cliques within groups. It helps to determine the scope of social alliances.

Communication is the use by one individual of symbols whose meanings are understood by other persons. The essence of language is a symbol and its meaning. The sentinel members of a flock of wild geese give warning cries which secure automatic responses of flight. If these cries were not followed by quick, automatic flight, the group would not long survive. Among higher animals a set of cries, calls, and similar symbols together

[1] Francis Galton, *Inquiries into Human Faculty and Its Development* (E. P. Dutton and Company, New York, 1908), p. 72.
[2] William McDougall, *An Introduction to Social Psychology*, p. 86.

with appropriate responses guarantee group life. With human beings these symbols and their meanings result in elaborate languages, and varied literatures.

A common means of communication enables individuals to work together advantageously. It is essential for coöperative action, but its presence does not necessarily guarantee coöperation. Communication multiplies both coöperation and conflict.

Communication between parent and offspring is a generic form of language. The human mother can easily recognize a half a dozen different cries on the part of her infant. From these simple sounds, a complicated language develops, so that at maturity, a person may have acquired a vocabulary ranging from two thousand to ten thousand words.[1] In addition he has acquired a large number of significant inflections of the voice and numerous silent symbols, such as facial gestures and pantomimic gestures of the hands, arms, shoulders, and of the body as a whole.

In its simplest form communication is characterized by feeling-symbols. The angry tone of voice is a symbol boiling over with meaning. It speaks far louder than words. Only under careful personal control are individuals able to keep their communicative-behavior from sinking at times to uncontrolled animal levels. It is the way in which a person says a thing rather than the thing that is said which carries the meaning. It is the pantomimic and facial gestures that accompany a statement which indicate the degree of conviction.

Language is a conversation of attitudes and appropriate responses.[2] It is "a conversation of gestures" of the hands, shoulders, face, and vocal apparatus. *Gestures* are either pantomimic (chiefly of the hands and shoulders), facial (centering about the eyes and mouth), and vocal (including spoken language). A gesture is the beginning of an act. Each gesture stands

---

[1] It is reported that a recent tabulation of 10,000 words heard over the telephone in a considerable number of conversations by different persons, showed that 80 per cent of the total number of words used was confined to only 155 different words.

[2] G. H. Mead, "Social Consciousness and the Consciousness of Meaning," *Psychological Bulletin*, VII: 397ff. Also see Floyd H. Allport, *Social Psychology* (Houghton Mifflin Company, Boston, 1924), Ch. VI.

for a whole act. As soon as the meaning is clear and an appropriate response is forthcoming, the gesture is discontinued. Sometimes we are obliged to act out the whole meaning that we have in mind. Again, the merest hint of a gesture conveys the total meaning.

A great deal of trouble arises at the point of misunderstanding of gestures. A person says one thing but his meaning is misconstrued. His gesture is taken out of the setting in which he conceives it, and is lifted bodily over into a different situation as experienced by another person. If we would understand one another, we must understand the social situations which generate and give meaning to gestures. Groups, as well as persons, fall into similar misunderstandings, but they may protect themselves from such grievous results by securing a comprehension of the social situations which lie behind the gestures of other groups.

As long as communication is pantomimic, facial, and vocal, its range is limited. When it takes the form of *writing* it expands its range in both space and time. "A drop of ink can make a million think." Writing is a form of communication that has undergone an interesting evolution. It began in putting very simple pictures and symbols on crude materials, and it has reached the level of hand-decorated tomes.

Writing was first (1) mnemonic, or memory-aiding. Some tangible object was used for a record between people who are separated. This object was used as a remembering device. It "carried" the voice of a friend beyond the time and place of its immediate expression. (2) The pictorial phase was that in which a picture of the object under consideration was reproduced. At a glance its story is revealed. (3) The ideographic phase, as the name implies, was that in which the pictures became representative. There was a shift from the actual to the symbolic, and written communication fell into line with all language with its symbols and meanings. (4) The phonetic phase is that in which sound signs are created, such as the letters of the alphabet, and are put together in the form of words. The alphabetic phase of written communication is characterized by signs or symbols for the basic sounds of the human voice. It was very long after man appeared on earth before he realized that all the words which he utters are expressed by a few sounds and that each of these sounds may be given a sign. When constant signs were used to represent constant sounds there occurred the invention of the alphabet, one of the momentous triumphs of the human mind. The alphabet was built on the principle that the sign of an eye picture suggests the sound, independent of the meaning of the sound.[1]

Over two hundred alphabets have been invented, but less than fifty have survived. India was the center of alphabet manufacture.[2] The chief alphabets today are the Chinese, Arabic, and Roman. The latter is the vehicle of the culture of Western civilization, and its children the English and French languages have become the main official languages of the League of Nations as well as of the world. Only through the invention of the alphabet was the preservation of all that is worth while in group and personal experiences made possible. Only so could educational systems develop.

As a special means of insuring accuracy to communication, *numbers* were invented. A debt of inexpressible magnitude is due those unknown and unhonored persons who first made the cipher and the nine strange looking marks known as the numerals of the Arabic system. These symbols represented a great advance over the Roman numerals, although the latter were truly remarkable. Special thanks is due him who invented the cipher, for without it modern banking, large-scale credit transactions, and the like, would be impossible.

Communication thus originated in the need to meet problems arising in social situations. It arose in inarticulate cries, which in term took the form of symbols and meanings. As communication developed, the growth of group life became possible. As a result of group history elaborate literatures have been built up gradually and have become an outstanding testimony to the permanent values in language.

[1] Edward Clodd, *The Story of the Alphabet* (D. Appleton and Company, New York, 1901), Chs. II, III. [2] *Ibid.*, p. 204.

INVENTION AND SUGGESTION

Out of the original nature of man and of the stimuli generated by social situations arises inventive ability. Original nature is not merely a repetition of past tendencies; it is also characterized by special talents and by *margins of uniqueness*.[1]

Inventiveness and uniqueness have origins in physical and mental energy. The concentration of mental energy on the part of nature sometimes explains the appearance of talent, aptitude, and of genius. The concentration of mental energy for a length of time by a person of standard ability gives that person an advantage over his fellows who do not so concentrate. It enables him to penetrate uncharted territory, and to discover unsuspected relationships. Concentration of mental energy, either by the "born genius" or the "hard-work genius," may lead to invention.

Nearly every person has inventive ability enough to contribute something to group life. This ability is rarely developed; it is often allowed to go little stimulated; it may be discouraged. A current report that only 4 per cent of the population of the United States has special ability is discouraging to all the rest of us. Fortunately not all of the remaining 96 per cent will accept such a report as final, and moreover, some of them will demonstrate a superiority above the average of the highly tooted 4 per cent.

Formal education has stressed copying, following accepted standards and established thought without inquiry. Low grades and failures are meted out to all who do not conform. There is soundness in some such emphasis only when invention, bona fide criticism, and creative thinking are at the same time put at a premium. It is often only by accident that inventive ability is discovered, stimulated, and set to work.

It has been said that it is as "natural to invent as to imitate," although the latter process as commonly understood is far

[1] For a fuller statement of the concept of "margins of uniqueness" see the writer's *Fundamentals of Social Psychology* (The Century Company, New York, 1931), Ch. IX.

easier. Inventing is defying the ordinary currents of life, while imitating is drifting or acting like other persons. Invention is largely a process of many trials and of final success in seeking new mental goals.

Imitation has several meanings.[1] (1) One who imitates may simply have behavior patterns like the one imitated. The actions of the latter are stimuli which release the behavior patterns of the former. Little if any conscious effort is involved. (2) One who has behavior patterns in process of development, may respond quickly and with little effort to stimuli in line with the inaugurated patterns. (3) One who has set up a prototype for himself will respond to stimuli in that direction even though a great deal of laborious effort is required. All the learning processes come under this phase of imitation. The deliberate copying of superior achievements of others even at great expense of time and effort is imitation, but so different from the first type mentioned in this paragraph that the two processes do not deserve the same label.

The child obtains the mass of his attitudes by imitating in one way or other the copies that are set before him in his family, play, school, religious, racial, and community groups. In these ways his impulses are organized in the early years of life in keeping with the culture patterns of his elders and associates. By the time the seventh or eighth year is reached the foundation lines of the child's personality are established. Since a child's stock of ideas is relatively small and his means of criticism are scanty, he easily adopts many of the culture patterns by which he is surrounded.

The need today of inventing in spiritual realms is greater than in material and mechanical fields. Technocracy has demonstrated all too well that material inventions and techniques have dominated man. Special talent and genius have been applied in the field of mechanical invention until the material

---

[1] See Ellsworth Faris, "The Concept of Imitation," *American Journal of Sociology*, XXXII: 367–78, and Floyd H. Allport, *Social Psychology* (Houghton Mifflin Company, Boston, 1924), pp. 239–42.

world has come to control both man's heart and brain, and then has given him a jiu-jitsu twist, throwing him down in despair and fear. Material inventions have so far advanced beyond the spiritual and social control of them that people have been either lulled into inertia or decay by a superfluity of luxuries, or else thrown out of employment, subjected to personal disorganization, and driven by hunger into revolution.

Talent and genius crop out in the inherited artistic, mathematical, mechanical, reasoning, and remembering tendencies. The appearance of talent and genius in any given person is difficult to predict. The biological mutant or sport appears unexpectedly; talent may spring into operation without announcement.

Human groups are wasteful of talent and genius. They often do not recognize such ability or else they label it undesirable because of its upsetting, creative behavior. The human genius is as likely to be born in the tenement as in the mansion. The former type is likely to be choked off by environmental pressures; the latter, to be soothed to inertia by environmental luxuries. Current attempts in schools to segregate the "superbrights" have so far been disappointing in that the "superbrights" have been made abnormal, and the rest have grown disheartened by an implied hopelessness. The aim is sound but the methods need to be perfected.

Suggestibility is a person's degree of readiness to respond more or less uncritically to stimuli. It is related to imitation, for it is the degree to which a person is likely to copy or to learn. One's suggestibility depends on what behavior patterns he already has acquired, what patterns he has inaugurated, what his goals are, and what is the nature of his prototypes. One's suggestibility varies from day to day according to his state of health, to his degree of fatigue; according to his temperament, sex, age, knowledge, critical ability; according to the source and volume of the stimuli.

Suggestion is the process of giving out stimuli that are accepted more or less uncritically. *A suggestion* is the particular stimulus which is accepted uncritically. Suggestion is the setting of examples and the giving out of stimuli; imitation in its various phases is the responding to or adopting of the "suggestions." *Direct suggestion* is the process of sending forth stimuli without disguise, plainly, in the form of orders. *Indirect suggestion* is "a flankwise movement." While a person's attention is centered on one idea another idea is presented. A person is taken "off guard." A college student is asked to sign a petition for a holiday. At once he "signs up" without reading the petition, which ends with a request that all who accept the holiday "be publicly beheaded" on the campus after their return! Indirect suggestion is a widespread and practical field for investigation.

Fashion suggestion is the process of advancing any new object or idea because it is new and because persons are likely to accept it. There are many bases of fashion suggestion. (1) The extensive reading of newspapers and magazines favors fashion suggestion. (2) Travel and migration result in attitudes that favor the new as opposed to the old. (3) Freedom of discussion breaks the spell of tradition and custom, and forward-looking teachers deliver the young from time-worn prejudices. (4) Individualism makes possible the reign of fashion. In attempting to set themselves off from each other, persons unwittingly promote fashion. (5) Competitive business deliberately furthers advertising and arouses countless new wants.

Competitive business is largely responsible for *fashion racing*.[1] By fashion racing is meant the process of setting a pace in adopting new objects, such as styles of dress, by some persons who regularly shift from one new object to another so as to elude the mass of alert imitators. Several different groups of persons participate at different points in the process. (1) There are the designers and the fashion-show merchants. These plan and put new objects on the market and work up anticipation in behalf of what "everyone will soon be wearing." (2) There are the pace-setters, that is, the persons who adopt a new fashion

[1] E. A. Ross in his *Social Psychology* (The Macmillan Company, New York, 1908), pp. 99, 103, has suggested the accompanying analysis.

as soon as it is put on the market. When any fashion is somewhat widely imitated, the pace-setter adopts a new fashion and thus the process continues. (3) There are the people who accept a fashion promptly so as to be taken for the pace-setters. (4) Another group are those who adopt a new fashion somewhat belatedly and in modified forms in order to avoid being conspicuous. (5) There are those who never conform.

The main law of the fashion process is that the persons or ideas which are rated as superior are copied by persons who are rated inferior.[1] Corollaries naturally follow, such as: the wealthy are copied by the poor; seniors in college, by freshmen; big business men, by little business men. A secondary law is that those who are rated inferior are occasionally and unwittingly copied by the superior especially in inferior particulars. Jazz, for example, originated on a low culture level, but made its way "upward."

ATTITUDES AND VALUES

An *attitude* is an acquired and established tendency to act with reference to some person or environmental object or matter. Attitudes arise out of experiences, either direct or derivative. A *direct experience* is one of specific personal nature. A *derivative experience* is based on hearsay. While direct experiences are usually the more effective, derivative ones may exceed direct experiences in number, and in total force and influence.

Toward those experiences which you have adjudged helpful to you, you hold favorable attitudes; toward those experiences which you have adjudged harmful, you possess unfavorable attitudes. If war has meant untold suffering, the loss of loved ones, and final disillusionment, you are likely to have an unfavorable attitude toward it. On the other hand, if it has meant a higher military rank, an increase in salary, adventure without much risk, and public applause, then your attitude will undoubtedly be highly favorable.

[1] Cf. Gabriel Tarde, *Laws of Imitation* (Henry Holt and Company, New York, 1903), pp. 213ff.

Personal experiences in social situations explain attitudes. If a person has had unfriendly contacts with one or two immigrants of a given race, he feels suspicious of the whole race. If his experiences on the other hand, have been wholly agreeable with a few members of a race, his attitudes may be friendly toward the entire race. On the basis of a limited number of personal experiences, one is quick to generalize regarding a whole class of people.[1]

The configuration of a person's attitudes explains his reactions to his new experiences and hence his new attitudes. Each new experience is interpreted or defined by a person in terms of his configuration or organization of previous experiences and attitudes. The way in which a person *defines his experiences*, or interprets them, is vital and to be explained in terms of configuration.

Those experiences which are accompanied by feeling and emotional reactions are most impressive and enduring. An attitude that springs from a social situation where sentiment surges high is difficult to change. A child who is terribly frightened by meeting an alleged ghost on a dark night is never quite able to throw off the resultant attitude. An Armenian immigrant who recalls seeing his parents brutally killed by Turkish persecutors can never wholly wipe out unfavorable attitudes toward Turks.

Every attitude is accompanied by a *value*. An attitude and a value are parts of the same process. The person or object toward which one has an attitude is a value. An attitude is subjective; it is a part of the mental equipment of a person. A value, however, is a part of a person's environment. Neither without the other would have any significance. All of human life that has any meaning may be included under attitudes and values.[2] Personal experiences are the whirlpools in which attitudes change regarding values. As environmental objects help or hinder a person they rise or fall in his scale of values.

[1] For further illustrative materials see E. S. Bogardus, *Immigration and Race Attitudes* (D. C. Heath and Company, Boston, 1928), Chs. IV–XI.
[2] See Thomas and Znaniecki, *The Polish Peasant in Europe and America* (Alfred A. Knopf, New York, 1927), I: 10–20.

Attitudes may be either favorable or unfavorable; and values, either positive or negative. We have a favorable attitude toward a positive value and an unfavorable attitude toward a negative value. Whatever furthers our status is likely to be regarded as a positive value; whatever hinders, is considered to be a negative value. A positive value is something that draws a person toward it; a negative one, something that drives one away from it. A lady illustrates a negative value as follows:

> As far as Mrs. S. is concerned I hope that I never see her again. She may be a fine person and a good neighbor but as for me I never want to have anything more to do with her. The sight of her or even her name brings up unpleasant and even disgusting memories.[1]

The welfare of loved ones is a fundamental personal value. For the sake of members of the family group and of closest friends, a person will face all manner of risks and dangers, and give up choicest treasures, even life. For their sake the laborer struggles on day after day in earning money for the bare necessities of life; and the man of wealth furnishes them with the finest comforts of life, all the advantages of travel, the ablest physicians in case of illness.

Another basic personal value is the opportunity to do creative things and to discover truth. To these ends the best years of life may be freely and enthusiastically devoted. Limitless joy is found in creative action.

A third fundamental social value is the group. At the crucial tests human beings give up their loved ones and their own lives for the sake of the group. Under the flags of the various national groups, millions marched to death in the World War. Self is hesitatingly if not freely placed on the altar of the group. Group opinion is almost all-powerful. Favorable group opinion expands personality; unfavorable group judgments constitute the severest forms of punishment.

Behavior is the test of one's attitudes. Since the latter are

---

[1] From personal interview materials.

subjective it is one's behavior over a period of time that affords a real criterion of them. One often does not know his own attitudes until he is required to act in a particular situation. The study of behavior, therefore, is the most worth-while approach to the understanding of human attitudes.

Opinions are different from attitudes. An opinion is what one thinks or says about something; an attitude is what he does about it. We have many opinions which are very shallow and fluctuating, but attitudes are more stable. An opinion may simply signify that one is not sure. Ordinarily we reserve a right to change our opinions, but not our attitudes.

Sometimes an opinion is merely an explanation of or a justification for an attitude. Some opinions are mostly "hot air"; some are put forth "for effect." A person may vigorously denounce certain conduct, but when he faces a pertinent situation himself he acts differently from what he said that he would do or not do.

Opinions range up into the realms of idealism; attitudes are confined to potential behavior. A single act may be camouflage, but a series of connected ones over a considerable period of time indicates an attitude.

The integrated opinions of a number of people create values, and remold attitudes. Favorable opinion gives value to an object; that which group opinion favors is reputable. Opinion attracts attention to persons and objects; and to the extent that it approves, new values prosper. Only here and there do we find a person well enough trained to review group opinion scientifically.

In times of group crises, such as war, attitudes and values undergo rapid modification. When the United States entered the World War there was no widespread tendency to send millions of soldiers to Europe. Pulpits, newspapers, motion pictures, government representatives, four-minute speakers joined in whirlwind campaigns throughout the country, starting far-flung currents of feeling and opinion "to make the world safe for democracy," and to fight "to end war." The results were almost miraculous. Millions of men left their accustomed pursuits, their homes and loved ones; they entered upon training to use guns, bombs, poison gas, and bayonets; they embarked on ships sailing with lights out over submarine-infested seas. They gave up the values of peace for those of war. Their attitudes shifted from earning money, following personal desires, and enjoying the comforts of home to responding to the call of the nation.

An attitude is a neuro-psychical mechanism that is expressed in either pro-social or anti-social ways. A general attitude is a viewpoint, or an integration of specific attitudes. "I have a religious attitude of life," is an example. A group attitude is an acquired, established tendency on the part of a number of persons to act.[1]

SOCIAL PROCESSES

Human interaction often follows certain sequences or processes. A *social process* is a mode in which a sequence of interaction occurs. To understand social processes is to understand social problems. To diagnose social processes is the main goal of sociology.

Isolation is the absence of social process, or at least, of interaction. The examination of any group at work, even of a committee, shows that some persons are not taking part, that some are holding aloof, that some are absent, or perhaps are present but are not paying attention. As a result they are isolated, and the group is isolated from them. The loss is mutual.

Isolation makes a person dead timber. He develops distorted attitudes and a "queer" personality. In a family, for example, one person may become separated from the rest in spirit, or he may desert. His isolation means a broken family.

The most important phase of labor-capital controversies today is isolation. As a result, labor does not understand capital, and for the same reason, the employer views his employees with prejudiced eyes. When industry was carried on largely by hand

[1] This type has been called a "social attitude" by E. B. Reuter in "The Social Attitude," *Journal of Applied Sociology*, VII: 97–101.

labor and employer and employee worked side by side, isolation was uncommon, but when the factory system developed and large-scale manufacturing arose, then a "great gulf" ensued.

Isolation between races is common and provocative of grave misunderstandings. Racial groups have developed in different parts of the earth and under various climatic conditions, with resultant differences in cultures and attitudes. Without contacts, isolation takes place and ill will, scorn, prejudices, and wars have been the harvest. Isolation prevents racial groups from viewing each other with understanding and sympathetic eyes.

Isolation is found in all international disputes. Each nation has built barriers around itself. When a world conference occurs progress is not great unless isolation can be overcome. In consequence of isolation and of implied competition, nations are mutually suspicious and unwilling to trust one another.

Isolation is absence of a sympathy and understanding. It involves an inability or unwillingness to put one's self or one's group in the position of the other fellow or group, and to consider problems in the light of mutual and larger situations.

Isolation is *mutual*. A disobedient child is isolated from his parents; they in turn are cut off from him. Both lose. In a labor-capital controversy the isolation is double-headed. Again both lose. Nations isolated from each other are mutual victims. All lose.

Isolation means *social distance*, which refers to the different degrees of sympathetic understanding that exist between persons, between groups, and between persons and groups.[1] A low degree of or no sympathetic understanding is isolation.

Interaction is the inclusive social process. It is a process of interstimulation. An infant could not possibly mature without social interaction, and an adult could not maintain a normal personality outside of social contacts. Groups likewise thrive through interaction with other groups, but shrivel without it. Interaction draws out, accelerates, and discovers unsus-

[1] See articles on "Social Distance" by the writer in *Sociology and Social Research*, Vols. XII–XIV, XVI–XVIII.

pecting powers. It increases mental activity, fosters comparisons of ideas, and multiplies achievement. It enlarges human horizons, sets new tasks, and electrifies life.

Conflict is the most striking form of interaction. Conflict is any clash of social forces. A conflict may be overt, as in the case of two fist fighters. It may be subtle, as when opponents contend surreptitiously against each other, seeking by calumny and chicanery to undermine one another. In the neighborhood group, families may gossip about each other to the destruction of each other's reputation. In politics whispering compaigns may be inaugurated to defeat a rival. In business, competitors may resort to pernicious under selling, and to steam roller methods of crushing out one another. Nations likewise may resort to trickery in diplomacy.

As a conflict waxes hot, it may degenerate into verbal gunplay, deception, and malicious lying. Any questionable cause whether slavery, alcoholism, narcotics resorts sooner or later to every conceivable means of misrepresentation.

Persons in conflict may fight viciously in broad daylight, and make no bones about it. War, the most objective form of group conflict, also maintains deceptive campaigns of propaganda in all the contending countries.

A conflict may take place between a small group and a large group of which the small is a part. Greater intensity of feeling may balance up the numerical weakness of the small group. A small committee may struggle vigorously in a college class meeting in behalf of a change in traditions. A lobby in Congress may work year in and out in behalf of a new measure or to support an endangered special interest. Any propaganda within a large association of people strives against the inertia or active opposition of the larger body.[1]

[1] Conflict between equals may bring out the best efforts of both. If it does not end in a helpless deadlock, it will effect a compromise or possibly a new and advanced stand. When two trained debaters of equal ability meet, each is likely to surpass his past record. When students and teachers freely question each other, the truth is promulgated. Children of about the same physique who compete in ordinary games may all gain physically and mentally.

Constructive conflict spurs each contestant to a maximum of effort and a maximum of gain for each. They compete in doing constructive enterprises and not in destroying each other. They are mutually stimulating and helpful.

Group conflicts may be *equal* or *unequal*.[1] Conflict that is somewhat equal (primary conflict) usually is a give-and-take process where each side learns something from the other. Even tolerance may result, and sometimes coöperation.

Unequal conflict (secondary conflict) occurs between unequal forces and means that the stronger swallows up or runs rough-shod over the weaker without learning anything or acquiring new skills. The weaker do not gain, for they are crushed. Neither do the stronger for they are not stimulated sufficiently. Equal conflict might be illustrated by a game between two championship football teams, while a contest between a college team and a kindergarten team would represent an extreme form of unequal conflict which in reality is no conflict at all.

Group conflicts may be either *destructive* or *constructive*. In destructive conflicts the aim is to get ahead by trampling someone down. The path to progress is believed to lie over the bones of adversaries. If anyone challenges an individual's or a group's march he is to be bowled over; if he challenges again, then deliver him a death blow.

The highest form of conflict is constructive. Neighborhoods may compete on "Clean Up" days to the advantage of all concerned. Farmers in a specific community may vie with each other in raising wheat so that the wheat yield of every farm is increased 50 per cent. Welfare agencies may contend against each other in rendering social service, and the best interests of everyone are advanced.

Competition is an indirect form of conflict. It is often a struggle for recognition, standing, or status. It occurs between students for scholarship ranking or for social rating. One of

[1] It was Franklin H. Giddings who drew the distinction between what he called primary and secondary conflict in his *Principles of Sociology* (The Macmillan Company, New York, 1896), pp. 101ff.

the unfortunate results of competition, however, is *prejudice*. Whoever loses out in a competitive undertaking may lose status, and at once finds it difficult not to feel prejudiced against the one who dethroned him. When "foreigners" take jobs away from native workers, the latter at once flare up with prejudice.

Antipathy is to be distinguished from prejudice, for its adverse reactions are based on unpleasant sensory impressions. Race antagonism, for example, may take the form of either antipathy or prejudice. Since these reactions are entirely different in origins, the reduction of them requires entirely different procedures.

Coöperation is a mutual working together. Persons may coöperate for self-centered gain, or for self-protection, or to do good. Groups, likewise, may coöperate for self-advancement, as in the case of a monopoly; or for mutual protection, as for instance France and Poland; or for the welfare of all groups.

Persons who coöperate may generate unbounded enthusiasm. There is almost no limit to the achievements of a thoroughly coöperating group. Coöperation not only stimulates morale but promulgates efficiency. In order that specialization may operate constructively there must be coöperation among the specialists.

Mutual aid is a special name for coöperation.[1] Kropotkin developed the theory that mutual aid has made evolution possible. Mutual aid is a powerful survival trait. Animals destroy one another through fighting and conflict, but they survive and grow in numbers through mutual aid. Primitive and modern people alike kill one another off through prolonged warfare but survive, multiply, and grow strong through mutual aid.

Coöperation may go too far; it may result in a cog-in-the-wheel organization. It may take away the identity of persons; it may degenerate into routine. Highly organized coöperation tends to crush creative effort and all the joy that goes along with creative activity.

Overorganization is a deadening form of coöperation. So

[1] P. Kropotkin, *Mutual Aid; a Factor in Evolution* (Doubleday, Page and Company, New York, 1902).

standardized are the "social" wasps, bees, and ants that they can hardly be said to have any social life at all. They are almost robots.

Overorganization means that there are too many groups. Student bodies are often overorganized. Modern city life may be so organized that many persons spend their entire time in going from committee meeting to committee meeting. Social life may become organized until life is a matter "of going to one bridge party after another" until the devotees suffer "a nervous breakdown" and must "go away for a rest."

On the rational plane coöperation is an acting together, but not so completely that the individuals become mere cogs, or slaves. It produces social morale, personal enthusiasm, and group efficiency.

Accommodation is the process of friendly give and take. It is the process of conscious adjustment by toleration, arbitration, and compromise. After contending for a time with few gains each side in a conflict learns to tolerate the other and perhaps to recede from earlier demands. It is the only feasible social process where the contending parties represent a worthy measure of truth and justice.

Passive accommodation is a process in which the environment makes over the individual.[1] *Active adaptation*, on the other hand, is the transforming of the environment by the individual. Some persons have played a dominant rôle in transforming their physical or cultural, or social environments, or all three.

Oftentimes the representatives of long-established classes fail to compromise, and go down in defeat. The leaders of economic, political, and other groups must be alert to social changes, and be willing to accommodate themselves to human needs. By such accommodation they may maintain themselves in positions of leadership indefinitely. When Bismarck inaugurated measures of social insurance he appeased the socialists; by such accommodation he continued in power.

[1] Adaptation, both passive and active, has been splendidly analyzed by Lucius M. Bristol in his *Social Adaptation* (Harvard University Press, 1915).

A privileged class always tends to violate the principle of accommodation. They become reactionary and in so doing provoke the liberal to turn radical. The result is generally conflict and revolution. Accommodation is the method of evolution. To block it leads to revolution.

Assimilation is a process whereby the attitudes of many persons are united, producing a unified group. It is the process of being conditioned to think as a unit. It is the integration of dissimilar attitudes and values, and it usually takes place unawares to those most affected.

Amalgamation is the process of making a new race out of various races. It is race mixture, or miscegenation. It is an exceedingly slow process, for it cannot be forced very well. When assimilation has occurred, amalgamation naturally follows. Without assimilation the amalgamation of races markedly different from each other is opposed strenuously and penalized by exhibitions of prejudice and ostracization.

Socialization is the process of working together, and of developing group responsibility. Each individual begins life in a self-centered way, as "a little anarchist," but slowly and surely his sense of social responsibility grows. In the early years of life the narrow and egoistic impulses dominate; in some cases they control throughout life. In fact their inherited force is so strong that life becomes a process of controlling and socializing them. In a sense discipline is a system of controlling the self-assertive impulses.

A child's gregarious and group nature also asserts itself early. The child seeks playmates. If he cannot do otherwise, he will imagine playmates; he will personify the material objects of his environment and talk to them, scold them, and love them.

While deeply grounded in inherited tendencies both social nature and self-centered nature are developed in and through group life. Environmental stimuli often determine whether the social or the self-centered forces will become supreme.

As a person matures, as he faces one harsh experience after

another, as he sometimes loses that which he values highly, he grows more sympathetic and wholesomely interested in the welfare of others. Providing it be not overwhelming, suffering socializes.

As a rule a person's socialized nature is likely to include few persons only. With an increase in far-reaching experiences a person may come to identify himself with a whole university, a community, or a nation. This identification of one's self with a large group may be propelled by self-centered impulses, that is, a person may identify himself with a group in order to become a hero, to secure election to office, or to promote his business. How many men, for example, join a national fraternal organization, a church, a golf club, in order to secure clients or customers.

A person may be socialized toward certain groups but not toward others. He may be a kind and sacrificial husband and father, but anti-social in dealing with employees, in his racial contacts, or wherever his prejudices may direct. On the other hand, some persons are arbitrary and unjust in the family circle, or toward certain neighbors, but at the same time they treat clients or customers with fine consideration.

In one sense socialization is participation; in another way it is identification for exploitation; again it may be identification without any expectation of reward.[1] It participates but does not ask: "What am I going to gain?" Socialization is a genuine and wholesome identification of a person with the welfare of other persons, of his own groups, and of other groups.[2]

A plea for socialized attitudes is made indirectly by John Galsworthy in his drama entitled *Strife* where it is shown how the bitter struggles between capital and labor are perpetuated because neither side is broad-minded enough to recognize the problems and needs of the opponent. When each contender

[1] E. S. Bogardus, *Fundamentals of Social Psychology* (The Century Company, New York, 1931), Ch. XXIII.
[2] For a discussion of moralization as a phase of socialization see C. A. Ellwood, *Christianity and Social Science* (The Macmillan Company, New York, 1923), Ch. III.

through suffering reaches a position where with unbiased eyes
it perceives the other's point of view, misunderstanding is
eliminated, and conciliation is in order. If both the opponents
in the destructive struggle between labor and capital had socialized attitudes, each would see that employers and employees
fundamentally have nearly everything in common, that their
primary aim should be to meet the needs of consumers as effi-
ciently and inexpensively as possible, and that coöperation
should dominate competition in all human relationships.

A person with socialized attitudes would not engage in any
business which is socially non-productive or which depends for
its maintenance upon destructive competition or upon gambling.
A socialized lawyer would not assist clients for pay to violate
the laws of the community. A socialized citizen would place
community and national welfare ahead of his own individual
gain. A person with socialized attitudes puts always and everywhere, the human standard of values above all else.

Social control is the process whereby a group regulates the
behavior of its members. It operates through social pressures
on one hand and social stimuli on the other. The group easily
accentuates the use of pressures. It often represses blindly,
and is suspicious of individual variations from the established
order.[1]

Social control also operates through the use of rewards,
honors, and prizes. It may stimulate individuals to act courageously, but it is chary with its rewards to those whose ideas con-
tradict revered ideas. It may emphasize rewards so much that
individuals serve the group not for the sake of the group but
of the rewards.

Social controls are the pressures or stimuli used in social
control. The controls are stimuli emanating from the group
which regulate the individual member. A law, an expression
of public opinion, a facial gesture of an official of a group—
these illustrate social controls.

[1] E. A. Ross, *Social Control* (The Macmillan Company, New York, 1901),
is a pioneer work in its field; it still retains a high rank.

Social controls become crystallized in *social institutions*. A social institution is a standardized set of human reactions, which tend to become inflexible, rigid, and to rule with an iron hand. They are slow to adopt new methods and hence sometimes rule with "a dead hand." As agents of social pressure they easily become tools of social repression. Undue and prolonged institutional pressure causes a virile group to remonstrate and to start a revolution.

Social institutions become *vested interests*. A vested interest is any social system which falls back on its past history and present connections rather than on its ability to meet human needs as a reason for its continued existence. A vested interest is one of the most dangerous agents of social control, for it grows haughty with age, and brooks little reform within itself.

The leading social institutions today are the home, the school, the church, government, recreation and amusement organizations, welfare, and art organizations. These are the main tangible agents of social control. They are the objective, crystallized integrations of social attitudes. They hold persons steady, sometimes too steady.

Law is a powerful agent of social control. *A law* is a rule laid down officially by a group for its members to observe. It is adjudged to be for the welfare of the group. By forceful, objective means it brings group standards before the attention of careless or anti-social members. By compelling the individual to live according to regulation, the group is protected, and the individual may learn to develop behavior patterns built upon group welfare. The process is often painful to the individual and costly to the group.

Group opinion is perhaps the most important phase of social control. Group opinion, or public opinion, is either *preponderant*, *majority* and *minority*, or *consensus*. Preponderant opinion is the unthinking and general feeling reaction of a group. Majority and minority opinions are the differentiated pro and con reactions of the members of a group after some discussion has occurred on a particular question. The majority opinion is often called public opinion, but it should not be confused with that public opinion which is a general opinion. A consensus opinion is the combined and common judgment of a group after each member has contributed to a truth-seeking discussion; it is quite superior to the argumentative discussion that precedes the formation of majority and minority opinions.

The psycho-social approach to the study of groups takes us into the very heart of group life. It lays bare the nature, development, and problems of personality. It furnishes the keys for understanding social problems. It points toward the prediction of human behavior.

PROBLEMS

1. What is an instinct?
2. Why has the term, instinct, proved unsatisfactory?
3. What are feelings?
4. Why are feelings so important?
5. Are women as a class more sympathetic than men? Why?
6. What is a basic urge?
7. What are the basic urges?
8. What is status?
9. How important is status as a social fact?
10. What is a prototype? How does it differ from a stereotype?
11. What are the differences between instinctive and habitual reactions?
12. What is gregariousness?
13. Are nations gregarious?
14. What is the essence of communication?
15. Why does an elderly person often talk aloud to himself?
16. What is an alphabet?
17. What is invention?
18. Do you invent much? Why?
19. Have you reached your maximum of invention?
20. What is imitation?
21. What is talent?

22. In what ways is talent wasted?
23. Distinguish between suggestion and a suggestion.
24. Distinguish between suggestibility and imitation.
25. What is fashion?
26. What is fashion racing?
27. Explain the main law of the fashion process.
28. Illustrate the difference between a direct experience and a derivative experience.
29. What is configuration of personality?
30. What is an attitude? Illustrate one.
31. Name an attitude and show how it originated.
32. Mention a change of attitude that you have experienced, and indicate how it came about.
33. Explain the difference between an attitude and a value.
34. What is the difference between an attitude and an opinion?
35. What is the best test of a person's attitudes?
36. Distinguish between an attitude and a viewpoint.
37. What is a process?
38. What is a social process?
39. Have you ever experienced isolation? Illustrate.
40. Is isolation always mutual?
41. Illustrate social distance.
42. How does social distance explain a social problem?
43. Why are conflicts so numerous?
44. How is competition related to conflict?
45. What is the difference between prejudice and antipathy?
46. For what different reasons do persons coöperate?
47. Distinguish between passive and active accommodation.
48. Explain the relation of accommodation to coöperation.
49. How are assimilation and amalgamation connected?
50. Illustrate any socialization experience of your own.
51. What is the difference between social control and a social control?
52. How have you felt social pressure?
53. Compare law and public opinion as effective agents of social control.
54. Illustrate preponderant opinion, majority and minority opinion, and consensus opinion.

READINGS

ALLPORT, FLOYD H., *Social Psychology* (Houghton Mifflin Company, Boston, 1924).

BOGARDUS, EMORY S., *Fundamentals of Social Psychology* (The Century Company, New York, 1931).

COOLEY, CHARLES H., *Human Nature and the Social Order* (Charles Scribner's Sons, New York, 1922).

——, *Social Process* (Charles Scribner's Sons, New York, 1918).

COYLE, GRACE L., *Social Process in Organized Groups* (Longmans, Green and Company, New York, 1930).

ELLWOOD, CHARLES A., *The Psychology of Human Society* (D. Appleton and Company, New York, 1925).

EWER, BERNARD C., *Social Psychology* (Henry Holt and Company, New York, 1929).

HART, HORNELL, *The Science of Human Relations* (Henry Holt and Company, New York, 1927).

KRUEGER, E. T., and W. C. RECKLESS, *Social Psychology* (Longmans, Green and Company, New York, 1931).

McDOUGALL, WILLIAM, *Introduction to Social Psychology* (John W. Luce and Company, Boston, 1914).

PARK, R. E., and E. W. BURGESS, *Introduction to the Science of Sociology* (University of Chicago Press, 1921), Chs. II–VII, VIII–XIII.

ROSS, EDWARD A., *Principles of Sociology* (The Century Company, New York, 1930), Part III.

——, *Social Psychology* (The Macmillan Company, New York, 1908).

YOUNG, KIMBALL, *Social Psychology* (Alfred A. Knopf, New York, 1930).

——, editor, *Social Attitudes* (Henry Holt and Company, New York, 1931).

PART TWO
SOCIAL GROUPS

CHAPTER V

THE FAMILY GROUP

Of all human groups the family is in many ways the most important. From its initial units, the father and mother, the child receives his physical inheritance, that is, a strong or weak mental and physical organism. "To be well-born is to possess the greatest of all gifts. To the ill-born there is nothing which this world can afford that will be adequate compensation for the lack of a good heredity." [1]

In the family the child learns the meaning of social responsibility, the importance of sportsmanship, and the necessity for coöperation. The family is the outstanding primary group, for in it a child develops his basic attitudes, patterns, ideals, and style or configuration of life.

When a child grows to adulthood he leaves one family group in order to establish another. After the experiences of courtship and romantic love he marries, having chosen thoughtfully or thoughtlessly a potential mother for his children that may be born into the new family group. A young woman possessing a mental and physical inheritance, and having received a social heritage and training from her parental family, likewise marries, having chosen thoughtfully or thoughtlessly a young man to be the father of the children that she may bear.

The two young people, the product of two different family groups, establish through the social institution of marriage, their own family group. Their attitudes change, for instead of being an irresponsible son and an irresponsible daughter who sometimes have remonstrated against parental direction, they now play the rôle of responsible father and mother, training, disciplining, and worrying about their children. Thus family

[1] S. J. Holmes, *The Eugenic Predicament* (Harcourt, Brace and Company, New York, 1933), p. x.

groups break up, new ones are established; and the process of personal growth and group change goes on. Individuals come and go, but family groups "go on forever." [1]

Early History of the Family

One may gain an understanding of the significance of the family group by considering its early history and development. Elemental forms of the family go back to the higher types of animal life. The mother and her brood or flock are everywhere evident from the domestic barnyard in America to the wilds of Africa. Here and there the father stands guard. Occasionally father and mother have effected a division of labor. Here and there the same mating lasts season after season, "till death do us part."

If the family has existed a million years, dating back to the early history of higher animals, it must be a highly significant type of social group. If it sprang up in response to need without being foisted upon any individual, it must be well founded. If nature prior to the advent of man instituted the family we may well treat it seriously. If it has continued in one form or other in an unbroken history since its first advent, we may ask: What is this marvellous institution?

Among primitive people the mother and child are the stable units of the family group. The father roamed far and wide, coming home irregularly, and staying away for periods of time. The helplessness of the infant compelled the mother to lead a home life. The irregularity of the father's habits made it necessary for the mother to gather fruit, to plant seeds, to develop hoe-culture. Engaged in the hunt and chase, the father led a more exciting life, made more social contacts, and enjoyed a wider variety of new experiences. [2]

[1] Except in those places experimenting with "free love" and state-raised children.

[2] There are two monumental works on the history of the family which represent a high type of scholarly research, namely, Edward A. Westermarck, *The History of Human Marriage* (Macmillan and Company, Ltd., London, 1902), and George Elliott Howard, *A History of Matrimonial Institutions* (University of Chicago Press, 1904).

In the early human family the mother rather than the father was the leader a great deal of the time. She stayed "on the job." Hence, it has sometimes been called the *metronymic family*, which means literally, "named after the mother." The child took the mother's name—the father was not always known. Property was transferred through the mother, since she was the stable member of the parent group. The metronymic family was well developed, for example, among many North American Indian tribes. The Iroquois Indians have been pronounced a typical metronymic people, among whom the government of the clans was to a degree in the hands of matrons as women councillors, elected by the males of the given clans.[1]

Where the pastoral form of life existed and where flocks and herds flourished, the father was the chief factor in the family group. Since the grazing of flocks and herds required considerable territory, the people moved about in small groups widely separated from each other. The wife and mother was removed from the influence and authority of her kindred. The husband's power over her by virtue of her isolation was supreme.

Under pastoral conditions, men owned and controlled the flocks. The owner of the family property literally owned the family too. The children took the father's name and inherited property through him. The eldest living son usually succeeded to the rulership of the family group.

Warfare gave men increased influence over women. The women captured in war were held as slaves and wives by their captors. The form of the family with the father at the head, possessing authority over if not ownership of the wife and children, is known as the patronymic (named after the father). It is the most common and best known type.[2]

The patronymic family of the early Hebrews has become world famous. The Old Testament affords many descriptions of

[1] A convenient volume containing helpful chapters on the history of the family is Willystine Goodsell's *A History of Marriage and the Family* (The Macmillan Company, New York, 1934).

[2] Metronymic and patronymic families are sometimes called matriarchal and patriarchal, respectively.

patriarchal families, such as those of Abraham, Isaac, and Jacob. The ancient Hebrew family is noted for the attention and care given the children. "Honor thy father and thy mother; that thy days may be long upon the land which the Lord thy God giveth thee." [1] Here is a fundamental principle which the Hebrew family bequeathed to the world, and which when observed but not overdone has given the family group a high degree of unity. Where children have not learned to respect their parents, the lasting qualities of the larger society have been rudely shaken. As a result of the unity and fidelity of the Hebrew family, the Hebrews have maintained a remarkable longevity as a people. It has been claimed that because of the unity of the Hebrew family the Hebrews, although national orphans, have survived through the centuries. Without a homeland of their own and forced to maintain themselves within other nations, often surrounded by hostile races, their family organization and their religious loyalty have been their salvation. Let their family life break down and their religion be discarded and they as a people will disappear.

Out of the early emphasis upon the family group came two universal principles of the Jewish and Christian religions. The rôle of the patriarchal father seems to have suggested the concept of the Fatherhood of God. The social responsibility developed within the Hebrew family is the apparent antecedent of the ideal of brotherhood of man.

An overemphasis upon parental control leads to ancestor worship. According to this pattern the welfare of the living depends upon the good will of the departed. In order to insure his happiness, a man's first duty is to rear a family that will continue the ancestral line unbroken. It has often been said that China's emphasis upon family stability and ancestor worship explains in part her long life as a people.

When we turn to the early Roman family of the seventh century B.C., we find that it was patriarchal. It maintained itself partly on the religious basis of ancestor worship. The

[1] Exodus 20 : 12.

family group was built around the ancestral gods, and the habitation in which the family group lived was virtually a temple, with the patriarchal head possessing the power of a god over the women and children. The house father had almost absolute power over all the members of the family. However, he could not always act arbitrarily, for he was controlled by what he believed was the will of the ancestors.

Property was held by the eldest living male member of the family; it was held in trust for the good of the entire family. In early Roman times, this eldest living male member or house father could not make a will. At his death the property passed automatically to the oldest living son.

At that time marriage was practically indissoluble and divorce unknown. It is said that for five centuries after the founding of Rome, the town had no divorces. This Roman family group possessed great stability. Although the family life was patriarchal and women and children were subjects of the patriarchal head the family reached a higher order than that of other ancient peoples save the Hebrews. It fell considerably below Hebrew family life, however, when the latter is considered at its best.

In the course of time the pendulum swung to the other extreme, and the family group began to decay. When this disintegration reached an extreme, Rome herself disintegrated. It would be an interesting problem to find out how far the breakdown of family life was responsible for the downfall of Rome. To turn the problem around: If a high level of family life had been maintained, would Rome have fallen?

The disintegration of the family group was accompanied by several interesting phenomena. (1) The family began to lose its religious significance. When marriage was viewed as a civil contract merely, the family was viewed lightly. (2) The authority of the father was broken. The right to make a will was established. The father was given first the right to divide his property among his children, and then to bequeath it to whom he pleased. When the family property was thus broken up in

units, and scattered, the family as an institution lost prestige.
(3) Women were given the right to hold property, and in the
second century B.C. to divorce their husbands. The women of
the higher social classes achieved "emancipation," and were at
liberty to do as they saw fit. (4) The personal liberty of both
men and women became personal license. Personal liberty
overthrew personal control of sex impulses. Marriages were
made and broken freely; temporary marriages were common;
sex relations were loose; and sexual immorality flaunted itself.
In reality companionate marriages were experimented with
widely. (5) The changes in economic conditions, such as the
expansion of commerce and manufacture and the growth of
cities, tended to destroy the social situations in which the family
had been the fundamental unit.[1] The decay of religious sanctions of the family, the growth of individual liberty, habits of
vice, particularly sexual vice, which were common among
Roman young men and winked at by young women, combined to
change the family from a strong primary social group into a
loose agreement of two individuals temporarily combined for
sensual pleasures. In swinging from extreme to extreme the
pendulum bore first the fruits of suppression and rigidity and
then of inefficiency and decay. In moving away from domination and slavery the momentum attained allowed the family
group to stop at no position of balanced integration. Neither
domination nor license was satisfactory. Balanced integration
was rarely reached.

Christianity was the next influence that vitally affected the
nature of the family group. Upon its Western invasion it
promptly began to reconstruct family life in Europe. It arrived
when the Roman family was at a low ebb with vice rampant.
It immediately attempted to reform the Roman family, and
succeeded in building an improved family life in Europe, somewhat like the old Hebrew patriarchal type.

(1) Christianity brought the support of religion to the family
again. It recognized marriage as a sacrament and opposed the

[1] Willystine Goodsell, *A History of Marriage and the Family.*

idea that marriage is simply a civil contract. It ascribed to marriage a religious nature and thus gave it stability once more.

(2) Christianity exalted the position of women and children. Women were treated in part as the equals of men. Motherhood was exalted, and children were put on the throne. The welfare of children began to receive attention. It was not a strict patriarchalism but a semi-patriarchal form of family group that spread under the banners of Christianity. The husband and father was still supreme but not wholly so.

(3) Christianity opposed divorce. When the church came into power in Western Europe, it discredited divorce as a legal institution. In the place of divorce legal separation was recognized. The church took a strict attitude against divorce and built up a type of stable, rigid family life.

The early Christian family, strict and stable, persisted in Western civilization until the latter part of the nineteenth century. In reconstructing the family in the early centuries of the Christian Era, even on semi-patriarchal lines, Christianity appears to have performed an inestimable social service.

Recent History of the Family

The stable, rigid family of Christianity like the stable, rigid family of the Hebrews and of the early Romans ultimately found itself under attack. As a result of its formal rigidity it was bound sooner or later to be shaken up. A reorganization, and a partial disintegration of the Christian family, began with the Renaissance. Many factors developed during the following centuries to create confusion in family life, with certain forces working for the improvement of the family and with others bringing about its destruction.

(1) With the Renaissance came the separation of church and state and the consequent weakening of the authority of the church. Hence the family again began to lose its significance as a religious institution. When marriage once more came to be regarded by many persons solely as a civil contract,

the way was open for divorces, which immediately mounted upward.

Where religious sentiments, beliefs, and attitudes have become disassociated from the family, many persons have gone to the other extreme of regarding marriage as a matter of personal convenience. If the religious control of the family has been too rigid, then without religion the family has often been wrecked on the rocks of personal pleasure.

(2) By the beginning of the nineteenth century the movement known as *individualism* had reached a remarkable growth especially in those countries in which pioneer conditions obtained. The rise of individualism was accompanied by the decline of authority in social life. The patriarchal family was called "old-fashioned" and the idea gradually spread that either party to the marriage vows could break these vows according to his or her individual desires.

An exaggerated spirit of individualism leads a person to find the guide to his actions in his own wishes, whims, or caprices. It gives him an attitude of carelessness toward the family as a social institution. This spirit, so often expressed in the phrase of "I should worry," has tended to make all social institutions unstable, and especially the family, for the family thrives only on attitudes of personal responsibility.

(3) *Economic changes* at the beginning of the nineteenth century seriously affected the status of the family. Under the domestic system of industry which reached its height in the eighteenth century, the family was the industrial as well as the social unit. All manufacture was carried on in the home, and all members of the family group as well as the employed help worked together on the same footing and ate at the same table.

The discovery of steam power, the invention of steam-driven machinery, and the development of the factory system all tended, however, to break up the economic unity of the family. The members of the family left the home for the factory as the place of work. With the breaking down of the economic unity of the family, there came also the social disintegration of countless families.

From primitive days until about a century ago the home was the center of manufacture. The use of steam-driven machinery was too expensive a procedure to be furthered in the family circle. The workers thus were called out of the home to labor in places where machinery had been set up, that is, in factories. The modern family scarcely manufactures anything at all. Even the immediate preparation of foods is likely to disappear and the kitchen to shrink into its primitive state of a few shelves and a cupboard.

(4) The opening of a large number of new industrial occupations to woman has rendered her to a degree economically independent of family relationships. Further, this movement has taken many married women out of the home to its neglect. Many homes have become simply dormitories. To tie woman up in the home is to make home a prison; to remove her entirely is the opposite extreme and makes home an empty gesture.

The employment in factories and shops of married women with small children has brought about the isolation and neglect of children, who have roamed the streets, acquired questionable habits, and fallen into delinquency. Married women with small children are unable to be real mothers if they must labor long hours in industry. When the mother goes out whether to work or to play bridge day after day, the home may go to pieces, and children may go astray.

Through the development of opportunities to work in factories and stores, many young married women have failed to learn the domestic arts, and to receive training in home-making. In fact they may get the idea that they are above such things. Therefore, when they come to the position of wife and mother they are unprepared and uninterested. Through lack of knowledge of and interest in home-making, they make home life unstable and miserable.

(5) Another influence affecting the family in Western civilization during the past century was the enormous *growth of wealth*.

The possession of wealth and the acquisition of the resultant social power has emancipated people from fear and stimulated them to defy many social rules. In other words the growth of wealth has favored a loosening of moral standards and of family bonds.

(6) In the next place, the growth of *science*, of knowledge, of a belief in a mechanistic universe, of behaviorism, has favored a view of the family as "merely another institution" and as "a device to be repudiated freely." Scientific data pertaining to sex and to birth prevention have made far-reaching inroads upon the belief in "the sanctity of marriage."

(7) Then, the nineteenth century was one of increasing *social unrest*. The family felt the effects of this unrest seriously, and found itself at the dawn of the twentieth century in the midst of change and confusion. People ranged in their attitudes all the way from those who accepted the family as "a divine institution made in Heaven" to those who felt that it was a device to be accepted or put aside according to personal desires.

(8) The *emancipation of woman* has sometimes increased family instability. The emancipation of woman in the sense of freeing her from those things which hold her personality in chains is entirely desirable, but this freedom has meant opportunities for going down as well as for going up. To some women it has meant license, licentiousness, and degradation.

The Roman women, it may be remembered, achieved emancipation, but that victory was accompanied by the fall of Rome. While the demoralization of Roman life was not necessarily caused by woman's emancipation, the latter doubtless played an important rôle to that end.

(9) The proportion of American families that are giving up their homes for "the cheerless existence in a *boarding house* or *hotel*" is disturbing. What does it mean, that a rapidly increasing part of the population finds the boarding house preferable to the home? Is the burden of housekeeping becoming too irksome to compensate for the maintenance of a home?

It is being asked frequently, what is to compensate for the giving up of home life by that increasing host of young married people who are living a superficial boarding house or hotel existence?

(10) The *growth of tenement districts*, high rents, and even depression at times, have operated against sound family life. It has been frequently declared that a normal home can scarcely exist in many of the crowded areas of the large cities. When a family group of three or four members, with perhaps a male lodger, are crowded into one room, normal family life is impossible.

(11) At the other extreme is the fact that *the high social standards of living* required in certain sections of the large cities are a cause of family instability. Many persons exhibit luxurious standards of living in order to maintain social status, but this is often done at the expense of family happiness. They are so wearied going to bridge parties, teas, dinners, and in "keeping up with the Jones's," that the family group disintegrates. To try to maintain standards that are out of all proportion to income is a cause of family breakdown.

(12) A *late age of marriage* is sometimes another disturbing factor. In the professions nowadays it is hardly wise for a young man to marry much earlier than the early thirties. At any rate an independent income in the professions is not possible much earlier. A person who marries after thirty sometimes finds difficulty in becoming adjusted to the habits of his (or her) mate; the maladjustments may lead to unstable family life. The high economic standard of living which a young woman of wealthy parents may require of a young man who is getting started in a profession often means that he must either postpone marriage or face marital unhappiness.

COURTSHIP AND MARRIAGE

Courtship is the interesting pathway to the family. An exciting volume could be written on the history of courtship. Higher animal life is replete with courtship antics in the mating season. Primitive people recognized courtship and built its manoevers into song and dance, sometimes degenerating into sex orgies and at other times reaching levels of chivalric human relationships. In a recent community study an interesting summary of inter-sex reactions is made as follows:

> Where we find the two sexes brought into contact with each other there will naturally be a pairing off to some extent. In these temporary companionships many phases of social life find expression. Thus there is an attraction and a repulsion between different groups of opposite sexes. Each person acquires a rating within both sexes, and companions are chosen with this idea in mind, depending on the contemplated activity. Thus some girls are sought after and some are not. A reputation for needlework or cooking does not mean that a person will be asked to attend some social event; however, such skill, other factors being equal, may prove an attraction. One chooses his temporary companion as well as his companion for life by weighing the various advantages of a prospective mate for the purposes in view. While the extremely social individual is desirable for parties and good times, the household talents of the individual are given very strong consideration when marriage is the object.[1]

Courtship had its origins in *force*. A young man after having made his choice would take the young woman away to his home bodily. Her parents in turn would develop a guarding technique so as to make the taking by force as difficult as possible, particularly by a strange and undesirable young man. She in turn would remonstrate against being taken by force, making a show of antagonism even in case she favored the particular man. Thus, male physical prowess won the fairest maidens, and a strong next generation was insured.

Courtship also had origins in *purchase*. Desiring a young woman a young man would offer to purchase her. The purchase price was offered on the theory that her rearing had been an expense to her parents and that since she had not yet had time to repay her parents the young man should recompense them for taking her away thus prematurely. Physical prowess

[1] William L. Leap, *Red Hill—Neighborhood Life and Race Relations in a Rural Section.* Phelps-Stokes Fellowship Papers (Bureau of Publications, University of Virginia, Charlottesville, Va., 1933), p. 112.

gives way to ability to pay. In Old Testament times Jacob paid for Rachel by working for her parents seven years, and then for seven years more.

Courtship had origins in the system of *securing parental consent*. Some parents were not mercenary and did not think in economic terms. They did not consider their daughters as economic values, but insisted that they themselves should evaluate the merits of all who came courting their daughters. The suitor thus found it wise to concentrate on courting the parents rather than the young woman. The latter's wishes were often ignored, denying to her the suitor of her choice and forcing upon her one whom she may have despised but whose status and wealth was such that the marriage would add greatly to the status of the parents and the family. The parents and elders had experience to guide them but were often moved by their own caprices and personal desires for prestige in "marrying off their daughters well."

Courtship reached a climax in the procedure of *securing personal consent*. Here the young man directs all kinds of artifices toward the inexperienced subject of his desires. She in turn grows coy or bold as events and her desires seem to require. While his courting is more or less open and widely recognized, hers is subtle and often the deciding factor. He courts her directly; she courts him indirectly.

Courtship is still evolving. The next stage may be that in which the advantages of securing the help and counsel of elders and of science are combined with the advantages of mutual thought and consent. Eugenic knowledge plus a mutually thoughtful decision by all the parties concerned is a goal beneficial to the race but not easily obtained.

The engagement period before marriage is a trial and error institution. With engagement a couple pass from formal to informal courtship. They are much in each other's presence and more intimately. Each makes a larger if not an all-inclusive claim upon the other's time and attention. A short engagement period of a few days is valueless; a long one of several

years is abnormal. A year, perhaps, gives the engagement institution a real opportunity to demonstrate the worth or the
weakness of the proposed marriage.

Extreme attitudes are found toward engagements. Some
persons have regarded an engagement as binding as marriage.
Others have treated it flippantly, believing that several engagements are desirable and not hesitating to obligate themselves
to more than one person of the opposite sex at a time. Very
few young people have fully appreciated the personal values
to be found in engagements and the ways in which engagements are defenses against the evils of hasty marriages.

A person furnishes half of the heredity of his offspring and
chooses the other half. It is of vast importance whom a person
chooses as his mate, for in so doing he may be selecting strong
or weak hereditary traits for his children. In the choice that
he makes of his mate and that she makes of him, the two together are selecting not one-half but the whole of the heredity
for their children.

Unfortunately a great deal of this choosing of mates, that is,
of parents for future children is done blindly. The usual procedure is that of "falling in love," which as a rule does not give
consideration to sound principles of eugenics. Moreover, if
two persons who fall in love marry almost immediately with no
engagement period ensuing, they ordinarily put themselves at
a tremendous disadvantage. By lack of method, foresight, and
common sense nearly everything is left to chance. Love often
is a tumultuous god who takes delight in freak matings.

Marriage is an institution admitting men and women to family life, that is, to living in the intimate personal relationships
of husband and wife for the primary purpose of begetting and
rearing children. This institution has social approbation and
religious sanction. It has had an interesting and varied history.

In certain parts of the earth *polyandry* has long existed.
Polyandry is a form of marriage where one woman has more
than one husband at a given time. For example, it is found in
sections of Tibet, where the conditions of social life are harsh

and where presumably the efforts of two or more men are needed in order that a family may be supported. It is a relatively rare type of marriage and exists only under peculiar and extreme conditions.

Another form of marriage is *polygyny*, a type where one man has two or more wives at a time. It should be noted here that *polygamy* is a general term that includes both polyandry and polygyny. It is more exact to use either one or both of the specific terms than the general concept. Polygyny is closely related to the institution of slavery. Women captured in warfare became the wives and concubines and slaves of their captor. A concubine is a kind of second-rate slave-wife. Under polygyny purchase is also common. For example, a chieftain may purchase a dozen women for wives, in the same manner that he would buy more personal property. The number of wives of one man sometimes reached a high figure, as in the case of Brigham Young with his seventy wives or of Solomon with his reputed 700 wives.

Polygyny did not develop much until human groups had accumulated some degree of wealth, at least an economic surplus to enable one man to support several families. Hence, even in countries where polygyny has been legal, as in Turkey and Egypt, only a small proportion of the people, namely, the wealthier, practice it.

Polygyny is usually based on the lower and degraded impulses of the male sex; it exists as a sacrifice to the development of the highest affections. It rests largely on the subjection and degradation of woman; it rarely allows any high regard for the feelings of woman. Under it, a woman is dethroned early from the affections of her husband because of younger and more attractive wives that are being added to the household. Moreover, children and aged parents often suffer grievous neglect.

Monogamy, the marriage of one man to one woman at a time, has been and is the leading type of marriage. In Western civilization, monogamy has been sanctioned by custom, religion, and law. The social advantages of monogamy are now well recognized; they have been stated by many writers and scientific observers.

(1) Monogamy secures the superior care of children. Under it, both father and mother unite their efforts in behalf of their children. A greater and better degree of attention can be given to the training of children by both parents under monogamy than under any other expression of marriage relationship.

(2) The monogamic family alone produces the highest type of affection, of altruistic love, of tolerant devotion. Under polygyny, the father cannot devote himself fully to his children individually, or to each of his several wives because there are too many of them. He is in reality the head of several households, and fatherhood in a real personal sense does not exist. Much jealousy exists between wives, and sets of children are isolated from each other. Under monogamy, on the other hand, both father and mother commonly sacrifice much in the mutual care of children.

(3) Monogamy creates more definite and stronger family ties than any other form of marriage. Affection between parents, between parents and children, and between children themselves is more wholesome. Legal relationships and blood relationships are simpler, less entangled, and less frequently the cause of permanent and annoying frictions. The cohesive power of the family is greater. As a result, it is probable that monogamic families tend to increase the unity and cohesiveness of society itself.

(4) Monogamy favors not only the preservation of the lives of the children but of the parents. It is only under monogamy that aged parents are cared for to any great extent by their children. Under polygyny the wife who has grown old is discarded for a younger woman, and hence she usually "ends her days in bitterness." The father is rarely cared for by his children, because the polygynous household does not give much opportunity for the growth of close affection between father and his numerous offspring. Under monogamy aged parents are likely to receive the favoring care of children; under polygyny they are commonly compelled to face a friendless old age.

The advantages, thus, of monogamy are many and far-reaching. Monogamy at its best presents superior opportunities for social interaction, and seems better fitted than any other type of marriage to produce the highest qualities of love and to lay the foundations for the finest forms of societary life.

Companionate marriage is the marriage of two persons on the understanding that as long as there are no children the marriage may be dissolved simply by mutual consent. Judge Ben B. Lindsey whose name has been connected frequently with the companionate marriage plan holds that this system is much better than free love or trial marriage as such, for it starts off with an official marriage and assumes that marriage is to be based on mutual responsibility.[1] The knowledge that divorce may be obtained freely in case there are no children, he claims, will make for more wholesome attitudes toward marriage. If there are children, then marriages are to be as binding as now. The opponents of companionate marriage claim the plan makes easy the way for persons to marry on the basis of sex alone, and remarry from time to time on the same urge. The opponents hold that the scheme has an unfortunate get-quick married and get-quick divorced trend that is in keeping with a jazzed-up civilization, that it will foster hasty marriages, and that it will irreparably cheapen marriage.

Unstable and Stable Marriage

Monogamic marriage has fallen far below its possibilities in many households and lands. Not all the evils attendant upon monogamic marriage today can necessarily be charged to the type of marriage itself. Many are doubtless the result of the misuse and abuse of a worthy system by incompetent and untrained persons who thoughtlessly rush headlong and blindly into marriage.

The institution of the family, particularly in the United States today, is unstable. Never were so many marriages being legally

[1] See Ben B. Lindsey and Wainwright Evans, *The Companionate Marriage* (Boni and Liveright, New York, 1927).

dissolved by divorce as now; never were there so many desertions. When maladjustments develop among the wealthy, divorce is resorted to; among the poor, desertion is more common. Divorce is often a sign that a third party has entered into the marriage situation, and that the eternal triangle has registered another victory. Desertion frequently means that the father has found many children a burden and economic support unfeasible, and so he disappears, leaving the wife and mother to carry on the best that she may, satisfying his conscience, if he has one, that public or private charity "will not let the kids starve."

For many decades the United States has held the unenviable position of leading European and American countries in the number of divorces granted. In 1906, it was found that there were 20,000 more marriages legally dissolved annually in the United States than in all the rest of the civilized world combined. At that time in France one marriage was legally dissolved to every thirty ceremonies performed; in Germany, only one marriage was legally dissolved to every forty-four marriages; in England, only one marriage was legally dissolved to every 400 marriage ceremonies performed; but in the United States the proportion was one to twelve, and in some of the cities the proportion was one to six or five.

In 1916, another survey was made, which showed that there were six counties in five states of the United States in which in a given year divorces actually exceeded marriages.[1] The entire state of Nevada showed one divorce to 1.54 marriages; while Indiana, the tenth state from the top of the list of high divorce rates, listed one divorce to every 5.94 marriages.

Still later, in 1921, estimates indicated that the increase in the divorce rate had not slowed down. In the United States as a whole, one divorce was being granted to about every nine marriages. The divorce rate in the United States had passed that of Japan, putting the United States in the position of

[1] In Pawnee County, Oklahoma, the ratio was one divorce to every .77th of a marriage. Washoe County, Nevada, Trinity County, California, Rutherford County, Tennessee, Union, and Clackamas Counties, Oregon, were the other communities with somewhat similar records.

leading the world. Interestingly enough, the divorce rate in Japan has been declining during recent decades.[1] In the United States as a whole in 1930 there was one divorce to each 5.9 marriages. While the depression has cut down both the marriage and divorce rates marriages have decreased more than have divorces and hence the divorce rate has been boosted still higher.

The statistics, however, need to be further interpreted. People migrate temporarily to a city, such as Reno, Nevada, and within a few weeks secure a divorce, and then return "home." In this way a community may acquire an enormous divorce rate that is entirely misrepresentative of the local situation.

Moreover, to compare the total number of divorces with the total number of marriages in a given year in a given country, such as the United States, may also be misleading. By contrast, suppose we think of comparing the number of divorces in a given year in a given country with the total number of marriages intact at the end of that year. The number of divorces granted in a given year should be compared with the total number of marriages in effect and not merely with the number of marriages that were performed in the particular year.

We do not reckon bank failures as some people do marriage failures —by contrasting the number of marriages with the number of divorces in a given year. If we were to compare the number of bank failures in a single year with the number of banks organized during the same year, I suspect that we should find that there were ten or perhaps twenty-five times as many bank failures as there were banks organized during that year. . . . Divorces occur from *all* previous marriages, not from the number of marriages that take place in the same year only. The figures of the federal marriage and divorce reports show that one marriage in 125 is dissolved by divorce annually.[2]

[1] For an interesting discussion of divorce in Japan see Y. Iwasaki, "Why the Divorce Rate Has Declined in Japan," *American Journal of Sociology*, XXXVI: 568–83. It is reported that education, increase in books, motion pictures, Christianity, and expansion of industrial life have combined to create new attitudes toward the status of woman, to raise the age of marriage, and to lower the divorce rate.
[2] James P. Lichtenberger, "The Changing Family in a Changing World," *Mental Hygiene*, XVII: 572 (October, 1933).

Not only does the United States lead the world in the number of legally dissolved marriages annually, but these dissolutions are increasing faster than the population. If this tendency is maintained, it will not be many decades before the family as a permanent union between husband and wife will no longer be common. If the United States should reach the place where one-half of all marriages are dissolved in the courts, the situation in that regard will be similar to conditions when Rome started on her decadent days.

As a reaction against the tradition that "marriages are made in Heaven," an increasing number of people have gone to the opposite extreme, and say that "marriages are for personal convenience." This self-centered view would appear to have serious evils not only in a personal way but from the viewpoint of creating sound pro-social attitudes of life.

The rate at which marriages are legally dissolved is higher as a rule in cities and industrial centers than in rural districts. Life is more personal, simpler, less keyed up, less sophisticated in the country, and in consequence young persons are better acquainted at the time of marriage, and have less disconcerting factors to contend with after marriage. As the country becomes urbanized, the difference in divorce rates doubtless will tend to disappear.

The divorce rate is from two to four times as high among childless couples as among those who have children, which is to be expected. Parental duties and privileges help to prevent a break in the marriage relation.

The divorce rate varies according to religion. In Western civilization it is lowest among Catholics, next lowest among Jews, next among Protestants, and highest among persons of no religious faith. Religious controls have been powerful in preventing a severance of the marriage ties, even though the parties to a given marriage have grown widely apart and become mutually antagonistic. Again, we have two extremes, one regarding a marriage as an iron-clad bond no matter how one party or the other may have been victimized or subjected to a living death. The other extreme is to divorce marriage from religion completely and to regard it in no way as sacred.

Approximately two-thirds of the marriages dissolved in the United States in recent decades have been broken at the request of the wife. This tendency indicates that women are becoming "emancipated"; that they are not submitting to abuses from their husbands as many women did formerly. Some perhaps are becoming too emancipated, developing too self-centered lives to meet the responsibilities of a family. Another conclusion is that men are more guilty than women of misdeeds and infidelity.

The grounds that are given in the courts for dissolving marriages are often misleading or insufficient. Desertion is often cited, but the question at once arises, What brought about the desertion? Incompatibility is more specific, but even then, one would like to know what led to the incompatibility? Neglect or mental cruelty likewise raises the question as to who is the more responsible. Sexual immorality, another common cause usually brings in "other women" with a train of complicating circumstances.

To an appreciable extent the legal breaking up of families is a symptom of more serious evils. Marriage itself is being viewed with decreasing seriousness, being treated as an ordinary promise. In certain classes of society, namely, the wealthiest and poorest, there is a noticeable decay of the social values upon which the family rests. Family life requires sacrificial living, personal chastity, and the assumption of social responsibility.

An increasing knowledge of the laws regarding divorce and an increasing laxity of these laws have furthered family instability. A few centuries ago the law was resorted to only by the wealthy or the socially powerful. Many people would not have thought of divorce three or four decades ago but similar people today know the laws concerning divorce and marry with the expectation of resorting freely to these laws if occasion arises.

The laws concerning the legal dissolution of marriage are freer in the United States than in almost any other so-called

Christian nation. The administration of these laws is also freer, being made a joke at times. Certain "divorce" judges seem to take pride in the number of divorces that they grant, although here and there is one who specializes upon reuniting separated couples instead of divorcing them as painlessly as possible.

Although the divorce rate is increasing in the United States, it is also true that the marriage rate is increasing. As E. A. Ross has suggested, the people of the United States are more married than ever before. Barring the recent depression years the number of persons who are married per 1,000 of the population has shown a somewhat steady increase over several decades. People are both marrying and divorcing more than formerly.

Moreover "the number of persons per 1,000 population who got married and did not get a divorce has shown an increase" during the period from 1887 to 1927.[1] The increase in the percentage of those who marry allows for both an increase in the divorce rate and in the stable marriage age. For example, in 1887, the marriage rate in the United States per thousand population was 8.67 and the divorce rate was .47. In 1927, forty years later the marriage rate was 10.12 and the divorce rate was 1.62. In other words in 1887 the stable marriage rate was 8.20 and in 1927 it was 8.50.[2] However, family instability is probably no worse than the instability in other phases of our current social life. An optimistic note may be found in the following observation:

In fact, I suspect that if we consider the matter broadly, we shall find that the family is really rather less disturbed than any of the others [phases of social life]. Certainly there is at present less stability in the domain of economics, of politics, of religion, or morals, and of education, than in the American family. Our industrial situation is much more perturbed than is our family life. To take it concretely the proportion of failures in business during this interval of depression is far larger than the proportion of failures in marriage.[3]

[1] Manuel C. Elmer, *Family Adjustment and Social Change* (Ray Long and Richard R. Smith, New York, 1932), p. 164.

[2] *Ibid.*, p. 163. However, in 1930, a depression year, the stable marriage rate had fallen to 7.64.

[3] James P. Lichtenberger, "The Changing Family in a Changing World," *Mental Hygiene*, XVII: 573 (October, 1933).

Sound family life depends on chastity. It requires a single or the same standard of morals for both men and women. The double standard or one standard for women and another for men breaks down at the points of personal happiness and social value. Sex chastity is essential to a true democracy of husband and wife. Unfortunately the discussion of sex values has been much avoided. It has been "tabooed by parents" usually through prudish considerations. It has been "slighted by the school," an institution that is supposed to give a well-rounded education. It has been "avoided by the church, which has stood for public and private morality." It has had "an open field chiefly among the gamins of the street," among hired men on farms, in low-grade fraternal groups, and in cheap motion pictures and houses of prostitution.

Illegal or immoral relations between the sexes have existed in all ages. The difficulties in the way of socially controlling the sex impulses have been and are almost insurmountable. When uncontrolled the sex impulses produce vice, "dirty" thinking, sterility, and obnoxious diseases, preventing a normal family life. They have taken thousands of girls and women in the larger countries of the world as an annual sacrifice. The virtues and bodies of girls and women have been commercialized, annually returning millions of dollars to evil-minded procurers and managers in every large country of the world, with the small countries not being immune. The segregation of sexually depraved girls and women in special districts has been and is an alarming blotch upon civilization, testifying that men and women have sunk lower in the control of sex passions than animals. In those countries where the so-called "red-light districts" have been done away with by law, the evil has persisted in a limited way, being diffused with certain hotels and rooming houses serving under cover as centers of vice.

Sex immorality leads to serious venereal diseases, so subtle in their nature that years after cures have been announced they may break forth, contaminating virtuous wives and helpless babies, and destroying happy home life. "The busiest speciality of medicine" is said to be that connected with venereal diseases. Disabilities, untold suffering, surgical operations, premature deaths follow in their wake. They "populate asylums and hospitals with human wrecks." Perhaps the most revolting phase of these deep-seated infections is the way in which many men having sown "wild-oats" in pre-marriage days are guilty of transmitting a dangerous venereal disease to helpless wives and of foisting misery upon innocent children.[1]

Unchastity may be defined as maintaining sex relations outside of marriage, that is, by a married party with persons other than his married partner. Ten causes of unchastity, an enemy of sound family life, have been noted. (1) The love of mammon is perhaps the chief factor; financial gain is placed ahead of personal virtue. For sake of money some persons will sell their bodies or worse still inveigle other persons into doing the same. (2) "Masculine swinishness" or uncontrolled sex desires rank as a close second cause. Some men exercise sexual "rights" that animals do not claim. (3) The practice of some girls and women of excusing their brothers or sons or sweethearts in being "a little wild" is another leading factor. To condone in such cases may be popular, but destructive of later human happiness and a wholesome family. (4) The countenancing of a double standard of sex morals operates disastrously against the family. A woman who succumbs once to her sex nature becomes a social outcast, but in that same community a man who violates sex and whose repeated illegitimate sex practices are known, may remain a "social lion" and be received with open arms by women in "polite society." (5) Feminine weakness for male adulation and flattery, and for the luxuries that some men offer to delude women are significant elements. The desire "to rate" may lead to the destruction of vital social values. (6) Closely packed populations in congested urban districts furnish breeding centers for sex immorality. (7) Some men

[1] *Damaged Goods* by Eugene Brieux carries the idea of using mechanical means to prevent or transmit venereal disease. Such a technique makes promiscuous sex relations "safe," and hinders chastity, unless coupled with adequate personal control of sex impulses.

and many women owe their initial sex debauch to the influence of alcoholic liquor and to the ill-regulated dance hall. (8) A double standard of medical regulations is also a factor. At present in certain countries, cases of smallpox must be reported to the health department but venereal diseases which may be as virulent as smallpox, must not be reported, for the reason that such reporting might incriminate men of standing in the community. Furthermore, public measures are not developed to prevent the spread of these diseases to the innocent. (9) Poverty leads many a girl to her sex downfall. She is enticed by the lure of expensive clothes and a so-called "easy life" which ordinary work and wages do not provide, and she gives in to a quick but demoralizing means of securing the lure. In times of economic depression many women succumb to sex in order to keep from starving. (10) A lack of adequate personality organization, of moral stamina, and religious idealism exists to a greater or less degree in nearly all cases of sex depravity.[1]

THE EUGENIC FAMILY

With the increasing knowledge of the laws of heredity, variation, and evolution certain persons have acquired a highly developed knowledge of plant and animal heredity.[2] In re-

[1] In sections of certain countries, such as India, and among some primitive peoples, sexual behavior has become ingrained in religious practices.

[2] An important biological consideration is the *gene* theory. In the germ cell there are carriers of heredity known as chromosomes, twenty-four pairs of them. One of each pair is inherited from the father; the other from the mother. It is now believed that in each chromosome are little particles called genes, arranged in two series of chains, one chain from each parent. If one parent has a gene for a defective trait, the corresponding gene from the other parent may come to the rescue with a normal trait. If both parents have corresponding genes for a defective trait, then the offspring may suffer defectiveness in that regard. Hence, when two persons marry who are related, the likelihood of an offspring inheriting two genes for some defective trait is high.

Moreover, the heredity of any given trait depends on the relationship existing between the genes in the germ cell. The geneticist speaks of the "environment" of the genes, and states that the development of any gene depends on what other genes are present in the chromosome, on the medium or fluid in which the genes function in the chromosome, on the media of the chromosomes in the germ cell, on the nutrition and other factors affecting the prenatal growth of the germ cell. Thus, to be "born well" involves many subtle but vital conditions.

cent years a movement has gained momentum to apply the laws of inheritance within the human realm and to improve the human race. This new movement is known as *eugenics*, a science which was inaugurated in England during the closing years of the nineteenth century by Francis Galton.[1] As the term, eugenics, implies, the science aims to work out a program whereby every child may be well born. It concentrates on applying the principles of heredity and variation to human life chiefly through the family.[2]

One eugenic method is to discourage by education and legal means the marriage of persons who are unfit physically or mentally. The aim is to prevent unworthy parenthood. It is planned to segregate feeble-minded men and women by sexes in public institutions and thus to prevent them from reproducing their kind. It is also planned to forbid the marriage of those persons whose health is constitutionally or organically below a certain standard. In line with this idea a movement has been inaugurated whereby only those persons who produce health certificates from a reputable physician shall be allowed to marry. It may be added that it is within the power of the government to raise by degrees the standards of health demanded of those who desire a license to marry. Thus the eugenist hopes to encourage the growth of a more healthy race of men and women.

The eugenist has to contend, however, with the problem of illegitimate parentage. To pass laws forbidding certain types of persons to marry does not hinder the birth of children outside of wedlock. In fact to make marriage laws more strict than public opinion will support is indirectly to increase the number of children born out of wedlock. Hence, the eugenist cannot wisely act too far in advance of public opinion.

[1] See Francis Galton, *Hereditary Genius* (The Macmillan Company, New York, 1914).
[2] Interesting books in the recent development of eugenics are H. S. Jennings, *The Biological Basis of Human Nature* (W. W. Norton and Company, New York, 1930) and Thomas H. Morgan, *The Theory of the Gene* (Yale University Press, New Haven, 1926).

A second and more constructive eugenic method is to establish a public opinion favorable to new and higher personal standards regarding *mating*. At present, attractions such as wealth or titles or social position frequently determine who may marry. If a marriageable person is wealthy he is considered highly desirable—irrespective of a possible unfit condition or absence of sex standards. The eugenist urges that a sound physique and heredity be ranked ahead of wealth or status, in fact, of all else. He holds that wealth without health, or rank without a sound heredity are false marriage guides.

Thus a strong hereditary stock, high vitality, and excellent health are emphasized as more fundamental marriage attractions than titles or gold. The eugenist asks that young people from childhood shall be trained to regard high vitality and dependable health as first essentials in an ideal man or woman. If this belief were to become accepted in a large social group it would influence personal fancy and "falling in love." However, the aim of eugenics is not to eliminate falling in love but to put it upon a superior level of vitality, heredity, and health. Thus would the eugenist strengthen every social group and help to build a superior human race.

Preventive eugenics refers to measures to protect parenthood from "racial poisons." [1] Alcohol is a poison which seems to affect the generative organs and even the germ cells. In preventing alcoholism a whole group may protect itself against a racial poison. Narcotics is another racial poison. By undermining the human organism, tubercle bacilli are weakening in their effects upon germ cell strength. Venereal diseases directly attack the generative organs of women, causing both sterility and untold suffering, and hence may be regarded as racially disastrous.

Disharmonic types are deplored by eugenists. When a pair of parents are widely different in traits their children may show disharmonic traits. Disharmonic physical types are more easily

[1] C. W. Saleeby, *The Eugenic Prospect* (Dodd, Mead and Company, New York, 1921).

observed than any other. A large heavy-set person may inherit a small heart, or *vice versa*. Thus, a person may have strong urges in opposite directions and must continually shift back and forth between his own lively tendencies. Disharmony in psychical traits may be produced in the offspring of two parents widely divergent in psychical natures. The result is an undue proportion of deep-seated mental conflicts; a person who might achieve is forever torn asunder by contending forces within him.

Inbreeding is an opposite tendency. The mating of persons who are closely related or who are too much alike may result in deficient or weak offspring. The eugenist contends against such practices whether found among the illiterate backwoodsmen or royalty. Blue blood dies out. The eugenist favors racial admixture but sets limits against inbreeding and outbreeding. The former increases deficiency and the latter disharmony.

Dysgenics is the study of the factors which hinder or prevent the birth of physically and mentally perfect individuals. Factors which cut down the birth rate unduly or make it excessive may be called dysgenic. Factors which undermine physical parenthood are also dysgenic.

Eugenics strikes at such a characteristic as mental defectiveness because of its relation to many social ills. While poverty or delinquency are not inherited, mental defectiveness, which is inherited, leads to poverty, pauperism, delinquency, and crime. The inheritance of feeble-mindedness and a phlegmatic temperament may lead to poverty, while the inheritance of feeble-mindedness and an energetic temperament is likely to result in delinquency or crime. In the case of longevity, or long life, traits such as high vital resistance and sound organic reactions have inherited bases.

Of those persons who are ordinarily considered well born, a large percentage possesses some inherited defects which sooner or later are manifested in low vital resistance, weak lungs, weak kidneys, a weak digestive system, a weak heart. Under the stress of modern speed, these defects grow into serious problems.

Hence to the extent that eugenic measures can safeguard individuals against inheriting such defects, it is rendering a valuable social service.

A weakness that is sometimes charged against eugenics is its apparent belief that a sound body and mind are sufficient to guarantee a sound citizen. By its nature it does not deal with human character, spiritual values, social responsibility, social or anti-social attitudes. Moreover it often overlooks the importance of environment. However, in its field of heredity it lifts a voice worthy of being heeded.

Human beings may be divided into three vitality classes.[1] (1) Low vitality classes include those persons, as a rule, whose birth rate and death rate are both high, whose physical and mental defectiveness is relatively high, whose vital resistance is low, and whose knowledge of eugenic and hygienic principles is meager. They are represented among the poorer peasants of remote areas and in the overcrowded districts of large cities.

(2) Medium vitality people are those whose birth rate and death rate are both low, whose intelligence is high, whose vital resistance is not equal to the countless demands of a speeded-up urban pace, and who do not live out the normal span.

(3) High vitality people are those who have been well born; who are without mental and physical defects; who have a substantial birth rate and a low death rate; and who live under a favorable environment. The higher culture groups among the rural land-owning classes will serve as illustrations.

An *optimum population* is one of a size and quality best fitted to achieve some social goal.[2] It varies greatly. A high birth rate and large numbers of people constitute an optimum population for war purposes. They also comprise an optimum population from the standpoint of "saving as many souls as possible." From an economic viewpoint an optimum population is a large

---

[1] As suggested by Georg Hansen, *Die drei Bevölkerungsstufen* (Munich, 1889), and Franklin H. Giddings, *Principles of Sociology* (The Macmillan Company, New York, 1896), pp. 342ff.

[2] Cf. W. S. Thompson, *Population Problems* (McGraw-Hill Book Company, New York, 1930).

one when there are many natural resources to be exploited, but a small one where resources are scarce. What would be an optimum population in prosperous times would be a surplus population when unemployment and starvation stalk the land. Capitalism often asks for a large population so that an excess labor supply will keep wages low, while social workers and tax payers protest because of the heavy expense upon public and private charity when "times are hard" and when millions are thrown out of employment. A "large population" is desired by real estate promotors, for land values rise with every addition to the population in "good times." A city of one million would be increased to a city of two millions or five millions by real estate "sharks" without being particular about the quality of population, or about the kind of housing and living conditions under which many of the proposed two or five millions will live. The "boosters" are inclined to ignore if not to defy all the sound principles of eugenics. Eugenics would shift the emphasis from quantity to quality of population; sociology, from plenty of people to plenty of opportunity and of creative stimuli.

History supports eugenics in its contention for a sound and a limited population. Population authorities stand with eugenists. In the early part of the nineteenth century an English scholar by the name of Thomas Malthus wrote an important essay on population and developed what has since been called the Malthusian doctrine in which he asserted that population increases faster than food supply, and that poverty and misery may be expected to result unless something is done to check the birth rate.[1] It is pointed out that by deliberately holding the birth rate down, a nation can prevent poverty and attendant misery.

On the other hand, if such a preventive check is not utilized, then certain *positive* or *natural checks* may operate, according to Malthus. These include famine, pestilence, war. The preventive checks and the positive ones hold an inverse relationship to each other. When the positive checks are operating strongly, the preventive ones are quiescent. When the preventive ones

[1] Thomas R. Malthus, *Essay on Population* (Reeves and Turner, London, 1878).

are holding down the birth rate, the positive are likely to be inoperative.

When a country is new, eugenics is likely to receive little consideration, and the Malthusian law is defied. A new country is often reckless in developing or exploiting its natural resources, and likewise may be careless regarding the birth rate and the heredity of its people. As it grows older, and its people grow more educated, the birth rate may decline but not so fast as the economic resources. Surplus populations seem to call for territorial expansion and to justify wars of aggression.

Some of the followers of Malthus have been known as Neo-Malthusians. They have urged *birth control,* or the use of artificial measures for the regulation of births. Birth control measures were adopted first somewhat spontaneously by the wealthier and better educated classes. Then, they were urged by reformers for the protection of women of lower economic and less educated levels from being burdened continuously by childbearing. Eugenists have favored the birth control movement in order to protect society from an increase in morons and the feeble-minded, for these types reproduce their kind extensively. Birth control is urged also by those who wish to protect the unskilled classes from becoming so numerous that wages for them will be kept at starvation levels.

The opponents of birth control have claimed that the wrong people use it most. It is pointed out that birth control has been adopted by the wealthy, the educated, and by society women in order to escape childbearing. It is used as a means of shirking a distinct duty to society. The educated and financially independent cut their birth rate so low that they do not keep up their numbers, and thus, society must rely on the lower cultural groups to replenish itself.

Orthodox religion objects to birth control on the ground that it "interferes with the will of God," and cuts down the number of souls that may be saved. If church people practice it, then church adherents are depleted. Church people who oppose birth control usually do so on strictly ecclesiastical grounds or because it is a poor substitute for that moral control by which people regulate the number of their children "by will power" and by keeping sex impulses well subordinated.[1]

Birth control is opposed also by militarists, nationalists, large-scale employers, and real estate "boosters," under the captions of "victory," "patriotism," "prosperity." Nearly all of these contentions are the products of wishful thinking on the part of self-centered "interests." The majority of social workers favor some form of social control for they are working with many people who are lacking in "moral control," or who are the victims of exploitation. Internationalists in general favor birth control for they fear "population pressure" as a leading cause of war. It is contended that no birth control leads to "standing room only," and the latter to misery and war.[2]

The *control of birth control* in some quarters is becoming a problem. In certain European countries the birth rate has been declining faster than the death rate and hence if this ratio continues the peoples of France, England, and Germany, for example, as they are now known, will pass away.[3] It is also argued that birth control makes promiscuous sex relations safe and that it is undermining marriage and normal family life and happiness. No control of birth control greatly increases self-centered existence on the part of many people. In a larger way the lack of international control of birth control is fast becoming a problem. The fact that birth rates are low in France and England and high in India and China is upsetting; it creates fear and military preparedness among certain low birth rate countries.

The widespread interest in *technocracy* has given birth control strong support. The relationship is indirect, but the figures of automatic machine production and of the wholesale discarding of workers in standardized industries has indirectly played into

[1] A clear-cut statement of this viewpoint is given by E. J. Ross, *A Survey of Sociology* (Bruce Publishing Company, New York, 1932), pp. 391–96.
[2] See E. A. Ross, *Standing Room Only?* (The Century Company, New York, 1927).
[3] Robert R. Kuczynski, *The Balance of Births and Deaths*, Vol. I, *Western and Northern Europe* (The Macmillan Company, New York, 1928).

the hands of the advocates of a widespread control and selection of populations. A world depression likewise supports the eugenic program of careful selection.

Eugenics has its best friend in education, for through education persons may learn what they can do in order to develop themselves toward high vitality, and at the same time guarantee a splendid physical start in life to the next generation. By education, a necessary improvement in environmental conditions may be made so that a eugenic racial stock may be built up, safeguarded, stimulated, and enabled to reach its full fruition. Through eugenics individuals and social groups alike may grow in stature and in mental and social worth.

HOUSING THE FAMILY

Of the many problems that have always accompanied the family not the least has been housing. Ever since the family and the race began the problem of housing has been baffling to the majority of people. It was pointed out by John Ruskin that after 6,000 years of human history we still find that a majority of mankind is inadequately housed. The genius of man has made tremendous progress in many material directions, but in one essential particular, namely, of housing the human family properly, the major problems are still unsolved for millions of people not only in uncivilized countries but in civilized as well.

The housing of the family is becoming more and more a social problem. Wage-earners desire to live near their work and yet cannot afford to pay rents which mount upward as cities increase in size. The wealthy overhouse themselves. The poor are underhoused. The middle class shift back and forth between renting and buying, trying in the latter case to escape the evil of high rents, and in the former, the evil of high taxes and special assessments.

The earliest family groups were very crudely housed. Cave houses and tree houses prevailed. The invention of the hall house, rectangular in shape, containing one room with the fireplace in the center, with no windows and perhaps no chimney for the fireplace, but accommodating several families, was a distinct achievement.[1] From these simple beginnings houses have developed until today they are limitless in variety, including many that are undescribably elegant. Despite this development, millions are forced to live in houses of the worst sort, in shacks and inhuman tenements, not much better than the houses of preliterate man. Moreover, millions of laboring persons desirous of modest homes find the ownership of these impossible because of forbidding prices.

The housing problem develops when more than one family try to live in a dwelling scarcely large enough for a single family. Each city in the United States, for example, has its housing problem, namely, how shall it house its people from a healthy and human welfare viewpoint? [2] Although New York City alone in the United States has a tenement house problem, all other large cities are tending toward tenement house conditions.

While overcrowding does not exist in country districts, yet poor sanitation and lack of hygienic conditions spell bad housing for whole regions. Ignorance and carelessness create bad housing in the country as well as in the city.[3] Thus, housing the family is a problem with many aspects everywhere.

(1) We may begin with overcrowding. Overcrowding is of two types, land overcrowding and room overcrowding.[4] The first is an overcrowding of limited areas of land with an undue population, in such a way that a fair level of living standards cannot be maintained. Under specific conditions a thousand people might be housed satisfactorily in a respectable, properly built, and well-equipped apartment house, whereas one-tenth that number living in shacks scattered over a considerable area "down by the river" might be ill-housed.

[1] R. E. Thompson, *The History of the Dwelling House and Its Future* (J. B. Lippincott Company, Philadelphia, 1914).

[2] See Lawrence Veiller, *Housing Reform* (Charities Publication Committee, New York, 1910).

[3] See H. B. Bashore, *Overcrowding and Defective Housing in the Rural Districts* (John Wiley and Sons, Inc., New York, 1915); and W. G. Savage, *Rural Housing* (T. F. Unwin, London, 1915).

[4] Lawrence Veiller, *op. cit.*

Room overcrowding means that too many persons are occupying a given number of rooms, especially sleeping rooms. In many cities there has been a standard of at least 400 or 500 cubic feet of air per adult per room. More important, however, than air space is the amount and kind of ventilation. Also important is the amount of light, particularly sunlight, that reaches in the daytime into sleeping rooms.[1]

(2) Closely related to overcrowding is the lack of health facilities. In addition to ventilation, light, and sunshine, health facilities include adequate plumbing, regular and frequent collection of garbage, and cleanliness.

It is surprising how anyone who breathes the foul air of the tenement continually can keep healthy. In "the dark, damp rooms" of the poor, the germs of disease live and multiply; sunshine and fresh air are not present to destroy them. Typhoid sweeps away its thousands because of impure water and lack of drainage, while tuberculosis takes a larger toll because of bad air and infected rooms.

(3) The rent problem is caused in part by a competitive economic system bent on obtaining as large profits as possible. As a result, people huddle together in close and mean quarters. With every increase in population or migration in times of prosperity rents and land values go up. In the months and years of depression, unemployment hinders or prevents the payment of high rents. Overcrowding and the breakdown of family morale follow.

Land speculation forces land prices up unduly high and makes housing conditions harsher for the poor. Housing speculation also results disastrously for the family, for many dwellings are "built to sell, not to house." Prices in large cities have reached levels where it is impossible for a majority of the people to own their own homes, no matter how thrifty and industrious they may be.

[1] It is better to permit a family to sleep in a room containing only 400 cubic feet of air per adult, of good quality and frequently renewed, than for them to sleep in a room containing three times that amount of air which cannot be renewed through ventilation.

With land near certain traffic centers in large cities priced at a thousand dollars a front foot and with tenements rearing their sooty heads a half a hundred feet high, with a housing problem so chronic that whole sections of a population live and die under the shabbiest of living conditions, is it not time that housing the family should be considered a question of national and world importance? Is it not strange that with all of our boasted scientific development, technological efficiency, and business acumen, a third of the nation's families are not decently housed? Civilized and uncivilized country, Christian country or not, housing is yet, after several thousands of years of human history, a major social problem.

When 60 per cent of the people of a country such as the United States with its three million square miles of land and its vast resources and "high-priced brains" are unable to own their own homes, and when they live all their days "on other people's land," a social situation has arisen that demands earnest attention. Moreover, when thousands on thousands who began adulthood expecting to own a home are giving up all such hope and resigning themselves to disillusionment and "a bare boarding-house existence," national welfare is at stake.

With more than 95 per cent of the people of New York City living in "hired habitations," and with other millions of the industrial classes being "homeless" in the sense of being renters and tenants, the family group is defeated almost at its start in developing a real home, and in creating social values which sound homes require. If individualism and capitalism were wise, they would modify the present economic system so that home ownership would be possible to all who desired it.

The own-your-own apartment plan has made some progress, but has not yet been adjusted to meet the wage-earner's needs. Farm land in the United States does not yield sufficient returns to enable a young man with slight means and with a family to pay for a home. An increasing degree of renting is a main factor in the social restlessness of the times.

(4) The taking in of *lodgers* is usually found along with over-

crowding and high rents. With unemployment, or with an increase in land values and rents, a lodger or two may be added to the family group, so that housing and home expenses may be met. The social effects of taking in lodgers in families already living in one or two rooms are serious.

(5) *Lack of play space* for children is the rule where habitations are congested. Hallways, dark stairways, side-alleys, and rear-alleys are the only places about the home where numerous children may play. Dark alleys foster not sound recreation but vice and delinquency.

The housing problem, then, is seen to arise, first, out of *too much individualism*, which is expressed vividly in a system of greedy profits. For the sake of profits, many landlords are willing to sacrifice the health and welfare of relatively helpless people. Many care little whether tenants as a class live or die, as long as financial returns are netted from property.

Even when the need for municipal and national action is clear, caution must be shown lest private enterprise take offense and raise the cry of socialism. Note the following statements taken from an Associated Press dispatch under date of September 3, 1933:

> Outlining the administration's objective in financing low-cost housing projects from public works funds, Secretary Ickes said today the program is designed to fill a gap by private capital's failure at slum clearance.
>
> The public works administrator in a formal statement denied the proposed construction will compete with private enterprise. He said it is intended first to create jobs, and secondly, to furnish satisfactory housing at a low cost.
>
> Asserting private initiative has failed to provide the type of housing contemplated by the public works administration, Ickes said "nothing could be further from the truth" than the suggestion the government plans competition with private capital.

A second leading cause of poor housing is *ignorance* and *lack of responsibility* on the part of poor people. There is ignorance concerning the nature of health, sanitation, and minimum living standards. Many people in large cities have never had the opportunity of learning about recent advances in sanitary science and household economics, despite the adult education movement. Whole sections of urban populations are still living in the Dark Ages. When they do obtain the needed knowledge they are unable or unwilling to put it into effect.

A third factor is the *ignorance* and *lack of responsibility of the public* regarding housing conditions. One-half of a city does not know or does not care how the other half lives. When bad housing conditions are known to exist, the failure of many citizens to take an effective interest in rectifying untoward situations is a startling commentary on a lack of welfare attitudes. These three causal factors [1] of bad housing, therefore, boil down to two psycho-social factors, namely, ignorance and lack of welfare attitudes.

At least eight different methods of controlling the housing of the family may be noted. (1) A *laissez-faire* reliance on private capital and on the law of supply and demand for houses encourages private building initiative, but does not meet the needs of families for well-built homes and does not prevent harmful speculation in a necessity of life. (2) The building of model tenements by individuals sets a fine example, but does not provide adequate housing for more than a fraction of those needing homes. (3) Municipally owned and operated tenements have been a success in Germany, Austria, and Great Britain. Their feasibility on a large scale in the United States is doubtful, because of the deep-seated antagonism to anything socialistic, and because of the inefficiency and political graft in municipal governments.

(4) The establishment of garden cities is praise-worthy, but meets the needs of only a small percentage of the people. (5) Better sanitary and health measures for regulating the activities of private builders are necessary. However, they do not hinder rents from rising in times of prosperity or overcrowding from becoming common during a depression.

(6) If not carried too far, the reduction of taxes on houses

[1] Cf. Lawrence Veiller, *op. cit.*

and improvements and an increase of taxes on land in cities graduated according to the unearned increment is being widely urged. (7) Rapid transportation at low rates gives the working classes a chance to house themselves well. Many people, however, prefer to live near their work. Rapid transit, moreover, affords only temporary relief unless terminals are continually extended, and people are encouraged to move farther and farther away from their work. The subways of a city like New York City carry people fast and far, but in a sense are dehumanizing. (8) Constant, persistent education of the public concerning housing conditions is essential. In order to secure needed economic improvements, adequate housing laws, and proper administration of these laws, public opinion must give steady and intelligent support to socially-minded legislators, administrators, and social welfare leaders.

If the chief end of life is to live helpfully, then it is a matter of prime importance that all the people live in houses which are conducive to health, safety, and morality. Adequate housing is so related to proper homing that it becomes a matter too serious to be left in the field of private speculation. It can be handled well only through wise methods of social control.

After many years' delay the United States through its NRA program announced in 1933 a federal policy of "slum clearance." Politics of the unsavory sort and economic greed will do everything possible to block slum clearance, and yet why should not all slums be removed and why should not all the citizens of a country such as the United States be entitled to a decent home no matter how humble?

In England the slum clearance or anti-slum campaign has made headway slowly. More important, according to E. D. Simon, once Lord Mayor of Manchester and for the past several years a leading housing expert in England, is the plan to build a house for every family in England, at suitable rents.[1] When that goal is achieved then a program to tear down and to rehouse

[1] E. D. Simon, *The Anti-Slum Campaign* (Longmans, Green and Company, London, 1933), p. 8.

families may begin. The building of new houses must take place on the outskirts of the present cities until land values are brought down in central urban areas that are zoned for housing to a reasonable level.[1] For housing the poorer families, private enterprise has not proven equal to the task and hence local city governments must continue and increase their home-building activities; in the same way that public money is used to educate children even to the point of constructing proper school buildings, so must public money be used to secure adequate housing, especially in view of the widespread breakdown of private enterprise as evidenced by the slums—such is an English view after years of experimenting with the housing problem.[2]

Reconstructing the Family

The family in Western civilization is undoubtedly in a transitional stage. The patriarchal family which has prevailed widely was good for its time and place, and still possesses meritorious features. Individualism has made inroads upon the older types of the family by emancipating women and sometimes by making children little autocrats, by challenging marriage, and even by advocating free love and state-controlled institutions for training all children.

The patriarchal family has been too rigid; individualistic attitudes toward the family, too loose. Perhaps there is a happy medium. A democratic family would be built on respect for age and experience, on consideration for the personalities of children, and on coöperation all around.

To change the family from one in which autocracy and ignorance are in the saddle to one in which a rational and mutual give-and-take rule applies, requires education in democratic relationships, sex relationships, parent-child relationships, and in

[1] A ground rent of four pounds per annum is generally agreed to be the maximum that a working-class family can pay. On the basis of forty flats per acre, and twenty years' purchase, this would amount to a price of 3,200 pounds per acre. It would seem reasonable to say that tenements should not be built on land that costs more than 3,000 pounds an acre, nor cottages on land that costs more than 1,000 pounds per acre (E. D. Simon, *op. cit.*, p. 97).

[2] E. D. Simon, *op. cit.*, Ch. XV.

an appreciation of the family group as a training center for social life.

In discussing the question, "Can the family have two heads?" Dr. Paul Popenoe [1] reports upon a study of 2,596 families which he classified into three groups as follows: (1) man-dominant, (2) woman-dominant, and (3) "50-50." [2] He found that in the 2,596 families, 35 per cent were man-dominant, 28 per cent were woman-dominant, and 37 per cent were "50-50," or approximately democratic. In answer to the question, Can the family have two heads? it appears that in more than one-third of the families studied the family not only can but actually does have two heads, but Dr. Popenoe at once asks: " Why is it that nearly two-thirds of the marriages in question have failed to reach a democratic basis at the present time? " Analyzing the data further, Director Popenoe found that happy marriages were distributed among the three groups as follows:

> Of the man-dominated marriages, 61 per cent are happy and 24 per cent are unhappy.
> Of the woman-dominated marriages, 47 per cent are happy and 31 per cent are unhappy.
> Of the "50-50" marriages, 87 per cent are happy and only 7 per cent unhappy.
> The figures leave no doubt that in marriages of the type studied, a democratic copartnership is associated with the greatest happiness; that man-dominated marriages come next in this respect; and that marriages dominated by the wife show a definitely smaller percentage of happiness than do the other two. [3]

The conclusion to be drawn from the above-mentioned facts is that education needs to be directed toward training children in democratic ideals for the family. At present, husbands and wives are encouraged to compete with each other. The need is to train them to coöperate with each other not only within but without the home.

[1] Director, Institute of Family Relations, Los Angeles.
[2] Paul Popenoe, "Can the Family Have Two Heads?" *Sociology and Social Research*, XVIII: 12–17 (September–October, 1933).
[3] *Ibid.*, pp. 14, 15.

The democratic family is one in which the husband and wife share the authority more or less equally and according to a pre-arranged division of labor. It is a group whose life is based not primarily on the fear and force of authority, but on the drawing power of mutual respect and affection. Rational love rules.

A democratic family rests on the principle of mutual self-sacrifice. In its sacrificial nature is its greatest strength as a social training center. If children do not learn to make sacrifices for the common good within the family, they have no adequate substitute, for large institutions become formal by their nature. If parents can be trained in the principles of democratic parenthood, and youth in principles of rational marriages then society will probably keep the family group as one of its basic institutions.

It has been well said that no child has a home if he cannot find it in the attitudes of a coöperative and companionable father and mother. He may have a kind guardian or a thoughtful father, or a loving mother, but the essence of a real home is found only in the attitudes of two parents united in genuine affection for each other.

The family group was "the first human school." Despite its weaknesses it has often been the best school. The most effective teaching is being done in and through the family. The informal education of every person normally begins in the family; the child's most important educational period, informal though it be, is spent in the family. The education of the children in the principles of health and sex hygiene may be given best by parents. There is no better place than the home in which a child can learn obedience, discipline, and socially sound behavior. Training in ethical behavior has fine possibilities in the home. The family may become the greatest socializing influence in the world.

It is within the home that individuals can acquire early and effectively the idea that marriage and the family have superior possibilities as social institutions. It is here that the social significance of fatherhood can be taught. Girls, and boys also, can learn here that motherhood represents the most important social service which a woman can perform, and that next in importance may be fatherhood.

Better marriages is an excellent starting point for improving the family. On the other hand, poor marriages are perhaps the chief cause of family instability, divorce, and desertion.[1] Since many persons assume that marriage is not a serious affair, they make hasty and ill-advised marriages and think that they can easily extricate themselves. The easier that divorce is made, the wider the assumption that marriage is unimportant and the more careless the attitudes regarding it.

Marriage on short acquaintance too often proves a delusion. The time element is necessary in order that young people may determine whether what seems to be love is real and lasting affection, or a passing fancy, or chiefly sex desire. Careful thought for a period of time, consideration of temperaments, consideration of cultural backgrounds, the advice of sympathetic and understanding elders are helpful if not essential in making one of the most fundamental choices of life, that of a husband or a wife.

Tentative statements of democratic marriage ideals would include a disapproval of the marriage of persons of widely different cultural and racial backgrounds, of persons of widely different ages, of any persons who have tendencies to mental defectiveness, or of persons with venereal diseases. The practice of requiring a health certificate from a reputable physician is intended to protect the innocent against hidden diseases. The requirement that a certain length of time should elapse between the securing of a marriage license and marriage is designed to protect society and persons alike from hasty and ill-advised marriages. If a person is required by law to go through a long period of training involving years before entering a profession, is it unreasonable to ask that persons give at least a few days' thought to entering the marriage relationship?

[1] George Elliott Howard developed this idea in his article, "Bad Marriage and Quick Divorce," *Journal of Applied Sociology*, VI, No. 2, 1–10.

Legislation alone is not enough. If marriage and the family are not supported by public opinion, then legislation cannot improve matters. Marriage needs to be viewed by public opinion not as an expression of purely individualist impulses but as a social safeguard. The family needs not to be considered lightly but as an institution socially necessary and sacred; not as a temporary contract to be assumed carelessly but as involving human feelings and intimate relationships that are to be treated as life-long in their effects upon personality. Lax family life rests in part on lax marriage attitudes, and lax marriages rest on lax public opinion. More knowledge about the means of securing sound marriages and stable family groups, and a wide distribution of such knowledge of this kind would produce a more wholesome social life.

Although the people of Canada and of England are similar in culture and institutions to the people of the United States, their divorce rate is relatively very low. This situation is partially explained by the fact that attitudes and laws in Canada and England toward marriage and the family are of a different order from those in the United States.

The instability of the modern family may go from bad to worse until a nation such as the United States hits the rocks, even as Rome decayed; or it may be met by new and constructive attitudes. While many factors, economic and so on, are vital to national morale, the outcome depends to a considerable extent on the attitudes toward marriage and the family that persons and groups elect to encourage. The destruction or reconstruction of the family lies within the realms of human attitudes.

The main function of the family is to train children to become worthy parents, neighbors, and citizens. So far the family has fallen considerably below its possibilities. Child guidance clinics report that a high percentage, sometimes as high as 85 per cent, turn out to be parental guidance cases. Parents as a class have been woefully untrained for parenthood. Fortunately, there are many new developments in parental education.[1] For example, in the United States the National Parents and Teachers Association with thousands of chapters and over a million members is promoting child study and parental education. The Child Study Association of America, dating back to 1888, is a leader in the development of parental education conferences. The United States Children's Bureau entered the field of parental education in 1924. Colleges and universities are now establishing courses and even divisions of parental education. Religious bodies are also beginning to give attention to this vital theme. Adult education classes for the training of parents are spreading in public evening schools in the United States.

Marriage guidance and *family relations clinics* are beginning to develop. They advise couples about to be married, and assist the married in meeting troublesome conflicts. They furnish the best books and other literature on marriage and the family. They conduct classes on preparation for marriage, and for family life. They are setting a pace for public education, and represent a pioneering type of social service of inestimable value.

In a current discussion of marriage guidance clinics Dr. Meyer F. Nimkoff has shown how family case workers are unable to effect adjustments for more than a small percentage of family problems because of heavy case loads and of lack of specific training. Domestic relations courts are able to effect adjustments in only a limited proportion of instances. The marriage and family guidance clinic has a trained director and offers special help of a psychiatric, psychological, and sociological nature, so that real assistance may be rendered to persons considering marriage as well as those who are maladjusted in marriage. Its thoroughgoing nature has been indicated as follows:

> Since the whole personality of an individual is involved in his life-accommodations, in dealing with a specific instance of maladjustment it is necessary to secure a complete case-history of the persons

[1] See George B. Mangold, "Some Recent Developments in Parental Education," *Sociology and Social Research*, XIII: 325–37.

concerned. Therefore, at the Institute for Family Guidance, the routine procedure calls for (1) a medical report, (2) psychological tests, (3) if needed, a psychiatric examination, and (4) a developmental or social history of the two persons up to the time of their marriage, and of their life together. The last-numbered item is of course the most important. The examinations and interviews then provide the data from which the "tensions" of the marriage may be diagnosed. Each case is analyzed in terms of its "constellation of tensions," and the sources of the stress are sought in the interaction of the personalities and in their social situation.[1]

Although too often the wife and mother has been a slave to her husband and a routine worker imprisoned within four walls called a home, another movement is now at hand, namely, of elevating home-making into a "career" as interesting and status-giving as are other high-class occupations. On a par with her husband she has equal status with him at home and in public; having regular avocational activities outside the home she has equal chance with her husband for personality growth and versatility; with adequate avocational training which she may turn into occupational activities when her children are grown, she has full opportunity for development, usefulness, and status in the later years of life.

After thousands of years of human history, nothing superior to or as good as the educated, democratic family has been found for the training of children. Marriage and the family determine the heredity of nearly all children; they convey cultural backgrounds; they furnish the primary stimuli for personality growth. Although it may be built of logs and possess humble appointments, the home may still function as "an informal school room of the human race and the noblest center of human affections."

PROBLEMS

1. Why is the family an important social institution?

2. Explain the statement that "woman has domesticated man."

3. In what ways is home life in the country better than in the city?

[1] Meyer F. Nimkoff, "The Family Guidance Clinic," *Sociology and Social Research*, XVIII: 233.

4. Why is marriage taken by many people with a lack of seriousness?

5. Explain: "No one marries the real man."

6. Define a good husband.

7. Define a good wife.

8. Define a good child.

9. What is feminism?

10. What are the effects upon home life of moving every year?

11. Why is dinner table talk of social value?

12. Explain the statement that the rich man's wife is often a parasite.

13. "Is the attitude of the public the same toward the man who has married money, as toward the man who made money?"

14. Should wealthy women resent being forced "to spend their time in the meaningless round of luncheons, teas, bridge parties, and stereotyped charities?"

15. Should every girl learn to cook?

16. Should every girl learn home-making?

17. Should every young woman be trained for an occupation outside the home?

18. Are women inherently better than men?

19. Should women become more masculine?

20. If so should men become more feminine?

21. What is the main function of an engagement period before marriage?

22. Why is the present form of courtship unsatisfactory?

23. Which are the greater, the advantages or disadvantages of being an only child?

24. In what way is heredity more important than environment?

25. How is environment superior to heredity?

26. Why did eugenics develop?

27. Explain the statement that although the death rate has declined in recent years, the race is less vigorous than formerly.

28. What is the significance of the statement: Man is "an outdoor animal"?

29. Distinguish between chromosomes and genes.

30. How does "the fittest to survive" vary under different conditions?

31. Explain: "Man is the sickest animal alive."

32. In what ways can "falling in love" be controlled to the advantage of all parties concerned?

33. How far is "falling in love" a sound guide for mating?

34. Compare eugenics and dysgenics.

35. What makes a disharmonic type?

36. How does an optimum population vary?

37. Why are real estate "boosters" often rated high as good citizens although they may be enemies of eugenics?

38. Can a large-scale employer be a good citizen and a violator of eugenic principles?

39. What is the strongest argument in favor of birth control?

40. What is the weakest spot in the birth-control argument?

41. Why has the control of birth control become an important problem?

42. Why are so many American families giving up their homes and moving into apartments or flats?

43. Which is better for the family, the single dwelling or the flat?

44. Explain the statement that every American city has its housing problem.

45. Why is there so much overcrowding in the United States when at the same time there is so much spacious territory?

46. Illustrate the statement: There is no room to live healthily.

47. Why are tuberculosis and crowded housing conditions found together?

48. Why are some good people who live in large apartments negligent as to how the janitor of the apartment building is housed?

49. Why do many poor people keep the windows closed in sleeping rooms even in the summer?

50. If you were a wage-earner and your rent were suddenly raised, would you take in lodgers or move into a smaller number of rooms? Why?

51. Are the people who own their own homes in the United States increasing or decreasing? Why?

52. Why do many landlords feel no responsibility for the poor health conditions which their properties generate?

53. How does unearned increment affect the question of housing?

54. Who suffers when people speculate in land values?

55. Why are municipal lodging houses maintained in some cities?

56. What percentage of a man's income should be spent for rent?

57. Explain the statement that "you can kill a man, woman, or child just as surely with a tenement as with a gun."

58. Is it true that the most successful person in the world is he or she who helps to rear socially-minded and socially-behaving children?

READINGS

ALLEN, E. L., *American Housing* (Manual Arts Press, Peoria, Illinois, 1930).

BASHORE, H. B., *Overcrowding and Defective Housing in the Rural Districts* (John Wiley and Sons, Inc., New York, 1915).

BOSANQUET, HELEN, *The Family* (The Macmillan Company, New York, 1923).

CALHOUN, A. W., *A Social History of the American Family* (Arthur H. Clark Company, Cleveland, 1917–1919).

COLCORD, JOANNA, *Broken Homes* (Russell Sage Foundation, New York, 1919).

DARWIN, LEONARD, *What Is Eugenics?* (Galton Publishing Company, New York, 1930).

DEFOREST, R. W., and L. VEILLER, *The Tenement House Problem* (The Macmillan Company, New York, 1903).

DOUGLAS, PAUL H., *Wages and the Family* (University of Chicago Press, 1925).

GALTON, FRANCIS, "Eugenics: Its Definition, Scope, and Aims," *American Journal of Sociology*, X: 1–25.

GILLIN, J. L., and F. W. BLACKMAR, *Outlines of Sociology* (The Macmillan Company, New York, 1930), Chs. X, XI.

GOODSELL, WILLYSTINE, *A History of Marriage and the Family* (The Macmillan Company, New York, 1934).

——, *Problems of the Family* (The Century Company, New York, 1928).

GROVES, ERNEST R., *The Drifting Home* (Houghton Mifflin Company, Boston, 1926).

——, *The American Family* (J. B. Lippincott Company, Philadelphia, 1934).

——, *The Marriage Crisis* (Longmans, Green and Company, New York, 1928).

GROVES, ERNEST R., and W. F. OGBURN, *American Marriage and Family Relationships* (Henry Holt and Company, New York, 1928).

HOWARD, GEORGE ELLIOTT, *History of Matrimonial Institutions* (University of Chicago Press, Callaghan and Company, 1904).

JENNINGS, H. S., *The Biological Basis of Human Nature* (W. W. Norton and Company, Inc., New York, 1930).

LICHTENBERGER, JAMES P., *Divorce, an Interpretation* (McGraw-Hill Book Company, Inc., New York, 1931).

MOWRER, E. R., *Domestic Discord* (University of Chicago Press, 1928).

——, *The Family* (University of Chicago Press, 1932).

——, *Family Disorganization* (University of Chicago Press, 1927).

NEUMANN, HENRY, *Modern Youth and Marriage* (D. Appleton and Company, New York, 1928).

PINK, LOUIS H., *The New Day in Housing* (John Day Company, New York, 1928).

POPENOE, PAUL, *Practical Applications of Heredity* (Williams and Wilkins, Baltimore, 1930).

POPENOE, PAUL, and R. H. JOHNSON, *Applied Eugenics* (The Macmillan Company, New York, 1933).

RATHBONE, ELEANOR F., *The Disinherited Family* (Longmans, Green and Company, New York, 1927).

REED, RUTH, *The Modern Family* (Alfred A. Knopf, New York, 1930).

ROSS, E. A., *Standing Room Only?* (The Century Company, New York, 1927).

SIMON, E. D., *The Anti-Slum Campaign* (Longmans, Green and Company, London, 1933).

THOMPSON, R. E., *The History of the Dwelling House and Its Future* (J. B. Lippincott Company, Philadelphia, 1914).

THURSTON, FLORA M., *A Bibliography on Family Relationships* (National Council of Parental Education, New York, 1932).

TODD, A. J., *The Primitive Family as an Educational Agency* (G. P. Putnam's Sons, New York, 1913).

TOWNROE, B. S., *The Slum Problem* (Longmans, Green and Company, New York, 1928).

VAN WATERS, MIRIAM, *Parents on Probation* (New Republic Publishing Company, New York, 1927).

——, *Youth in Conflict* (New Republic Publishing Company, New York, 1925).

VEILLER, LAWRENCE, *Housing Reform* (Charities Publication Committee, New York, 1911).

WEILL, BLANCHE E., *The Behavior of Young Children of the Same Family* (Harvard University Press, Cambridge, 1928).

WESTERMARCK, EDWARD, *A Short History of Marriage* (The Macmillan Company, New York, 1926).

WOOD, EDITH, *Housing of the Unskilled Wage Earner* (The Macmillan Company, New York, 1919).

——, *Housing Progress in Western Europe* (E. P. Dutton and Company, New York, 1923).

WOODHOUSE, CHASE G., "A Study of 250 Successful Families," *Social Forces*, VIII: 511–32.

CHAPTER VI

THE OCCUPATIONAL GROUP

Human life is focused not only in the family but also in occupational groups. In the family group bread and butter problems, money matters, and occupational activities arise from time to time for comment and discussion. Dinner table talk frequently relates to the day's work.

If work is regular and remuneration is received, an occupational status has been achieved. An *occupation* is any type of activity to which a number of persons give themselves regularly for pay. A *profession* is a specialized type of occupation which maintains formal standards for admission.

OCCUPATIONAL ORIGINS AND ATTITUDES

Among early human groups, the elemental impulse of hunger, perhaps more than any other influence, led to industrial activity. Primitive people satisfied this impulse by searching for food and by living upon what they could raise. Hence they gorged and starved, feasted and fasted, according to their skill or luck in finding food.

As an aid in this search for food, primitive people invented crude weapons and tools. Man, the only tool-using animal, invented knives for cutting, scrapers for abrasing, hammers for fracturing, needles and awls for perforating, tongs for grasping, and so on, throughout a long list of complex implements.[1] It was a remarkable advance when man learned how to kindle a fire, and could cook. Another achievement is represented by the discovery of drying foods in the sun or before a fire, as a means of preserving them for times of scarcity.

[1] O. T. Mason, *Origins of Inventions* (Charles Scribner's Sons, New York, 1910), Ch. II.

Man moved forward again when he learned to domesticate animals. This domestication resulted in giving the human race valuable assistance in its industrial activities; in the dog, man had an assistant in the chase; and in the ox, a beast of burden. Then there developed the raising of domesticated animals for food, which guaranteed a dependable defense against hunger, relieving the human group of its dangers of famine, except occasionally.

The digging stick, as the forerunner of hoe-culture and later of agriculture, was used to scratch the surface of the soil for the planting of seeds. For long centuries, doubtless, women with digging sticks and similar crude implements managed to raise a few herbs and roots, and thus to provide against periods of famine. In the meantime men were engaged chiefly in the hunt and the chase, and in fighting.

The early occupations were twofold, and each was a double-header. The main division was made on the basis of sex. Women did the work pertaining to the raising of children and also to the raising of foodstuffs near the habitation. Men divided their time between hunting wild game, and in defensive and offensive warfare.

The domestication of animals became a group undertaking, and a few domesticated animals grew into extensive flocks and herds. Group life changed when pastoral and nomadic life developed. In order to secure pasturage, the human group followed the flocks up the valleys and mountain slopes in the summer and back again in the winter. Not only was a stable food supply made fairly certain, but materials were always at hand for clothing. Social organization took on new aspects. Instead of human life being organized around the mother and children, the center shifted to the flocks and herds, women were subordinated, and men came into a larger dominance.

Along with the development of hoe-culture, field-culture, or agriculture, and pastoral occupations, there arose the institution of *private property*. Tools and weapons were early considered to be the private property of their maker. With the increase of flocks and herds the institution of private property seems to have become well established. Land and pasturage, however, were first considered *group property*, but flocks became private property with group protection. Each tribe or group possessed its generally recognized territory throughout which its members might wander with their cattle, sheep, and goats.

The use of land as an occupational activity is primeval and universal. Hoe-culture including the protection of roots and tubers for future consumption developed into tillage of the soil with oxen and plow. When men turned from the hunt as a means of livelihood to hoe-culture which was developed first probably by women, they made application of some of the technical skill which they had acquired in hunting and fighting. New tools were developed, and hoe-culture was supplemented by crude field-culture on a relatively larger scale. Thus agriculture was born.

With the rise of agriculture, primitive groups passed from the flesh diet of nomadism to a larger use of vegetable foods. The roaming life of hunting days and pastoral nomadism gave way by degrees to the more settled life of agriculture and to the farmer. The farming occupation developed its own attitudes and values, based on an individualistic, stationary life located close to nature rather than to people.

With the cultivation of the soil and the accompanying vast increase in food supply, population multiplied. Agriculture made fixed abodes necessary, and led to the establishment of village communities. The village group grew out of gregariousness, and of the need for protection against human enemies and against storm, famine, sickness, wild beasts, evil spirits.

All these changes were accompanied by the creation of new forms of wealth. The making of money itself became an occupation which has added greatly to human welfare but which has also created an unlimited amount of human ill will and misery, and which has dominated other occupations as well as life itself.

With stationary abodes, the holding of slaves became feasible. *Slavery* acquired an occupational status. Under nomadism and earlier forms of human existence the food supply was so small and uncertain, and life was so migratory that it was usually necessary to kill captives taken in warfare. With the rise of agricultural occupations it was better to enslave captives than to kill them. The cultivation of the soil by slave labor represented at first an advance. It was wiser to put captives at work than to put them to death. Slavery, however, developed brutal phases. It ran counter to many human impulses. It treated human beings as mere property and the traffic in them became disreputable.

Slavery gradually became economically unprofitable and was ultimately supplanted by free labor and the wage system. Even if human sentiments had not been deeply affronted by such practices as selling children and women "on the block," the factory system would have bowled over the slave system.

Down to the middle of the eighteenth century, agriculture was the leading occupational activity of mankind. The serf system of cultivating the soil which existed for centuries permitted a small percentage of the people, sometimes known as lords, to own not only the land but also the people who worked on the lands and who were known as serfs.

With the Industrial Revolution which began in England in the latter part of the eighteenth century, and with the manufacture of tools on a large scale there developed a new type of agriculture. The division of land into farms under independent ownership became common. An increase in population and in the demand for food brought about a change from a superficial and extensive type to an efficient and intensive type of farming, and inaugurated the scientific agriculture of the twentieth century. Likewise free labor paid for on a monthly or day basis developed.

The Industrial Revolution furthered *specialization*. Instead of being a Jack of all trades, each person became a specialist in one. Along with specialization in industry and in agriculture, there developed many occupations and with them occupational attitudes. These attitudes and their accompanying values are basic to a further discussion of occupational groups.

If an occupation is a set of repeated and somewhat standardized activities, it is natural that certain attitudes toward life should develop out of it. Any type of doing and thinking concentrates the attention upon certain objects or values. The continued seeking of the values produces established tendencies to act or attitudes. Each occupation thus has its characteristic attitudes and corresponding values. An *occupational attitude* in general is an acquired and established way to act with reference to some value offered by a regular means of earning a living.

Each occupation has its own peculiar problems, its own demands upon the attention of its representatives, and its special influences upon the latters' attitudes. Doing a thing or a set of things according to certain formulae every day, in season and out, tends to create mental patterns. The occupation of driving ox teams will produce a slow-moving mental pattern, while driving a taxicab in a large city will lead to quick-moving mental habits. Acting as a motorman with the sign before one of "Don't speak to the motorman" gives one a day's work in a partial mental vacuum, while teaching college classes of wide awake, inquiring young people sharpens one's wits and creates alert mental patterns. Correcting children's mistakes in arithmetic, spelling, and reading for several hours daily over a period of years produces a mistake-hunting pattern.[1]

A person who has enjoyed his work in a given occupation and has succeeded in it is likely to feel that his occupation or profession is the most important of all. Life becomes organized habitually around or conditioned by occupational activities. Moreover, as J. M. Williams explains, "A man's business becomes precious to him as it is that for which he has given his life, just as children are precious to the mother as that for which she has given her life." "Life is precious and whatever one gives it for becomes precious."[2] In this way life comes to revolve around one's occupation, and an occupational egocentrism develops.

[1] Adapted from E. S. Bogardus, "The Occupational Attitude," *Journal of Applied Sociology*, VIII: 172.

[2] *The Foundations of Social Science* (Alfred A. Knopf, New York, 1920), pp. 57, 58.

A professional attitude is a specialized occupational tendency to act, arising from skill in a highly complex and limited field. A profession may be distinguished from a trade in that the latter deals primarily with transforming material things into useful commodities, whereas the former renders personal services and at its best promotes health, knowledge, happiness, better government, and better living. The professional groups maintain high entrance standards. They foster an occupational ethics and occupational organizations. They have usually been allied with the higher well-to-do classes. Often they have represented middle class attitudes and served as a steady mean between the economic extremes. Each profession has developed a high degree of pride and even of self-sufficiency. This tendency has produced biases, narrow-mindedness, and intolerance, due in part to overspecialization.

MODERN CAPITALISM

Modern industry has gone a long ways from those early days when occupations were divided into only four types, with women engaged in child-raising and hoe-culture, and men, in hunting and fighting. Modern industry has shifted greatly from the days when settled agriculture arose and slavery and serfdom prevailed. It has its immediate origins in the changes which supplanted the slave and serf systems by the wage system. In the wage system workers found a new measure of personal independence, and in consequence did more work per day than slaves or serfs did, and hence supplanted the latter groups.

The rise of the factory system in the latter part of the eighteenth century and in the early nineteenth century drew free laborers together under single roofs, giving rise to *class consciousness*. They were drawn away from the homes of their employers where they worked under the domestic system of industry and where they and their respective employers kept in close touch with each other. In the factory they lost touch with their employers and a social chasm developed between the two groups. When employer and employee lost contact with each other, modern industrial troubles began. When the industry divided into two antagonistic groups labor-capital conflicts arose.

The application of steam as a motive force in operating machinery revolutionized industry. Hand-driven tools were supplanted by power-driven machinery; and the home as the unit of production gave way to the factory. Although the factory system and large-scale production imply mutual dependence, the loss of personal contact between employer and employee has led to endless industrial troubles. Labor began to organize for its own protection; capital likewise organized for its own advancement. Labor wished to secure control of industry; capital wished to dominate. Two large and powerful classes have arisen with a black gulf between.

The use of steam-driven machinery and the rise of the factory system created a demand for large units of capital. Modern business is conducted (1) by individual *entrepreneurs*, (2) by partnerships, or (3) by corporate organizations. The first method puts everything in the hands of one person. It is satisfactory for conducting a small business. The second is adequate where capital larger than one person can supply is needed. The corporate form is not only the largest and most important type of business group, but it wields vast power, and its public control has become very difficult. The leading business occupations which have adopted the corporate form of organization are banking, insurance, manufacture, mercantile enterprises, and transportation. Some types of business, such as investment banking, have developed sinister international connections.

Corporate business units first existed independently of each other. Then in the last half of the past century in the United States there came a period of competition, and even of cut-throat competition, as it was called. When that competition between business units in the same field became disastrous, these units began to combine into larger groups. The following summary is based on the analyses of several leading economists.

(1) One of the earliest types of combination was represented by the agreement of independent concerns to fix prices, and hence to increase profits by restricting competition. (2) The next step was the agreement of business groups to divide the field; each enterprise contracted to limit its activity to a particular section of the field.

(3) A third phase was the pool, or the attempt to restrict the output rather than the price or the field. According to this type of agreement, each member of the combination accepted an alloted percentage of production. (4) Then came the formation of "trusts." By this method, each of the constituent companies turned over the operation of its respective shares of the business to a board of central trustees, and in turn received trust certificates. Each essentially abandoned to the "trust" the entire operation of the business.

(5) The "holding corporation" developed as a successor to the "trust." In this connection a new central corporation was formed in order to purchase a majority interest of the stock of individual corporations. Each constituent corporation was operated as a separate unit. The control rested largely in the hands of the parent company. The holding corporation was a "trust" in a new and more effective form.

(6) Then the so-called system of "community of interests" developed. By this method the same group of directors possesses a controlling voice in the management of each constituent company. It is exceedingly difficult to prevent combinations of this sort from taking place. Their ramifications are difficult to trace. Moreover, a few individuals can command vast power. They can control legislation, political appointees, and newspapers, and they can manipulate profits to the advantage of themselves and their friends but to the loss of all who are not "on the inside."

Big business sometimes runs into an orgy of speculation, and speculation easily becomes legalized gambling on a gigantic scale. Big business likewise promotes overproduction, and sometimes it produces little minds on everything except business.

Combinations of capital eliminate competitive costs and permit the purchase of large quantities of materials at lower prices than the proprietor of the small independent business can obtain. They permit the undertaking of vast enterprises extending over many years, with the result that the small, independent producer generally suffers. The large corporate group becomes impersonal, and its responsibility to the public often disappears. The corporation develops attitudes of economic superiority, of class aloofness, of legalism, of profitism, of competitive shrewdness, of worshipping the god of things as they are, and of opposing needed economic and social improvements. A fundamental evil of capitalism is that it promotes acquisitive attitudes instead of contributive attitudes.[1] It makes great projects of human welfare possible, but all too often defies national and even international control.

The *business cycle* is coming to be known as a serious evil of capitalism. On a rising wave of business there develops overproduction, overextension of credit, overspeculation, even gambling with the idea of making millions out of nothing. Prosperity reigns. Then someone gets scared and decides to "cash in," which requires that others collect the debts owed them. Still others join in selling out until selling exceeds buying. As long as the buying exceeds the selling prices rise, sky high, but when the selling becomes dominant, prices fall; speculators are caught with promises and obligations that they cannot possibly meet. A crisis ensues, the worst business offenders are sent to the penitentiary or exile themselves from the country, and the populace are thrown out of work and suffer all the miseries of a long-drawn-out depression. After a few have lost millions but still live in comfort, the millions who have lost all of their hard-earned savings also lose what is worse, namely, their faith in government and human nature, and they grow revolutionary. Then business slowly starts all over again,

---

[1] R. H. Tawney in his *Acquisitive Society* (Harcourt, Brace and Howe, New York, 1920), brings out strikingly the "acquisitiveness" of the competitive economic system.

which is after all a very poor and miserable method of economic procedure, and which in 1933 in the United States was ostensibly repudiated in favor of a socially-controlled system.

LABOR UNIONISM

The movements to remedy and to prevent the evils arising out of modern labor-capital conditions and the competitive economic system are many. As the laboring man has come to realize the extent of economic injustices, he has organized for his own protection. The *labor union* is a protest against the evils of capitalism. The labor union probably would not have developed in its present form if capitalism had had the social vision and willingness to correct its own weaknesses.

It was during the nineteenth century that labor unions in the United States rose from the status of local organizations to national trade unions, and then into a general federation, the American Federation of Labor. The evolution of the labor union was slow and painful. The labor union had to fight its way upward against the powerful and sometimes unscrupulous methods of capitalism. It learned to fight fire with fire. It too often found the courts on the side of vested interests, and hence took the law into its own hands. It often showed the same shameful indifference of public welfare that it observed on the part of those corporations whose spokesmen sometimes proclaimed: "The public be damned."

Labor unionists believe in *collective bargaining*. They contend that the representatives of unions shall meet with the representatives of an employing concern, and that together they shall determine wage scales, hours of labor, and other conditions of work. Claiming that labor has the same right to organize as capital does, they logically insist on collective bargaining, because as individual bargainers for wages they are helpless in dealing with gigantic corporations.

Labor unionists as a class believe in *arbitration*. They are usually willing to abide by the rule of arbitration, providing they are sure that a fair board of arbitrators has been chosen. Reasonable labor unionists believe that broad-minded employers and they after friendly discussions of disputed points, will agree. They prefer the personal method of settling disputes. They ask that the representatives of organized labor be accorded a fair hearing by the representatives of organized capital, and that the chairman of an arbitration board be a public-spirited citizen. They usually object to compulsory arbitration for fear that the arbitration board will be "stacked" against them, and that they will have no recourse.

If denied what they consider a fair hearing labor unionists resort to *strikes*. They lay down their tools and walk out. If there is a likelihood that other workers will be brought in to take their places they resort to picketing, that is, others are prevented from taking their places. The strike is a powerful weapon. It stops production and profits. Moreover, it advertises to the world that a group of workers feel that some employer is treating them so unfairly that they are willing "to walk out."

In recent decades the strike has become a menace to the public. For example, a general railroad strike paralyzes the transportation of food, and brings starvation to the doors of the poor. It puts the travelling public into embarrassing situations. If the public denies the right of labor to strike, then the public is under obligation to provide labor with other means of obtaining justice. If labor cannot strike, then employers, it is claimed, should be forbidden to exercise the *lockout* or "to fire" without notice. Thus, the control of labor-capital problems becomes in part a public affair and subject to social control.

The moderate trade unionist, as V. S. Yarros has suggested, is not a revolutionist. He does not think of overthrowing the present economic order. He does not object to the wage system, or to the institution of private property.[1] In the United States he has generally been conservative in his demands.

[1] V. S. Yarros, "Social Science and What Labor Wants," *American Journal of Sociology*, XIX: 308ff.

They [labor] are the real victims of unemployment and economic distress. They are firmly convinced that industrial management and those who actually control the financial and industrial affairs of the nation have refused to accept the remedies which labor proposed and have failed to deal with a great emergency in a constructive and practical way.[1]

The labor unionist asks for more pay, shorter hours, and safer and healthier conditions of work. He will "always be making these three requests." He wants more pay (in normal times), for the same reason that the capitalist always wants more dividends. He urges shorter hours, for he sees many people who are no more worthy citizens than himself, who are not working at all, but who are living luxuriously, and as it seems to him, at his expense. He will always possess a desire for better conditions of labor, because he feels that he is entitled to share in the advances that are being registered by inventions and discoveries.[2]

The moderate trade unionist in the United States has been aptly described as having no Utopian schemes, as dealing with immediate problems, as priding himself "on his reasonableness and practicality," as believing in private capital if it is not used as an instrument of special privilege,[3] and as protesting against the prejudices, the lack of sympathy and comprehension, and the distrust shown by the capitalist. On the other hand he has often created a trade union autocracy and personified narrow class control. At times he has been obdurate and inconsiderate, hindering works of mercy because trade union rules would be broken thereby. He has worshipped the rules of the union at the expense of both the employer and the public.

In England at the present writing (1934) the trade unionist is becoming a state socialist. He would nationalize all the major or basic industries. He would have the government take charge

---

[1] From statement made by William Green, president of the American Federation of Labor before the New York Board of Trade, March 8, 1933 (Associated Press).

[2] V. S. Yarros, *op. cit.*, pp. 309ff.   [3] *Loc. cit.*

of all large-scale business because otherwise he believes that business is dominating government and manipulating it to its own pecuniary ends.

In Mexico in 1933 the labor provisions in the Constitution were proving to be an interesting experiment. If a worker feels that he has been dismissed unfairly he may appeal his case and if he wins he may receive three months' wages and additional wages at the rate of 20 days for every year that he has been employed by the given firm, and for overtime. Many difficulties have pursued the enforcement and operation of these labor laws.

Sociology believes in the principle of "Come, let us reason together," and in methods of adjudicating differences by discussing them frankly, and in a friendly manner.[1] It believes that labor and capital have the same need to organize, recognized at last in 1933 in the United States by the NRA, and that the representatives of organized labor have the same need for a fair hearing as have the representatives of organized capital. Neither have any rights to organize if they use such organization to work against the common weal.

In 1933, labor in the United States responded to the NRA because the latter recognized the principle of collective bargaining. In the "codes" employers at the request of the NRA agreed to recognize the representatives of labor unions without prejudice and not to ignore or discriminate against them in favor of independent workers.

Sociology does not approve of the arbitrariness and desire for class control of either unionists or capitalists. It does not excuse union labor in its schemes of using dynamite; neither does it condone organized capital in its schemes of stock-watering, and speculating in the necessities of life. Labor makes capital possible; herein lies the merit of Abraham Lincoln's statement in his first presidential message to Congress: "Labor is the superior of capital, and deserves much the higher consideration."

[1] *Loc. cit.*

Socialism

Socialism is a protest on one hand against the evils of private capitalism and profitism and on the other hand an announcement that labor unionism as such is too mild and inefficient. The socialist believes that labor unionism is in the long run the cat's paw of capitalism. As a result of the evils caused by private property and the corporate group, the movement known as socialism has developed into a world-wide prominence. In general, socialists having grown hopeless regarding the labor union method of appealing directly to the employer, advocate national ownership of the main instruments of production and transportation. When the representatives of organized capital refuse to meet the representatives of organized labor, then socialism is advanced as the only recourse for meeting the needs of labor.

Socialists as a class are opposed to the use of private property "to produce more private property." They make no war upon capital as such, but believe in capital providing it can be owned and operated for the benefit of all. Instead of having only a small percentage of the people reaping the major benefits from capital and land, they would have both owned by the state, and a managerial system developed for operating them, in the same manner as the postal service is governmentally owned and operated in many countries.

Instead of the returns from economic enterprise being divided into four parts, namely, rent, interest, profits, and wages, the socialist urges that all the returns should go to labor, recognizing different types of and gradations in labor service. Since land would be owned by the state no one would need to pay any rent, and since capital would be state owned, no interest would be charged. Since both land and capital would be used by individuals under direction of the state there would be no need for individuals to secure profits to themselves. Thus all the returns from industrial enterprise, according to the socialist's plan, would go in one major direction, namely, to labor, ranging from the highest type of superintendence and administrative labor to unskilled labor. No one would receive an income unless he worked; and the income would be determined by the skill or managerial ability which the individual showed, and by the social value of his activities.

The socialist does not believe that governmental regulation of gigantic private monopolies will succeed. He contends that the monopolies have become so powerful that they regulate governments. He points to case after case where private monopolies have become entrenched in governmental positions, even in Cabinets of the President of the United States, in Congress, and in gubernatorial chairs. The socialist says that the alternative is for government to go all the way and take over the large private businesses, beginning with the so-called national banks, the transportation systems, the basic industries of iron and steel, and so on. The socialist secretly smiles when he sees a gigantic monopoly developing, for he believes that such a monopoly is putting itself into a position where the next logical step will be for the government to take it over. He sees no alternative but for governments to own and control the major industries of their countries on a non-profit basis.

State socialism, or the ownership of and control by the national state, of the major instruments of production, as described in the preceding paragraphs, has several strong and several weak phases. The strong points will be considered first. (1) Justice is an effective plea. The ideal of socialism is to have everyone rewarded in proportion to his services, not to himself, but to society. Socialism urges a more just distribution of wealth; it desires to eliminate special privilege. It protests against an economic system which pays one man a million dollars annually merely because he is the son of his father, another man, $10,000 a year for managing the father's business, and other men, $750 or $1,500 a year each for furnishing the bulk of the labor. In all sincerity socialism argues that the big economic rewards should not go to the shrewd and the cunning. It asserts that the big prizes should not go to those favored by inheritance irrespective of their social worth. It insists upon a more just distribution of wealth.

(2) Socialism asks for a more scientific organization of the exchange factors in economic life. It asks that the multiplicity of middlemen be reduced. For example, there are perhaps three times as many milk wagons and drivers today in the United States as are required to serve the people. No one would think of returning to competitive postmen, that is, of having three or four postmen delivering mail on a given street at the same time and in the employment of as many different companies. When the farmer sells apricots on his trees at a cent a pound and the consumer a hundred miles away pays twenty-five cents a pound for those same apricots, there is room for a more economical organization of exchange, the socialist claims.

(3) Socialism would eliminate the commercialized spirit. The producing of goods and the rendering of service for profit would be stopped, as the latter has already been stopped in the postal service. It is contended that today many goods are manufactured primarily for profit, that is, primarily for selling purposes rather than because of usefulness. Under socialism it is said that the business of the shop-keeper would be to help the customer find out what he really needs, whereas under capitalism it is often to his interest to sell the customer what he does not need or what will return the largest profits.

(4) Socialism fearlessly proclaims the truth about unjust economic practices. It uncovers the worst conditions in industry. It engenders a critical public spirit. It holds the mirror of publicity before weak spots in economic life.

The first weakness of socialism that may be mentioned is (1) its attempt to put into practice a new economic system before people are ready for it, or before they are trained to assume responsibility under it. In Russia during the first ten years of the soviet régime a great deal of difficulty was encountered because a new economic system had been thrust upon a people unprepared for such responsibility. Socialism would move too rapidly; it often overlooks needed evolutionary measures. (2) Socialism tends to underestimate the premium that is placed by the present system upon thrift and energy. Under socialism there would be grave danger that individuals would succumb to the tendency of relying upon the state. The watchword might become: "What does it matter, the state will take care of me anyway." (3) Under socialism there would still be serious danger to personal liberty. Under capitalism when political rulers and business magnates combine, the majority of the people are helpless. With socialism in charge vast political power and absolute economic monopoly would be in the hands of a few persons at a time; moreover such concentrated authority would be fully legal. (4) Socialism puts nearly all its emphasis upon a new *organization* of society. It holds that if you would change the structure of society, you would *ipso facto* secure the desired improvement. It does not provide for adequate and immediate changes in personal character and in personal attitudes toward other classes of people. It makes no primary effort to change the self-centered attitudes which govern so many people so much of the time.

Fabian socialism has developed in England among the educated people. It is the product of the thinking of a select group who put their chief faith in intellectually spreading an evolutionary state socialism rather than in working out an organized political movement. The group, however, has remained weak in numbers but strong in its personnel.

Christian socialism also began in England. The Christian socialists find the basis of their beliefs in the teachings of Jesus. They claim that Jesus taught an essentially socialist view of life and that the first Christians set out to practice a form of communism. Theirs is an evolutionary type of state socialism based on religious zeal and motivation. Maurice and Kingsley are the two best known founders of Christian socialism. The movement has gained considerable sporadic strength but nothing equal to the expectations of its founders.

Guild socialism is another movement that has developed in England. It is struggling toward the organization of manufacturing establishments as industrial units with the workers in charge and in virtual ownership. It centers its efforts not on securing political control of society but on obtaining a new industrial organization of society. It has not made great headway.

Syndicalism is an extreme form of socialism, which aims at a complete overthrow of society by violent means in order to put society in the control of the workers. It has had its major development in France. Like its partial counterpart in the United States, the Industrial Workers of the World (I.W.W.), it believes that the program of the state socialist is too mild, and that the political method of securing economic control will fail. The syndicalist would have his *syndicats*, or unions, assume general control in society. The syndicats would be loosely bound together and exercise a working-class control.

Syndicalism holds that when state socialists are elected to office they become conservative. The syndicalist therefore advocates direct action. Do not try to get control of government by slow evolutionary means. You will get nowhere. Direct action is the only recourse.

A part of the syndicalist's method is *sabotage*, which originally referred to throwing a shoe into a machine so as to stop production and to further revolution. In this way if carried out extensively business confusion would result. "If you are working in a freight office and asked to ship oranges from Florida to Illinois, then change the shipping address to some town in New Mexico." By so doing business will break down, profits will be cut off, the consumers will protest against capitalism, and ask for "a new deal." Business under capitalistic control will be defeated, and a new syndicalist order can be set up. The *general strike* is also advocated. Let all employees cease to labor, and capitalistic business cannot go on—it will fail, leaving the way open for syndicalism. Syndicalism has not made much headway in the United States but has made itself felt in Europe, particularly in France.

Marxian socialism is best known through its left wing exponents in Russia, namely, through *bolshevism*. Karl Marx in his well-known work, *Das Capital*, showed how class struggle is a necessary result of the autocracy of capitalism. Revolution is the way out. In Russia during the World War the Marxian socialists came into power but not until they had split into bolsheviks and mensheviks, that is, into majority and the minority wings. The majority were the more radical, and took charge, establishing a dictatorship of the proletariat. They carried on their political activities through councils, or *soviets*.

The World War had killed many of the Czar's army officers; and the men in the ranks, as they became officers, finally swung the proletariat into power through a bloodless revolution. For the first time in the history of the world, the propertyless classes overthrew the propertied classes and assumed political control in one of the largest countries of the earth. Under the direction of Lenin, they established a dictatorship of the proletariat, using the same autocratic methods that they had become acquainted with under the lash of the imperialistic forces of the czars. They represent class control, but with a new class, the presumably weakest class in charge of society. Their success or failure depends on their five year plans, on their educational programs, on the degree of democracy which they will permit, and on the socialized attitudes which they achieve.

Communism is expressed in various movements, but Russian sovietism is often referred to as a fair sample. In communism ownership and control of everything would be in the hands of a small group presumably representing the common people. Marx advocated an equal distribution of wealth, a phrase which is widely misunderstood. Marx did not mean an equal distribution of all property among all the people pro rata, but a distribution primarily of income according to the service rendered or the work accomplished.

Communism would do away with nationalism and unite the world on a working-class basis. Its internationalism has given that term a special meaning that has painted it red in the eyes of many. According to Marx, nationalism separates the workers and on occasion divides them into warring armies that shoot each other down.

Marx developed the class struggle idea, namely, that the interests of capitalists and workers are so far apart that they cannot be united. In fact the chasm is bound to widen. The struggle between the laboring classes and the employing classes will go on from bad to worse until by revolutionary means and by sheer force of numbers the laboring class will come into control of governments.

Then there is the surplus value theory as developed by Marx. The capitalist by virtue of being in control pays the workers a wage which is less than the exchange value of the goods produced and keeps this surplus value for himself. On occasion the system is especially bad when the capitalist pays the worker less than a living wage, or employs children and women at low wages, and thereby is enabled to pocket a huge surplus.

Communism has made rapid strides in recent decades, but it has basic weaknesses, for example, its arbitrariness and its dictatorship programs, which put it on the level with some of the worst characteristics of capitalism. Its materialism has led it into atheism and a repudiation of religious values. Its ruthlessness in regard to personality and initiative, when these do not "toe the mark" subserviently is an evil portent.

In many parts of the world communism is greatly feared today. While its methods of control are ancient, it is a very real expression of the increasing unrest of the times. To denounce it feverishly and to jail its leaders will strengthen it. The chief thing needed is that economic and social injustice be rooted out.

Fascism

In a radio address in the presidential campaign of 1932 in the United States, a candidate for president proclaimed fascism as the last stand of capitalism against communism. In 1922, fascism came into power in Italy under the powerful directing hand of Mussolini. Although once a socialist, Mussolini had become disgusted with the weaknesses of the masses in their self-governing plans and had violently disagreed with their internationalist and pacifist tendencies. Consequently he shifted his allegiance and promoted the formation of groups of ex-service men, augmented by members of the middle and upper classes in the cities and by the land-owners in the rural districts. These *fasci di combattimento* sometimes took charge in cities when the government failed. The *fasci di combattimento* were ex-soldiers aided by those who wished to stave off socialism. Fascism originated in part as a defense mechanism against socialism.

Capitalism has been undergoing modifications in Italy under fascism. At first employers were left a relatively free hand, but since April 3, 1926, the fascist government has been putting into operation its so-called "corporative" law. By this law, "corporations" of workers and also of employers "in each industrial activity are created as legal units" and hence are subject to the will of the fascist government. There are no private labor unions or large business organizations outside of fascism. Only corporative units exist. Moreover they operate only as they respond to the will of fascism. If a business enterprise is conducted in a way judged detrimental to the state it receives first a warning and then an order to cease its questionable practices. Both strikes and lockouts are forbidden by law.

The corporative state involves thirteen national corporations. There is a corporation of employees and also one of employers in each of the following six fields: agriculture, industry, commerce, banking, land transportation, and maritime and air service. The thirteenth is the national corporation of professional men and artists. These thirteen giant national corporations operate through the national council of corporations and under the direction of the minister of corporations, who is the head of the corporative state. If the fascist state should fall there is its powerful child, the corporative state, which might be able to stand, to continue functioning, and to become the government.

Under the corporative state both the employee and the employer are feeling the effects of an authoritative control. Those persons who do not belong to the corporative state, however, do not count for much.

Fascism does not take stock in traditional economic principles such as, "competition is the life of trade," or that prices should be regulated by the law of supply and demand. In fact, in 1932, the minister of corporations began to regulate prices on the basis of what he and his advisers judged to be fair prices, and to regulate supply and production on the basis of needs. The private promoter, the real estate "shark," the blatant advertiser are likely to be regarded as enemies of the state, and treated accordingly. Private property and capitalism exist in fascist Italy but are under autocratic control with the interests of the nation being made paramount.

A basic idea of fascism is: Everyone shall work, but no one shall work against the state. A nationally planned economy is thus in operation with individualism in industry and property being maintained but under rigid and often arbitrary control. This control goes to the extreme of preventing freedom of speech, freedom of the press, freedom of assemblage, if that freedom is used to criticize the fascist system. It is promised, however, that some day when fascism is more accepted than now that a measure of personal liberty will be returned to the people.

Coöperatism

Coöperatism is a term that covers all collectivist movements that are proceeding by evolutionary means to increase good will. Coöperatism changes human attitudes so all people may express themselves not only in behalf of themselves but also in behalf of others. Coöperatism is a working together of all for the well-being of all. It is an integration of individual initiative and coöperative action. It includes the various forms of coöperation and industrial democracy.

Consumers' coöperation has made considerable headway in many countries. Its aim is to enable consumers to work together so that all may obtain commodities, such as food, clothing, and so on, at wholesale rates, of selling them at special retail rates, and of dividing the profits if there be any among all participants on some equitable basis.

Producers' coöperation is somewhat different. While the aim of consumers' coöperation is to give the purchaser the advantage of lower costs, the purpose of producers' coöperation is commonly that of maintaining or of raising prices. Associations of workingmen have employed managers and acted as their own employers. While uneducated and untrained persons do not respond to producers' coöperation, highly trained people are often not much more effective because of their specialized individualism. Other difficulties in connection with producers' coöperation are a lack of sufficient capital, endless trouble with incompetent and shiftless members, the problem of securing and keeping efficient managers, the inability to bear losses, and insufficient intelligence and socialized backgrounds of the rank and file.

Profit-sharing is a form of partial coöperation that a few employers have inaugurated whereby "the employee receives a share, fixed in advance, of the profits." It is a plan of paying to employees a share of profits in addition to wages. It is assumed that the profits which are shared will be created by the increased diligence and care of the employees. It also assumes that the employees help to create profits as well as wages. It implies that if profits are shared, then losses should also be assumed but this the employees are unable to do. Hence, it becomes a prosperity measure only.

Management-sharing gives the employee a part in the operation of a business. Management-sharing in small ways has been extensive. Workers, for example, have been given places on shop committees. In some instances, employers have shared management with their employees to the extent of establishing joint committees for determining hours of labor, wages, and the settling of other difficult points. Sometimes the committee is composed of an equal number of representatives of the employing firm and of workers with a public-spirited citizen as chairman. Management-sharing probably has reached its greatest growth in the form of shop committees. It increases the status of employees. On the other hand, many employees are not qualified to assume a share in management while others are adverse to assuming such responsibility.

Social insurance is the insurance of the working classes through state action. The funds are furnished in part by the employer, in part sometimes by the employee, and in part sometimes by the state. There are several types of social insurance, such as accident insurance or workman's compensation, sickness and old age insurance, and unemployment insurance.

In the case of *accident insurance* or *workman's compensation*, the employer usually pays all the cost of an accident, on the theory that the workman who is injured is paying his share through his suffering. Moreover, when a $5,000 machine in a factory wears out, its loss is charged to the costs of production; when a $5,000 employee suffers death as the result of an accident while at work, this loss is also being charged to the cost of production, and the sum of $5,000 is paid in installments to the widow or children, or both.

Sickness and old age insurance is a godsend to the workman. When he is ill his wages cease, unlike the situation of the temporarily disabled salaried person. Old age insurance greatly increases the workman's sense of security. The horror that every honest workman faces is to be forced out of work because of old age or sickness accompanying old age and not to have any funds. Many employing firms have a pension system for their employees who have been with them many years, but this procedure ties up a workman with a given firm, and leaves him unprotected in case he should change employers. State old age insurance gives the workman more freedom and at the same time the needed security.

Compulsory *unemployment insurance* which was introduced, for example, in England in 1912, in two leading trades, was greatly extended in 1921. Although this insurance fund was deeply in the red in England in 1932, many persons from various walks of life were saying that unemployment insurance was the only thing that stood between England and revolution. The socialists and communists were opposing it on the ground that it kept the working people contented and thus postponed a revolution. Employers and Tory members of Parliament were viewing unemployment insurance as a necessary evil; they could suggest nothing better. The usual plan is for the state, the employer, and the employee to contribute approximately equal amounts per labor unit. If an unemployment insurance fund is started on a large scale at the beginning of a period of prosperity it is likely to be built up to a level where it can meet all payments in case of widespread unemployment, providing the unemployment period does not last too long.

Social insurance in its main forms as discussed in the foregoing paragraph has the merit of providing industrial workers with a degree of freedom from anxiety in normal times, and of increasing their happiness and efficiency. It keeps them self-respecting. Social insurance is sometimes criticized as being an opening wedge for socialism, a point that is exaggerated in the minds of the fearful. A more serious objection is the danger to individual initiative. It may undermine a full sense of personal responsibility. In a way it might be better to provide higher than living wages and to promulgate habits of thrift, so that full personal responsibility may flourish, always of course toward socialized ends.

Free national and state employment bureaus are a logical part of any coöperative plan. If it is to the basic interest of the nation to keep its subjects employed as far as possible, then such employment service may well be furnished free of cost. It is less expensive for the nation to operate such bureaus than to have large numbers of persons needlessly idle.

Adult education for the unemployed that fits them for the trades or for better work than they have known previously is a natural accompaniment to a system of national employment agencies. For the persons whom the employment bureau cannot place, an educational program of some kind or other is desirable, enabling the temporarily unemployed to be busy, to improve in skill and become master of more than one trade. Any nation can ill afford to have a large unemployed class, whether the individuals be rich or poor. In these ways a percentage of the unemployed problem would be solved. Everybody would either be working, or if out of work, would not be lying around idle acquiring dangerous habits.[1]

Welfare work is a phase of coöperatism. The provision in a business establishment for organized recreation, social clubs, restaurants, rest rooms, and free dental service, baths, illustrates welfare work in its simplest forms.[2] As a result the employer is usually repaid in the form of the increased efficiency of and improved personal relations with his employees. For him welfare work is a paying proposition.

The American workman, however, has been peculiarly sensitive to anything that suggests charity. It has been well pointed out that persons who understand workmen at all, realize that they do not want to be the recipients of that type of charity which would place them under lasting servile obligations. Welfare work is either a natural claim or a charity. If the former, the workman should have it as a basic condition of work; if the latter, he is put under questionable obligation. It is being urged that the benevolent works of employers in the form of welfare activities which at first seemed to be gracious and liberal gifts, should be required by law. Real welfare is fair wages, shorter hours of labor, a larger voice in management, better conditions of working and living, more certainty of work, and more guarantees against old age dependency.

[1] Sidney and Beatrice Webb, *The Prevention of Destitution* (Longmans, Green and Company, New York, 1912), Chs. V, VI.

[2] C. R. Henderson, *Citizens in Industry* (D. Appleton and Company, New York, 1915).

Industrial democracy carries the idea of coöperation to its fullest limit. For many years employers were prone to confuse welfare work with industrial democracy. Genuine industrial democracy, however, involves three main factors, namely, the public, labor, and capital. The needs and welfare of the public are primary; the interests of both labor and capital are secondary. Any economic system which gives the entire management of business to labor is unsound; and likewise capital is in error when it wishes to monopolize control. Labor and capital alike are striving in part for material ends; one wants more wages, the other more profits. Both goals are materialistic; the higher spiritual needs of life are likely to be sidetracked.

It is thought by many persons that the main solution of economic problems is to give labor representation on boards of directors and in the management of industry. Capital opposes this plan and labor is not trained for it. The joint control of industry by capital and labor is no certain cure-all for industrial evils. Capital and labor have shown signs of combining against the public. At times capital has profiteered and labor has grown arbitrary. In a given corporation an increase in selling costs was proposed some time ago with the understanding that one-half of the profits that might accrue should be turned into dividends, and the other half into wages. Capital and labor thus combined against the consumer.

In the matter of wages, hours of labor, dividends, and hence of prices the third party to industrial enterprise needs to have a voice and representation. Without the consumer neither capital nor labor would have much to do. A *tripartite organization of industry* is inevitable. It is essential if all interests vitally concerned are to receive a square deal. The public is bound to come into the picture. If capital and labor, or either one separately takes the bit into its own mouth, the public will insist upon national control, if not of ownership. It might be better to give the public definite representation on boards of ownership and control. Still more important is the development of socialized attitudes on the part of all who are involved.

As a reaction against profiteering, overinflation, and high prices, a new economic phenomenon on a large scale occurred in the fall of 1919 in the United States. It was *a buyers' strike.* This strike continued for some time as a protest against high prices. For a time both capital and labor were so engrossed in their struggle against each other that they did not observe that the public was striking in reality against them both. Again, in the depression which began in the latter part of 1929 and continued for a number of years, business attempted in every way possible to start people buying, but the public did not have money with which to buy. Moreover, they learned how well they could get along on little. Even during the national bank holiday of about ten days declared by President Franklin D. Roosevelt soon after he took his oath of office on March 4, 1933, people generally were surprised by the way in which they could manage their affairs for a short period of time without buying but by "simply trusting each other." In the fall of 1933 the NRA urged widespread buying as a recovery matter and a patriotic duty but still the public did not buy extensively, for they lacked money. Buyers' strikes demonstrate the necessity of including the public in the management of industry.

It is claimed that industrial democracy will shift the emphasis from rights to functions. Instead of capital employing labor, labor will employ capital and grow wise in so doing. Instead of goods being produced for profits, business will purge itself of profitism, as teaching, medicine, the ministry have purged themselves, and will produce goods for needs.

According to these principles, capital will be entitled to standard rates of interest, dependent upon the amount of risk involved and determined by labor-capital-consumer agreements. Any returns above the standard rates would go back into the business, for promotion and insurance. The professions have been changing from a profit to functional and standard income bases. Teachers once were paid directly by pupils; the larger the number of pupils the larger the pay. It was a distinct advance when teachers reached a salary basis. If business does not follow some such procedure, it will be in danger of suffering revolutions and of bringing about labor class control.

Under industrial democracy it is claimed that instead of as high dividends as possible being voted and of workers being paid as low wages as they will accept, the material component represented chiefly by capital will be secured at as low a rate as possible, and the human element, the workers, will be paid as much as possible. Instead of a prospective investor in stocks asking first, how large dividends are paid, his initial inquiry will be, what service does the company perform. Social welfare, after all, will be the standard to which all classes must ultimately render an accounting. Good will and the spirit of "Come, let us reason together," are basic to industrial democracy.

An illustration of the democratic spirit in business is that of a leading shoe manufacturer who some years ago announced that the main business of his factories is to help the employees to become better men and women and that the secondary business is to turn out better and better shoes. Only by such methods can evolutionary change take place and revolution made unnecessary.

After all the most important product of a factory are the men and the women who are employed. Are they becoming better persons and citizens, or are they shrinking or becoming radical? Coöperation is a good substitute for destructive competition. Socialized attitudes in industry would help to make a new earth.

OCCUPATIONAL DISORGANIZATION

Occupational disorganization has created many social problems. One is the question of *child labor*, which, however, is different from child work. The former involves putting children at work for wages in factories, sweatshops, canneries, and so forth, thus depriving them of health, play, and education. The latter involves a well-occupied childhood, keeping children in school, giving them work to do at home, providing for their health, and allowing full opportunities for development. The former is wasteful and stunting; the latter, educational and developmental.

Since the rise of the factory system, children have been employed at gainful occupations for eight, ten, or twelve hours a day while still at the beginning of their adolescence. The industries which have been the greatest sinners in employing children at too early an age are cotton manufacture, silk manufacture, glass manufacture, agriculture, the canneries, the sweated clothing trades, and the street trades.

The costs of child labor are heavy. (1) The effect upon bodily growth and physical development is serious. Child labor operates against a symmetrical development of strength, vigor, and substantial healthfulness. It generally causes a one-sided development of the body, or the overuse of certain muscles at the expense of others scarcely developed at all. (2) The boy who begins work in industry at an early age will have a total earning power much less than that of the youth who does not begin his working life until he is physically developed. (3) The boy or girl who goes to work in industry in adolescence is prevented from completing a well-rounded education. His training is cut short and he is handicapped for life. (4) Delinquency problems seem to be greater among working boys than among those of the same age who are in school. The working child often falls in with the rougher type of unskilled labor and acquires harmful information; the influence of some of his companions is vicious. He has money to spend, and hence does not feel a full sense of responsibility to parental control. He suffers from adequate guidance in sophisticated social situations.

The causes of unfavorable child labor conditions are numerous. (1) The greed of ignorant parents is often a factor. Many parents among both the foreign-born and the native-born consider their growing children as economic assets from which financial returns in the form of wages may immediately be received. The idea once prevailed that the larger the number of children in the family, the larger the family income might grow. Boys on the farm have often been taken out of school because of their capacity to labor, but at the expense of a needed education. (2) A second cause is real economic need. Many gainfully employed children belong to families suffering from actual economic pressure.

(3) The child's attitudes are significant. For various reasons, sometimes his own shortsightedness, and sometimes the school's inflexibility, he becomes dissatisfied with school life and seeks work. Boys are prone to develop a spirit of independence and become anxious to demonstrate their working capacity. The impulse grows because the boy has friends who are earning money and boasting about it. Few experiences thrill a boy more than the first wages he receives. (4) The attitudes of the employer are responsible for much child labor. He is responsible because he willingly accepts or invites children. He often encourages parents and child workers in their willingness to continue the evils of child labor.

(5) The rise of the factory system with its minute subdivisions of labor has made it possible to separate the lighter forms of labor from the more difficult, and thus to encourage the employment of children. Many types of work have developed, as in the cotton mills and the glass factories, which chiefly require time, and running to and fro, and hence have been assigned to children. Thus adolescents are substituted for adults but at a heavy human sacrifice. (6) The public must bear a share of responsibility for child labor, because it has the power to correct the evil. The public thoughtlessly, or otherwise, permits child labor. Public opinion does not fully realize the ultimate effects of premature child labor.

In 1933, President Franklin D. Roosevelt in signing the codes in the cotton and other industries prohibiting children under 16 years of age as a rule from gainful employment wiped out a great deal of child labor in the United States. It remains to be seen how well the codes will be observed and how long they will remain in force. Depression has done at least for the time being what the prolonged efforts of reformers had not previously accomplished.

Women in industry constitute another important occupational problem. The rapidity with which women entered industry in the United States after 1880 has been amazing. The number of women and of girls over ten years of age who are in gainful employments passed the ten million mark about 1912. The World War caused a leap forward in the employment of women in industry. The emancipation movement is another leading factor, for in becoming emancipated from the home, women have turned to industry in order "to be doing something," or to make themselves useful.

Women have entered nearly all occupations that men enter, although the former sometimes do so at a tremendous sacrifice to health and motherhood. It has been demonstrated many times that one of the saddest chapters in human history is connected with the fact that the machine which was invented to relieve people of labor has led to the factory system of labor, and that women and children are forced "to follow their work to the factory." Continues W. I. Thomas as follows:

> The machine which was invented to save human energy, and which is so great a boon when the individual controls it, is a terrible thing when it controls the individual. Power driven, it has almost no limit to its speed and no limit whatever to its endurance, and it has no nerves. When, therefore, under the pressure of business competition the machine is speeded up and the girl operating it, is speeded up to its pace, we have finally a situation in which the machine destroys the worker.[1]

When subjected to long hours of industrial labor for years, women are likely to become low-grade mothers. Their children suffer. Both mother and child are subjected to the danger of nervous and physical breakdown. The girl who rapidly performs the routine operations of wrapping caramels every day, or who threads the almost invisible Tungsten filament through a tiny hole at the rate of three every minute, or one thousand a day, or who operates an electric sewing machine that carries ten needles sewing ten seams at a speed so fast that the needles become ten streaks of light, this girl becomes less than human, hardly fit to be a citizen and much less fit to be a mother.

[1] William I. Thomas, "Woman and the Occupations," *The American Magazine*, 68: 463–70.

Then there is the comparative lack of ambition on the part of many working girls and women to advance above certain low levels. This attitude is due partly to the "I should worry" spirit of the times, partly to the expectation of marriage, and partly to the lack of adequate opportunities for advancement.

The employment of married women in industry has serious phases. Several years ago in the United States the number of married women gainfully employed passed the one million mark. Homes and young children are neglected. On the other hand, married women whose children are grown need an occupational or organized avocational pattern of life.

Another vexatious problem is that of *organizing women in industry*. Some decades ago, the members of men's labor unions refused to admit women to the unions. Today a changed attitude exists. In fact, many unions now try to induce women to organize, and to ask collectively higher wages and better working conditions. The new idea is to prevent women from competing with men on low wage levels.

There are great difficulties in organizing women in industry. Large numbers of women are only temporarily employed; they have simply a passing interest in the conditions of their work. The majority are in their twenties and are not as seriously interested in their work as older persons would be. Another difficulty is that there are relatively few good leaders among women wage-earners.[1]

The need of protecting women in industry received unique recognition in New York City in the winter of 1889–1890, when the National Consumers' League was organized out of what had been the Working Woman's Society. The Consumers' League operated by maintaining a "white list," that is, a list of stores whose owners treat their employees justly. It is expected that shoppers will patronize these stores. Then a label stamped with the name "Consumers' League" was devised.

[1] See Alice Henry, *Women and the Labor Movement* (George H. Doran Company, New York, 1921).

This label on a piece of goods assures the purchaser that the goods have been made under standard conditions of labor.[1]

The need for the protection of women in industry against the harsh influences of organized capital is being met by the National Women's Trade Union League, which was organized in 1903. It has done an important work in helping women workers to organize and thus voice their needs effectively. As Alice Henry says, organized women are "the only women quite free to express opinions without paying for freedom of speech in the loss of a job."[2]

To the extent that the wife and children enter industry, the wages of husband and father are thereby reduced. There is much evidence to show that the income of the male wage-earner when working alone is as great as the combined wages of the man himself, his wife, and the children when the wife and children enter into industry in competition with him. The composite wage of all the members of the family is not likely to exceed the income of the male wage-earner when employed alone. A unique suggestion for meeting this problem has been made by Paul H. Douglas.

The way out, therefore, lies in the fixation of a minimum wage sufficient to support single men with added allowances for dependent wives, children, and other adults. The natural danger which such a plan would create in causing employers to discriminate against those with dependents in order to reduce their wages bill can be prevented, as is later explained, by the creation of funds which generalize the burden over a group of employers as a whole. Such a plan, moreover, would make it possible to pay women an equal minimum with men and hence remove the dangers of their undercutting the men's rate.[3]

Dangerous occupations comprise a real problem. Fatal industrial accidents among wage-earners in the United States passed the 25,000 mark per year some time ago. The number of non-

[1] Mrs. Florence Kelley was the prime mover in the organization and development of the National Consumers' League.
[2] *Women and the Labor Movement* (George H. Doran Company, New York, 1923), p. ix.
[3] *Wages and the Family* (University of Chicago Press, 1925), pp. ix, x.

fatal industrial accidents involving a disability of two weeks or more also reached the million a year mark a number of years ago. The most dangerous industry is mining. Navigation and railroad transportation are also high on the list. Then follow occupations, such as electrical work, quarrying, lumbering, building, and draying. Air transportation is the most spectacular in its accident rôle.

According to John B. Andrews, industry maims more men than war ever did. H. R. Seager has pointed out that the United States has shown a larger proportion of industrial accidents in its mines and factories and on its railroads than has any other civilized land. "Industry is doubly wasteful of life and efficiency," says G. L. Campbell. He continues:

> It [industry] may be charged not only with the extravagance of killing and maiming yearly thousands of workers, but it seems to choose for its victims many persons in the prime of manhood, normally with years of life before them, and with obligations but partly discharged to wives and children. . . . Yet it is evident that the victims are usually young men, that the majority of them have families, and that the standard of living of these families is greatly lowered by losses due to injuries. The tale of industrial accidents is at best a tale of destitution, blighted hopes, and arrested development.[1]

Occupational diseases are common. They consist of those diseases which are caused directly by the nature of the occupation in which the wage-earner is working, such as lead poisoning, caisson disease, or even tuberculosis. The worker himself may be quite ignorant of such sickness-producing conditions. The employer may be only slightly interested in the welfare of the employees, and neglect to protect them against danger. In some cases the poisonous character of the materials used produces diseases, for example, in the printing trades, in plumbing, and in making phosphorous matches. The poison seeps into the human organism day by day, and in time becomes a main cause or a secondary cause, of disease.[2]

---

[1] *Industrial Accidents and Their Compensation* (Houghton Mifflin Company, Boston, 1911), pp. 21, 27.

[2] These major hazards of industry, thus, may be summarized as: infections and poisons, trade dusts, humidity, air pressure, and fatigue.

Overfatigue is a serious occupational problem. Despite all the talk about short hours in industry and unemployment there is still a great deal of overtime work for many people in the world. Overtime means overfatigue.

Overfatigue represents one of the most subtle effects of occupational activity. It involves a chemical process that continually tears down muscle and nerve tissues. Fatigue substances or toxins circulate in the blood, poisoning brain and neural system, muscles, glands, and other organs.

Overfatigue causes industrial inefficiency. As a rule poorer and less work is done in the last hours of a long day's work than in the earlier hours. Overfatigue likewise causes industrial accidents. In general, liability to accidents increases with the passing of the hours of the day. After a study of the records concerning 36,000 industrial accidents in the United States and Europe the writer arrived at the following conclusion.

> The more or less regular increase in the number of accidents, hour by hour, from 9,113 to 12,230 and from 12,230 to 15,064, indicates quite definitely the results of fatigue in terms of industrial accidents —inasmuch as extraneous elements have been largely accounted for and not included in these figures. . . . Continuous work, other things being equal, is accompanied, hour by hour, by an increasing number of accidents.[1]

Overfatigue assists the advance of disease. An overworked person is more susceptible to pneumonia, tuberculosis, and typhoid fever than is one whose vital resistance is normal. With fatigue toxins in the body, the organism is seriously handicapped. It has been pointed out that a not uncommon succession of events is, first, overfatigue; then colds; then pneumonia or tuberculosis; then, death.

Overfatigue accentuates nervous diseases. Long hours of work at a feverish pace lead to nervous breakdown. Unscrupulous employers who are abusing the principles of scientific management are guilty of turning many of their employees

[1] *The Relation of Fatigue to Industrial Accidents* (University of Chicago Press, 1912), p. 55.

into lightning-like machines. The neural system, not built for such a pace, breaks down after a time.

Future generations will suffer from the fatigue of the present generation. The children of perennially tired parents are in danger of being physical weaklings. Overfatigue has an untoward effect on morals. It increases human susceptibility to temptation, causes a person to turn almost anywhere for relief, and leads him to neglect his own welfare and also that of his family.

Labor turnover is an important phase of unemployment. It is an outgrowth of the "hiring and firing" system of capitalism. In many industries men are "hired and fired" freely, and a labor turnover of 100 per cent in a year has been known to occur. When the whole body of workers in a given establishment changes in a year (100 per cent turnover), then the costs to the employer of "breaking in" new workers and of supervision are excessive. To the workers "hiring and firing" is obnoxious. The honest laborer who comes to his work daily with the fear that he may be notified that his services will not be needed tomorrow develops an unbearable state of mind. If he has a wife and little children dependent on him, such a state of mind creates antagonism against "a heartless economic system." [1]

Occupational disorganization is evident in depressions. A depression is usually a resultant of the follies of prosperity. People overspeculate, overbuy on the installment plan, overadvertise, and overstimulate the wants of each other, until perhaps 60 per cent of the workers are engaged in making luxuries. When a limit in overspeculation is reached, people cease buying on a large scale, and limit themselves to necessities, throwing the 60 per cent of workers out of work. [2]

The depression beginning in 1929 was unique because of its world-wide character. In the United States in 1933 President Roosevelt pushed the idea of national control of capitalism

[1] See Brissenden and Frankel, *Causes of Labor Turnover in Industry* (Ronald Press, New York, 1921).

[2] According to an analysis made by W. B. Munro of California School of Technology in 1933.

further than had ever been done before. With powers greater than those accorded President Wilson during the World War, President Roosevelt went ahead with a nation-wide NRA program. One large industry after another was brought under a code decreeing minimum wages and maximum hours of labor per week (usually 40). In the main capitalism responded favorably as a means of getting back on its feet. Likewise there was an extensive acceptance on the part of labor, for the NRA gave collective bargaining a new status besides cutting down the labor week and setting up minimum wages. The system is known as *state capitalism* and is an attempt to remedy the evils of too much individualism and too much competition in business.

The day of unlimited individualism is gone, and *laissez-faire* methods are out of place in a complex industrial society. The main question industrially today is not whether we shall have social control or not, but how much. If a small amount does not suffice to keep powerful interests in line with the common welfare, then a large degree of public control will be demanded. If this is inadequate to keep special interests from taking advantage of the general welfare then state ownership or socialism will be tried. If that fails then communism will have an inning. After all, however, the socialization of human attitudes is the highest goal, for then persons will assume a full measure of social responsibility in whatever they are doing and will put the common good first and personal pecuniary gain in a second place. With everyone assuming a full measure of social responsibility, economic power need not be centralized in an omnipotent government, but may be distributed to all socially-responsible persons.

PROBLEMS

1. What is labor?
2. Should everyone work?
3. What is an occupation?
4. What is meant by an occupational attitude?
5. What is occupational egocentrism?

6. What are the main reasons why a laboring man works?

7. What are the main reasons why a capitalist works?

8. What are the average laboring man's attitudes in the United States toward the capitalist?

9. What are the average capitalist's attitudes in the United States toward the laboring man?

10. What is the best test of a successful laboring man?

11. What is the best test of a successful capitalist?

12. Can you name any occupation in which capital produces without the aid of labor?

13. Can you name any occupation in which labor and capital produce without the aid of the consumer?

14. Is either the average capitalist or average socialist in a position to pass an unbiased judgment upon socialism?

15. Is socialism to be judged by its ideals or by the way it works?

16. Does it make any difference who owns the wealth providing it is socially administered?

17. Under socialism, what is to take the place of the present rewards of industry as an incentive to the exertion of a person's best efforts?

18. Explain: "Luxury at present can be enjoyed only by the ignorant."

19. Can business enterprise survive if, as in the case of the teaching profession, the element of profits were eliminated?

20. What is the difference between an acquisitive society and a functional society?

21. Why do some business men put profits above human values in treatment of their employees?

22. Why was there no such gulf between the laboring classes two centuries ago as exists today?

23. Why have capitalists insisted on the right to organize but have fought the efforts of labor to organize?

24. Does anyone in the United States earn more than the President, and hence should he receive a larger income?

25. Should anyone be paid as much as he earns?

26. Should anyone be paid who earns nothing?

27. Who is the chief gainer from child labor? The chief loser?

28. Explain: "Child labor is child robbery."

29. Why does an adolescent boy have strong desires for earning money?

30. Explain: "The newsboy needs your protection, not your patronage."

31. How far is the presence of women in industry to be encouraged?

32. What are the effects upon the home of careers for women?

33. What factors would you consider if you were a member of a wage board and asked to determine a minimum wage for women in a given occupation?

34. Should equal wages be paid to men and women doing similar work in the same occupation?

35. Should unmarried and married men doing similar work in the same occupation be paid the same wages?

36. Make out a minimum budget for a self-supporting young woman who is employed in a department store.

37. What is thrift?

38. Does the miser or the spendthrift set the more unworthy example?

39. Distinguish between poverty and pauperism.

40. Is it true that "abnormally large incomes make abnormally small ones"?

41. Why do some people do charity work as a kind of sport?

42. Who constitute the greater social problem, the idle rich or the idle poor? Why?

43. What are your reactions to the NRA as a form of social control?

READINGS

ATKINS and LASSWELL, *Labor Attitudes and Problems* (Prentice-Hall, Inc., New York, 1924).

BALDERSTON, C. C., *Group Incentives* (University of Pennsylvania Press, Philadelphia, 1930).

BEVERIDGE, W. H., *Unemployment: A Problem of Industry* (Longmans, Green and Company, New York, 1930).

CALKINS, CLINCH, *Some Folks Won't Work* (Harcourt, Brace and Company, New York, 1930).

CALLCOTT, MARY S., *Child Labor Legislation in New York* (The Macmillan Company, New York, 1931).

CHASE, STUART, *Men and Machines* (The Macmillan Company, New York, 1929).

DAVIS, JEROME, *Contemporary Social Movements* (The Century Company, New York, 1930).

DONOVAN, FRANCES R., *The Saleslady* (University of Chicago Press, 1929).

DOUGLAS, P. H., *Wages and the Family* (University of Chicago Press, 1925).

ESTEY, J. A., *The Labor Problem* (McGraw-Hill Book Company, New York, 1928).

FEIS, HERBERT, *Labor Relations* (Adelphi Company, New York, 1928).

FILENE, A. F., *A Merchant's Horizon* (Houghton Mifflin Company, Boston, 1924).

FULLER, RAYMOND G., *Child Labor and the Constitution* (Thomas Y. Crowell Company, New York, 1923).

GILLIN, JOHN L., *Poverty and Dependency* (The Century Company, New York, 1926).

HENRY, ALICE, *Women and the Labor Movement* (George H. Doran Company, New York, 1923).

LAIDLER, H. W., *History of Socialist Thought* (Thomas Y. Crowell Company, New York, 1927).

LA DAME, MARY, *The Filene Store* (Russell Sage Foundation, New York, 1930).

PAGE, KIRBY, *A New Economic Order* (Harcourt, Brace and Company, New York, 1930).

PARKER, CORNELIA STRATTON, *Working with the Working Woman* (Harper and Brothers, New York, 1922).

PATTERSON, S. H., *Social Aspects of Industry* (McGraw-Hill Book Company, New York, 1929).

ROCKEFELLER, JOHN D., JR., *The Personal Relation in Industry* (Boni and Liveright, New York, 1923).

ROWNTREE, B. SEEBOHM, *The Human Factor in Business* (Longmans, Green and Company, New York, 1921).

——, *Poverty* (Longmans, Green and Company, New York, 1922).

SELEKMAN, B. M., *Sharing Management with the Workers* (Russell Sage Foundation, New York, 1924).

SLATER, GILBERT, *Poverty and the State* (Constable and Company, Ltd., London, 1930).

TAWNEY, R. H., *The Acquisitive Society* (Harcourt, Brace and Company, New York, 1920).

TODD, ARTHUR J., *Industry and Society* (Henry Holt and Company, New York, 1933).

WARNER, QUEEN, and HARPER, *American Charities and Social Work* (Thomas Y. Crowell Company, New York, 1930).

WATKINS, GORDON S., *An Introduction to the Study of Labor Problems* (Thomas Y. Crowell Company, New York, 1929, Revised Edition).

WILLIAMS, WHITING, *What's on the Worker's Mind?* (Charles Scribner's Sons, New York, 1920).

WOOD, L. A., *Union Management Coöperation on the Railroads* (Yale University Press, 1931).

CHAPTER VII

THE PLAY GROUP

Work and play, occupation and recreation, are complementary. Family life, occupational activity, and play are a natural triumvirate. Play is coming to be recognized as one of the main activities of life, and leisure time is becoming more extensive than work time. Moreover leisure-time problems are increasing faster than are work-time problems.

While recreation has always been a matter of deep human interest, it now occupies a more fully accepted position in the scheme of human affairs and finds ready justification on the grounds of health and efficiency as well as relief from the routine of daily toil. In a very real sense recreation has forged to the front as one of the compelling interests of human life and has already developed to the point where it makes extraordinary demands upon time and energy and requires large financial expenditures to cover its mounting costs.[1]

The play group is one of the primary groups in which the child's earliest attitudes are developed.[2] It usually originates within the family group and hence as a primary group within a primary group.

If one will ask himself, "What was my earliest play group?" perhaps the answer will be "Other children in the neighborhood." Further thought will probably reveal a parent or a brother or sister within the home as forming with one's self the original informal play group. By the time the child is two or three years of age he begins to participate with some regularity in playful activities with other children, within or without the

[1] Jesse F. Steiner, *Americans at Play* (McGraw-Hill Book Company, New York, 1933), p. ix.
[2] C. H. Cooley, *Social Organization* (Charles Scribner's Sons, New York, 1909), p. 24.

home, or both, and the play group becomes an important nursery of child life. Under normal conditions childhood and adolescence have their main setting in play group life. Moreover, play attitudes are normal throughout life.

The significance of the play group is found in its pleasing nature. It is full of interesting stimuli. It is lively. The play group is an ideal combination of pleasing atmosphere, stimulating events, and changing scenes of action. It is composed not of one's elders, but of one's peers or of individuals posing as one's peers. It usually contains chums or pals. The reason that college activities often win out over college studies in their bid for the student's time is because they represent the spirit of play, often serious play to be sure, in association with one's peers.

The play group has had a long history, dating back to primitive life in every land. It has varied greatly in different ages of human development and among various peoples, and yet throughout time and everywhere it has had common traits, such as its informal character, its social composition of peers, its activity nature, its stimulating, changing program, its primary rôle of forming and changing attitudes and ideals.

History of Play Attitudes

(1) To primitive people play was merely the expression of energy irregularly in contests of physical skill or prowess. They had neither work nor play attitudes. Life was activity or inactivity, with the former possessing varying degrees of interest. Activity that was interesting was play; other activity was work. Neither work nor play arose as distinct concepts among earliest peoples.

(2) It was a long leap forward that is represented by the Greeks who carried the idea of contests into regular spectacles involving large numbers of persons who submitted themselves to long periods of training. Play rested on physical education and culminated in group pageants, often symbolizing the finest and best aspirations of people. A perfect human physique was

idolized and a widespread participation was secured. Commercialization of play did not exist. A community consciousness was promoted without cost. Play, to the Greeks, had a therapeutic social value. Widespread play is healthful to a large social group, for it enables that group to express itself wholesomely rather than in riots, mob action, and social unrest.

(3) The Romans, particularly in the days of Nero, held that play is a natural expression of life energies which should be gratified without restraint. The social product was often uncontrolled licentiousness and demoralizing situations. Each person was free to give way to any feelings or passions that he experienced. Morals were taboo, and amusements were self-centered.

(4) Early Christianity promptly reacted against the Nero interpretation of amusements and swung to the opposite extreme of urging that play be suppressed. Live seriously as a preparation for the next world, became the Augustinian doctrine. Alcuin, the celebrated English educator of the Middle Ages, developed further this theory, helping to make it dominant in Europe for many centuries. The rigid control of play impulses was accepted by the Puritans and was brought to the United States by them. Puritanic attitudes prevailed widely in the United States until recently.

It was believed that play is useless, or worse still, it is frivolous. Play should be discouraged and suppressed. At best it is a relatively harmless way of amusing children who are too young to be doing anything useful.

(5) In the closing decades of the last century several other theories of play developed. For example, Herbert Spencer, following the suggestion of Schiller, argued that play is essentially an expression of *surplus energy*. When a growing child accumulates an overflow of energy, he plays. This theory, however, does not account for the girl, for example, who "jumps the rope," until she falls from exhaustion. In other words, the Spencer-Schiller theory accounts for a part of but not for all play.

(6) The recapitulation theory of play, promoted by John Fiske, held that a child in his play life is primarily living over rapidly the stages of human development. In his earliest plays he is experiencing the days of savagery of the race. Then he becomes interested in play activities which represent the days of barbarism. When he later comes to take part in team plays and coöperative sports, he is said to have reached the stage of civilization. From fist action or teasing animals or fighting in gangs he moves up to highly controlled social plays. Again we have an incomplete theory, covering only a portion of play phenomena.

(7) Play has also been defined as an instinctive preparation for life.[1] Play is practicing for life. In playing with a spool, that is, in rolling and catching a spool, a kitten is getting ready for the serious business of catching mice. The kitten is thereby developing claw and eye coördination which will in due time be useful in procuring food. In like manner the plays of a lamb are a preparation for the life of a grazing animal. The plays of a small boy are preparing him for activities of building, constructing, and acquiring. The plays of a small girl with her dolls are fitting her for motherhood.

Play teaches respect for law. In no other way can a boy so fully realize for himself the value of law as on the playground. By the same token he learns respect for others, acquires habits of coöperation, and sacrifices personal ambitions for the welfare of the group. According to this interpretation, it would seem that play is "a first-rate educational process."

If we accept this theory that play is a preparation for life, we might go one step farther and say that play is a preparation *for more life*. He who ceases to maintain play attitudes, ages rapidly and dies, he shrinks within himself. It is an important accomplishment to be able to turn from a day's work and to forget the perplexities of that day's work in healthful play. Play has been called "the sovereign recreator," necessary especially for the adult worker. Play is no luxury. It is a natural

[1] K. Groos, *The Play of Man* (D. Appleton and Company, New York, 1911).

184 SOCIOLOGY

technique for the development both of self-control and of pro-social attitudes. It needs to be maintained throughout life. The play impulses have been pronounced nature's way and God's way of developing body, mind, and character. "The Creator has purposely set the beginning of life in a joyful mood." Such a theory, like the others, is significant but does not account for all play.

(8) Play as one of the natural expressions of personality is John Dewey's explanation.[1] The difference between play and work is largely in "time-span." Play consists of those activities which are not consciously performed for the sake of any reward beyond themselves. They contain their own stimuli. Prizes do not need to be offered in order to get children to play. When prizes are offered, the goal in play becomes objective, and play itself becomes work.

Play attitudes are tendencies to throw one's self whole-heartedly into any interesting and stimulating situation. If in responding to social stimuli and social problems one forgets himself in the activity of the moment, he is experiencing play attitudes. Anticipated stimuli, as in the case of boys who clear a lot for a baseball diamond, may be so vivid that they color the current routine task and make it seem like play.

None of these theories is entirely adequate, but each contains some truth. A complete explanation doubtless would combine the valid elements in all the theories, and add newly discovered ones. More attention is needed in working out an inclusive, well-balanced theory of play.

COMMERCIALIZATION OF LEISURE

Commercial enterprise has taken advantage of play impulses and turned them into dollars for the benefit of the promoters of amusements. It has furnished amusements for every period of life, for every social level, and for all degrees of ignorance. This movement began in an organized way in the United States as early as 1890.

[1] John Dewey, *Democracy and Education* (The Macmillan Company, New York, 1924), pp. 237ff.

In 1907, Simon N. Patten, the economist, declared that we had gone little further than to permit men to exploit for private gain the human craving to be amused. In his words: "The workman is drawn hither and thither by the uncorrelated motley devices of selfish promoters and is often solicited by them until he has dissipated his vigor and lowered his moral tone." [1] Wherein is there any personality growth, any social welfare, any social sense in such an unregulated, individualistic régime?

When the workman comes from "the barren industrial grind" of the day's work, where is he invited most loudly to turn, if not to a great variety of amusement institutions in which the melodramatic and overexciting presentations stand out foremost. For several decades the leisure of the people in the United States has been capitalized by private enterprise to the extent of billions of dollars. The play impulses of people have been used not to increase the total welfare or to build up personality but to make money. "Cheap seaside resorts have sprung up over night, vieing with one another," it has been observed, "in enticing patrons thither by patriotic or salacious posters and advertisements," and in furnishing them with new sensations. The regular frequenters of such places of amusements are getting "so much excitement for a small outlay of money" that they find the attractions irresistible.

The dance hall often has a more disorganizing influence than does the academy. The proprietors of certain dance halls knowingly permit men and women of questionable character to prey upon young girls. Where drinking of liquor is also permitted, the effects are likely to be vicious. The combination of sexually vulgar dancing, of drinking liquor, of noisy but exciting jazz is one that many participants find hard to withstand.

Theaters may be divided roughly into at least four types, namely, vaudeville, burlesque, standard, and motion picture. In regard to the average vaudeville theater the chief characteristic has been called "simple stupidity." No person it has

[1] *The New Basis of Civilization* (The Macmillan Company, New York, 1912), p. 132.

been stated can attend a dozen vaudeville performances "without being disgusted at their vapidity." Moreover, some of the acts are "wholly crude," a few "decidedly clever," and the majority, "trite and stupid." The vaudeville is like many exciting occurrences, stimulating but disorganizing to personality. It excites the onlooker transiently; it is unlikely to offer him recuperation or recreation. It represents hyperstimulus on a low personality plane.

The *burlesque* has been found repeatedly to be the most undesirable type of theater performance. It has been diagnosed as "artistically crude" and "intellectually stupid." Its appeal is based on physical prowess and lewd sex relations. No improvements in it in recent years have occurred.

The *standard theater*, partly because of the admission charged, draws only a small proportion of the theater-going public, perhaps not more than 10 per cent. The working classes, isolated partly because of the admission prices, are unable to attend the best plays. The "high brow" character of certain plays, such as the Shakespearean, is also a deterrent in the eyes of the "low brows."

The standard theater produces a small percentage of plays of lasting value. Herein is an opportunity for the citizens of every community to encourage wholesome plays of cultural worth. When young people come to have a vital appreciation of worth-while drama, they will no longer be satisfied with low, unrefined theatrical performances.

While drama influences human attitudes, it also has a recreational value to many people. Although the following excerpt represents an extreme case, it reveals clearly the playful significance of drama.

And then again, I always distinctly remember an old neighbor of ours, a woman who was such an inveterate theater attendant that one might say she lived the greater part of her life in an orchestra seat. Now, one could tell from her behavior just what play she had seen the day before, for her actions were but imitations of those heroines she admired most. Let a *Sappho*, a *Zaza*, a *Mrs. Dane*, or a

Camille be played before her, and for the next few days, she fancied
that she and these ladies were identical. Their very affections became
hers, their sayings, hers, their manner of receiving guests, hers, smiles
and sighs, hers. And all this, much to the embarrassment of her family
and friends, bore strong testimony to the vitality of the theater! [1]

The *motion picture* began to attract attention in the United
States at the close of the last century. By 1905, it was becoming
well known, although the cheaper type predominated; by 1915,
the theaters producing elaborate motion pictures were common
in the large cities. By this time motion picture producers were
combining into powerful nation-wide organizations; the demand
for censorship had already been expressed strongly, and public
opinion had begun to turn against motion pictures.

The "nickelodeons" of 1905 were supplanted by better theaters and higher prices. Physical conditions have been greatly
improved, for the fire-traps have been largely done away with,
ventilation systems have been developed, and film projection is
not the strain on the eyes of the spectator that was once the
case. The technical quality of the films has made vast strides.
By 1930, there were in the United States, the leading motion
picture country of the world, about 22,000 motion picture
theaters, with a combined seating capacity of 11,000,000, representing an investment of two billion dollars, drawing into the
box offices an annual total of admissions amounting to one and
one-half billions of dollars, and having a weekly attendance of
100,000,000 individuals.[2]

The great popularity of motion pictures has been pointed
out by various individuals. The main reasons may be boiled
down to the following points: (1) The fascination "of not knowing what one will see," is effective. (2) No punctuality is required; a person can enter and take a seat at any time and
leave at any time. (3) "No special degree of intelligence" is

[1] Melvin J. Vincent, "The Influence of Drama Upon Human Attitudes,"
Sociology and Social Research, XVII: 142–52.
[2] From data furnished by the Motion Picture Producers and Distributors of
America to Jesse F. Steiner, *Recent Social Trends* (McGraw-Hill Book Company,
New York, 1933), II: 940.

required; "no attitude toward anything" is needed; "no convictions on anything" are necessary. No knowledge of any language is essential; consequently, the immigrant is reached by the motion picture before he understands the language of the community. (4) A fairly good eyesight and the price of admission are the main requirements. As "a direct and immediate appeal to the feelings" and to an elemental understanding the motion picture is far-reaching. (5) Appeals to one's love of children, of home, of flag, of courage, of romance, are usually made, but these worthy tendencies are often accompanied by tantalizing appeals to the melodramatic, the brutalizing, and the sex impulses. (6) The family as a group, among poorer people with small children, often finds it feasible to attend, although the jumbling of the wholesome and unwholesome scenes before the eyes of impulsive children and adolescents not to mention child-like adults, is unfortunate.

We may now turn to the oft-repeated need for regulation of motion pictures. Perhaps the need arises chiefly from the use of *indirect suggestion*. This principle operates strongly both constructively and destructively. The constructive tendencies are found in the emphases on the worth-while values of the home, recreation, art, morals, social life. The destructive tendencies have been effectively stated as follows:

> We now are freely setting before our children an unrestricted volume of pictured representation of every immorality in the world in the film theater under the name of entertainment. . . . Sin is exploited insinuatingly for amusement. . . . The picture is a graphic story, clear and complete to the last detail, a hundred times easier to comprehend than reality. . . . To seductively illustrate the life of a moral reprobate for an hour, and then for a minute to say "that such living is wrong will not excuse such a performance." [1]

Motion pictures vary from the developmental to the demoralizing. The positively developmental constitute only a small percentage of the whole. Then come the major group which have been labelled "entertaining" and "merely entertaining."

[1] E. P. Oberholtzer, *The Morals of the Movie* (The Penn Publishing Company, Philadelphia, 1922), p. 85.

After these come the "undesirable" and "demoralizing" which run up to perhaps a third of all scenes and which include a great deal of violence.

Most pictures stir up unduly the feelings and emotions. By being so designed, they draw the largest audiences and hence the largest profits. The effects of operating motion pictures primarily for profit instead of for social welfare are disconcerting.

A leading producer has said that the picture which draws the largest audiences represents the level of intelligence of an adolescent; therefore the common run of film is made on that intellectual level. Managers who have attempted to show films of a higher educational value than the average, report that the audiences immediately decrease in size to a point where the showing of such pictures is no longer profitable. It appears that the public does not go to the motion picture show to be educated but to be amused. The immense popularity of the "Mickey Mouse" and similar pictures is a case in point. The public does not attend to reason or to think hard, but goes in a passive and subjective sense to be amused.

The motion picture exercises such subtle effects upon adult minds that it operates continuously as a powerful psychological force upon an entire national group. The public is hardly yet aware of this far-reaching form of control. If the public is receiving but one-fourth to one-third of the constructive values which it might from the billions of dollars that are spent on this popular form of entertainment, if motion pictures pour a steady stream of questionable influences along with the good influences upon the youth of the nation, if they exert a generally hypnotic influence upon the adult mind, arousing in it a greater and greater thirst for the excitable, the criminal, the sexual, then the public is entitled to ask for public control and regulation of pictures.

Inasmuch as the motion picture has catered so often to the lower elements of human nature, it has had to face censorship. Three times has an adverse public opinion arisen. (1) The first angry wave of public opinion came about 1907 to 1909,

when for example, Mayor Gaynor closed all the motion picture
houses of New York, and when the Chicago *Tribune* denounced
the cheap theaters and films. As a result reels and show houses
were improved.

(2) The questionable picture, however, continued, but on a
higher level of technique. Public opinion demanded but did not
get an improvement, and in consequence, censorship achieved
a widespread vogue. City after city and even states passed
censorship laws. Censorship, on the whole, has not been satisfactory, partly because it is negative, partly because it is enforced by untrained persons, and partly because it "cuts"
pictures after large sums of money have been spent on their
production. By 1921, the adverse public opinion had acquired
such a momentum that the motion picture industry undertook to
reform itself. It secured a member of the Cabinet of the President of the United States to direct the reorganization. Adverse
opinion quieted down only to rise again with new force about
1929. This time it was the women's clubs and liberal church
press, such as the *Christian Century*, that led the adverse opinion. A sample of the unfavorable opinion is expressed by Mrs.
Robbins Gilman, president of the Federal Motion Picture
Council in America:

> The industry claims that it has twenty million people viewing
> films a day. These people cannot go to motion pictures for one month
> without realizing that the worst accusations that have been made
> are self-evident in the moving picture theater. There is no need to
> prove—even if this writer were willing to present the sordid details—
> that, even with due regard for good pictures, the screen is permeated
> by exaggerated sex appeal, criminal practices, ridicule of marriage,
> disregard for law enforcement, desecration of religious ideals, and
> questionable ethics. . . .
> The facts show that motion pictures are influencing unfavorably
> the education and character of citizens in this and other countries;
> that they are undermining the prestige of Americans in foreign lands;
> are causing the loss of confidence in the leadership of the white race;
> and are menacing the good will among peoples and endangering the
> peace of the world.[1]

[1] *Woman's Journal*, XV: 11.

From the motion picture producer's viewpoint the problem is complicated. The producer is often under pressure from many directions. An analysis has been made as follows:

> The problem of the producer is to make a picture of such wide appeal that the adult, the child, the moron, the intellectual all will find something in it to enjoy. The producer has first to pay the big salary to the actor, and then along comes the director asking even more, and now the author is clamoring. The picture must pay all of them. So it must have a great audience—not of thousands, but of millions.[1]

The third adverse movement reached a climax in a widespread belief that the "movies" are unable "to reform themselves," that the securing of well-known people to act as "reorganizers" means little, and that nothing short of public control and regulation will suffice. Consequently measures have been developed that would put the industry under the control of a federal commission in a way similar to the regulation of the railroads by the Interstate Commerce Commission.

In the public control of motion pictures the principle is involved of regulating pictures at the point of production rather than to wait and censor the finished picture. The federal regulation of what pictures shall be produced and sent to foreign countries is considered to be as vital as granting passports and deciding what citizens shall go abroad.

The motion picture industry protests against federal control. This protest is in strange contradiction to its own system of "block-booking" and "blind-booking" whereby the industry controls arbitrarily what films shall be shown by each of the theaters in each of the circuits. As a result of this control by the industry a particular theater must show good and poor films as they are sent out from headquarters, or else get out of the circuit.

The talking picture "arrived" in 1926. It greatly increased the cost of picture production and cut off foreign markets. Foreign stars, if they could not speak the native tongue, could

[1] Associated Press, April 20, 1933.

be no longer employed. The realism of motion pictures was greatly increased, unless the synchronizations were faulty, or unless voices were reproduced poorly.[1]

It is in leisure hours that *alcoholism* becomes prominent. The use of alcoholic liquor has been common to many peoples. It has met various types of craving, ranging from the desire for excitement to the wish to deaden one's feelings and drown defeats and sorrows.

In European countries such as France and Italy the drinking of wines with varying degrees of alcoholic content is significant because they are drunk regularly with meals, and as agents of sociability. They are drunk up to their maximum stimulative levels and occasionally to an intoxication stage. In Germany, for example, it is beer with a low alcoholic percentage that is drunk with meals regularly and in beer gardens. It is drunk slowly while listening to classical music or while conversing with friends. Again, it rarely is drunk until it produces drunkenness.

In other countries, such as England, where hard liquor, or liquor with a higher alcoholic content is used the "public house" or "pub" where liquor is sold under government supervision becomes a "hang-out" not only for men but for women, day after day. Often the "pub" becomes a rendezvous for "old sots." The poor spend their earnings at these "pubs" with nothing to show of value as a result. Reports indicate that in

---

[1] In 1933 the publication of a remarkable series of thirteen research studies of motion pictures was begun. They were made by the Committee on Educational Research of the Payne Fund and published by The Macmillan Company. They include: *Motion Pictures and Youth: A Summary*, by W. W. Charters; *Getting Ideas from the Movies*, by P. W. Holaday and G. D. Stoddard; *Motion Pictures and the Social Attitudes of Children*, by Ruth C. Peterson and L. L. Thurstone; *The Social Conduct and Attitudes of Movie Fans*, by F. K. Shuttleworth and Mark A. May; *The Emotional Responses of Children to the Motion Picture Situation*, by W. S. Dysinger and C. A. Ruckmick; *Motion Pictures and Standards of Morality*, by C. C. Peters; *Children's Sleep*, by S. Renshaw, V. L. Miller, and Dorothy Marquis; *Movies and Conduct*, by H. Blumer; *The Content of Motion Pictures*, by E. Dale; *Children's Attendance at Motion Pictures*, by E. Dale; *Movies, Delinquency, and Crime*, by H. Blumer and P. M. Hauser; *Boys, Movies, and City Streets*, by P. G. Cressey and F. M. Thrasher; *How to Appreciate Motion Pictures*, by E. Dale.

some sections on the East Side of London the people spend more for liquor than for bread, milk, rent, and taxes combined.

In the United States hard liquor and saloons grew worse until 1919 when national prohibition went into effect. Drunkenness was common and a disgrace. The licensed saloon became a disreputable institution, often a "hang-out" of "bums" and "crooks," a door to the "underworld" of vice and crime, prostitution, and debauchery. Unlike the German or Frenchman who sips his mild liquor while eating and drinking, the American became notorious for gulping down his hard liquor by the glassful until he succumbed in a "drunken spree."

The widespread misuse of liquor in the United States has been due on one hand to individual lack of control, to the speed with which everything is done, to the belief that a person can do as he pleases, and that if a person wants to get drunk such a debauch is his own affair. The commercialized dealers have sold liquor to Indians until they became "crazy," to youth until they became "fools," to the working man until he had no money with which to buy bread for his wife and children, to the man in "high society" until he sank lower than the brutes. Commercialization of liquor created the disreputable "pub" and the saloon. Concerning the latter says an observer:

> How well I remember the saloons in our town. Big, fat bartenders with red noses, lines of hard-handed working men in blue jeans at the bar; now and then one would come out "blubbering away" to himself and unsteady at the knees, reeling listlessly; at the back door was a poor sot "sleeping off" his over-indulgence. Worst of all was the man who went by our house yelling with "delirium tremens," on his way "home" to wife and children, led by a friend. How one man could sell another, glass after glass of poisonous drink until the latter sank beneath the human, was more than I could understand.[1]

Many of the European nations during the World War declared officially against alcoholism, but they reverted after the War to pre-war attitudes. If the use of alcoholic liquor militates against efficiency in war the argument is strong for the rigid

[1] From personal interview materials.

control of it in connection with the strenuous activities and conflicts in times of peace, for it is in these periods that a nation grows strong or weak, and builds the foundations for future successes or defeats.

In the United States the Eighteenth Amendment to the Constitution and the Volstead Act, prohibiting more than one-half of 1 per cent of alcohol in drinks of any kind, were bitterly opposed as soon as they were passed, although prohibition as a social movement developed slowly in the United States over several decades. Prohibition was fought by the liquor interests and their friends; it was defied by many people of wealth, aided and abetted by some immigrants and others as "bootleggers." Within ten years after prohibition went into effect, it had become a dead letter in many urban centers; and between the presidential elections of 1928 and 1932 public opinion swung measurably toward repeal. An interesting problem arises, namely, what factors operated to bring about this change in public opinion. Was it the depression? Was it a breakdown in moral control throughout the nation? Was it a decline in religious influence? Was it a rise in materialistic, mechanistic behaviorism? Was it all of these?

Alcohol is a turbulent and intractable element in society. From the Whiskey Rebellion which Washington had to suppress in his first administration, to the criminal gangsters of New York and other American cities in the middle nineteenth century, and down to the first decade of the administration of the Eighteenth Amendment in the United States we have witnessed one long history, not of violence in the attempt to improve the lot of men through eliminating alcohol, but primarily and consistently of schemes to circumvent the reform.[1]

A survey of the facts over a period of time seems to show that intemperance produces destitution among the poor, increases insanity, adds to delinquency and crime, augments automobile accidents. Alcoholism produces harmful effects upon heredity, causes degeneracy, destroys happiness in the home, breaks down personal control, and is economically wasteful.

[1] Arthur J. Todd, *Industry and Society* (Henry Holt and Company, New York, 1933), p. 560.

LEISURE-TIME PROBLEMS

Mankind started out with a great deal of leisure on its hands. In the beginning there was no organized work and leisure predominated. Then developed slavery and feudalism with one class having all the leisure and another class having all the work, which was often mostly routine. Relief from routine was often secured through idleness or carousal, sometimes fostered by the master class. A century and a half ago steam power was harnessed to the machine and the factory system arose with many gradations of labor. Those at the top had as much leisure as they wished; those at the bottom had little if any leisure. The long hours of labor of those at the bottom, again, were often punctuated by periods of idleness and carousal.

In our day the machine age has reached a climax. The shorter working day began to arrive for the industrial masses through the efforts of organized labor and benevolent employers. In the fall of 1932 it was proclaimed boldly by the Technocrats that a four hour day four days in the week would soon be sufficient. The machine would do the rest. The new leisure is for everyone.

The depression that began in 1929 brought the "staggered" week in which a week's work for one person is divided up between two or three persons with doubled or trebled leisure for all. Depression brings its millions of unemployed with its leisure for millions.[1] Technocracy has proclaimed that the United States will have a permanently unemployed class of five millions or more even in times of prosperity, and hence a

---

[1] The attendance at outdoor playgrounds for 1932, reported at 235,632,553 by 516 cities (out of 1,012 cities of the United States and Canada), was thirteen millions more than the similar attendance reported by 565 cities for the previous year, according to the Year Book of the National Recreation Association for 1932. Attendance at indoor centers also rose materially. The greatest increase in participation was in connection with facilities offering water sports.

"As compared with the cost of public recreation, keeping men and boys idle has been found a costly and painful mistake," Howard Braucher, secretary of the National Recreation Association, points out. "Even in a desperately hard year, recreation has been continued as deserving of tax support. Cities have met the challenge of curtailed budgets and reduced staffs in responding to the need for recreation service which has continued to grow by reason of unemployment."

new permanent leisure class. This new leisure class from the masses will supplement the one from the wealthy classes that has existed since the human race created wealth and allowed it to become concentrated.

The new leisure is that which comes in normal times with the short working day and the short week. If both the machine and production are properly controlled, everyone will again have leisure, as in the primitive days of mankind. This new leisure will be enjoyed or wasted under entirely different conditions from those of earliest human days. The new leisure is really the old leisure of primitive days but under entirely new conditions.

The new leisure means that every week end will be a set of holidays for everyone. New inventions in transportation will mean increasing journeys in number and length not only in summers but throughout the year, for every week will have its vacation as well as its vocation aspect.

With the development of the ideal some years ago of eight hours for work, eight hours for leisure, and eight hours for rest, the leisure-time problem became a problem of prime importance. With a growing emphasis on a forty hour or shorter week the problem increases. When every week end becomes a short-term vacation, the leisure problem grows.

Leisure becomes the problem of what to do with at least a third of life. The leisure hours are becoming as important as the work hours. In a way they are more significant, for during work hours there is standardization, but during leisure hours there is likely to be lack of regulation and a tremendous waste of time. The problem is especially acute when commercial interests prey upon the leisure hours of people, creating great excitement, leaving people nervous and befuddled, and stripping them of their possible savings. It is about time that prosocial uses of leisure became known and practiced.

It was once asserted that civilization depends largely upon the way people use their leisure time.[1] Leisure may mean re-

[1] Frederick C. Howe, *The Modern City and Its Problems* (Charles Scribner's Sons, New York, 1915), Ch. XXI.

cuperation from work or the acquisition of vicious habits, the invigoration of body and mind, or the destruction of life itself. The leisure hours of a hundred million people and more are becoming as important to the nation as the hours spent by the adult at work, or as the time that the school claims of children. If technocracy is a correct prophet, then leisure hours are going to multiply and work hours will diminish. Controlling the leisure of a national group will become a staggering problem.

The social situation regarding play in a country such as the United States has changed greatly in the last century. A hundred years ago all the natural activities of life centered in the home. They could be expressed largely within the physical limits of one roof and its environs and under home control. They were simple, non-commercialized, and more or less in the open.

The modern city has changed this social situation. Formerly boys could expend their energies upon hillside and meadow and in the dooryard and barnyard of the rural home. Parents maintained a watchful eye. Today in the city, boys play on narrow streets traversed by speeding cars and heavy trucks. The parents are relatively helpless. Said a boy to the writer in connection with the " Boys Work Survey " of Los Angeles, "There are no vacant lots in our neighborhood any more; we can't play on the streets without getting 'pinched,' the school playground closes at seven, but what boy wants to go to bed at seven? " [1]

In giving boys and girls opportunities to earn money at an early age and in leaving them free and often unguided in spending their money "as they choose in the midst of vice deliberately disguised as pleasure," the modern city is grossly negligent. [2] Apparently, continues Jane Addams, the modern city sees in working girls, for example, two main possibilities, both of them commercial: first, a chance to use day by day their new and immature labor power in its factories and shops, and then another

[1] Cf. E. S. Bogardus, *The City Boy and His Problems* (Rotary Club of Los Angeles, 1926).

[2] Jane Addams, *The Spirit of Youth and the City Streets* (The Macmillan Company, New York, 1912), p. 8.

chance in the evening to extract their wages from them by catering to their love of amusement and play.[1]

A vital question is: Shall the leisure-time and play attitudes be monopolized by commercial interests, or shall pro-social uses of leisure be taught and generally adopted? Which shall it be: The commercialization or the socialization of leisure? Shall leisure of all be exploited for the financial gain of a few, or turned into activities building up both personality and group welfare?

The promulgation of wholesale community projects such as has been sponsored in Czechoslovakia where thousands come together not as spectators but as participators, under the direction of physical education leaders is needed. In this way a new community consciousness may be developed for large groups of people.

If "the use of leisure is the architect of character" and if leisure is to be more extensive than ever before, then social recreation has an enlarged responsibility. If as Samuel Johnson said: "No man is a hypocrite in his recreation," then physical education leaders are to be congratulated for they are working with people when they are most natural. If instead of "leisured classes" we are to have considerable leisure for all classes then let social recreation step into the breach before commercialized agencies take charge.

To what use will the new leisure be put? The answer depends largely on what leisure-time stimuli are set before the people. (1) One possibility is to leave the use of leisure in the hands of commercialized amusements operated for profits for a few, and characterized to a large extent by excitement and melodrama. In fact commercialized amusement interests will leap forward with all sorts of devices to steal away not only the leisure hours but the potential savings of the multitude.

(2) A second possibility will be to allow a great deal of leisure to go to waste. Between the hours given over to commercialized amusements and the actual working hours will be a con-

[1] *Ibid.*, p. 9.

siderable margin of hours spent in simple "fooling around," flitting from one nerve-wrecking hour to another, "loafing," gossiping, despite the fact that life is "too precious for a single hour to be wasted."

(3) A third use of the new leisure will be an interesting emphasis on "the sitting amusements," that is, on those in which people "sit down" and talk or read, or listen to the radio, or ride in an automobile, or otherwise watch and listen to others. The intellectual values may be great or small, but physical exercise values are likely to be negative.

(4) The fourth possible use of the new leisure may come through socialized recreation. It will be an expansion of activity programs for families as such, for individuals of similar ages, sex, and tastes, and for communities. It will be a further development of the play movement that has already made excellent headway.

SOCIALIZATION OF LEISURE

Broad-minded persons have led the way in creating institutions that develop constructive play attitudes, irrespective of financial gain. Of the various constructive activities, developed for their own sake or for welfare purposes, and irrespective of monetary ends, the playground movement easily leads. This movement began in the United States about 1880; won widespread public attention about 1900; and by 1920, had secured wide recognition. Within the first decade of the present century, over $60,000,000 were expended in this country in furthering the playground movement.

In 1920, the cities above 2,500 population that maintained public playgrounds numbered 428. In 1930 they had increased to 695. During this ten year period the number of playgrounds grew from 4,139 to 7,240, a gain of 74.9 per cent. Their growth has been more rapid than city population, for in 1910 there were 3 playgrounds per 100,000 urban population; in 1920, 7.6 per 100,000; and in 1930, 10.5.[1]

[1] From *Recent Social Trends in the United States*, Report of the President's Research Committee on Social Trends; by permission of the publishers, McGraw-Hill Book Company, Inc. (New York, 1933), II: 917.

Play supervisors increased from 3,345 in 1910 to 24,949 in
1930, "showing an unmistakable trend in the direction of better supervision of playgrounds by persons technically trained
for their task." [1] All this has been done in order to make play
activities possible at a nominal cost or free of charge to huddled
urban children.

Seven main stages in the playground movement in the
United States have been clearly analyzed by Clarence E. Rainwater. [2] These are: (1) the sand garden stage, beginning with
a box and a pile of sand for small children; (2) the model playground stage, with a small playground to a million people perhaps; (3) the small park stage, for walking and sitting or for
the playing of a few games by selected individuals; (4) the recreation center stage, with first a public auditorium, a school auditorium, perhaps, for pageants and lectures; (5) the civic art
and welfare stage, with an emphasis on esthetic factors and a
public consciousness; (6) the neighborhood organization stage,
where neighborhoods developed a concrete consciousness through
widespread and active participation; and (7) the community
service stage, originating in part in "war community service"
during the World War. This exhibit reveals the trend of an
important social development.

These stages were accompanied by the growth of an all-year
playground service of play facilities for youth and adults as
well as for children. In the adult world the play movement has
meant the organization of whole communities, giving them an
opportunity to decide upon the type of recreation that they
need, encouraging them to provide recreation for themselves
at a minimum charge, and withal indirectly developing in them
a social consciousness and a community participation which
lies at the heart of any truly democratic life.

The play movement has had not only stages or levels of growth
but it has had transitions, or evolutionary changes. The stages

---

[1] *Ibid.*, II: 918.
[2] *The Play Movement in the United States* (University of Chicago Press,
1922). This book gives an excellent analysis of the play movement.

are testimony to the operation of organic growth. These evolutionary emergencies have been ably summarized by C. E. Rainwater,[1] namely, (1) from provisions for little children to those for all ages of people; (2) from facilities operated during the summer only, to those operated throughout the year; (3) from outdoor equipment only to both outdoor and indoor facilities and events; (4) from programs for congested urban districts to programs for both urban and rural communities; (5) from philanthropic to community support and control; (6) from "free" play and miscellaneous events to directed play with organized activities and correlated schedules; (7) from a simple to a complex field of activities including manual, physical, esthetic, social, and civic projects; (8) from the provision of facilities to the definition of standards for the use of leisure time; and (9) from appeals to individuals to appeals to group and community activities.

The public school in the United States has had but few organized play activities until recent decades. However, it has caught a new impetus from the public playground movement, and consequently boards of education are providing playground directors not only for school days but for the holidays and vacations, when in fact in large cities such directors are more needed than during school days. In a particular school district in L. the boys have complained with reference to school vacations, especially holidays, saying:

> During the Christmas Holidays the school playground is closed, and we can't have a good time. There is no regular playground in our neighborhood. We will get "pinched" if we play ball in the street. Only the alleys and hallways are left. Christmas is the dullest time of the year for us, for there is no place to play.[2]

Social settlements and similar institutions have been known for their recreational programs, although they have often been inadequately equipped and forced to rely on volunteer or poorly paid workers. They have been located in the heart of con-

[1] *Ibid.*, Ch. IV, "The Transitions in the Play Movement."
[2] From personal interview materials.

gested areas, and hence have been quick to appreciate the few constructive opportunities for play which the poorer people have at their command. They have responded to this need nobly, despite the limited means at their disposal. They have been heroic pioneers. They understand the masses, and hence are in a strategic position for formulating a widespread recreational procedure for those most in need. The successful methods which they have worked out have sometimes been adopted by the city or local area and put into operation on a large scale with the use of public funds. They have contributed ideas for a city-wide public school and playground program financed by tax money. Many of their functions thus have passed into a larger expression, leaving them free to develop other and newer ideas through experimentation.[1]

The churches are beginning to recognize that wholesome play activities are normal. The recreation impulses are such powerful forces for the good or ill of children, youths, and adults alike that churches are assuming positive attitudes toward them. Some churches have built splendid recreation halls and developed a diversified community program.

In certain instances churches have led in combating destructive amusements. They may well go further and assume the leadership in developing a new public opinion, a public opinion that will insist on socialized play provisions for all the people young and old.

The play movement, thus, grows out of the principles that the dominant interest in the life of youth is play, not work, and that the best development at this age comes from play rather than from work. It also includes the principle that adults need wholesome and constructive play which will offer true recuperation from a neurasthenic urban pace.

In providing for a larger socialization of play a comprehensive

[1] Small and large parks alike have offered only a minimum of recreation until recently for the working people. Located usually in the same areas where the wealthy or well-to-do live, their beautiful expanses have afforded chiefly a walking or sitting type of recreation. In the last few decades the extension of play facilities and equipment to public owned spaces has proceeded apace.

vision is a prime essential. Play needs are varied and may be met in a number of important ways. (1) The greatest need, possibly, is to educate all the people regarding the principles of recreation. For example, the public should perceive how modern industry and the city have created home conditions for the masses that are too congested and ill-arranged to permit the enjoyable spending of leisure time in the home area, unless radical changes are made in eliminating the congestion. The public may well understand how commercial enterprise has taken advantage of the play attitudes of people, catered to the play impulses of every age-period in life, and "to every grade of intellectual, artistic, and moral development." The public needs to appreciate how commercialized amusements, developing under a *laissez-faire* public policy, have led often to the economic and moral exploitation of both children and adults. It is quite clear that under modern complex conditions recreation can no longer be left to individual and commercial control.

Public control cannot neglect the fact that children and adults alike require and will have amusements of some sort. If such control is chiefly repressive it may do more harm than good. It is best when regulatory and constructive. Every community, rural as well as urban, may well have a recreation committee or commission, private or public, voluntary or paid, to study the play needs of the particular area and to see that as many of these needs as possible are met, and that their cost is kept low.

(2) A recreation body will find its greatest work in planning and providing for the future, although in crowded urban districts it will be swamped in providing simply for current needs. Local recreation bodies will not be enough. State recreation commissions are necessary in order to coördinate properly the local programs. Many cities now own mountain and winter as well as summer camps many miles away from their business centers. Regional play facilities are a necessary part of a real leisure-time program for all the people. In fact, so great is the scope of recreation needs that a national recreation commission

has important functions to perform in correlating the activities of state commissions, in promoting new types of play programs, and in formulating new principles for the socialization of play.

(3) The development of home recreation is essential. Even in comfortable homes there has arisen a tendency for young people to get away before the dinner hour is over in order to enjoy themselves, thus eliminating the few remaining hours now available to the members of the family as a unit. After all, the home has perhaps the best requisites for becoming a socialized recreation center, particularly for children. The opportunities are many for the development of play as an activity of the family as a unit.[1]

(4) The provision of many small playgrounds for young children is a standard need. In Philadelphia a study some years ago of the attendance at playgrounds showed that 74 per cent of the attendance of the younger children was from homes within three blocks, or a five minutes' walk, of such playgrounds. The radius of efficiency of a playground, according to a Milwaukee study, was from one-fourth to one-half a mile.[2] Later studies have verified this conclusion.

For adolescents over fourteen years of age in cities of size, larger playgrounds, play fields and parks are needed within a twenty minutes' walk of every home. Another safe rule is to spend twice as much on supervision as on any special form of equipment, for the human element in play and its supervision and direction is by far the most important consideration. A play leader performs vitally in the development of the personality of his followers. He leads in the most engaging form of human interest, namely, play relationships. He sets examples when examples most easily condition the behavior patterns of others.

[1] The development of home yards for play purposes is important. Many small yard spaces are available but totally unequipped and improperly used. Parents as part-time instructors might easily double the home play facilities in particular city areas.

[2] "Recreation Survey," Milwaukee Bureau of Economy and Efficiency, 1912, p. 22.

(5) A most difficult task is to secure proper inspection, control, or suppression where needed, of commercialized amusements that are run for profits rather than for welfare, such as low-grade dance halls and academies, drinking-inns and "roadhouses." In suppressing commercialized amusements that are destructive of the best values of life, it is necessary to provide constructive substitutes. In controlling them, it is usually necessary to defy "politics" and "pull," and to substitute standards of recreation for destructive amusements.

(6) Socialized play distinguishes between amusement and recreation. Amusement is passive, non-participating but often exciting; it creates "spectatoritis." The amused person is one who looks on while someone else plays or works or overworks. Recreation, on the other hand, is active and recreative; it is constructive and invigorating.

A current tendency is to accentuate amusement at the expense of recreation. The emphasis may safely be reversed. The majority of adults and many adolescents can secure ample amusement in real, enlivening recreation; in fact, many persons obtain genuine recreation through their work, providing it contains sufficient opportunities for creative expression. Work which is so specialized that it possesses no interesting elements compels the worker to look to the end of the day or of the week for his recreation. Leisure hours spent in idleness or in melodramatic excitement are also abnormal.

(7) The need for community recreation, that is, for recreation provided for the community and by the community, is paramount. A splendid step to this end is taken when a whole community is stimulated to provide organized recreation for itself at cost. The ideal is for each community to provide its own recreation at a minimum expense. "Community recreation by the community," is a sound slogan.

AVOCATIONS AND LEISURE

Leisure may be defined as the time that remains after work hours, sleep and rest hours, dressing and eating hours are deducted from the twenty-four hour day. Leisure time may be classified as follows: (1) waste time, (2) pastime, (3) hobby time, and (4) avocation time.[1] (1) *Waste time* includes "fooling around" and "killing time." Some persons waste nearly all their spare time, while nearly everyone is guilty of squandering some time. Indecision is an explanation of much waste time. Waiting by one person for other persons is another common source of waste time. Lack of personal system and of well-defined personal goals also explains wasted time.

(2) *Pastime* is a short-term diversion. Perhaps it is reading a work of fiction now and then; perhaps it is something entirely useless. A pastime usually has little meaning, or as the term indicates, it is something by which "to pass the time." Note this example:

> I had a few minutes to spare and picked up a jigsaw puzzle that lay on the living room table. I spread out the pieces and they fascinated me. They went together well for a time and then I was balked, but I did not want to admit defeat even to myself. I kept on for hours and finally won. I am not much interested in jigsaw puzzles but now and then I get caught in the net. They take my mind off my work. Once a start is made I never give up until the puzzle is completed. It is not a hobby with me by any means.[2]

(3) *Hobbies* are interests to which a person devotes considerable time over a period of years but irregularly. Personal pleasure is a chief result. Making collections of some object, for example, of paintings, or butterflies, or books, playing bridge for enjoyment rather than to win, gardening, are examples.

> My garden is my hobby. I belong to several garden clubs and I am learning the Latin names of flowers. My family laugh at me because at times I take the garden clubs so seriously. The trips to visit the elaborate gardens of the wealthy are marvelous but I shall not keep them up, although I shall be arranging and re-arranging my garden from time to time. There is where my real interests lie. I like a garden for its own sake. It is "a lovesome thing." You can't

---

[1] This classification has been tested by Marion Flad in her study of the "Leisure Time Activities of 400 Persons," *Sociology and Social Research*, XVIII: 265-74.

[2] From personal interview data.

work with flowers without thinking beautiful thoughts. Of course I get pleasure out of showing the new flowers or the best ones to my friends. Maybe I'll compete in a flower show soon.[1]

Hobbies are sometimes pursued with abandon for a time. A hobby may take one to the extreme of high tension. At a close game the baseball fan wears himself out. The bridge fan strives so hard to win that defeat is bitter and the mistake of a partner an unpardonable sin. The "night-out" devotee goes to his work the morning after with a thick head. In other words, hobbies may be carried too far and a check is required. The best antidote is perhaps having a hobby with a purpose, but this safeguard carries it over into the nature of an avocation.

> Making the hobby the end in itself is a waste of time. Having a hobby with some definite purpose in view is everything. If you ever think of taking up a hobby, try rare book collecting. But specialize in a certain type of rare book. You'll be astonished how much enjoyment you get out of it. At the same time if you acquire a large collection and keep it intact, you will be performing a great service to scholarship.[2]

(4) An *avocation* is a spare-time activity that is followed regularly, seriously, and that has recreational or other useful values. Regular hours are devoted to it each week. It may be illustrated by the person who faithfully plays golf twice a week for the sake of recreation and health. If a person played a dozen games of golf in rapid succession three or four times a year he would be treating golf as a hobby. One who gives regular hours each week to physical exercise has an avocation. The worker who spends some time daily in improving his mind or in developing a new skill, or the business man who teaches a church school class every Sunday has an avocation. Another type of avocation is found in the case of the Latin or mathematics teacher who perfects herself at the piano daily for the enjoyment of friends.

[1] From personal interview data.
[2] Harold D. Carew, "Otto h.f. Vollbehr Discusses the World's Greatest—and Other—Books," *Touring Topics*, XXV: 8.

An avocation is pursued in a business-like way. Attention is given to details, without allowing these to overwhelm one. While an avocation is pursued purposely and without thought of remuneration it may lead to the development of useful skills and be rewarded by an occasional fee. One may grow so proficient in an avocation that it may be substituted for his regular vocation.

Most persons fall into their avocations. There is little scientific study of avocations being made, and yet with the increase in leisure time now taking place avocations are important

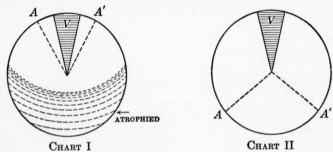

CHART I   CHART II

aspects of personality organization or reorganization. The choice of an avocation requires a great deal of thought and care. Avocational guidance is coming to be as important as vocational guidance. Avocational planning already deserves a place in school curricula.

A basic principle in avocational choosing is *balance*. The teacher whose avocation consists of professional activities is using her leisure time in ways that are too closely related to her vocation to give the necessary balance in personality growth. Moreover, most persons who choose avocations that are different from their vocations usually participate in such avocations with persons of their own callings which do not thereby fulfill all the requirements of balance.

Chart I is a personality diagram in which *V* represents one's vocation and *A* and *A'* his avocations. The latter are related to his vocation, either in the nature of the activities, or of associates, or both. They are therefore likely to further the development of a one-sided or overspecialized personality. Whole sections of personality may atrophy.

If we examine this principle of balance further, we find that it calls for avocational activities that will balance the vocational program. For example, a person whose vocation keeps him indoors will choose an outdoor avocation. He who has a strenuous mental vocation requires a physical-exercise avocation.

Chart II illustrates the principle of balance. The avocations *A* and *A′* indicate activities that are quite different from the vocation; they give a person a breadth of outlook that he needs in view of the delimiting influence of a specialized occupation, afford him contacts with people entirely different from his vocational associates, and enable him to develop a balanced personality.

TABLE I. BALANCES IN AVOCATIONS [1]

Vocation			Avocation
1. Indoor	balanced by		outdoor
Outdoor	"	"	indoor
2. Mental	"	"	physical
Physical	"	"	mental
3. Sitting	"	"	standing
Standing	"	"	sitting
4. Individual	"	"	social
Social	"	"	individual
5. City	"	"	country
Country	"	"	city
6. Noisy	"	"	quiet

If all individuals could be trained to select and maintain well-chosen avocations a large part of the recreation and amusement problem would be solved. Leisure would become constructive and personality would mature in socially valuable directions.

PROBLEMS

1. Distinguish between play and work.

2. What is the main function of a football game?

3. Why is making artificial flowers, work; and climbing Mont Blanc, play?

---

[1] This table of Balances grew in part out of the study by Marion Flad on "Leisure Time Activities of 400 Persons," *op. cit.*

4. Explain: "Milwaukee spends a thousand years of leisure each week."

5. Why is it often true that an American's idea of a holiday is a fatiguing journey?

6. What is the tenement child's most common playground?

7. Who are in greater need of provision for play, the children of the poor or of the rich?

8. Explain the statement that the parks are often too far away from the individuals who need them most?

9. Why do many people prefer so much passive amusement when active recreation is their real need?

10. How was the play of the children of primitive people different from that of the children of tenement areas today?

11. What was the best feature of the recreations of the early Greeks?

12. What was the major weakness of Nero's notion about recreation and amusements?

13. What is the strong point of the Puritans' theory of play?

14. What is the main flaw in the recapitulation theory of play?

15. Is the theory of play as a preparation for life or for more life wholly satisfactory?

16. Can you see any advantages in commercialized amusements?

17. What are the chief disadvantages?

18. What is meant by the phrase, "Our movie made children"?

19. Characterize the motion picture public in the United States today, that is, those who weekly or oftener attend motion picture shows?

20. What types of persons rarely or irregularly attend motion pictures?

21. What results may be expected from treating the motion picture industry as a public utility under regulation by a federal commission?

22. In what ways is alcoholism a social problem?

23. Why did so many of the states of the United States in 1933 vote against the Eighteenth Amendment?

24. What can be said in favor of alcoholism?

25. What is meant by the "new leisure"?

26. How is recreation closely related to personal character?

27. What is "socialized recreation"?

28. What is meant by "stages" in the play movement in the United States?

29. How are the "transitions" in the play movement related to the "stages"?

30. Why are holidays miserable days for many children?
31. What is the relation of recreation to avocation?
32. What is the principle of balance in choosing an avocation?
33. Distinguish between a hobby and an avocation.
34. What are the merits of a well-chosen avocation?

READINGS

ADDAMS, JANE, *The Spirit of Youth and the City Streets* (The Macmillan Company, New York, 1912).

BOWEN, W. P., and E. D. MITCHELL, *The Theory of Organized Play* (A. S. Barnes and Company, New York, 1927).

BURNS, C. DELISLE, *Leisure in the Modern World* (D. Appleton-Century Company, New York, 1932).

CHARTERS, W. W., *Motion Pictures and Youth: A Summary* (The Macmillan Company, New York, 1933).

CRESSEY, PAUL G., and FREDERICK M. THRASHER, *Boys, Movies, and City Streets* (The Macmillan Company, New York, 1933).

DALE, EDGAR, *Children's Attendance at Motion Pictures* (The Macmillan Company, New York, 1933).

DAVIE, MAURICE R., *Problems of the City* (John Wiley and Sons, Inc., New York, 1932), Part V.

DYSINGER, W. S., and CHRISTIAN A. RUCKMICK, *The Emotional Responses of Children to the Motion Picture Situation* (The Macmillan Company, New York, 1933).

ELSON, J. C., *Community Recreation* (The Century Company, New York, 1929).

FORMAN, HENRY J., *Our Movie-Made Children* (The Macmillan Company, New York, 1933).

GROOS, KARL, *The Play of Man* (D. Appleton and Company, New York, 1910).

LEE, JOSEPH, *Play in Education* (The Macmillan Company, New York, 1915).

LEHMAN, H. C., and P. A. WITTY, *The Psychology of Play Attitudes* (A. S. Barnes and Company, New York, 1927).

MAY, H. L., and DOROTHY PETGEN, *Leisure and Its Use* (A. S. Barnes and Company, New York, 1928).

MITCHELL, ALICE M., *Children and the Movies* (University of Chicago Press, 1929).

OBERHOLTZER, E. P., *The Morals of the Movie* (The Penn Publishing Company, Philadelphia, 1932).

PETERS, CHARLES C., *Motion Pictures and Standards of Morality* (The Macmillan Company, New York, 1933).

PETERSON, RUTH C., and L. L. THURSTONE, *Motion Pictures and the Social Attitudes of Children* (The Macmillan Company, New York, 1933).

RAINWATER, CLARENCE E., *The Play Movement in the United States* (University of Chicago Press, 1922).

STEINER, J. F., *Americans at Play* (McGraw-Hill Book Company, Inc., New York, 1933).

WARD, E. J., *The Social Center* (D. Appleton and Company, New York, 1913).

WOOD, ARTHUR E., *Community Problems* (The Century Company, New York, 1928), Part IV.

CHAPTER VIII

THE EDUCATIONAL GROUP

The family, occupational, and play groups are all highly educational, but they represent *informal* education. They do not teach directly and do not resort to formal methods. By indirect suggestion they create atmosphere, furnish lasting impressions, and give a setting whereby formal facts are interpreted.

The school represents *formal education*. The school is direct and systematic. It begins with the nursery school and ends in the university and the professional college. Education of the formal type has been recently defined as "a social process directed by the community or by individuals of the community toward the realization of socially accepted values." [1]

Education in one sense begins with the thousands of years of experience into which each individual is born. Into these experiences crystallized in the form of culture patterns each child is born and from them he obtains his fundamental concepts of life. This culture heritage includes a marvellous technique of alphabet, language, a system of writing, literature, traditions, customs, inventions. Education consists in getting the meaning of the culture heritage and of life.

The most vital part of the culture heritage is the ensemble of inventions. An account of human inventions is a story of the creative efforts of quick witted or deep thinking persons and of alert, vibrant minds. It is the story of group change and advancement. Through inventions the human group has advanced from the dug-out to the palace, from skin breeches to elaborate costumes, from the uncooked aboriginal meal to the seven

[1] Samuel L. Eby in George A. Hedger, editor, *An Introduction to Western Civilization* (Doubleday, Doran and Company, Inc., New York, 1933), p. 659.

213

course dinner, from the digging stick to the twenty-furrow steam plow, from the carrying stick to overland trains, and from the gourd with a cord stretched across it, to modern oratorios and symphonies.[1] Educationally, it is the child's problem to learn the meanings of this culture heritage, to acquire methods of mental analysis, and to function as a critic and a molder of the culture heritage.

Leading elements in the culture background are preserved in poetic and prose literature. Literature is "the best expression of human thought reduced to writing." In early human society the first formal educators were the priests. They compiled the tribal chronicles; they were the rhapsodists who celebrated the prowess of tribal chiefs in the presence of the worshipful tribal people. Since man feels before he reasons, and since poetry is the language of the feelings, poetry developed before prose. Hence sacred writings and war songs became the first educational source materials. Then the epic records of past glories developed and were supplemented by the lyrical records of contemporary events.

The development of reasoning tended to deprive poetry of its ornamentation and to provide man with a simpler and more accurate educational instrument. Prose of permanent value soon found expression in the form of oratory, which reached an exemplary level in Greece. Public speaking became a powerful educational force. During the early centuries of the Christian Era and the Middle Ages, no new educational methods were produced. The invention of the printing press in the fifteenth century made inexpensive books possible. Invention has followed invention in recent centuries until the printing press, the telegraph, the telephone, the radio have made education available to all.

The scientific method insists on definite proof; it struggles for accuracy. It strives to know the truth, the whole truth, and nothing but the truth. Although the known is but a small part

[1] See O. T. Mason, *The Origin of Inventions* (Charles Scribner's Sons, New York, 1910), p. 17.

of the unknown, no student today can hope in his education to encompass all knowledge. He must choose and specialize. He cannot familiarize himself with all the knowledge that has been discovered. However, he can learn enough truth to free himself from superstition, to be able to go through life with an open mind, and to get the message of courage and hope which comes from scientific inventions and the achievements of mankind.

Broadly speaking, education includes both the feeling elements of personality, or literature, and the reasoning aspects, or science. The average student often scorns one or the other, neglecting to see that a well-educated person must be familiar with the advances being made in both literature and science.

The well-educated child learns not only to feel and to think, but also to do. Education has generally been weak in training behavior. It has neglected the doing process. For example, it has taught people to think about democracy more than it has taught them to do democracy. Mankind, however, has been active, energetic, and even original; the lists of human achievements are beyond ordinary comprehension. Sound education whether informal or formal, whether operating in the family group, the play group, the occupational group, or the school group emphasizes in a balanced way the affective, the cognitive, and the activity phases of personality. Otherwise education produces incomplete personalities and one-sided groups.

Schools

The *nursery school* receives the child at two years of age or younger. It is a recent development which appeals to poor and wealthy parents alike. The latter have had nursemaids and tutors for their children, but the nursery school furnishes necessary group stimuli. The former are inadequately trained (many wealthy parents are equally untrained) to give their children the proper start in life and hence welcome the efficient nursery school.

As the child advances in the grades, education begins to take on formal aspects and to develop routine phases, symbolized by the checker-board seating arrangement in the schoolroom. The learning processes become more difficult and intellectual factors become segregated from the affective and behavior elements. The children organize school "activities" which are conducted outside school hours, supplanting the "passivities" of the regular routine.

The *kindergarten* is "more social than other grades or years" of school life, and hence possesses a greater appeal to pupils than does any other stage of school life. The child's work is organized on a group basis. The group stimuli coincide so well with the child's play attitudes that play pervades work. Activity and freedom predominate. The child learns almost entirely through doing, and reacts enthusiastically to the process.

The first two or three years of a child's life are spent in learning muscular coördinations and in developing basic feeling patterns. The years from three to twenty-three or more are the period in which the individual acquires meanings for the human experiences of the past thousands of years of history. In this age period he becomes somewhat adapted to his physical and social environments. On the basis of this training a person is expected to earn a living and to make a contribution if possible to the sum total of social culture and human happiness. At least if given opportunity he should not be found among that "stupid procession that never had a thought of their own."

Many interesting developments in the way of socializing school life are taking place all the way from the early grades to and through college. According to one of these experiments, reading, arithmetic, and geography are no longer being studied as such. Instead, in every grade, people are being studied. For example, the second grade children give their attention to Indians, but in studying about Indians they learn more than the usual quota of reading, arithmetic, and geography. In so doing they do not develop any of the customary adverse reactions to routine and formal studies.

While education may take cognizance of play attitudes and

of organizing the study process around interesting stimuli, the child needs to keep in mind that education is incomplete if it fails to train him to do gladly some things that are uninteresting and unpleasant. Education based only on desires and pleasant stimuli is negligent, for life itself contains unpleasant tasks that must be faced, and faced with a smile, even though it be a forced smile. The sooner every child learns to face some disagreeable tasks with a degree of stoicism, the better balanced will be his personality.

The emphasis in school studies has been one-sided. Self-culture studies and the physical sciences, splendid as far as they go, give an unbalanced development. In the main, languages and literatures represent self-culture, and the sciences help in securing control over natural resources but too often in terms of individual success and power. The importance of the social sciences and of a social welfare emphasis is but slightly appreciated by many school leaders and still less by some boards of education or by the public.

Any serious attempt, however, to train in terms of public welfare must begin in the first school years because the majority of children do not go beyond the elementary grades and yet when they become adults they will cast deciding votes. Moreover, social studies need to be given a primary place in high schools and normal schools. Training in the public welfare viewpoint is more important than training in individual success and efficiency, for the latter by itself creates a nation of exploiters and racketeers.

Education that is acquisitive may suffice in pioneering areas, but is destructive in vast population centers. Acquisitive education needs to be supplanted by functional education, that is, by an education that trains in rendering service. Instead of emphasizing the acquiring of knowledge as the alpha and omega of education, the current tendency is to view education as "a learning by doing" process. He who would learn the best things, must do the best, that is, render service without seeking personal reward.

Another important social conception is that the whole child needs to be educated, and hence every phase of the child's personality requires development. The school is not simply a place to train a child's intellect. Intellectual development without concomitant training of the feelings and emotions is dangerous. It puts powerful tools in the hands of the independable and the reckless.

At the vital point of spiritual development, the average public school official is nonplussed. The whole child is not trained properly if spiritual and religious values are neglected. The increasing rôle of science in education brings the physical and the material and the measurable into increasing prominence, while the intangible, the spiritual, and the religious are in danger of losing out entirely, although they represent the essence of personality.

One of the most difficult problems confronting the school is that of training youth in *social* and *group responsibility*. A child who learns the Constitution of the nation does not *ipso facto* become a good citizen. There is little transfer of a memorized Constitution into terms of real national loyalty. Children and youth need to be taught the significance of becoming good neighbors, good fathers and mothers, and good citizens, by doing neighborly, fatherly or motherly, and citizenship acts regularly. Training in social responsibility is as important if not more important than the teaching of the trades and of methods of earning a living. The school needs to overcome the failure of many parents in performing intelligently their parental duties and in developing in their children behavior habits of group responsibility. The school needs to concern itself with training a new race of parents, of neighbors, of citizens both of the nation and of the world.

Of social merit is *sex education*. The ignorant and vicious perversion of the sex impulses as manifested in illegal sex relations, false marriages, and divorce evils constitute a set of pernicious social conditions. Segregated talks on sex hygiene are inadequate. The best procedure for sex education is through the natural study of subjects such as botany, zoölogy, physiology.

Industrial education and *vocational guidance* are enabling children and youth to orient themselves with reference to life. There is danger, however, of forgetting that the chief value in learning a trade is that the child may discover himself. He should be trained for one or more occupations for the purpose of earning a living, essential as that is, but also that he may through his occupation develop his personality to the fullest and richest extent. To teach a trade or to learn one for the purpose of acquiring individual success may prove anti-social. A person who has attained high individual efficiency but who has not learned to work well and wholesomely in society is an unbalanced person.

The *continuation* school is performing a worthy social function. If all boys and girls would attend school a few hours each day until eighteen years of age the increased capacities would more than counterbalance the cost. A chief merit of the continuation school is that it combines work and school in a way that education takes on the meanings of the actual work-a-day world and that work satisfies educational needs. The continuation school enables society to exercise guidance over thousands and hundreds of thousands of youth who would otherwise be thrown into a sophisticated environment and surrounded by many temptations at a time when they may have developed only partial control over turbulent desires.

Education needs to take cognizance of three types of youth.[1] The first type is "flaming youth," undisciplined and pampered, seeking chiefly "to get by" and making mad plunges here and there. Second are the social crusaders, interested in pacifism and social justice. Third is the largest group of all, intellectual gropers, many of whom are loath to learn from their elders and yet are blindly experimenting with life. For each of these groups, education needs to develop a distinctive program.

[1] As indicated by Clarence M. Case, *Social Process and Human Progress* (Harcourt, Brace and Company, New York, 1931), pp. 192ff.

Adult education is developing extensively. Its main emphasis has been on meeting the needs of immigrants and the backward; its new accent is on education for every adult, for a person may often profit most from systematic education after he has gained considerable experience. It assumes that no one's education "is ever concluded at any point." It would have everyone go to school for at least some time every year throughout life in order that his personality may continue to grow richer and more socially useful.

The *visiting teacher* takes education into the homes of the persons who cannot come to the school. To the multitudes of poorer people the visiting teacher introduces scientific knowledge concerning the proper care of children during their first years of life.[1] Countless children are so handicapped by lack of proper care in their homes before they reach the regular schools that "they are not in a fit condition to have public money spent upon them." Countless others receive an improper orientation toward life. To meet needs such as these the visiting teacher movement has developed.[2]

The visiting teacher is a boon in immigrant neighborhoods. She carries not only knowledge but the spirit of helpfulness and of human sympathy and understanding into homes where wholesome contacts with natives are few. To the immigrant mother with her slight opportunities to know the life and institutions of the natives, the visiting teacher is an angel of light as well as of mercy.

More important than methods of teaching or than subjects taught is the personality of the teacher and the atmosphere

[1] See Julius J. Oppenheimer, *The Visiting Teacher Movement* (Joint Committee on Methods of Preventing Delinquency, New York, 1925); also see Mary B. Sayles and H. W. Nudd, *The Problem Child in School* (Joint Committee on Methods of Preventing Delinquency, New York, 1925).

[2] The visiting teacher offers the homes of the less fortunate a knowledge of sanitary living conditions, of sound purchasing methods, and of home-making. Large numbers of people are still living in darkness as far as their knowledge of sanitation, bacteriology, and sound health is concerned. Many are unable to go to a night school or to adult education classes, and so the visiting teacher comes to them. Not only are they taught better ways of living but under the actual conditions that they daily face.

created. The personality of the teacher may kill a worthy subject or enliven a dead one. It may stimulate common clay into superior effort or smother throbbing aspirations. It may transform human energy into social sacrifice or social sacrilege.

Specialization in education is a necessity and a danger. It is a necessity, for the fields of knowledge and skills have become too many and complicated for any one person to master more than one or a few. It is a danger, for it narrows a person's vision and concentrates his viewpoint until he becomes unappreciative and often intolerant of other fields of specialization. If successful in his speciality he tends to develop superiority feelings regarding it, and to look down upon other and equally important lines of work.

A young man entering college wishes to become a specialist as soon as possible, and sometimes "to get out into the world immediately" where he can make money. Consequently he shuns or submits unwillingly to the cultural courses, and demands the practical. The practical courses to him are those that train for individual and pecuniary efficiency. Public welfare is slighted and education becomes indirectly unpatriotic and dangerous to the common weal. Moreover, a young man in avoiding the cultural is building his personality upon narrow and shallow foundations. He is cutting off his future possibilities of development.

NEWSPAPERS

While the school is a primary group there are informal educational groups such as those who comprise a newspaper public. Such a public is being daily educated by what it reads, that is, by the pictures of society which it receives every morning or evening from the columns of its favorite newspaper. Such a public is largely the adult's educational group. If in the United States the schools reach practically all the people while they are young, the newspapers reach practically all when they are adults.

The rise of the newspaper in recent decades has been meteoric and marvellous. In catering to the casual, the ephemeral, and the melodramatic the newspaper has often belittled its high educational calling. In bowing to advertisers, because the latter pay so large a proportion of newspaper costs, the newspaper has often become a one-sided organ of public opinion. By playing the game of party politics, it loses the confidence of independent thinkers.

The newspaper, together with the telegraph, the telephone, the radio, has created a special degree of social consciousness. It has even made at times a world consciousness possible. It has made Paris, Rome, Berlin, London, New York, Tokio, and Peiping neighbors, or at least nigh-dwellers. It is a marvellous spectacle to contemplate, namely, a hundred million persons, or more, leaders and common people, reading simultaneously about one national or world happening after another, hour after hour, the whole day through as the earth continues its endless revolutions. More significant is the fact that each reader knows that thousands and hundreds of thousands of other persons are reading and thinking about the same human success or tragedy at approximately the same time. He also knows that many if not nearly all are responding to startling happenings in the same way as he is responding. This gives him a place in a large and almost incomprehensible social group. Therefore, the newspaper constitutes a powerful instrument of creating public opinion, social consciousness, and good or ill will; and newspaper publics become interesting and powerful social phenomena.

Today a million dollars is hardly sufficient for establishing a metropolitan newspaper of size. The capitalist-owner has supplanted the editor-owner. As a rule, the editor is no longer the owner unless he is a millionaire. An editor like Horace Greeley or Charles A. Dana who owns his paper and makes it the projection of his personal character and social ideals is rare. Many editors now are hired. They are not expected by their employers to put their own ideals into the paper.

The highest social usefulness of the newspaper has been compromised by commercialization. The securing of financial returns has become the yardstick for measuring what will be printed. Often the profit standard overrules the public welfare standard. A part of this untoward situation is due to the fact that a large proportion of the total receipts in the newspaper business is derived from the sale of advertisements. The subscriptions represent a decreasing percentage. When advertising furnishes two-thirds and more of the earnings of a daily newspaper, the advertiser rather than the subscriber or the general public supports and controls the newspaper and the newspaper public becomes an advertiser-created phenomenon.

Corporations which are extensive advertisers are referred to in newspaper offices as "sacred cows," and nothing in the news or editorial columns is printed that would in any way offend the "sacred cows," no matter if the latter be the community's leading racketeers. A difficulty lies in the fact that the selling of advertising is purely commercial, while the printing of news and editorials is a matter of social values. Edward A. Ross has declared that the modern metropolitan newspaper is in danger of becoming a factory where ink and brains are so applied to white paper as to turn out the largest possible marketable product.[1] Under such conditions a newspaper's public is in danger of being a narrow and bigoted group.

The general public takes a rather irresponsible attitude toward its newspapers. To be sure it criticizes them freely and ceases to buy them at times, but as Walter Lippmann has pointed out, no one is willing to pay for his newspaper. He is willing to pay just a fraction of the cost.

> We have accustomed ourselves now to paying two and even three cents on weekdays, and on Sundays, for an illustrated encyclopedia and vaudeville entertainment attached, we have screwed ourselves up to paying a nickel or even a dime. Nobody thinks for a moment that he ought to pay for his newspaper.[2]

[1] *Changing America* (The Century Company, New York, 1912), p. 112.
[2] Walter Lippmann, *Public Opinion* (The Macmillan Company, New York, 1922), p. 321.

The newspaper as an authority is both reliable and unreliable. It is dependable to bring many important matters and much trash to public attention. It is not dependable in bringing all the important happenings to the public eye, in giving proper weight to the various events that are reported, or in getting all the essential details correct.[1]

It is clear that more newspapers are needed which ignore the dubious influence of certain advertisers and whose owners avoid the rôle of propagandists. Newspapers are needed which will consistently print the truth about police protection to vice, corporate tax-dodging, and non-enforcement of laws when money buys its way to freedom. The public does not fully realize the actual situation; it is not aware how little of the real news it receives on many questions. It does not know the degree to which coloration of news takes place. Newspaper owners and the public together have the power if they wish to bring about a day when public welfare will be the test of newspaper efficiency. The need for a nationally endowed press has been strongly advocated.[2] Perhaps a privately endowed newspaper would be better providing there were no strings attached to it.

To offset the biased newspaper a number of independent weekly journals of opinion have developed in the United States. In the main they are liberal in viewpoint and play a considerable rôle in the formation of opinion among the more openminded. Many people, however, grow tired of much opinion and read semi-scientific monthly journals as a basis for their attitudes on public questions. Only a small percentage of the total population, however, read the scientific journals; there is a need for a monthly digest in popular terms of all scientific journals. In this way the latest facts and analyses of facts would be made available to everyone.

[1] Lucy M. Salmon, *The Newspaper and Authority* (Oxford University Press, London, 1923).
[2] See V. S. Yarros, "A Neglected Opportunity and Duty in Journalism," *American Journal of Sociology*, XXII: 203–11.

Radio and Cinema Publics

The *radio* has created new and gigantic publics. The listeners in at a given address or concert often extend over an area with a radius of several thousand miles. With the development of "hook-ups" the radio can turn a whole nation into one gigantic public, creating a primary group feeling. It has now been several years since the first open forum of the air was inaugurated. The speaker asked the listeners-in to telephone questions to the radio station as he was speaking; then these questions were answered over the radio. Debates are held via radio and the members of the public who wish to participate may register their decisions over the telephone. International "hook-ups" and short-wave lengths have made possible the beginning of a world community group. The radio defies the storms that snap telephone wires and reaches into polar regions as well as around the world. It is hastening the day of a common world language and of one comprehensive world group.

Radio plans to establish broadcast theaters. "Thousands of seats will be provided and the admission will be free," at least at the beginning. At first radio concerts and plays were broadcasted from "silent rooms" with no one being present except the necessary directors. Today the situation has changed. Audiences are admitted, for it has been found that the presence of spectators helps to make the broadcasting more realistic. The performers are more natural than when receiving no responses from their remote unseen audience. "The chuckles and applause of the audience give them 'that feel' that the trouper needs to tune him up." The performers thus have a double audience— a primary group at hand, and a secondary group "on the air." Each group requires a special type of presentation with the result that a happy combination in style of presentation may be effected.

The radio is developing at a time when immigration is being restricted. Nationalism and depression stop migrations but the radio recognizes no national boundaries. It is an international carrier of culture patterns. It levels culture up and down. Economic opportunities will become more uniform when world radio functions freely. It will no longer be necessary to migrate in order to enjoy the finest music of another country. International radio, broadcasting regularly from a common world center like Geneva, "the capital of the world" could create an international-mindedness little dreamed of today.

The *cinema* is an educational agency of tremendous force. Each star has his or her public which includes people of many nationalities around the world. Cinema publics also may be classified according to the type of stars who are worshipped.[1] As an educational force the cinema utilizes indirect suggestion to its fullest extreme. While the direct suggestion is indescribably great, indirect suggestion emanates not only from the pictures themselves but also from the lives of the stars. The motion picture uses many characters that move rapidly, that dramatically pass before the eyes of the spectators in countless rôles, and that stimulate them in a multitude of unsuspected ways. If the spectators are youthful, freedom-loving, enthusiastic, uncritical they are thereby usually susceptible to the indirect suggestion of the film. The star in his personal life, styles of dress, forms of amusement, and the like, are copied in detail far and wide.

The use of carefully selected and produced films in schools and churches is increasing; they bring the farthermost reaches of the earth into the schoolroom or church hall with accurate vividness. They envisage the best of the past of all races; they enable persons to relive events of human significance that occurred thousands of years ago. They personify the greatest religious ideals, giving the spectators immeasurable inspiration.[2]

The talking motion picture was introduced to the public in 1926; it added to sight the influence of sound in making realistic

[1] The significance of the cinema in terms of amusement and recreation has been considered in the chapter on "The Play Group."

[2] For a manual prepared for the use of high school students see Edgar Dale's *How to Appreciate Motion Pictures* (The Macmillan Company, New York, 1933).

whatever it reproduced or set forth. It multiplied the realism and the force of the screen. Its educational possibilities are forecasted in the "language laboratories" that are being set up in many universities.

Television carries marvellous new possibilities. Television publics will exhibit powerful crowd characteristics. A press item raises such interesting questions as these:

> When will the first television wedding occur? The bride and groom may be a thousand miles apart, and the clergyman some distance from either of them, yet each will be able to see and hear the other, and they will be in full view of an assembled congregation.
>
> It is thought that this new science may be used to speed up the machinery of the law. Why should not a witness give evidence by television and submit to a cross-examination through the air?
>
> Will a doctor be able to visit patients without leaving his office? Will a business man carry on his work at home?
>
> Will an engineer responsible for construction of a bridge direct operations from his office, where he has all the details in front of him? He can instruct his assistant on the site to carry the television transmitter to any point he wishes to examine.[1]

Television bids fair to open a new era of social life. In a way it represents a movement opposite to that of the talking picture, for in the latter case "sound caught up with sight," while in the former, "pictures are catching up with sound." With pictures accompanying sound at lightning speed to the ends of the world the time is truly at hand when all the world may be summoned together in one vast public and by picture and sound be made to feel the force of a common cause.

Television is bringing the motion picture into the home. Although the motion picture theater will continue, it will have a serious competitor when vision and audition carry the same films into millions of homes simultaneously the world around. A social evolution will have occurred when television unites the people of every country. Television and radio together will usher in the long heralded day of a world language, a world culture, a world public.

[1] *Los Angeles Times*, April 10, 1933.

Socially Illiterate

Basic informal educational groupings of all people may be made in two different ways. First there is the intelligence-heredity test. The result is fivefold as follows: (1) geniuses, (2) talented people, (3) persons with intelligence quotients ranging from 90 to 110, (4) mental defectives, and (5) morons. A telic society will endeavor through eugenic programs to eliminate classes 4 and 5 as far as possible, for they are a more or less dead social weight. Individuals in these classes easily and unwittingly commit some of the most heinous offenses, although the shrewdest crimes are committed by members in the first two classes.

The other test is educational and the result is also fivefold: (1) university and professionally trained persons, (2) the college trained, (3) the high school trained, (4) the elementary school trained, and (5) the illiterate. This classification is based first largely upon opportunity. A telic society today aims to move all its members into the first three classes as far as possible. The task of overcoming illiteracy, however, is gigantic. Even in the United States which has long prided itself on having one of the best and most advanced educational systems in the world there were 4,283,753 illiterates reported by the Census of 1930, or 4.3 per cent of the total population. Progress is being made for the number is 648,152 less than in 1920 although the total population increased about 17,000,000 in the decade.[1] A few countries of the world boast of a smaller percentage of illiteracy than does the United States, notably Germany,[2] Switzerland, Denmark, Sweden, Norway, England, Wales, and Scotland. Literacy is an essential to progress and to democracy.

Certain countries still have excessive literary rates, such as India, Egypt, China, and until recently Russia and Mexico. Where the illiteracy is 50 per cent or more, the majority of the people would not recognize a map of their own country. Political democracy under such conditions would have little chance.

---

[1] The percentage of illiteracy thus decreased from 6 per cent to 4.3 per cent.

[2] Germany ceased to keep a record of illiteracy after 1913 because it had reached such a negligible figure.

After illiteracy is cut down to a negligible level, a telic society still has the problem of socializing its literates, that is, of training and conditioning them to react intelligently in behalf of the common welfare first of all and then in behalf of themselves.

"Social imbecility," as Dr. Clarence M. Case uses the term, apparently ranks high in most literate nations today. Evidences of social imbecility are found in those obnoxious signboards that clutter up the landscape in American cities and on country roads, in the habit of getting off of street cars backward, in throwing lighted cigarettes away carelessly, in endurance tests such as marathon dancing, in thinking that getting drunk is "smart," in the "Valentino hysteria," in publishing glaring newspaper accounts (with large head lines) of startling but disgusting behavior, in "night-riding," in honking horns, so as to make the pedestrian jump for his life, in settling national disputes by mutually killing the largest number of the finest specimens of young men. It does not matter much what name or label is used, whether boobery, foolhardiness, moronishness, idiocy, or stupidity—the problem is the same. In mental age many people may rank high but low in "social age." Despite their big brain power they are still little children in their sense of social responsibility. They have never grown up. Concerning social stupidity in general and war in particular, Dr. Case states:

The social stupidity in question is the work of the great mass of non-psychopathic, apparently adequate, normally intelligent human beings who carry on the daily work and play of the world. Yet the result of their quite intelligent (?) activities is a notably stupid world at home and abroad—a world that not only suffered the World War, but actually and inevitably, and through no sort of accident, produced it as a legitimate product. The stupidity, even moral and social idiocy, of such a world cannot be characterized in words. It might be said to represent the ideal for a perfectly stupid world, especially since it now seems bent on repeating the recent orgy of destruction.

Apologists for "the system" may attempt two defenses. One is that war is an affair of humanity in its vast, unwieldy, international aspects, but no fair measure of our associated life on the smaller and more manageable scale. The other is that such blind folly belongs only to the less lucid moments of social experience and not to the steady run of affairs. Both arguments are vain, for the sober fact is that behavior essentially of that kind is the daily and hourly experience of all human groups everywhere. Such foolishness is the stuff that associated human life is made of, and I have been able to hit upon no better name for it than social imbecility.[1]

Educational groups, thus, are seen to be both formal and informal. The formal is well organized and characterized by informative action. The informal is unorganized, indirect, and characterized by personal appeal. One moves in the rational realm; the other in the feeling sphere. One provides facts; the other, atmosphere and stimuli. One is represented by the carefully directed classroom; the other, by personal followings and by publics. Both are educationally essential.

PROBLEMS

1. Explain: "Better than time to read is time to think."
2. Why are relatively so few people engaged in doing original thinking?
3. Why do students "cram" for examinations?
4. What would be a better method than "cramming"?
5. Why is the better method not followed?
6. How many months should there be in the public school year?
7. What is education?
8. Explain: Every student should have a target.
9. Do you see any values in being stupid?
10. Should society spend more money per capita upon wealthy or poor children?
11. What are the arguments for and against a national university?
12. Which function of teaching should be given the greater attention: imparting information or developing critical thinking?
13. What is the relation of the daily newspaper to public opinion?
14. What is the major effect of coloration of news?
15. In what ways does a newspaper hinder its readers from forming opinions freely?
16. Describe a socially ideal newspaper.

[1] Clarence M. Case, "Social Imbecility and Social Age," *Sociology and Social Research.* XII: 22.

17. In what ways is a radio public different from a newspaper public?

18. How might a national radio public become exceedingly dangerous on occasion?

19. What is the double social significance of the "broadcast theater"?

20. What is the relation of the radio to culture diffusion?

21. Explain the twofold indirect suggestion that the motion picture wields.

22. What social changes might be effected by television?

23. What is meant by the socially illiterate?

24. Why is there so much social illiteracy even when ordinary illiteracy has been wiped out?

25. Describe in a sentence the probable state of society in the United States if all the schools "were to be closed tomorrow and kept closed for one full generation."

READINGS

ANGELL, R. C., *A Study of Undergraduate Adjustment* (University of Chicago Press, 1930).

CHARTERS, W. W., *Motion Pictures and Youth* (The Macmillan Company, New York, 1933).

FORMAN, HENRY J., *Our Movie Made Children* (The Macmillan Company, New York, 1933).

GIDDINGS, FRANKLIN H., *The Mighty Medicine* (The Macmillan Company, New York, 1929).

GOOD, ALVIN, *Sociology and Education* (Harper and Brothers, New York, 1926).

GROVES, ERNEST R., *Social Problems and Education* (Longmans, Green and Company, New York, 1925).

HART, J. K., *A Social Interpretation of Education* (Henry Holt and Company, New York, 1929).

HOLADAY, P. W., and GEORGE D. STODDARD, *Getting Ideas from the Movies* (The Macmillan Company, New York, 1933).

KATZ, DANIEL, and FLOYD H. ALLPORT, *Students' Attitudes* (Craftsman Press, Syracuse, New York, 1931).

OPPENHEIMER, J. J., *The Visiting Teacher Movement* (Joint Committee on Preventing Delinquency, New York, 1925).

PETERS, C. C., *Foundations of Education* (The Macmillan Company, New York, 1930).

ROBINSON, JAMES H., *The Humanizing of Knowledge* (George H. Doran Company, New York, 1923).

SAYLES, M. B., and H. W. NUDD, *The Problem Child in School* (Joint Committee on Preventing Delinquency, New York, 1925).

SMITH, W. R., *Principles of Educational Sociology* (Houghton Mifflin Company, Boston, 1928).

SNEDDEN, DAVID, *Educational Applications of Sociology* (The Century Company, New York, 1924).

WICKHAM, E. K., *Children's Behavior and Teachers' Attitudes* (Commonwealth Fund, New York, 1928).

CHAPTER IX

THE RELIGIOUS GROUP

At any early age the average child is likely to find himself under the influence of a religious group. If so he begins to respond in one way or another to religious stimuli. He may react favorably and grow in religious faith and wisdom. He may fall away for a time, for years, and then as life wears on, troubles come, losses of loved ones occur, return to his childhood faith and spend his closing years in a renewed religious hope. He may react adversely and proudly call himself an atheist, although most atheists are reacting against "an inadequate conception of God" and not against a wholesome religious spirit.

When one person worships with other persons a special religious spirit develops. Fellowship creates first a religious group, and then a religious institution. The process has been well stated:

> If the person is alone naturally he must worship by himself or not at all. If there is a small company of people of similar faith they will come together from time to time for common worship. After such a group has settled and has become large and strong enough they will build a house of worship near their habitations. They will then hold services as often as convenient and attempt to secure a person to visit them at intervals and perform the functions of priest or pastor. If the neighborhood grows and the pastor is successful in increasing the membership a resident pastor will be engaged to look after the ministrations of the group. When this happens we may say that the religious life of the neighborhood has become institutionalized. It is this objective manifestation of religion with which we are mainly concerned here.[1]

[1] William L. Leap, *Red Hill—Neighborhood Life and Race Relations in a Rural Section*. Phelps-Stokes Fellowship Papers (Bureau of Publications, University of Virginia, 1933), p. 80.

RELIGIOUS ATTITUDES

The religious group is everywhere an expression of the need for extra-human aid. At best every person suffers a degree of isolation. Many of the hardest blows in life one cannot shift to others, and hence he may resort to religious aid.

Religious impulses have been and are universal. They were common among primitive groups and are found today nearly everywhere, but lo, in what different forms—Christian, Mohammedan, Buddhist, Jewish, and so on. In many of their narrow and bigoted expressions they have been socially destructive but in their finest and truest developments they have been socially helpful. In recent centuries they have found expression in definite religious groups with elaborate rituals, costly cathedrals, and powerful social organizations. What an array and a tribute to religious zeal are St. Peters, Westminster Abbey, the Cathedral of Milan, the Cologne Cathedral, not to mention Mohammedan mosques, Jewish synagogues, and Buddhist temples.

To comprehend the significance of religious attitudes it is necessary to analyze religious behavior. The universality of religious attitudes is due to the universality of certain overwhelming human needs. For example, there come times in every person's life when he is confronted with the fact that he does not know very much after all. The most highly educated and cultured, the wealthiest, the politically most powerful as well as the poor and the ignorant, are all in the same category when it comes to placing themselves, their achievements, and their powers alongside of the powers of the universe and the realms of the unknown. Miracles and marvels and mysteries face man at every turn. Life is filled with baffling problems and death remains the greatest conundrum.

At best it appears that human beings are but little organisms moving hopefully for a short moment through a vast sweep of mystery. As Charles H. Cooley once stated, human beings are like "a party of men with lanterns making their way through an immeasurable forest."[1] To all except the intellectually blasé or to the stupid, the perplexities of life sooner or later are recognized as being too great for man to meet out of his own resources. Herein is the explanation of the permanency of religious attitudes and groups.

Religion has developed out of human needs that cannot be met in mundane ways. When the sense of need urged primitive man to attempt to communicate with a higher Power, there religion made its first appearance and there prayer became the first religious tool. Religious attitudes have developed from both feelings and thought, leading on one hand to faith, and on the other to beliefs about life and the universe. In its essential nature religion is a conscious and coöperative relationship of puny human beings with the powerful Creator of the universe.

At its noblest, religion perceives human society not as an end in itself but as an emergence of the superhuman, the endless, the Divine. To consider human life in its finest and richest aspects as an emergence of an Eternal Personality lends greater value and an increased dignity to human society. Through religion man sees himself as a functioning unit of a social group far larger and more significant than any visible human group. He views himself as a part of a society extending back into the centuries, struggling up the steep and slippery road of human endeavor, but at times falling back. He sees himself as an immortal part of a society extending into endless time. When he views the hard-fought victories of the past he braces up with renewed courage for the tasks of the day, and when he catches a glimpse now and then of the vista ahead he steps more lightly to his day's work. Thus religion is one of the main sources of those enthusiasms of life without which gloom, pessimism, and cynicism would settle down over all and engulf all.

[1] *Social Process* (Charles Scribner's Sons, New York, 1918), p. 362.

PRIMITIVE RELIGIOUS GROUPS

Primitive groups were elementarily religious. At first innumerable spirits were worshipped. Man early conceived the sun, the moon, the wind, the heavens, as being like himself and as guided by feelings and attitudes like his own. Even the thunderstorm was worshipped as a mighty being which had power to end a drought. Some objects called fetishes, were worshipped not because of their intrinsic value, charm, or power, but because a spirit or god was supposed to reside in them. Animals were worshipped, and revered for the qualities in which they excelled. Ancestor worship was common. The simple folk of Thibet, for example, are described as the most religious people in the world in that they are continually praying, that they literally pray in five different ways at once, and that their political and social organizations are subordinate to their religious life and organization.[1]

The worship of innumerable spirits became burdensome and confusing, hence many spirits were supplanted by a relatively few deities and religious beliefs. Polytheism in turn became a source of conflicts; the deities constituted too large a group to be efficient. Then it seems that the main deity of the leading tribe in a given area became supreme. Here is found the beginnings of monotheisms and of national religions.

In early times a man's religion consisted largely of the religious acts which he performed rather than in the beliefs which he held. In modern days the emphasis is often reversed. Sacrifices were invaluable features of early religions. By this method the relationships with the gods were renewed and strengthened. Prayer was the ordinary concomitant of the sacrifice; it was the means by which the worshipper explained the reason of his gift, urged the deity to accept it, and asked for the help he needed. Worshipping, thus, was a series of social acts, a phase of social behavior, and an outgrowth of group relationships.

There were few temples, idols, and no churches in the early

[1] Dorris Shelton, "Culture Traits of the Tibetans," *Sociology and Social Research*, XVIII : 150–57.

human world. The worship of natural objects did not suggest the enclosing of a space for religious purposes. There were no formal religious organizations. Everyone in the social group was assumed to take a part in the religious exercises and every group organized thus had its religious phase. In later centuries, religion became somewhat set apart from the rest of life and manifested itself in distinctive institutions.

Taboo developed. In order to maintain religion intact certain acts were forbidden. Particular objects became taboo. The earthly belongings of a deity could not be touched. By taboo a chieftain, because of his close relationship with a deity, might save to his own use or pleasure, objects of special value. Religion thus furnished society with one of its earliest tools of control.

Taboos were enforced by invoking fear. The wrath of the gods would come down upon the offender, and punishment would strike him down. Thus along with taboo came the appeal to fear and the concept of punishment. Rewards and punishments for here and now were not sufficient to induce or to deter certain behavior, and hence the individual was promised a Heaven of bliss or threatened with a Hell of agony. The behavior problem thus is shown to be one that even religion could not deal with except by glorious or terrible stimuli.

The religion of the tribal group developed into the religion of the nation group. Instead of partisan tribal gods, a higher and impartial deity was conceived, who belonged to and watched over all the tribal groups. New social bonds developed. There was no longer the tie of blood which bound the people to their gods; the tie became more spiritual and more social.

The Inca religion, Confucianism, and the worship of Yahweh or Jehovah, may be conceived as national group religions. With the coming of the Hebrew prophets, religion assumed broader aspects and finally culminated in Christianity with its claim as a religion fit for the world group.[1]

[1] Not exactly a national religion is Judaism, for the Jews have been nationless for many centuries. Neither is it a world religion although its adherents are found all over the world, because Jews have not proselyted or sent missionaries to win non-Jews.

Judaism, or the religion of the Jews, is based largely on the teachings of the Hebrew prophets and has a strong social content. It has conserved the family group as a socializing institution, and has pictured Jehovah as a God of both righteousness and mercy. A better human society is sought. Its attention has not been centered on other-worldly affairs as much as on the problems of this world. It has borne fruit in calm and well-organized social programs.

Sometimes national religions have been officially adopted as state religions, but in recent decades the tendency has been in the opposite direction. The state and church are no longer one in most countries. The combination has sometimes led to undue concentration of power, and created difficult problems. If religious needs, however, are vital to the development of the finest type of persons and citizens, then perhaps the religious phase of life cannot be entirely neglected by the state.

WORLD RELIGIOUS GROUPS

In its essence *Mohammedanism* which has aspired to be a religion for all the world, holds to the doctrine of the unity and omnipotence of Allah, and of the responsibility of every human being to Allah.[1] The submissive tendency, the implicit surrender, and entire obedience to Allah are emphasized. Allah, however, does not inspire the worshipper with ideals of goodness, although an influence against evil is exerted; he is abstract. He does not come in close contact with people; he seems to have little personal interest in human welfare. He does not inspire persons to strive after high social standards; he does not seem to be related to humanity and cannot figure extensively in group welfare.[2]

The central movement of East Indian religious thought has culminated in *Buddhism*, another world religion. Gautama, the founder, in his early manhood began to realize that suffer-

---

[1] See Allan Menzies, *History of Religion* (Charles Scribner's Sons, New York, 1906), Ch. XIII.
[2] *Loc. cit.*

ing accompanies all existence, and scorned a life of rank and ease. In rising from a period of contemplation this remarkable leader proclaimed himself as Buddha, the Enlightened One, the one who beheld the true nature of things.[1] Sorrow and evil had lost all hold on him; he had reached emancipation by the destruction of desire. Moreover, if people are to be "saved," they must do it by their own efforts; no mediator can relieve them of any part of the burden.

Buddhism is based on the social concept of equality. All human beings are to be paid respect; hatred is to be supplanted by love; life is to be filled with kindness. On the whole, however, Buddhism is not a positive force. The believer does not trouble himself about the world but chiefly about his own salvation. Buddhism does not aim at an ideal society, such as a Kingdom of God. It checks rather than fosters enterprise; it does not actively interest itself in the advancement of civilization. It favors a dull conformity to rule rather than a free cultivation of various gifts. It does not train or condition the attitudes toward virtuous and harmonious group action. It seeks "selflessness" and "quietism." It would escape life and its problems rather than attain "the development of life through mastery over its conditions." It is socially depressing; it furthers isolation rather than coöperation.

Christianity early made its world claim. Its first great missionary, St. Paul, carried it to Gentiles as well as to Jews. Its doctrine of brotherhood of man also gave it a world flavor. Its later missionaries have braved disease and death in order "to evangelize the world," and to set up Christian churches in all lands. Its social emphasis is implicit in the injunction of its founder "to love thy neighbor as thyself;" social ideals and service have been carried far and wide. In it religion assumes extensive social expressions and accepts varied social obligations.[2]

[1] Allan Menzies, *op. cit.*, Ch. XX.
[2] In Christianity also religion finds intolerant, dogmatic, and vicious behavior, but at its best it rises to cosmopolitan claims.

SOCIAL PHASES OF CHRISTIANITY

The social principles of Christianity originated in the teachings of the Hebrew prophets and the other founders of the Hebrew or Jewish religion; they received a dynamic impetus in the teachings of Jesus; then they lay dormant for centuries, in fact, until about 1885, when they began to be reinterpreted.[1] For centuries the individual and the social interpretations of Christianity remained divorced. Theology tended to build up the individual principles of religion at the expense of the social. On the other hand, Jesus apparently made them inseparable, for he insisted upon the test of loving one's neighbor as a test of loving one's God.

Within the decades since the social principles in the teachings of Jesus have been discovered they have been attacked by fearful theologians and by narrow-gauge laymen. These social principles are not to be considered as the whole of Christianity but as "the lost tribes of Christian thought." When given their due emphasis they enable Christianity to take a lead in directing the solution of the world's problems. They furnish the vision and the dynamic for solving the labor and capital problem, divorce, housing, and even war. Christianity could not prevent the World War, for its social principles had been submerged for eighteen centuries while the war pattern of settling disputes had been practiced and ingrained into the body politic of many nations for eighteen centuries and more. During the World War many people in the fighting nations reduced Christianity to a national religion headed by a national god; many lost sight of the social principles of Christianity entirely in the midst of the killing.

It became the task of St. Paul to work out some of the world-wide implications of Christianity. In Christianity it was expected that all racial differences would disappear. "In Christ there is neither Jew nor Greek."[2]

---

[1] By religious leaders such as Washington Gladden and Josiah Strong.
[2] Romans 3: 29.

As Jesus taught, God is the Father and human beings are his children unless by their behavior they belie or decry the relationship. All that a person needs to do is to live in communion with man and God on a socially responsible level. Religion thus becomes the active communion of children with their father; the father and children are to dwell together in loving behavior. Religion is not an apparatus but a process of love. He who acts on a lower level than love breaks the tie and by that act grows irreligious. Prayer is necessary, for the child must keep in tune with the father. The process is simple, deep, broad, mutual, dynamic, constructive, and holy.

In its essence Christianity inspires a person not to withdraw from the world, but to realize his own richest possibilities in and through group life. Its ideal of a Kingdom of Heaven may find elementary but genuine expression on earth, and through human personalities. In fact the perfect society has begun in the personalities of those who live in terms of love and social responsibility. Realization of religion means living according to the principle of the brotherhood of man and the principle of the Fatherhood of God. Only in these two principles when integrated can a person realize his complete emergence; nothing less is satisfactory to the whole person.

Not only is Christianity personally developmental but it is socially constructive. In its finest expression it not only identifies itself with a large measure of human freedom but it tends to unite all persons in a vast world brotherhood. It has taken the richest sentiments connected with the family, namely, the ideas of brotherhood and fatherhood, and given them the largest possible group application. It has possibilities of becoming the super-socializing force of all times.

The Kingdom of God is both a spiritual and a social ideal; the two elements are inseparable. Those religious persons would seem to be mistaken who say: "We are not here to make the world any better; we have to pass through it on the way to glory." Equally mistaken are those who conceive of the Kingdom of God as a social ideal only, who are simply humanitarian, and who proclaim: "Every man a well-fed, well-housed, and well-cared-for human being." The Kingdom lays stress upon character, love, and social ideals. It implies "good conditions, a perfect environment, justice to all, wholesome dwellings, the fair reward of labor, opportunity for men to realize themselves,"[1] and in addition spiritual growth and the development of stimulating social bonds.

As a social and spiritual dynamic Christianity has operated in three directions. It has furnished social ideals, it has formed character, and it has evoked service.[2] (1) It gives new ideals of life, of personal, family, and group life. It affords a vital interpretation of marriage, and has "founded the Christian home." It emphasizes the child as a center of sacrificial living. It sets up ideals that are to transform human personalities and the world. It would create high-minded, sympathetic, and progressive groups everywhere.

(2) "Christianity has produced the highest type of character known to man," says David Watson.[3] Without constructive character, it may be added, all group life would become a farce, and the world would disintegrate. Christianity lays heavy emphasis on moral traits. At its noblest it moves persons and peoples away from lives of selfishness, idleness, and vice to lives of sacrifice, fidelity, and service.

(3) The dynamic of Christian love has operated not only through high ideals and sturdy character, but also through social service. It has stood for doing good, for philanthropic endeavors, and self-sacrificing behavior. It has stimulated endless numbers of men and women to inaugurate and carry forward reform movements. Nearly every philanthropic movement in recent centuries had Christianity as one of its major dynamics. Countless missionary activities, full of sacrificial deeds, have been born of Christianity. Scientific training and the spiritual dynamic of a wholesome religious outlook combine to make an excellent foundation for social service.

[1] David Watson, *Social Advance* (Hodder and Stoughton, London, 1911), p. 28.
[2] *Ibid.*, Ch. II.   [3] *Ibid.*, p. 35.

After social and economic programs have been put into action, the spirit of constructive religion will be as useful as ever. After everyone reaches a level of material comfort, religion is still needed. No social or economic program suffices to abolish sorrow, or pain, or infirmity, or human regrets, or heartaches, or death. There come times in the lives of everyone, no matter how well padded his environment may be, when none of these things suffice, when the best of friends can do little more than stand by, mutely by. The religious spirit in its greatest sweep contains the largest group idea possible. It dares to include all human beings. It dares far more—to include all those who have lived well and died, those who are to live, and God—all in one almost inconceivably large group, living on, and ever developing.

Socio-Religious Problems

Religion like other phases of life tends to grow professionalized, to become narrow, to develop bigotry, and to fail to adjust itself to changing social needs. Persons have difficulty in living up to their religious expectations; religion fails to meet personal hopes. Many socio-religious problems or socio-personal problems in the religious realm, arise.

(1) A difficult task is that of affording all persons an appreciation of the highest attained religious concepts. Underlying this problem is that of coming to an agreement as to what are the highest religious concepts. Also basic is the problem of discovering new religious truths and of seeing more clearly the relation of the finite life to the infinite. However, if present religious truth and faith in their most helpful phases were known, accepted, and put into practice generally by mankind, the leading social and personal problems would be met.

(2) The tendency of religion everywhere is both socially and personally conservative. On one hand it ties up with vested interests, as in the case of Russia under the Czars, until a widespread adverse human reaction goes to the opposite extreme of atheism. On the other hand, it ties up with a person's prejudices and biases, his outworn sentiments, until his religion no

longer appeals to the new, inquiring generation. When a given practice has once been sanctioned by religion, it has been almost impossible to eliminate it until long after it has ceased to serve a useful purpose. At times the church has been one of the most conservative of group institutions. It has tended to identify itself with the conditions of a given decade and then to cling to the established methods long after the situation has changed.

(3) Generally in their social living persons fall below the religious ideals which they profess. Many instinctive impulses and tendencies are so persistent and so subtle that even some religious persons fail at unexpected moments. It is not possible of course that persons subject to the weaknesses of human nature should attain to religious perfection without a long struggle.

Then there are those who profess religion, but who live as hypocrites. The hypocrisy may be either conscious, or more or less habitual and unconscious. It is such behavior which harms religion unmeasurably. A man who supports the church but employs children, men, and women at less than living wages is a concrete example. A church member who gambles with the savings of hard-working people and through the failure of stock-manipulations causes elderly people to spend their days in virtual pauperism is another notorious example. Still another illustration is that of the lawyer who conducts a church school class but who at the same time for a liberal fee helps a client to dodge the legitimate laws of his country.

"He is an angel at home," said the chauffeur for a big business man, but he is "a devil in business, driving his employees as though they were slaves and crowding his competitors to the wall." The reverse is also true of other church members. "He is an angel to his stenographers and customers, but a devil at home to his wife." There is the churchman in good standing who boasts that he can always hire unskilled labor at less than the market rate. The exploited laborers however curse him, and worse still, they curse religion and the church. Men may be good husbands, good fathers, and good church members, but bad employers or employees, bad patriots, bad citizens.

(4) Religious, church, denominational rivalries do inestimable harm. It is such conflicts that belie the Christian's profession of love and brotherhood. If Christians, for example, cannot make their brotherhood principle work among themselves, how can they conscientiously ask unbelievers to accept their doctrines? Present sectarian divisions are socially, economically, religiously wasteful. Union and coöperation need to be substituted for sectarianism; fair play and love, for religious conflicts and hatreds. In a small experimental way the community church is developing as an antidote to religious division. The experiment has many weaknesses but also achievements to its credit. It serves not only the religious needs of the entire community, but in certain instances has taken the lead in reorganizing and building up the entire life of an entire community.[1]

(5) It has been one of the weaknesses of religion that it moves persons as individuals, but does not affect their behavior vitally in their group or social relationships. The process of saving individual souls has often failed in saving persons in all their group activities. It has been pointed out that the custom of appealing to individuals to seek personal salvation first of all is to arouse egoistic attitudes. A religion that leaves a person satisfied with saving his own soul is socially obstructive; religion must go further if it is to command widespread respect. Some claim that the best way for a person "to save his soul" is through saving the souls of other persons. The truly religious church, it has been claimed, is not the one which seeks primarily to build itself up, but that which builds up the community in which its members live and work.

(6) *Social service* as evidence of a religious attitude has grown rapidly in recent decades. It has also met with serious-minded rebuffs. It has been misunderstood and in places has misunderstood itself. The social service movement of the churches has developed particularly in the United States. In other countries

[1] Cf. A. C. Zumbrunnen, *The Community Church* (University of Chicago Press, 1922).

such as Europe, religion has been both other-worldly and charity-minded. Social service denies its high calling when it stoops to substitute "a soup and soap salvation" for spiritual regeneration. Moreover, it was never meant to provide bait for enticing the unchurched laboring man into the house of worship. Its chief concern is not with externalities or comforts but with getting the dynamic of divine love into all human groups and processes. One of its exponents explains:

> A religious community is not necessarily one that is full of churches, each seeking its own peculiar formulas and practices. It is rather a community which has become aware of its organic nature, which has found its soul, repented of its sins, come to conscious realization of its powers and needs, and is coördinating its forces, including its churches, in harmony with a power greater than itself, for the working out of its salvation.[1]

A church is purblind, if while it is satisfied with saving a few hundred souls, the lives of thousands are being gradually snuffed out in the same community by sinister agencies. While the church is engaged in individual soul saving, "evil gathers its corporate power, puts its hand upon the forces of social control," and nullifies the gains that come from evangelizing individuals. "Preach the Gospel and the rest will take care of itself," is a narrow creed. Any church which holds itself aloof from constructive human activities "is setting itself off from God, now and forever."

The important features of social service programs of religion are many: (a) These programs are based on the social injunctions of religious leaders, on the group character of religion, on social principles such as brotherhood of man and Fatherhood of God. They supplement, not supplant, the individual phases of religion; they indicate whether or not the individual is sincere and intelligent in his religious professions. They furnish a medium by which a religious person may test his religion and grow more genuinely religious. They represent a form of group worshipping.

[1] Harry F. Ward, *Social Evangelism* (Missionary Educational Movement, New York, 1915), p. 21.

(b) These programs call for a service procedure, organization, and training. They require a paid and volunteer corps of social service workers. They imply that everyone in the parish will become something of a service worker from the minister down. The minister will become an expert case work adviser regarding personal problems of maladjustment in religious beliefs, in marriage procedure, in parent-child training problems, and so on. He will develop both educational and activity programs of service within his parish.

(c) The church program includes social service classes, divided into study groups and training groups; addresses and sermons according to a schedule on all the leading social problems at home and abroad. In some parishes the Sunday morning service is distinctly devotional and worshipful, and the evening service is likewise devotional and worshipful in the sense of considering community, national, and world problems involved in the injunction: "Thou shalt love thy neighbor as thyself." [1]

(7) Christianity is developing a concrete social creed. In 1912, for instance, the Federal Council of Churches of Christ in America perfected a creed which however was revised twenty years later in 1932.

In comparing the Social Creed of 1932 with the first one adopted in 1912 new developments appear, such as: injunctions to the church to stand for (a) "subordination of speculation and the profit motive to the creative and coöperative spirit," (b) social "control of the credit and monetary systems and the economic processes for the common good," (c) "educational preparation for marriage, home-making, and parenthood," (d) "economic justice for the farmer," (e) "protection of the individual and society from the social, economic, and moral waste of any traffic in intoxicants," and (f) "repudiation of war" and "drastic reduction of armaments." [2] The new creed indicates that the churches are keeping up well with the social trends.

[1] Matthew 22:39.
[2] Graham Taylor, "The Church Keeps Up with Social Trends," *Survey*, LXIX:64-66 (February Midmonthly, 1933).

So important are the social creeds of religious bodies that the one adopted by the Federal Council of Churches of Christ in America in 1932 may be given here for careful scrutiny. It declares that the churches should stand for:

1. Practical application of the Christian principle of social well-being to the acquisition and use of wealth; subordination of speculation and the profit motive to the creative and coöperative spirit.

2. Social planning and control of the credit and monetary systems and the economic processes for the common good.

3. The right of all to the opportunity for self-maintenance; a wider and fairer distribution of wealth; a living wage, as a minimum, and above this a just share for the worker in the product of industry and agriculture.

4. Safeguarding of all workers, urban and rural, against harmful conditions of labor and occupational injury and disease.

5. Social insurance against sickness, accident, want in old age, and unemployment.

6. Reduction of hours of labor as the general productivity of industry increases; release from employment at least one day in seven, with a shorter working week in prospect.

7. Such special regulation of the conditions of work of women as shall safeguard their welfare and that of the family and the community.

8. The right of employees and employers alike to organize for collective bargaining and social action; protection of both in the exercise of this right; the obligation of both to work for the public good; encouragement of coöperatives and other organizations among farmers and other groups.

9. Abolition of child labor; adequate provision for the protection, education, spiritual nurture and wholesome recreation of every child.

10. Protection of the family by the single standard of purity; educational preparation for marriage, home-making and parenthood.

11. Economic justice for the farmer in legislation, financing of agriculture, transportation and the price of farm products as compared with the cost of machinery and other commodities which he must buy.

12. Extension of the primary cultural opportunities and social services now enjoyed by urban populations to the farm family.

13. Protection of the individual and society from the social, economic and moral waste of any traffic in intoxicants and habit-forming drugs.

14. Application of the Christian principle of redemption to the treatment of offenders; reform of penal and correctional methods and institutions, and of criminal court procedure.

15. Justice, opportunity and equal rights for all; mutual good will and coöperation among racial, economic and religious groups.

16. Repudiation of war, drastic reduction of armaments, participation in international agencies for the peaceable settlement of all controversies; the building of a coöperative world order.

17. Recognition and maintenance of the rights and responsibilities of free speech, free assembly, and a free press; the encouragement of free communication of mind with mind as essential to the discovery of truth.

Catholics and Jews likewise have well-worded creeds, declaring for needed social ideals. In fact it is at the point of social welfare needs that Catholics, Jews, and Protestants have been able to work together better than in any other connection. When Catholic, Jew, and Protestant stand shoulder to shoulder on a commonly accepted social welfare program, a new social order may be envisaged.

(8) The social service activity program of religion refers to meeting neighborhood needs and the building of a community of forward-looking and forward-moving persons and groups. It would condition persons in terms of national and world welfare. It would eliminate all behavior that blights human hopes and lives. It would so meet the needs of people in terms of better working and living conditions if it had half an opportunity that the churches would be crowded to the doors "by the people who now shun them."

Social service attitudes are neither the whole of religion nor a disconnected adjunct; they are an integral, organic phase of genuine religion. Neither welfare-minded persons who are outside of the church nor individually-minded persons inside the church are representative of religion at its best. The integration of personal religion and social service presages a new type of religious dynamic that may yet transform the world.

Life is surrounded on every hand by mystery, miracle, and the unknown. That which is not known far exceeds the known and the understood. Through feeling-thinking-behaving man may interpret the mysteries of life, acquire faith in God, and stand up against the odds of life which at times are almost overwhelming. These interpretations often take the form of poetry, music, and other forms of art as well as the forms of philosophy and religious treatises. These forms are the vehicles of those things which are felt to be true but whose truth has not been proved or disproved. The child who early learns to perceive the handiwork of the Creator in the beauty about him, to feel inspired in the presence of such handiwork, and to act as a worthy person in a creative world will hate ugliness, imperfection, meanness, littleness, pettiness, and narrowness; he will create beauty, and justice, and love, which are the finest fruits of a socio-religious personality.

PROBLEMS

1. Distinguish between individual religion and social religion.
2. Why is neither adequate?
3. What is social salvation?
4. In what ways may religion make a person more individualistic?
5. In what ways more socialized?
6. Why are many religionists intolerant of social welfare plans?
7. What forces besides religion produce high types of character?
8. How is religion the most radical social force in the world?
9. What is the leading social ideal which Christianity has given to the world?
10. "Is it an advantage or a disadvantage to Christianity that it began among the working classes?"
11. What is your church doing as a social service institution?
12. What change of any kind would you make in the "Social Creed of the Churches"?
13. How is modern religion different as a social force from primitive man's religion?
14. What is your own definition of religion?
15. What are the essentials for a world religion, that is, for all mankind?
16. Compare the social emphasis of Christianity with that of Judaism, of Mohammedanism, and of Buddhism.

17. Why has Christianity failed to stop war?

18. Why is it difficult for one to live up to the social teachings of his religion?

19. Why have there been so many divisions and persecutions in a religion that stresses the principles of love and brotherhood of man?

20. Is there a contradiction between a personal and a social religion?

READINGS

BATTEN, S. Z., *The Social Task of Christianity* (Fleming H. Revell, Chicago, 1911).

CASE, S. M., *The Social Origins of Christianity* (University of Chicago Press, 1923).

DAVIS, JEROME, editor, *Christian and Social Adventuring* (The Century Company, New York, 1927).

DOUGLAS, H. PAUL, *The Church in the Changing City* (George H. Doran Company, New York, 1927).

——, *How to Study the City Church* (Doubleday, Doran and Company, New York, 1928).

EDDY, SHERWOOD, *Religion and Social Justice* (George H. Doran Company, New York, 1927).

ELLWOOD, CHARLES A., *Christianity and Social Science* (The Macmillan Company, New York, 1923).

——, *Reconstruction of Religion* (The Macmillan Company, New York, 1922).

FRY, C. L., *Diagnosing the Rural Church* (George H. Doran Company, New York, 1929).

GLADDEN, WASHINGTON, *Social Salvation* (Houghton Mifflin Company, Boston, 1902).

HOLT, ARTHUR E., *Social Work in the Churches* (Pilgrim Press, New York, 1922).

JOHNSON, FREDERICK E., *The Social Work of the Churches* (Federal Council of the Churches of Christ in America, New York, 1930).

KIRKPATRICK, CLIFFORD, *Religion in Home Affairs* (John Wiley and Sons, Inc., New York, 1929).

MATTHEWS, SHAILER, *The Social Teachings of Jesus* (The Macmillan Company, New York, 1909).

McCOWN, C. C., *The Genesis of the Social Gospel* (Alfred A. Knopf, New York, 1929).

PEABODY, FRANCIS G., *Jesus Christ and the Social Question* (The Macmillan Company, New York, 1900).

RAUSCHENBUSCH, WALTER, *Christianity and the Social Crisis* (The Macmillan Company, New York, 1908).

——, *Christianizing the Social Order* (The Macmillan Company, New York, 1912).

SOARES, T. G., *Social Institutions and the Ideals of the Bible* (Abingdon Press, New York, 1915).

TAYLOR, GRAHAM, *Religion in Social Action* (Dodd, Mead and Company, New York, 1913).

VOGT, PAUL L., *Church Coöperation in Community Life* (Abingdon Press, New York, 1921).

WALLIS, LOUIS, *Sociological Study of the Bible* (University of Chicago Press, 1912).

WARD, HARRY F., *Social Evangelism* (Missionary Educational Movement, New York, 1915).

——, *Which Way Religion?* (The Macmillan Company, New York, 1931).

WEGENER, A. B., *Church and Community Recreation* (The Macmillan Company, New York, 1924).

WINCHESTER, B. S., *The Church and Adult Education* (Richard R. Smith, Inc., New York, 1930).

ZUMBRUNNEN, A. C., *The Community Church* (University of Chicago Press, 1922).

CHAPTER X

THE RACIAL GROUP

Every person possesses racial traditions, prejudices, and pride. Every small child is conditioned, as a rule, to believe that his race is the best race, but only a few persons perceive how impossible it is for every race on the earth to be "the best."

Since nearly everyone is proud of his race it is very easy for race conflict to flare up, especially when everyone holds premises concerning his own race which are partly false. To have one's race praised is to feel a sense of race superiority, but to have one's race attacked in any way is to experience race antagonism.

While the human race probably had a common origin in regions extending roughly from England to Java, its earliest groups wandered in many directions. These aborigines settled in and increased in the various inhabitable areas of the globe. As a result of different physical, climatic, ecological, psychical, and social conditions, early peoples developed separate cultures and became more and more differentiated from each other, and with the rise of ethnology they have been designated by definite racial names.

In a sense racial groups are the product of migration. It is migration that has been basic to the making, the remaking, the conflicts, and even the assimilation of races. It is largely migration that has created new races, caused invasion by a race of an area already occupied by another race, and separated mankind into various population centers.

RACIAL MIGRATION

Many social groups are composed of two classes, the native-born and the immigrant, those born within the group and those who come in as outsiders from other groups. The native-born persons have been called genetic members, and the immigrants, congregate members. The invaders are especially significant for they come from other groups bringing a special set of culture patterns with them. At once culture conflicts arise and acculturation begins.

Man has always been "a wanderer on the face of the earth." Since earliest times he has wandered to and fro in search of a better living. He has always been more or less dissatisfied with his situation at any given time, and has felt that if he were elsewhere he would have a better opportunity and would be happier. Society seems to be made up of many persons in whom this spirit of unrest and dissatisfaction is inherent. In fact persons who are easily satisfied have rarely developed fully. Civilization itself is a product largely of aspiring, hopeful, energetic attitudes. Persons looking for larger opportunity are prone to migrate.

The leading single cause of migration is perhaps economic, that is, the desire to make a better living. Among primitive peoples hunger was a primary force which set the human race in motion. Recently the immigrant became "a seller of labor seeking a more favorable market." Since the economic advantages of the United States, Canada, Argentine, Australia, New Zealand, and Brazil have been striking, these countries during the past century have been the chief immigration countries of the world. Italy, Germany, Poland, South Slavic countries, Scandinavia, England, and Ireland have been among the leading emigration countries. Political oppression, religious persecution, adventuresome urges, and desire to join relatives, together with economic dissatisfaction are the main causes of migration.

Migration was at first characterized by aimless *wandering*, as in the case of primitive tribes moving up and down valleys in search of food for themselves and their flocks.[1] It sometimes expressed itself as a *mass wandering*, in which a whole population

[1] This analysis of the types of migration is based on A. C. Haddon, *Wanderings of Peoples* (University Press, Cambridge, England, 1911).

moved slowly from one section of the earth to another, notably the movement of the Huns into Europe.[1]

Migration was sometimes *forced*; weaker peoples or offending groups have been exiled or driven out of one country and compelled to seek refuge elsewhere. Then there came a period known as *colonization*, when for three centuries or more, beginning with the latter part of the sixteenth century, nations officially sent out small groups of people as colonists to take possession of a given area in the name of the parent country.[2]

Immigration is an unofficial movement of people, either as individuals or families, who on their own initiative move from one established country to another, usually to a newer country, for the major purpose of improving their living conditions.[3] Whenever the economic advantages of two countries are noticeably unequal, population will flow to the more favored nation, providing there are no restrictions. When the advantages become somewhat equalized, the population movement slows up. As the newer countries of the world have become populated, their free lands occupied, and their natural resources exploited, immigration has declined.

There are still millions of people, however, living in poverty in India, in China, and in other parts of the world, who if they learned of more favorable conditions elsewhere and were aided would form a wave of migration that would be engulfing. Nearly all the immigration countries of the world have experienced economic depression, widespread unemployment, and an increase in poverty in recent years, and hence have put up legislative barriers against immigrants. These barriers constitute another important factor in the recent decline in immigration.

Wandering, mass migration, forced migration, colonization, immigration—all these forms of the movements of people have in turn pretty largely ceased. If immigration, the latest form

[1] Cf. Henry P. Fairchild, *Immigration* (The Macmillan Company, New York, 1925), pp. 13–17.
[2] Cf. A. G. Keller, *Colonization* (Ginn and Company, Boston, 1908).
[3] Cf. Henry Fairchild, *op. cit.*, p. 26.

of population movement, is reaching an end, what will be the result on racial conflicts, and what new form will migration take?

At the time that immigration restrictions are being put into operation, radio is beginning to carry the ideas of one culture group through the air to other groups. Legislation stops the migration of peoples but radio multiplies the migration of ideas and other culture patterns. Sooner or later it will not be necessary for people to migrate in order to take advantage of opportunities elsewhere. As culture programs are carried back and forth from one country to another over national boundaries and immigration barriers by air there will come about a levelling down and up of all cultures. Declining migration will tend to cut down racial conflicts; increasing international broadcasts if kept on a constructive level will foster good will and similarities if not cultural unity.

Migration is also a social phenomenon of importance within a nation, for people move extensively from rural areas to urban; from one part of a city to another; from the city to rural regions. In a country covering a large area such migration brings different culture patterns and people into contact, conflict, and accommodation.

Since the person who changes groups takes with him culture patterns different from those in the group to which he goes, many problems arise. The greater this difference in patterns or values the greater the problems. When different standards of living, different types of governmental views, different religious beliefs come into contact, problems of adjustment are created.

The industrial problems arising from migration are many. The immigrant often experiences trouble while striving to find acceptable work at satisfactory wages. To the extent that the conditions under which he works are agreeable to him the immigrant learns to love the new country and desires to become a citizen. If these conditions are disagreeable, or if the immigrant is mistreated or exploited, he becomes suspicious and develops a sense of injustice. He moves toward radicalism and revolution, and away from loyalty to the country to which he has migrated.

The living problems of the immigrant are also important. In the United States the influx of immigrants for several decades has usually been to the overcrowded sections of the population centers. The immigrant finds that congested housing in a big city is more serious than poor housing in the rural area from which he has come. Moreover, he may have had his expectations too high and as a result suffers a severe jolt when he finds that living conditions are no better than they were at home or perhaps that they are worse.

The social problems of the immigrants are many and troublesome. If the immigrant does not know the language of the adopted country, he is isolated and has difficulty in understanding many of its culture patterns. A real barrier exists between immigrants and natives where neither group speaks the language of the other. Misunderstandings due to differences in cultures easily arise. The stranger, foreigner, and immigrant are generally regarded with prejudice. This sentiment usually expresses itself in condescending attitudes, in scorn, and sometimes in derision. The problem emerges in racial conflicts.

RACIAL GROUP CONFLICTS

Wherever racial groups markedly different exist together in considerable numbers, race problems may become insuperable. A race characterized by physical differences wears a racial uniform that cannot be removed. A race whose members arouse *adverse sensory reactions* in others feels the sting of *antipathy*. The persons against whom antipathy is expressed usually cannot help themselves; they generally find such antipathy almost impossible to allay or to overcome, especially if it be due to color of skin or to facial angle.

A race which *competes* for a livelihood, for an occupation, for a neighborhood foothold, or for any other form of status, social, economic, political, religious, educational, with natives suffers the bitterness of *prejudices* expressed against it that at times is unbearable. When the competition is removed, then race prejudice will be alleviated. The two entirely different

of antipathy and prejudice are worth pondering; the
need to be kept distinct even when the general or inclusive
term of race antagonism is being used.

Some persons would like to show no race prejudice but circumstances hinder them. Rather than to suffer loss of economic
or social status they ignore their best attitudes. A fair statement of this predicament is given herewith:

> There is no question but that to have Japanese and Negroes move
> in here would lower the value of our property. It is an economic
> problem much more than an ethical one. Even now with the Negroes
> as close as they are, white people simply won't buy property in this
> block. Yet it is not only an economic problem. The people have
> lived here in this district a long time and they feel at home. We, for
> example, have lived here thirty-one years. Some have lived here
> longer. Our feeling is that if the Japs and Negroes had not moved in
> so close to us, all this property would have boomed with the Stadium
> and the Park not far away. It is a lovely place to live but their com-
> ing has made it less desirable.
>
> The situation is rather difficult for us too. If we want to raise
> money on our property, for example, the banks hesitate to loan as
> much on property where the colored people or the Japanese are
> encroaching. . . .
>
> We neighbors must really stand together, for it is clear that if the
> man next door sold his house to a Negro or to a Japanese my
> property would immediately become worth a thousand dollars less.[1]

Often a person who claims that he possesses no race prejudice has the most deep-seated kind. He has learned to protect
his status by keeping members of another race "in their place"
and is unaware of the serious character of his race antagonism.
A case in point follows:

> I have no prejudice against the colored people. I have always
> had colored servants and nurse girls for my children and I like them.
> I have never known them to be dishonest. My husband employs
> seven colored men and his experience has been the same as mine. I
> don't care to live next door to a colored family nor across the street
> and if they do come this side of Raymond, I certainly will move out.

[1] Quoted by Bessie A. McClenahan, *The Changing Urban Neighborhood* (University of Southern California, Los Angeles, 1929), p. 85.

I like the colored people, they are excellent people but they do not know their place. It is one thing for me to invite the children of my colored woman who has worked for me for twenty years to come over and see our Christmas tree, but what do they do but the next week turn around and invite my children to come and see their tree. That shows how well they know their places, as if I would allow my children to go down there to "Nigger" town to see their tree! [1]

The most far-reaching race conflict in the Western hemisphere is between the white and colored peoples in the United States. It all started in 1619 when white Virginia colonists brought in a few Negroes as slaves. The evils of slavery received increasing public attention during the middle of the nineteenth century. At that time slavery was growing industrially unprofitable in competition with the wage system. It was attacked bitterly by abolitionists and during the Civil War it was ended. With freedom came suffrage that threw illiterate Negroes into political power alongside of white Southerners who liked Negroes as slaves and as long as they stayed "in their place," that is, on a distinctly lower level socially. To have Negroes rule over them was unbearable and hence the suffrage amendment to the Constitution of the United States was nullified.

Slavery, then freedom, then disenfranchisement—this was the sequence until Booker T. Washington added a fourth factor, namely, industrial education. In the early part of the present century Booker T. Washington's program developed widely. Washington urged first industrial efficiency, then professional efficiency, claiming that as the Negro showed himself capable and worthy and friendly the white man's antagonism to the Negro would gradually disappear. In social relations the two racial groups are to remain separate as the fingers of the hand, but in other matters they are to work together. [2] By showing his worth the Negro can undermine the antagonism of the white people.

[1] Quoted by Bessie A. McClenahan, *op. cit.*, p. 84.
[2] Booker T. Washington, *Up from Slavery* (A. L. Burt Company, New York, 1900), p. 221.

The white man in turn has a definite responsibility, which consists in being able to recognize true worth, ability, and dependable personality wherever they may be found irrespective of color. It is assumed that in a democracy the white man will return the vote to the Negro as soon as the latter is really qualified. An educational test would be meritorious, for the mere fact that a person is born in a country and has reached 21 years of age is no guarantee that he is a competent voter. Of course an educational test would need to be applied indiscriminately to all persons alike, Caucasians, Negroes, Indians, immigrants. It is claimed that as the Negro reaches the higher educational levels his birth rate drops to the level of the white race and hence that political justice can be made possible without creating special problems.

In turn the Negro must assume a special responsibility, namely, of putting his case upon the achievement and merit level rather than upon the boasting and "fighting back" planes. A great deal of race prejudice is engendered by the less developed race flaunting its successes before the more developed group. There is a vicious circle here, for when the more advanced race "lords it over" the less advanced, the latter are likely to retaliate by the most striking weapon at their command, namely, by the assumption of superiority on the slightest excuse, which reaction in turn creates more "lording it over" on the part of the more advanced group purely as a defense mechanism.

In recent years the Negro opponents of Booker T. Washington have gained widespread recognition under the able leadership of such men as Dr. W. E. B. DuBois. The opposition urge the Negro to assert his "rights" and to fight vigorously against the injustices being done to their race. Only in this way it is claimed that the Negro may get the real opportunities which he needs. Only in this way will the white race give heed to the fair claims of the colored race. Any procedure that is less mild will leave the Negro suffering from wage slavery and loss of status. This procedure, however, may easily aggravate race friction and lead to bloody disturbances.

The World War and the post-War developments have increased the social distance between the white and colored peoples in the United States. The Negro soldiers to the number of 400,000 were in the American Expeditionary Forces; one-half of this number went to France. They were told that they were fighting for democracy. To their surprise they found that for the most part the color line was not drawn in France and Italy, especially among the peasant peoples. Far more to their surprise, to their chagrin, and their bitter resentment they found upon their return to the United States that "the color line" was drawn tighter than when they went merrily away to fight to make "the world safe for democracy." This resentment spread among nearly all Negroes and culminated in a troublesome social unrest that was countered by a recrudescence of Ku Klux Klan activities, by night-riding, and other threatening moves by white people. These counter activities have used fear as a weapon of social control, but fear suppresses and aggravates. It never settles anything but multiplies the sense of injustice among those against whom it is directed.

One of the worst features of racial group conflicts is lynching and rioting. Fear and brutality are miserable tools of social control. They produce undying hatreds besides failing to settle difficulties justly. They create a greatly embittered atmosphere in which the ordinary race problems are made unusually difficult to solve.

As long as lynching is considered to be a local offense and lynchers are tried in local courts, no justice can be expected. The local jury will exonerate their fellow citizens, for their feelings are similar. When lynching is viewed as a federal offense and tried in a federal court sitting at a distance from the area where a lynching occurred, the chances of a dispassionate judgment are greatly improved. Lynching is a form of intimidation, bad in itself, and defiant of the established law of the land.[1]

[1] For a current statement of the laws in the United States concerning lynching, see J. H. Chadbourn, *Lynching and the Law* (University of North Carolina Press, 1933).

The most promising method of dealing with both "the Negro problem" (as seen by white people) and "the Negro's problem" (as seen by colored people) is through local joint committees in every community where white and colored people reside. In the Southern states at least 800 interracial committees, generally under religious auspices, have been formed; perhaps one-third of these have achieved worth-while results. White people in the South have taken the initiative, and in the main, have selected conservative colored people to serve with them on the same committee. Liberal white people and conservative colored people meeting together can iron out many difficulties, and most important, can create good will, whereas conservative Southern white people and radical colored people could not even meet together around the same table. When trained and broad-minded white and colored leaders meet at the same counsel table to discuss in good faith the problems which concern them mutually in any community the results are incomparably superior to leaving these same difficulties to be settled by race riots, which usually are begun by the hoodlums of both the conflicting races. Upon the basis of these local conferences and adjustments it will be possible to work out methods for solving race problems on a larger scale. From the concrete and specific and local to the general and national and world-wide is a logical sequence for a racial adjustment procedure.

Race antipathy can be undermined only by agreeable experiences, and race prejudice can be destroyed only by eliminating competition. Much race antagonism arises from misunderstanding, and from the ignorance of the potential worth of "the other fellow." When the Negro permits his increasing worth to speak for itself and is enabled to work out his advancement without creating competition, and when white people treat colored people on their merits, race problems are on the way to a satisfactory solution. If the Negro's problem can be solved then all other race problems can be met, for none seem more difficult to handle.[1]

[1] For a valuable symposium of eight articles on the Tuskegee Institute point of view see the *Journal of Educational Sociology*, VII : 149–205.

RACE RELATIONS CYCLES

When races of similar physical traits and culture patterns come together without competing, assimilation occurs. When races widely different in physical type or in cultural patterns or in both come in contact, or when they compete, a conflict ensues that pursues a definite cycle of relationships.[1]

(1) Newcomers of a strange race are viewed first with *curiosity*. Sympathy is aroused in favor of the peculiar stranger. His strangeness coupled with fewness of numbers and apparent helplessness arouses a harmless interest in him. He may be pitied or even laughed at but in a friendly way.

(2) If he comes to do work that natives find disagreeable he meets with an economic welcome, particularly on the part of employers. They see in him a source of "cheap labor," and encourage him to send for compatriots from his own country. If wages are higher than at home his compatriots respond in large numbers.

(3) When many immigrants come, especially if they come rapidly, industrial antagonism develops. When native workers find the wage scale going down because of the competition of foreigners, the latter at once feel the brunt of antagonism. Propaganda starts and the flames of prejudice leap upward until the newcomers are helplessly encircled by mistrust, fear, antagonism, and possible hatred. Organized labor often leads the defense campaign.

(4) Political antagonism quickly follows. Politicians see a chance to win votes from natives by denouncing the dangerous foreigners. The politicians grow bold and reckless in attacking immigrants, for the latter not being naturalized during their first five years in the country have no vote. The immigrants are depicted as bringing in degrading customs or as becoming the parents of hordes of children who one day will become voting citizens and will favor the parent's homeland. Patriotic societies take up the cudgels against the foreigner.

[1] Based on an analysis made by the writer in the *American Journal of Sociology*, XXXV: 612–17, under the title, "A Race-Relations Cycle."

(5) Social antagonism arises sooner or later. Native-born parents object to the presence of the children of foreigners in the same school and on the playground with their children. Low-grade conditions where the foreigners live are deplored, but if some of the more progressive of the latter desire to better their living conditions and attempt to move into a better neighborhood, they feel an outburst of bitter antagonism.

(6) Legislative antagonism is the climax. All the antagonistic forces combine to secure restrictive legislation. Sometimes it is legislation debarring immigrants from entering the country; sometimes it is legislation preventing land ownership. At any rate the further advance of the "undesirable immigrants" is blocked.

(7) A period of quiescence sets in. With the danger past, the antagonism subsides. Even a degree of friendship may be professed for the immigrants whose increase by migration has been stopped. Prejudice gives way to indifference and in a few cases to sympathetic interest. The persecuted immigrants are left to get along as best as they may with their wings clipped.

(8) Ultimately the second generation problem develops. Children grow up as persons without a country. In theory they are the heirs of two countries, but actually they are out of touch with the country of their parents and are not fully accepted by the land of their birth. They learn the language and customs of the latter country but are not accepted because they look like their parents, and hence are treated as foreigners. At the same time they have broken away from parental attitudes and values so far that they are partly disowned by the parents and they would never be satisfied to return permanently to the parental homeland.

(9) The third generation problem duplicates the second generation one. However, it is less severe. The third generation are more like the natives of the adopted country than were the second generation in personal appearance, physical type, and in culture patterns. They are less likely to be taken for foreigners; they are given more opportunities and on the whole

their difficulties are ameliorated considerably. They are on the road to assimilation and to general acceptance but have a long ways to go.

Another type of race relations cycle begins (1) in a curious interest in new immigrants, (2) in an economic welcome, and then moves on not in a spirit of antagonism but (3) of friendly approval, (4) of adjustment and accommodation, (5) of assimilation, acculturation, naturalization, and (6) of amalgamation. The essence of this cycle is found in the type of native-born persons whom the immigrant contacts and in the conditions under which the contacts are made. This type of person is known for his tolerance, good will, and cosmopolitanism. The favorable conditions are devoid of competition, and hence race prejudice is not aroused.

RACIAL GROUP ASSIMILATION

The presence together of persons racially different not only leads to conflicts but also to *assimilation*. In its original meaning assimilation refers to the adoption by one people of the culture patterns and the personal attitudes of another people. In a more developed sense it means giving as well as receiving; it involves a unifying of culture patterns and of attitudes. Both the incoming race and the native race mutually contribute to the building of a synthesis of attitudes and values.

It was once thought that the immigrant should give up his traditions and customs and adopt *en toto* those of the country to which he migrates. If he is not willing to do this he should hurry back home, or should not have come at all. Such a method usually means that the immigrant is to shift from one group to an intolerant group. He is to put off one culture and put on another, pretty much as he would exchange one coat for another. This demand by the native group is based on ignorance concerning how personality develops; it is also grounded on an exaggerated race pride and group egotism.

Another theory is that the immigrant should be "melted into the body politic." He should throw himself, culture patterns and all, into the melting pot, and lose his racial identity in his adopted national group. Although there is merit in this theory, it does not allow sufficiently for personality traits; an immigrant cannot easily and jauntily throw away his connections with his homeland, with his childhood days, and with the country in which perhaps his parents or other relatives live. No one wants to lose his identity suddenly and entirely.

The belief that an immigrant should give up and forget his native language as soon as possible is begotten of false local pride. In his native language the immigrant brings a precious gift to any country. A truly cultured group is one in which many of its members are bilinguists. Through the languages that they bring immigrants represent open doors to the cultures of the world. Through the language which they learn immigrants are able to understand the culture to which they come. Through both languages, immigrants become culture interpreters. If the new culture synthesis represents the best culture patterns of the races concerned, the product will be superior to either of its parts.

After the melting pot theory of assimilation became common in the United States,[1] the average American rested content in the belief that immigrants were being satisfactorily assimilated. He was not disturbed by the open fact that in all the congested districts of all large cities, the immigrants were living in ever enlarging colonies, having few contacts with Americans at their best.

The World War made evident to the American people that by virtue of their neglect, millions of persons had been allowed to live in the country without having any reasonable opportunity to become Americans in spirit. Thereupon Americanization of a narrow type was put into operation with a vengeance; it used compulsion, neglecting the fact that loyalty is a delicate human sentiment that cannot be forced. In fact the more you demand loyalty the farther away you drive it.

[1] Following the appearance of the drama, *The Melting Pot*, by Israel Zangwill, in 1909.

Immigrant children as a rule become assimilated first, immigrant fathers next, and mothers last of all. The fathers do not make their contacts under as broad or as favorable conditions as do children. Their contacts are found in factories and mills, where often they learn profanity and obtain their first impressions of the new culture (new to them) from the curses of foreman and bosses. Public schools and social settlements, however, have come to the rescue and have helped immigrants to learn the strange language and to acquire favorable impressions.

Immigrant mothers usually have the fewest opportunities to become assimilated. They have few contacts with the adopted land, its culture, for they are often circumscribed by the life in their own immigrant colony. They live in a small and isolated world. Fortunately, the visiting teacher [1] has helped to save the day for immigrant mothers. She serves as a beneficent friend and guide; she brings the best of the local civilization into the home of the immigrant mother and her family.

Closely related to assimilation is *amalgamation*, which is a biological union of peoples and the creation of new racial stocks. Racial intermixture or *miscegenation* may take place through marriage or outside of marriage and illegitimately. It is a process that cannot easily be forced and that is hard to control. It is a slow process of the generations and even of the centuries.

However, when assimilation has occurred, amalgamation naturally follows. When peoples come to think alike, possess somewhat similar culture patterns, and give each other equal status, then no objections are raised to amalgamation. For this reason different cultures with proud exponents resist assimilation as long as possible.

The amalgamation of races that are somewhat different from each other is to be favored. The result of such intermixture has often been a race stronger than either of the parent races. The English, Germans, Scotch-Irish are outstanding examples of at least partly amalgamated peoples.

[1] See the chapter on "The Educational Group."

The amalgamation of races widely different in physical types and in cultures has never taken place under normal or favorable conditions. It has occurred illegitimately, or where bitterly opposed by race prejudices and adverse public opinions. Nature apparently does not object to such intermixture of races but social standards forbid. The age-long controversy still rages around the "racialists," that is, around the people who claim that race represents distinct biological gaps with some races inherently superior and with others inherently inferior. The data against this theory are slowly but surely outbalancing the data that favor the theory. Apparently all races are blood relations. Apparently there is one human race with marked differences in external appearances and in acquired culture patterns.

Of all the major immigration countries Canada has perhaps shown the most intelligent understanding of the assimilation problem. Canada has analyzed her needs, determined upon the types of immigrants that she has needed, and then sent for them to come—from the United States, England, Scotland, Ireland, Scandinavia, and so on. She has officially encouraged certain types of persons to immigrate, namely, those for whom she has felt a specific need. When they have arrived at her gates she has helped them to become adjusted to the new conditions and tried to protect them from exploitation. Her immigration halls and employment offices have rendered free service. By softening the harsh conditions of adjustment, the immigrant's good will has been won.

Responsibility for non-assimilation rests upon both immigrants and natives. If the immigrant will show himself coöperative and a willing learner, and if the native will be tolerant, kindly, and afford opportunity, assimilation will take place more or less automatically. Favorable experiences at vital points condition immigrants so that they are turned into loyal citizens.

In the past the United States has placed emphasis upon the individual, and allowed the masses to increase and to become disgruntled. She has been busy developing or exploiting her natural resources to the advantage of a few. During her haste to exploit her natural resources, her masses, the immigrant masses, the farming masses, and the industrial masses, have become recalcitrant. The development of material values has gone ahead so fast and furiously that the spiritual values of good will and loyalty have been neglected.

New attitudes of helpfulness are needed in a polyglot racial nation such as the United States. When one comes to know the history of any race and to understand the struggles and disappointments of that race, he grows more friendly and in turn secures more friendly responses. If it is true that "in the highest and lowest spheres of thought and activity, all races are alike," [1] they have proved their essential unity, and the exponents of democracy may take hope.

Naturalization is partly an administrative procedure whereby an immigrant forswears allegiance to one country in favor of another. It has often been conducted in formal ways, with immigrants memorizing parts of the Constitution and of the laws of a country. It has at times represented merely a legalistic shift. Real naturalization is based on an actual change in the center of an immigrant's loyalties from his native country to his adopted country. Such a change comes about through no legalistic formulae but only on such grounds as better working conditions, better living conditions, and better personal treatment than was found in the home country.

The current tendency is to move toward an educational basis for naturalization. In the United States a curious situation exists, for the naturalization laws developed spasmodically. At first, in 1790, naturalization was opened chiefly to "free white people," and later, in 1870, naturalization was opened to Negroes. It has thus been made available to persons of the extreme colors of white and black but denied to intermediate shades.

Oriental immigrants thus are denied naturalization privileges.

[1] Edward A. Steiner, *Against the Current* (Fleming H. Revell, New York, 1910), p. 229.

It is a mistake to admit representatives of any race into one's country and then to hold them aloof by giving them no opportunity to assume the responsibilities of citizenship. It would be much wiser through educational training and tests to set the standards high for citizenship and for suffrage and then to open such priviliges only to such native-born and foreign-born persons as can qualify. Without question some foreign-born persons attain a higher standard of citizenship than do some native-born. With personal worth and potentiality being required for admission to a country, and with personal worth and public welfare activities as tests for voting, no racially discriminatory legislation would be needed.

PROBLEMS

1. Why do people migrate?
2. Have you or your parents moved from one house to another? Why?
3. Distinguish between inter-migration and intra-migration.
4. Distinguish between colonization and immigration.
5. How does migration cause progressiveness?
6. Why have immigrants tended to go to the already overcrowded areas in large cities?
7. "What is the underlying reason for permitting immigration to the United States?"
8. What is race antipathy? How may it be overcome?
9. What is race prejudice? How may it be reduced?
10. What is the Negro problem in the United States?
11. What is the Negro's problem in the United States?
12. What is a race relations cycle? Name two types.
13. What causes race conflicts?
14. What is assimilation?
15. What is amalgamation?
16. What is miscegenation?
17. What is naturalization?
18. What is a race?
19. How long does it take to make a race?

THE RACIAL GROUP 271

READINGS

ABBOTT, EDITH, *Historical Aspects of the Immigration Problems* (University of Chicago Press, 1926).

BOGARDUS, EMORY S., *Immigration and Race Attitudes* (D. C. Heath and Company, Boston, 1928).

Chicago Commission on Race Relations, *The Negro in Chicago* (University of Chicago Press, 1922).

DOWD, JEROME, *The Negro in American Life* (The Century Company, New York, 1926).

DUNCAN, HANNIBAL G., *Immigration and Assimilation* (D. C. Heath and Company, Boston, 1933).

EMBREE, EDWIN R., *Brown America* (The Viking Press, New York, 1931).

FAIRCHILD, H. P., *Immigration* (The Macmillan Company, New York, 1925).

FELDMAN, HERMAN, *Racial Factors in American Industry* (Harper and Brothers, New York, 1931).

GAMIO, MANUEL, *Mexican Immigration to the United States* (University of Chicago Press, 1930).

GARTH, T. R., *Race Psychology* (Whittlesey House, McGraw-Hill Book Company, Inc., New York, 1931).

JOHNSON, C. S., *The Negro in American Civilization* (Henry Holt and Company, New York, 1930).

LASKER, BRUNO, *Race Attitudes in Children* (Henry Holt and Company, New York, 1929).

MACLEAN, ANNIE M., *Modern Immigration* (J. B. Lippincott Company, Philadelphia, 1925).

MUNTZ, E. E., *Race Contact* (The Century Company, New York, 1927).

PANUNZIO, CONSTANTINE, *Immigration Crossroads* (The Macmillan Company, New York, 1927).

REUTER, E. B., *Race Mixture* (Whittlesey House, McGraw-Hill Book Company, Inc., New York, 1931).

WIRTH, LOUIS, *The Ghetto* (University of Chicago Press, 1928).

YOUNG, DONALD, *American Minority Peoples* (Harper and Brothers, New York, 1932).

YOUNG, PAULINE V., *The Pilgrims of Russian Town* (University of Chicago Press, 1932).

CHAPTER XI

THE COMMUNITY GROUP

A community is a social group with some degree of we-feeling and with definite human boundaries. To develop a real community of spirit it is necessary for all the members of a community to participate and to acquire a sense of belonging. A community may be limited to a specific area or it may extend to all who commune together in the fellowship of similar attitudes and values. A community may be composed of several neighborhoods; it may extend to a nation; it may reach beyond national boundaries. A community has been currently defined as "a group of people living in a contiguous geographic area, having common centers of interests and activities, and functioning together in the chief concerns of life." [1]

Community organization is the basic way in which people react concerning the various phases of life. The older Chinese have a family-clan-village community organization. The older Japanese have a feudal-bureaucratic type. In the United States an individualistic-industrial form of community organization has prevailed. In the family-clan-village organization nationalism is slow to develop and China today suffers from being a house divided into many parts against itself. A bureaucratic organization makes the individual an automaton. An industrial type hampers spiritual vision.

Community organization also has an administrative aspect. A community may organize itself to meet many of its needs. In the concrete a local community may be organized for recreation and pageant purposes, to send representatives to a city council in support of needed local measures, to work for more

[1] Loren D. Osborn and Martin H. Neumeyer, *The Community and Society* (American Book Company, New York, 1933), p. 8.

reasonable water or transit rates, to take care of its own needy persons, and in so doing it may develop a genuine community spirit.

Communities are becoming *communalities*, that is, a grouping together of persons with common attitudes and values, but who are spatially scattered.[1] The closely-knit community of a few decades ago in the United States is being supplanted by psycho-social unities of people possessing a wide spatial "scatter."

> This situation suggests that a type of association, supplementary to neighborhood or community, is being developed, which is located wherever the means of transportation can carry the person; which is defined in social contacts not limited spatially; and which may be called the *communality*. The communality is a social grouping for carrying on an activity, whose members are drawn together on the basis of the common interest or interests subserved. Neither the communality itself nor its total membership is specifically related to any local area. It is an activity-circle. It is functional and not spatial.[2]

THE NEIGHBORHOOD

As a child the neighborhood came to one's attention through playmates, through family participation with a few persons living near by, and through family conversation, often uncomplimentary, about other persons living in the vicinity. In large cities today the neighborhood is largely a group of "nigh-dwellers"; it is a group characterized chiefly by the fact that the members live within a certain geographic area. In a rural neighborhood people may live somewhat apart although within a specific area, but they know each other well. A village neighborhood involves persons living closely together and being well acquainted with each other. An immigrant neighborhood includes people from a foreign country and their children, who are mutually acquainted, who live in close proximity to each other, and who possess a common group loyalty.

[1] See Bessie A. McClenahan, *The Changing Urban Neighborhood* (University of Southern California, 1929), Ch. I.
[2] Bessie A. McClenahan, *op. cit.*, p. 108.

The neighborhood is a loose integration of several family groups. Most people like to live near other people even though they do not have much to do with the nigh-dwellers. Children and women feel the neighborhood appeal more than do men. Social bonds, however, are rarely organized, except when a neighborhood enterprise develops, such as a demand for material improvements. A neighborhood often has no specific form of group control except unorganized group opinion borne hither and yon on the wings of gossip. Its lack of organized social aims explains its main weakness as a group phenomenon.

The neighborhood feud is common, spectacular, and lasting. Since the neighborhood is composed of family groups living in close proximity and experiencing personal contacts of all sorts, conflict is likely to arise at any time. As a result of the highly personal nature of the neighborhood, people easily take sides. The neighborhood feud usually begins with a disagreement between two families over a boundary line between property, over live stock, over children, or over a disparaging remark that one person is reported to have made about some member of another person's family. The imagination works feverishly, tongues wag freely, and an alleged wrong is multiplied. Gossip does its deadly work, and a neighborhood becomes divided into opposing camps.

The feud illustrates the neighborhood group in its worst behavior. It may run for years. In remote mountain districts it may lead to murder, and last until all the thirty-two MacGregors have been killed, and all but one of the thirty-three McIntoshes, leaving only one McIntosh alive and thus demonstrating to a disinterested world that the McIntoshes have won.

In the modern large city the neighborhood is losing its former entity as evidenced by the fact that nearly everyone can stand in his front door and behold the homes of a number of his neighbors whose names he does not know. Many people do not wish to neighbor with their neighbors. Old time neighbors are giving way to nigh-dwellers, while people "neighbor" with persons "living all over town."

I don't know anything about the neighborhood. I don't like it and take no interest in it. We have been here a year and bought only for investment. We have nothing whatsoever to do with my neighbors. I don't even know their names or know them to speak to. My best friends live in the city but by no means in this neighborhood. We belong to no clubs and we do not attend any local church. We go auto riding, visiting, and up town to the theaters.[1]

We are renting and have been here six years. . . . We like to live here because of the conveniences, the local shops, and the junior high school. I don't want to neighbor and I do not know how people neighbor. . . .

I know nothing about the neighborhood and I never did have anything to do with my neighbors. I lived in the N. apartments in S. for ten years and never spoke to a neighbor in the house. I find it best not to, you are much safer. Then no one knows your business and I don't care to know any one else's.[2]

THE RURAL NEIGHBORHOOD

Human groups have been chiefly rural. Human society began in rural groups, developed to the level of civilization in rural groups, and only about a century ago began an extensive movement into urban groups.

Primitive groups evolved a crude form of village life, from which the men went out at first on the hunt and chase and in later centuries to cultivate the soil. At first women stayed at home but when soil cultivation became extensive and arduous the women folks were also taken along to assist in the harvesting tasks. Today in many regions people live in villages, from which they go out, perhaps a considerable distance to the land that is often divided in strips and cultivated intensively.

The rural group remained basic even after the rise of military strongholds, the establishing of special shrines or places of worship, and the creation of trading posts. In the Middle Ages when commercial centers surrounded themselves by walls, and included congested populations living by commerce and trade, rural influences were still dominant. With the rise of the modern metropolitan city, the urban group began to dominate civiliza-

[1] Quoted by Bessie A. McClenahan, op. cit., p. 68.
[2] Ibid., p. 70.

tion. The American farmer has been referred to as "the forgotten man except at election times."

Despite urbanization it is still true that the population of the world is largely rural, that urban life is still dependent on the farm and what it produces, and that in times of widespread depression the back-to-the-farm movement is revived. While the unemployed city man is walking the streets, the unemployed rural man can at least raise his own food supply, meet his needs for shelter, and partially provide his clothing needs. "Where two years ago there were countless empty houses and abandoned farms all over the Quincy area in Illinois, Missouri, and Iowa, now every available house is occupied and there are no unoccupied farms." [1]

The force of depression produces what is probably only a temporary migration from city to country. While no permanency can be guaranteed to this population transfer, it is nevertheless an interesting social phenomenon. With a million people in a year transferring their allegiance even for a time from urban to rural life something worth studying is taking place.

> A gain of more than 1,000,000 persons was registered in the nation's farm population during 1932, the Agriculture Department announced today. This evidence of the back-to-the-land movement was accompanied by a report showing that the vacant habitable dwellings in rural sections have been "largely reoccupied" and city families are experiencing increasing difficulty in locating places in farm communities.[2]

The rural group is built around the family. The country is a relatively safe place in which to rear children, although lacking in urban advantages. There are fewer false attractions in the country than in the city. The rural family lives together as a unit, eats three meals daily together, works together, and goes together on picnics.

The long hours and hard work of the farmer represent the exceptional day's work, instead of the regular routine as in the case

[1] Associated Press, March 5, 1933.
[2] *Ibid.*, April 19, 1933.

of the steel worker, the miner, or factory employee. Moreover, the farmer is in a way master of his own time. The introduction of labor-saving machinery has shortened farm hours, decreased the difficulty of labor, and increased the amount of leisure time.

The rural school is undergoing transformations. Through the consolidated school and the rural high school, a new day for rural life may be expected. The rural school with adequate educational and playground equipment, with a permanent residence for the principal and his family, with a teaching staff that is somewhat continuous from year to year, and with a community and civic center program, is creating a new type of rural life.

In many regions the rural church has been unable to meet the situation. There has been overchurching, and also sectarian conflicts. Many small rural groups have tried to support three or four denominational churches where one strong church would have been better. Near-by city churches with their high-salaried ministers, chorus choirs, and well-organized church activities guided by energetic leaders have drawn rural people away from rural churches. Rural young people especially have felt this pull.[1]

A specially trained rural religious leadership would transform rural life and make religion a truly dynamic force. The rural pastor is in a strategic leadership position. In addition to a modern religious training, he should be well versed in sociology, that is, in a knowledge of the laws of personality growth, group development, and social processes. He should understand the technique of making community surveys and community case histories; he should be trained in methods for making the church a leader among rural institutions. He must be as interested in community reorganization as in personal regeneration.

[1] Rural ministers have rarely been rural leaders. Their salaries have been ridiculously low. The rural church has suffered from an absentee ministry; it cannot progress satisfactorily with non-resident leadership. The rural minister has often been a misnomer; he has been a clergyman ministering to a rural parish but having his eyes set upon a more desirable city pulpit, especially if he has initiative and leadership ability; or else he has been a worn-out city preacher who has been transferred to rural parishes to spend the closing years of his ministry.

The rural church has lost a large part of the social center function that it once exercised. Decades ago in the United States the meeting house was the only place of social stimulation. Today with good roads, automobiles, rapid transit lines, the rural church is no longer the chief place at which people can meet for social interaction.[1]

If the rural school, the rural church, and other rural institutions would coöperate and work together toward dynamic community ends, they could make the country so attractive that the ablest young people who now flock to the cities, would stay and add their abilities to the process of redeeming and magnifying rural group life.

Many farmers are reconstructing their farm dwellings and grounds artistically. A small lawn with an artistic arrangement of shrubs and trees and of driveways, creates a large amount of personal satisfaction in rural life. A rural community of such homes gives rise to a great deal of group pride. With the passing of the unattractive, barren, and drudgery features of the farm home, there comes a new appreciation of the deeper rural values. Rural groups may yet develop many of the advantages of urban groups without acquiring many of the latter's disadvantages.

In many countries today the *rural mind* is closely circumscribed. It sees life through a microscope. It revolves about a few people only. It represents a great deal of mental inbreeding. In most countries of the world the rural mind is essentially an undeveloped mind; it has not been fully or freely stimulated; it flares up occasionally in feuds; it has strong opinions, prejudices, and faiths.[2]

---

[1] The lot of the farmer's wife has usually been and still is full of routine. Many of the conveniences and comforts of the city, however, are being introduced into rural homes. With an electric motor to operate sewing machines, washing machines and churns, with vacuum cleaners, with electricity and gas for cooking, heating, and lighting, the farm may become attractive to the farmer's wife and daughters.

[2] The rural mind is highly tinged with reactions involving nature. It includes friendships with pet animals and identification with green valleys, woodlands, and streams. The spectacular demonstrations of nature, especially in storms, arouses awe.

The farmer, subject to sudden weather changes, destructive frosts or storms, and sometimes losing the gains of a year because of fruit or grain pests, or cattle plagues, develops attitudes of reserve and of independence based not on social laws but nature's laws. He enjoys standing upon a piece of land that he can call his own, and off of which he can order anybody of whom he does not approve. He enjoys planning his day's work and even a year's work to suit his own ideas. He pities city people who must work according to orders given by other persons. He reacts against the endless committee meetings, "the clatter and clash, the rush and pandemonium of sound" in the midst of which the city man is doomed to spend his best days.

Rural life is not stilted or formal, except when an occasional individual attempts to ape the city. It does not lead to an enslaving night life. Rural people generally are frank, open, and genuine; they scorn the kow-towing and the artificiality of city life. The rural mind is built on sturdy strength, physical endurance, continuous physical activity, freedom from nerve-destroying speed, and that fast-living which turns night into day. At its worst it is crude and outspoken.

With the development of scientific agriculture, the farmer is becoming increasingly independent of climatic changes and insect pests. He is still subject to the manipulations of a Wall Street and of unscrupulous politicians. With the introduction of free mail service, the telephone, and the automobile in rural life, the rural group mind began to expand. Narrow individualism is disappearing; interest is growing in large-scale organization, and in world affairs.

While the farmer has little chance of becoming a millionaire, he usually can make a comfortable livelihood. He is not obliged to live upon an imported food supply, as is the city man. He has plenty of room in which to live; he is not forced to live as a cave-man on the sixth floor of a dingy tenement, or to spend his savings as a slave to fashion's dictatorship.

The farmer has the satisfaction of being a genuine producer of the necessities of life. He generally becomes a representative of the middle classes; he rarely is an exploiter or grafter; neither does he devote his life to financial speculation. His opportunities to develop an intellectual life have been slight. His reading centers in the intensely practical farm journals and also in the daily newspapers, although in many rural areas of the world these publications are unknown. Rural life does not offer many inducements for intellectual study, although wherever labor-saving machinery is being introduced and communication and transportation are developed, the situation is changing.

Many studies have been made of rural community groups which show that considerable progress is under way despite great difficulties. In the United States the ideal unit for rural social organization appears to be an area varying from thirty to fifty square miles. This area is represented in certain regions by the consolidated school district. It usually contains one or more trade centers, one or more religious centers, a community hall or two and four or five neighborhoods ranging from twenty to fifty families.

The scientific study of rural groups is known as rural sociology. This science, which has been developing rapidly in the United States, points the way to a new era, not only for rural groups but also for the national group of which rural groups constitute a vital part.[1]

Five special rural problems will now be stated. (1) It is difficult to maintain upon farms in the United States persons of superior ability, for most of them have their eyes upon the city and move to the cities, thus depriving rural areas of their experiences and abilities. They "retire" to the cities, leaving the rural community at the time when they might be free to render much community aid. (2) Closely related is the problem created by the young people of initiative and education who leave the farms for the cities. Energetic rural leadership is depleted.

[1] A long list of books on rural sociology have appeared within the last ten or fifteen years. The most recent addition is Carl C. Taylor's *Rural Sociology* (Harper and Brothers, New York, 1933), Revised Edition. A pioneer work was John M. Gillette's *Constructive Rural Sociology* (Sturgis and Walton Company, New York, 1913).

(3) In the United States ruralites are characterized by a degree of isolation that is not found in rural Europe with its many village aggregations. Farm houses are separated in the United States and life is less associative.

(4) Tenant farming is on the increase in the United States. It is becoming more and more difficult for a young man without means to marry, rear a family, and pay for a farm. (5) A related problem is that of land speculation. If in times of depression a young man cannot buy a farm because farm produce sells too cheaply, then in times of prosperity prices of land are run up too high. The rise of land values under private ownership in prosperity times tends to bring about the concentration of land ownership in the hands of a small percentage of the population. This system of "absentee landlords" rarely works well from the larger social viewpoint. The evils are so serious that it may be necessary to limit the amount of land that one person or a group of persons may own, and to regulate rentals. Either speculation in land or depression prices for farm produce works untold hardship on young people who have initiative and character but who possess no economic advantages. In its methods of social control of land a nation may well encourage rather than penalize young men and women who wish to establish homes on rural acreages of their own.

The village has been in many countries a real neighborhood, the starting point of all social life as well as of civilization. It has avoided the evils of both isolation and of congestion. It has been the center of group life for the majority of mankind, but in the United States the village as a social group has degenerated. The village has often been a dead center. The deadening life of the village is unfortunate but real. People move away from their isolated farm dwellings, pass by the village, and locate in the large city.

The village, however, is a socially strategic unit especially in a country where the isolated farm dwelling is common. The village possesses all the potential advantages of urban neighborhoods and affords expression for the gregarious impulses of people living a half mile or more from neighbors. It is or may be large enough to maintain nearly all the advantages of the city, and yet avoid the hustle, the superficiality, the soot, the squalor, and the homelessness of the large city. The village might become a happy medium between isolated farm living and congested urban living.

THE CITY COMMUNITY

The urban group is a loose organization of people living compactly in a limited area and possessing a relatively high degree of intercommunication. Industrial and business pursuits and social life comprise the main lines of the picture. Inasmuch as the people are removed from agricultural enterprise and from direct contact with nature, they live in a somewhat artificial, man-made world. They are subject to a superficiality which leads them to assume to be what they are not. Urban society is notorious for its haughtiness, its cocksureness, its "high life," its wastefulness, and its uselessness. Urban society often defeats that industry, frugality, and satisfaction in work well done which is essential to national welfare.

Urban groups are the products of complex social forces. They have often originated in trade centers, such as those located at "breaks" in transportation lines or near the centers of agriculture or mining. Sometimes they are the products chiefly of population momentum; again, they have been produced by modern industrial and commercial enterprise. Nearly all cities have profited greatly by an immigration of rural people whose ambitious eyes have been caught by the flashing of urban opportunities.

In 1790, in the United States only about 3 per cent of the population lived in urban groups of 8,000 or more people. Today over one-half of the population is congregated directly under urban group influence. In 1800, there were only five cities in the United States which had a population of 10,000 or over; in 1900, a century later, there were 447 such cities. Every large city is the center of a constellation of smaller centers of influence. Each of the smaller centers becomes integrated with the large center. We must consider a large city, therefore, not so much in terms of population but in terms of its "sphere of influence." Every large city becomes a powerful super community.[1]

The development of the urban group is due to many factors. (1) As it grows the city gives increasing status to its inhabitants. The social contacts in cities are numerous and compelling. The ordinary person is afforded pleasure simply by being one of a large group, even if he does not know more than a few persons.

(2) The invention of machinery, the increasing use of steam power, and the application of capital in commercial and industrial enterprises have created gigantic manufacturing plants. For the sake of working with others and of high wages men will forego the more independent forms of rural work. Thus, large-scale production has furthered the growth of cities.

(3) The development in methods of transportation and communication, the increased desire for communication, and the facilities which cities offer for satisfying the desire for communication and exchange explain urban growth. The compactness of a city, its telephones, and its rapid transit system greatly facilitate interstimulation.

(4) There is more opportunity for personal advancement in cities than in rural districts. Modern business and commerce draw young men to the cities, offering the chance of "getting rich quick." Religious leaders achieve high rank in cities. Educational leaders have special recognition in cities. In all lines of activity the urban possibilities of achievement far eclipse the opportunities for power and honor in the country.

(5) The city offers superior educational advantages. Until recently all high schools were in cities. Elementary schools

[1] R. D. McKenzie, *The Metropolitan Community* (McGraw-Hill Book Company, Inc., New York, 1933), p. 312.

are better equipped and developed than in the country; normal schools, colleges, trade schools are urban. Prominent national leaders give lectures and addresses in urban centers. All large libraries are located in cities. Operas and art productions are urban.

(6) Amusement and recreational agencies in cities are drawing cards. The city worker is able "to go out" every evening. By making appeals in every conceivable way to the feelings, sentiments, play impulses of children and adults alike, commercialized amusements are powerful magnets.

Urban groups have a reputation for *namelessness*. Its citizens meet and speak without knowing each other's names. One may live for years in a city and not know personally one-half the people whose homes are located in the same city block. Extensive secondary group relationships take the place of primary group ones.

Homelessness is another disturbing characteristic of cities. Boarding-house life and hotel life does not permit the development of real homes. An automobile first and a home afterward or perhaps never is frequently an urban slogan. To give to children a genuine home life on the sixth floor of a flat with hallways and flights of stairs as the only play space is almost impossible. A husband and wife with pet bulldogs can rent elegant quarters with ease, but not so if they possess sons. The city environment often puts a premium on childlessness.

Class extremes characterize the city. The worst racketeering and the best forms of ethical behavior are both to be found in cities. The direst poverty often exists in the shadow of the most elegant mansions, while superior creativeness and chronic unemployment are alike urban characteristics.

Energy and *speed* are traits of the American city. Young and ambitious people set a tremendous pace both by day and night. Stimulation and interstimulation are endless, but generally on superficial planes. The pace soon exceeds the ability of the human organism to maintain; it is "the pace that kills." Hence cities have been called consumers of population. They stimulate persons to almost inconceivable efforts, but often at tremendous sacrifices.[1]

The rural group furnishes deeply genuine attitudes, nerve stability, indifference to luxury, and vast undeveloped ability; the urban group offers social stimulation, chances for personal advancement, opportunities for superior creative efforts, and the advantages of a developed social life. Rural life reflects in a large measure the life-giving and health-restoring advantages of an out-door existence. The city tears down nerves and wears people out while giving them superior opportunities in countless directions.

The history of mankind seems to indicate that any people who are chiefly rural or chiefly urban is at a disadvantage. In the first instance the people are understimulated and subject to inertia; in the second, they are in danger of being smothered by numbers, of being overstimulated, or of being exhausted nervously. A nation somewhat equally representative of healthy rural and healthy urban groups is likely to prove in the long run to be the strongest.

The *suburban* group lives at the edge of the urban group. It is essentially a part of the urban group enjoying favorable living conditions. The suburban group have their occupations in the city but by virtue of the automobile or of commuting are able to live where light and air and space for homes are plentiful and in the main reasonable in price.

Somewhat related is the satellite city,[2] which springs up near a large city, sometimes as an industrial center. When a large factory moves out from a city into an adjoining unsettled area a small city tends to develop at that point. Its proximity to a large city and the original low values of the land involved are its outstanding features.

[1] Interdependence is pushed to a high degree in cities. The average city person is utterly dependent with reference to the purity of the water supply or the milk supply. Highly organized fire and police departments are required to protect the individual against nature and against other individuals. Traffic officers are needed to keep people out of each other's way; or from destroying one another accidentally.

[2] See Graham R. Taylor, *Satellite Cities* (D. Appleton and Company, New York, 1915).

The *rurban* group, a term coined by C. J. Galpin,[1] refers to that phase of rural life which is becoming urbanized in certain particulars but which retains various rural features. The rurban group is a rural group in a state of urbanization. It has numerous urban advantages due to rapid transit, the telephone, daily newspaper, and the like; it still retains its rural setting and some of its rural customs and traditions. It is in transition from rural to urban. It represents the extreme disadvantages of neither rural nor urban groups, but many of the substantial advantages of both.

The Nation Group

The nation group is composed of rural and urban groups, of neighborhood and community groups held together by a commonly accepted set of collective representations or symbols of unity. The nation group is a social control group with its activities centered in some form of an organized government. When danger from attack from outside forces is greatest, the nation group is likely to be strongest.

The nation group originated in the need for protection. Individuals who live under a group organization survive, while others perish. As wild horses developed a group organization in order to withstand the attacks of ferocious animals, so primitive people lived in groups and submitted themselves to the rules and regulations of a crude, arbitrary government, especially in times of crises and danger. In the presence of a common enemy, primitive peoples developed a keen sense of the need of protection and responded to group or governmental control.

The *horde* was the group organization in which the modern state had its origin. It was a sort of temporary oligarchy based on respect for those whose personal prowess enabled the group to meet attack successfully. The horde may be distinguished from the clan or an organization of families; from the household or a group organization for economic purposes; and from the phratry or a group organization for social, recreational, and religious ends.

[1] Of the United States Department of Agriculture.

The horde possessed three of the fundamental elements of the modern nation. It had (1) the idea of the authority of the leaders; (2) a notion of law, in the obedience given to the commands of the chieftain, and in the customs governing the group while fighting and hunting; and (3) an extensive unity, since all members combine for a general purpose.

Under the protection of group organization, such as the horde, primitive people acquired occupational stability and inaugurated social advance. Here also were found the origins of private property. As a result of the horde organization man early possessed a measure of protection from the "outside," and had a little world in which ordinarily he could live at peace, a peace which was one of the first conditions of progress. He also had a measure of protection from enemies within the group, which led to an increased unity and strength of the whole group. He thereby secured release from certain elemental fears.

In the *tribal* group, which was an advance over the horde, the need of protection stands out prominently. As in the case of the horde the ties of blood relationship functioned as a bond of union. The common descent of members from a fictitious ancestor was postulated, and the ruler or king was invested with the absolute authority of a father. Religion, also, especially in the form of ancestor worship, rendered important service in developing the habit of obedience. It enforced with supernatural sanctions the customs, political and otherwise, of the past.[1] The tribal group was based on the need for protection, on ties of blood-relationships, and on the strength of a common religion.

The *city state* was in part an outgrowth of tribal group life. The need for protection was greater than ever, as opposing groups increased in size. The ties of blood-relationship were still strong. Religion was an affair of the state and a bond of political strength. The authority of the city state was greater, more regular in its exercise, than that of the tribal group. The

---

[1] It is at this point, also, that religion has been severely criticized, for it has tended at times to support the *status quo* blindly and to hinder progress.

city state developed an elaborate administrative machinery, promoted art and education at times, and achieved considerable recognition and historical significance.

The *feudal state* was no longer an enlarged family as was the tribal group. It was "more like an army." The government of the feudal state was semi-military. In theory the king owned the whole feudal group. He parcelled out the land to his nobles, who in turn distributed it among their subordinates. The members did not live so much for the feudal group as for the ruler. Everything was concentrated in the monarch. Personal allegiance to the king overshadowed other loyalties.

The *absolute monarchical group* was an overgrown feudal organization. For centuries in many lands the monarchs treated their respective states as their private property; concessions were secured from them with the greatest difficulty. The absolute monarch was a dictator. Any limitation of the authority of the monarch was rarely obtained except at the cost of bloodshed. Political parties began to develop, but of course as secret organizations. In Russia, for example, political parties existed largely as secret organizations until 1017. In fascist countries today, a reversion to secret political groups naturally occurs.

The *constitutional monarchical group* afforded some privileges to the constituency. The people slowly but surely obtained certain rights from the ruler. The people secured a parliament through which to express their wishes. The monarch lost his status of a superior being with divine rights. Political parties grew stronger; they developed into open organizations representing conservative and liberal attitudes on the various questions of interest to the constitutional group. The sovereignty of the members of the group became recognized.

The *fascist group* is a reversion to a dictatorship. The leader rules by might. The group gives over its powers of governing to one man who by support from an army suppresses and imprisons opponents. Freedom of the press, of assemblage, of speech are denied to all except those who agree with the dictator. The schools become propagandistic and a generation of automatons are produced.[1]

The *democratic nation group* abolishes the office of king and establishes the sovereignty of the people. By means of representatives the people attempt to express their wishes. A general election of officials gives the people a chance to express their approval or disapproval. Gigantic political powers develop. There are generally no more than two leading political parties in the democratic state at a given time, although in European countries such as Germany before the Hitler revolution in 1933, there were several strong parties which were deadlocked to the point that no majority could be obtained by any of them. The deadlock created inefficiency and brought on Hitlerism.

Political parties perform a definite social function. The party in power rarely initiates new programs after having come into authority for any length of time. It generally has more than it can do in fulfilling preëlection promises.[2] The party not in control renders a service in prodding up the party in power, and in insisting that the latter live up to its promises. The party out of power usually stands for new measures in order to bid successfully for the suffrage of the people.

The democratic nation group is in danger of breaking down or has broken down because of too much individualism and by the indifference of individuals to group welfare. The multiplication of private interests invites neglect of the more fundamental affairs of government. The complexity of modern city life is so great that the ordinary person has difficulty in determining the truth about candidates for office. It was Elihu Root who once publicly expressed the belief that there are too many persons who are trying to get something out of their country and too few who are trying to serve it. Too many persons have accepted

---

[1] See E. S. Bogardus, "Fascism as a Social Movement," *Sociology and Social Research*, XVII: 569–74.

[2] The activities of Franklin D. Roosevelt upon coming into the presidency in the United States in March, 1933, seem to be an exception. However, he acted to meet a long-standing depression and national emergency, having been given temporarily extended executive powers by Congress.

government positions for the sake of the offices, the appropriations, the class benefits, and "too few have sought to preserve liberty and to do justice" for the sake of their national group.

Some persons give their attention so largely to their private affairs and neglect governmental affairs so generally that politics has fallen into the hands of racketeers. Hence, many worthy persons refuse to run for public office lest their own good names become smirched. Many politicians work in a realm of irresponsible secrecy and government decays at the core. That a public office is a public trust is a principle exceedingly difficult to realize.

The larger a nation becomes the more likely are the people to regard their government, even a democratic one, as "a ruler operating from above." It is not easy for the government of a hundred million people to remain in touch with the people, or to act promptly and flexibly in response to public need. It is also difficult for public opinion under such circumstances not to be influenced by propaganda.[1]

The nation, thus, is a group of people living within a specific territory and exercising organized control over its members. Its activities are threefold: (1) activity with reference to its citizens, guaranteeing them both security and liberty; (2) activity in promoting constructive measures for group advancement; and (3) activity with reference to other states for the interchange of goods and services and the defense of citizens abroad or of its territory at home.[2]

In the first instance the state defends the law-abiding citizen and punishes the anti-social individuals. It enforces contracts between persons when properly drawn; it affords

---

[1] The taxation problem, or the problem of paying for government, is especially troublesome in a democracy. Personal property, for example, is reported to assessors so inaccurately that the honest person who reports all his personal property, pays more than his share of taxes. He is confronted with the choice, as Charles R. Henderson of the University of Chicago once said, "of being robbed or of perjuring himself." Many forms of taxation have led to deception, and perjury has become respectable among many people.

[2] This analysis was made by Arthur Fairbanks, in his *Introduction to Sociology* (Charles Scribner's Sons, New York, 1910), pp. 195ff.

damages for accidents; it aims to protect individuals against fraud; it gives protection to persons organized in corporate groups for business or other purposes. It is a powerful agency of social control; it incarcerates for life and it takes life.

In the second instance, the state promotes social and economic measures. It coins money and assumes charge or responsibility for banking. It has become an extensive employer of labor; it carries the mail; it builds and maintains highways. The question may be raised: How far should the state go in the economic sphere? The answer varies. The capitalist says: "Just as little as possible, and still maintain national unity"; the socialist, "As far as possible, and still maintain individual participation." The present tendencies are in the main toward an increasing degree of government supervision and control.

In the third instance, the state carries on an elaborate set of diplomatic and military activities. The citizen expresses his indebtedness to the state through *patriotism* which often is built up largely as a defense mechanism against other states. The strength of patriotism becomes apparent only in case of national emergency, especially when some other state becomes aggressive. Patriotism sometimes unwittingly contributes to national egotism. Sometimes it denies the full obligation of the nation to other nations. Sometimes it creates chauvinism.

The nation is a group which needs citizens of strong moral character, but which is not in position to create that character directly. Moral character cannot be created by force. The nation, however, does something in this connection, such as preventing the circulation of obscene literature, and of regulating the sale of intoxicants. The national group that is wise provides training for adequate rural leadership and rural social organization. It endeavors to transform its village groups into active intermediaries between rural and urban life, providing through them many of the advantages of urban life with little of the neural wear and tear for which cities are notorious. It strives to make its cities into social groups where constructive home life prevails, where "slums" are abolished, where persons are stimulated to do their best but not at the expense of other persons, and where socialization reigns.

WORLD COMMUNITY

The succession of horde, tribe, city state, feudal state, monarchical state, and democratic national state has but one next stage and that is "world community." Hundreds of international organizations have been formed in the last fifty years; all of these connote progress in world community thinking. Although many of these international bodies are loosely organized, although they rely on a great deal of volunteer effort, and although they do not carry the force of law or national decree, they are creating world opinion and are stimulating coöperative international activities.

The Hague Tribunal has attracted the attention of the world in the settlement of many international disputes, some of which could easily have led to war. It has demonstrated the need for a more widely effective world instrument of adjudication. The League to Enforce Peace set a new ideal clearly before the world [1] and pointed the way to a League of Nations, the formation of which constituted another step in the direction of world community. President Woodrow Wilson's memorable statement before the Chamber of Deputies in Rome, January 3, 1919, that the need of the hour is "to organize the friendship of the world" is still fundamentally true.

International law is an evidence of world community at least in an incipient form. International law is a body of rules, generally recognized by civilized states, which determines to a degree the conduct of modern states in their mutual relations. The coexistence of many national groups spatially near each other has made it necessary that they develop standard rules of action in their interaction.

In war times and similar crises the principles of international conduct are likely to be violated. Owing to the absence of an adequate world opinion or of some other social force, inter-

[1] Despite its unfortunate title.

national law may break down. The function of international law, however, is to regulate the conduct of national groups in all their contacts, hostile as well as pacific. Modern international law is based on the principle that nations are organic units in a larger society, and possess mutual obligations. Grotius [1] was one of the first outstanding leaders in bringing about a recognition of the international concept.

World community is developing despite many and serious setbacks. The spirit of nationalism is still far stronger than the spirit of world community. The World War demonstrated how nationalism in Europe is more powerful than Christianity, with its doctrine of the brotherhood of man, for Christians split up into their respective national camps, and viciously mowed each other down while calling upon the same God to give them victory. Likewise the World War showed how nationalism is stronger than socialism with its international premises, for horny-handed workers divided up into the opposing national camps and tried to annihilate each other with poison gas.

The League of Nations has been seriously handicapped because it was built upon so many nationally narrow concepts. Some feared it as an organization of nations for the promotion of an autocratic capitalism. Others suspected it as a post-war weapon for defending the Versailles Treaty. Still others felt that it was in reality a league of European nations. Even its very limited power to deprive nations of a small part of their sovereignty for the sake of world community was deplored by nationalists everywhere.

The Washington Conference on Limitation of Armaments was based on the principle that independent nations should come to agreements on world problems without giving up even a slight degree of sovereignty to a world agreement. The Conference furthered the development of a world public opinion. The Kellogg-Briand or Paris Peace Pact made considerable headway in a world community direction. Its pronouncement is remarkable:

[1] The distinguished Dutch founder of international law.

ARTICLE I

The High Contracting Parties solemnly declare in the names of their respective peoples that they condemn recourse to war for the solution of international controversies, and renounce it as an instrument of national policy in their relations with one another.

ARTICLE II

The High Contracting Parties agree that the settlement or solution of all disputes or conflicts of whatever nature or of whatever origin they may be, which may arise among them, shall never be sought except by pacific means.

On July 24, 1929, President Herbert Hoover proclaimed the Pact in full force. World community was definitely promoted by it. However, in September, 1931, Japan, one of the signatories to the Peace Pact, sent her armies into Manchuria and to Shanghai and opened her guns on the Chinese, violating the spirit of her own signature to the Peace Pact. Secretary of State Henry Stimson in January, 1932, declared that any territory taken over by Japan in violation of the Peace Pact would not be so recognized by the United States. Japan did not actually declare war, and hence it is claimed that she did not violate the Peace Pact. At the League of Nations in 1932 it was proclaimed that a declaration against war was not enough to meet the world situation. The phrase in the Pact "condemn recourse to war" shall become "condemn recourse to force." Thus, the movement to safeguard world peace and promote world community is a contest of wits, a struggle to solve the problems created by hyper-nationalism, and a desperate race between warlike forces and attitudes of peace.

The London Economic Conference of 1933 made little headway partly because three underlying national principles were in conflict. From London William Allen White [1] pointed out that three systems of control were deadlocked, namely: democracy represented, for example, by Great Britian, France, United States; fascism, represented by Italy and Germany; and com-

[1] Correspondent of the North American Newspaper Alliance.

munism, represented by Russia. Nationalism was blocking internationalism, with fears, hatreds, and prejudices being in the saddle. Moreover, it was proclaimed that the public conference method is inefficient, because while the speakers are addressing the assembled multitude of newspaper reporters and political attachés of one kind or another, the real decisions are being made by the representatives of the respective nations behind closed doors or via telegraph and cable dispatches in code to each other. However, there never was a time when so many people as now in each country are aware of the nature of international dilemmas and hence in position to exercise effective influence through public opinion.

The world has reached the place where public opinion speaks of Western civilization or Eastern civilization, of Occidentalism or Orientalism, but where the differences between the two, not the likenesses, are emphasized by the chauvinists on both sides of the Pacific. The average members of the Western social order are widely proclaiming its superiority. They fail to understand or to study the worthy phases of Orientalism; they see and magnify its defects. They often fail to feel humble for the weaknesses of Occidentalism but go on their way boastfully blind. Likewise many of the adherents of Eastern civilization are silently and politely feeling a sense of their own superiority. They pity Western chauvinists. Now and then someone such as Rabindranath Tagore openly expresses himself, calling Western society black and dwelling upon the superiorities of the East.

On the constructive side an excellent analysis of Western civilization has been made by Charles A. Ellwood [1] who has outlined the following attributes: (1) a set of ethical and religious values was derived from the Hebrews and early Christians. In the former the major concept is justice; and in the latter, love. (2) Philosophical and ethical values were contributed by the Greeks. (3) A set of administrative and legal values stressing the rights of property originated with the

---

[1] *The Social Problem* (The Macmillan Company, New York, 1919), Ch. II.

Romans. (4) Personal liberty values were developed by the early Teutons and given concrete modern expression under the *laissez-faire* doctrine of the nineteenth century in Western Europe and the United States. Within recent decades additional values have been produced by Occidentalism, namely, (5) scientific methods, (6) business and industrial techniques, (7) universal education, and (8) as an antidote to economic inhumanity, a set of humanitarian values.

Eastern civilization is known for (1) its sacrifice values, which to the Oriental makes the Occident seem synonymous with organized selfishness. (2) There are contemplative values in Orientalism, culminating in mysticism. (3) In the East there is veneration for parents, for customs and traditions, for law, order, and stability. (4) There are important conventional standards expressing themselves in courtesy and in an appreciation of the finer values of life. (5) Orientalism is esthetic and mystic, not rational-philosophic. (6) Orientalism has a sense of social solidarity, and strong sentiments of patriotism. The social group past and present ranks far above the individual. (7) Family stability extending back into past generations is given prominence whereas in the West the convenience of the individual is often put first. (8) The Oriental lives in generalizations rather than in particularizations. He glories in the abstract more than in the concrete.

When the positive elements in Western and Eastern civilizations are brought together apparent differences are present. We see the rationally versus the mystically philosophic, action versus contemplation, the physical versus the psychical, individualism versus solidarity, the individual over against the family unit, facts against concepts, utility versus estheticism, anxiety as opposed to tranquillity, and the means of life versus the sake of living.[1] These apparent contrasts, vividly stated by Dr. Nitobe, upon reflection provide nothing less than adequate bases for building a world community that will be superior to

[1] Inazo Nitobe, *Bushido the Soul of Japan* (Teibi Publishing Company, Tokio, 1911).

either Western or Eastern civilization. Many of these seeming contrasts represent different poles on the same social axis.

As now developing, world community possesses a number of important tendencies. Apparently (1) the world will become more psychically and culturally united than at present. Mankind had common origins but dispersed early in many directions over the earth. In various physical, climatic, and social environments mankind became widely differentiated into races and cultures. The cultures are now being reunited. Whether one accepts a polygenetic theory or a monogenetic theory of the origin of mankind the main point still obtains, namely, that a unity of culture patterns is developing. The process of social evolution is producing one world civilization. The common culture will achieve an increasing degree of assimilation and amalgamation. The different climatic areas of the earth, however, will continue to function in producing sunny and serious peoples, light- and dark-skinned peoples, distinctive culture traits here and there over the face of the globe.

(2) World community is engaged in producing a political structure that will become superior in strength to the most powerful nations today, and that will guard the special needs of individual nations both small and large. It will be built out of the values of the individual nations and will regulate these nations, even their internal affairs, where such regulation is needed to guarantee world community. It will not abolish nations, but foster them as long as they work for the planetary good. It will do away with hyper-nationalism, provincialism, and chauvinism. It will need to eliminate the balance of power theory, the secret treaty practice, and territorial aggrandizement.

(3) It appears that world community will ultimately be democratic, for no permanent world structure can be built out of autocracies. Rulership from the top down exclusively, bears its own seeds of destruction in the power which it gives the few over the many. Not autocracy but aristocracy will exist with democracy in world community. It will be an aristocracy that

will be guided by the needs of the many allowing them a voice in determining their needs, that will not waste itself in extravagant living, that will continually endeavor to raise all persons to its own level, and thus create a democracy of superior men and women with pro-social attitudes and values.

World community is moving toward an industrial democracy. Neither labor nor capital will control. One has as its goal, wages; the other profits. Both ends are materialistic and low grade. Service values will rule both capital and labor. Persons will strive with one another in rendering service to all instead of viciously competing in order to grab from each other. Service will supplant profitism and speculative gambling.[1]

World community is moving toward a working together although not necessarily alike of all peoples toward the realization of world values. A world situation in which there are sixty nation groups, each setting up its own standards of right and wrong conduct, and each passing judgment on all the other fifty-nine, makes necessary a new world order, a socialized citizenry, and a widespread community consciousness. Some force, such as the dynamic of love, is needed to put into effect the foregoing principles of world community. Humanitarianism, having no goal outside itself tends to become self-centered, concentrated, and professional. The principles of love and brotherhood are humanitarian, and more; their ultimate goal is located outside and beyond humanity. Thus they provide a dynamic guiding force for world community.

PROBLEMS

1. What is a community?
2. Describe a good neighbor.
3. How may neighborhood consciousness be developed?
4. In what ways is a rural population useful to a nation?
5. Why is there a dearth of leadership in rural communities?
6. Who need the better schools, urban or rural children?

[1] Cf. John H. Randall, *A World Community* (Frederick A. Stokes Company, New York, 1930), Ch. X.

7. What is a city?
8. In what sense are cities consumers of population?
9. Why are cities overcrowded?
10. What is a city for?
11. How might a village be made an ideal social group?
12. Describe a good citizen.
13. "Are laws that are framed in the interest of classes of individuals of permanent advantage to the nation as a whole?"
14. "How may men sin against the welfare of society without breaking any law of the land?"
15. What is patriotism?
16. What is hyper-nationalism?
17. What causes hyper-nationalism?
18. What is a world community?
19. In what ways may world friendship be developed?

READINGS

ANDERSON, NELS, and E. C. LINDEMAN, *Urban Sociology* (Alfred A. Knopf, New York, 1928).

ATKESON, MARY M., *The Woman on the Farm* (The Century Company, New York, 1924).

BALDWIN, B. T., et al., *Farm Children* (D. Appleton and Company, New York, 1930).

BIZZELL, W. B., *The Green Rising* (The Macmillan Company, New York, 1926).

BUELL, R. L., *International Relations* (Henry Holt and Company, New York, 1925).

BURGESS, ERNEST W., editor, *The Urban Community* (University of Chicago Press, 1926).

CARPENTER, NILES, *The Sociology of City Life* (Longmans, Green and Company, New York, 1926).

DAVIE, MAURICE R., *Problems of City Life* (John Wiley and Sons, Inc., New York, 1932).

DOUGLASS, H. P., *The Little Town* (The Macmillan Company, New York, 1919).

——, *The Suburban Trend* (The Century Company, New York, 1925).

GALPIN, C. J., *Rural Social Problems* (The Century Company, New York, 1924).

GILLETTE, JOHN M., *Rural Sociology* (The Macmillan Company, New York, 1928).

GIST, NOEL P., and L. A. HALBERT, *Urban Society* (Thomas Y. Crowell Company, New York, 1933).

HARLEY, J. EUGENE, *Toward International Understanding* (Stanford University Press, 1931).

HART, J. K., *Community Organization* (The Macmillan Company, New York, 1920).

HAWTHORNE, H. B., *The Sociology of Rural Life* (The Century Company, New York, 1926).

HAYES, A. W., *Rural Sociology* (Longmans, Green and Company, New York, 1929).

HOFFER, C. R., *Rural Sociology* (Ray Long and Richard R. Smith, Inc., New York, 1930).

LUNDQUIST and CARVER, *Principles of Rural Sociology* (Ginn and Company, Boston, 1927).

MacIVER, R. M., *Community* (The Macmillan Company, New York, 1928).

PARK, ROBERT E., editor, *The City* (University of Chicago Press, 1925).

RANDALL, JOHN H., *A World Community* (Frederick A. Stokes Company, New York, 1930).

SANDERSON, DWIGHT, *The Rural Community* (Ginn and Company, Boston, 1932).

SIMS, NEWELL L., *Elements of Rural Sociology* (Thomas Y. Crowell Company, New York, 1928).

STEINER, J. F., *The American Community in Action* (Henry Holt and Company, New York, 1928).

——, *Community Organization* (The Century Company, New York, 1930).

STRATTON, G. M., *Social Psychology of International Conduct* (D. Appleton and Company, New York, 1930).

TAYLOR, C. C., *Rural Sociology* (Harper and Brothers, New York, 1933).

TAYLOR, G. R., *Satellite Cities* (D. Appleton and Company, New York, 1915).

WILLIAMS, J. M., *Our Rural Heritage* (Alfred A. Knopf, New York, 1925).

ZORBAUGH, H. W., *The Gold Coast and the Slum* (University of Chicago Press, 1929).

PART THREE
GROUP ORGANIZATION

CHAPTER XII

GROUP CONTROLS

Organization is the technique whereby a group controls its members. Organization gives configuration to a group. It sets limits and keeps human energies from spreading out in all directions and from being dissipated. It gives boundaries to human behavior and channels this behavior toward helpful or harmful ends.

Organization includes all the direct and indirect, the formal and informal ways by which a group controls the attitudes and values of persons. Some group controls are stimulative, for instance, promotions, honors, prizes, grades; others are repressive, for example, physical punishment, taboos, sneers, or hard names. *A group control* is any stimulus originating under group auspices, while *group control* is the sum total and integration of all concrete controls emanating from a group. Group controls indicate the nature of group values.[1]

PERSONALITY AND CONTROLS

The need for group controls arises from the conflict between the group and the individual. A human being is born into a group which has standardized rules and regulations. An infant, however, possesses countless unorganized impulses. He is "a little anarchist," whose anarchistic impulses conflict with group standards. He lacks social vision and does not perceive the value of standards. He yells at the top of his voice in protest. Facing group control suddenly he struggles violently to overthrow it. If he does not go into a temper tantrum, he may try non-violent coercion by sulking, or by refusing to participate.

[1] For a pertinent and timely discussion read the chapter on "What the American Citizen Values" in James H. Tufts, *America's Social Morality* (Henry Holt and Company, New York, 1933), Ch. II.

If largely extrovertive he goes into a tantrum; if largely introvertive he grows sullen. He may use his fists, or he may silently sneak away.

In his earliest activities a child is usually unsocial; he seeks the satisfaction of his own inherent impulses. This elemental behavior soon becomes conditioned to social ends through personal experiences. The best social control is that which operates through the normal experiences of the individual and which conditions him in group welfare ways. After slamming a door shut on his finger once, a child is generally cautious thereafter, and after acting contrary to the judgment of a calm, self-controlled parent and suffering bitterly from his own misbehavior he learns to be at least considerate of the judgment of broad-minded elders.

Most individuals feel control first as a member of the family group. Parents sometimes exercise control over the child through force and sometimes through love. The child full of energy and without experience wants so many things because they are bright or make interesting appeals (devils in enticing garbs) that parents find themselves saying "don't" more often than "do," and hence using negative instead of positive controls. The more active a child the larger the number of "do" situations that parental control must provide. If parents resort to anger as a control they arouse angry feelings in the child, and the control problem grows worse. The child is likely to grow defiant when controlled by angry parents, and if anger is shown many times, the child first loses all respect for parental control and then develops hatred for the parents. Sooner or later he manifests defiant attitudes.

The social significance of exercising parental control with a combination of love and firmness cannot be overestimated, for thereby children are conditioned in terms of group participation and responsibility. That type of control which secures wholesome participation in the life of the family by the children conditions the children against self-centered lives, against yielding to impulses for mere personal pleasure, against establishing anti-social attitudes. More important, it conditions them in terms of sympathy, of give-and-take, of group responsibility, and of seeking pleasure in the advancement and enjoyment of other persons. By the use of wise controls the family is probably better fitted than any other group for the training of children, because the family is a miniature society with varied opportunities and problems.

Each of us has felt the control influence of play groups. By virtue of play controls, the child is conditioned to submerge his desires, and gladly so, to the welfare of other children. In the case of boys this lesson sometimes is learned from the fists of other boys; girls have less overt but equally effective ways of regulating the irregular member. In the play group a child will sometimes take severe punishment from other and older children without whimpering, whereas slight punishment from a parent may produce sullenness or anger. In a play group children will often obey a leader of their own selection more readily than they will a parent, for there is not the disparity in viewpoints. In other words the play group is an excellent support to the family group in conditioning children in a sense of group responsibility.

We have all experienced social control in school. Perhaps that control has been felt in regular and routine assignments, in standard hours of work, or in a formal seating arrangement. Perhaps it has come from the teacher's encouraging remarks or from his disciplinary rules; perhaps, from the derisive laughter of the classroom group. The loud guffaws of boys or the scornful glances of girls may be more effective in bringing a recalcitrant individual into line than a teacher's stern remarks.

Then there is community control exercised through the police. As long as a person keeps within the law and the customs he does not experience this form of control, but let him violate a traffic law, for instance, and control begins to operate. Let laws be repeatedly flaunted and control is felt.

A religious group exercises control through its dogmas and beliefs. To many persons the eye of God which sees in secret, which penetrates everywhere, which watches when there are no human observers, which penetrates the secret places of a person's inmost thought, is a powerful control. A person thus may regulate his behavior according to the concept of God held by his religious group.

Group control and personal initiative are two poles of social life. Both are essential yet either in an extreme form can destroy the other and wreck the group itself. Both must operate with due consideration of the other. Group control is usually sound which has for its main standard the criterion of personality emergence and richness. In turn personal initiative is well founded if it operates within the limits of social welfare.

By stimulating certain impulses of the individual the group may condition a person to a broad type of self-control or by stimulating other impulses arouse anti-social behavior. The group may develop self-respect in its members or stimulate destructive tendencies.

As a result of his experiences within group life a person develops two general standards. One standard is used for judging self and friends; the other, for judging mere acquaintances and strangers. Each person has both an "in-group" and an "out-group" ethics. He excuses unworthy behavior by himself and by members of his in-group that he despises when exhibited by the out-group. That which is lying when perceived in the out-group is mere "stretching the truth" if indulged in by the in-group. That which is vicious when countenanced by the French is justifiable when practiced by the Germans, if one is a German; and *vice versa*.

A group of 105 students were once asked this question by the writer: "Is your personal ethical standard higher in your dealing with your instructors or with your fellow students?" Sixty-six replied that they exercised higher standards of personal control in dealing with their fellow students; twenty-eight declared that they held themselves to a higher standard of behavior in dealing with instructors than with their fellow students; while eleven asserted that personally they behaved according to the same standard in their relations with their instructors and their fellow students. The explanation of the reaction of the majority is that there is a more personal relationship between student and student than between student and professor. The group with the greater fellow-feeling exercises the greater control over its members. Even a gang of thieves may exhibit a fine type of social control among themselves at the very time that they are engaged in robbery and burglary with reference to the public.

Ethical dualism is in reality *ethical polyism*. A person may have one standard of control for himself, another for his nearest friends, still another for other friends, and yet another for strangers. It is possible for a person to have a different standard for each group and each person whom he contacts. These varied standards mean that a person is in conflict within himself. Since different groups have different standards of right and wrong, a person wholly subject to group control may have as many standards of right and wrong as there are groups to which he belongs.

Since there is a close relation between a person's behavior standards and the controls exercised by his groups, an excellent way to study group control is by considering the behavior of persons as group members. In one class no student cheats in examination; in another class composed of similar persons cheating is common. In the first class group control is constructive and helpful; in the other, loose and demoralizing. In the first instance the class may be small and the instructor fair; in the other, the class may be large and the instructor judged to be unfair.

Everyone finds his personality being modified by the control exercised by his in-groups, that is, by his family group, play groups, his social club groups, business associates, although now and then someone modifies the group controls. Now and then a person goes to prison because he refuses to abide by group demands. The difference between such a courageous soul, or conscientious objector, and a criminal, is that the former is striving to improve his group's standards, while the latter is endeavoring to lower group standards.[1]

Fashion is an autocratic ruler. Too often it represents control by the ephemeral, the unessential, the superficial, the foolish, and yet from fashion comes now and then some elements of lasting value. Fashion control is as often irrational as is custom control, hence the need for critical examination of it by its devotees.

If I act in line with group demands merely in order to succeed, I am living on a relatively low behavior plane. If I act in line with group standards merely in order to maintain personal status, I am still living on a low level. If I act socially because of having thought through my behavior in terms of human welfare I have attained a higher plane. In the last instance I am likely to start new currents of constructive group opinion and to create new and better social controls.

Control by Custom and Tradition

A large part of group control is found in customs and traditions or in the ways of doing and believing by which persons are conditioned chiefly in their childhood. Customs and traditions are group accepted techniques of control that have become well established, that are taken for granted, and that are passed along from generation to generation. They represent methods of doing and thinking that have been successful, and hence have acquired prestige. They are group sanctioned, and the individual members of the group are constrained to conduct themselves according to the dictates of these customs and traditions.

The real authority behind the mores, or those customs and traditions that are proclaimed essential to group welfare, is the group itself. It includes not simply the living members, for the memory of those who have departed from this life may exert a powerful influence. The group develops "collective representations"[2] or symbols. It may create a flag which becomes

---

[1] Of course the conscientious objector may at times be mistaken.

[2] "Collective representations" is one of the main concepts contributed to sociological thought by Émile Durkheim, one of the most eminent French sociologists.

sacred. It promotes group songs; confers honors and assigns rank, or position to the faithful.

The group enforces its will sometimes through ridicule, which is so powerful that most persons cannot long withstand it. In their overt behavior many persons live on higher planes than they would if they were not afraid of inviting group contempt.

Negative control includes the use of taboo. Taboo is a "don't" with a penalty attached to it. In order, for example, to protect a cocoanut crop, a primitive chieftain may place a taboo upon it, and in consequence, whoever violates the taboo will be stricken to death by unseen beings. More significant perhaps is the fact that some of the group's members take the taboo so seriously that if they violate it they die from fear.

Among civilized peoples group control is often exercised through a modern form of taboo, which includes a threat and a penalty although the latter is inflicted directly rather than by invisible powers. For example, intermarriage of whites and Negroes is taboo in the United States.

Every group organization contains some degree of *ritual*, which is a positive control. Ritual is crystallized custom and tradition. It operates by "the charm of orderly movements," by "the impressiveness of ordered masses in processions," by the appeal to mystery.[1] Ritual secures the actual doing and also at the same time the formation of habits. Ritual conditions persons to the actual carrying out of certain group-desired customs and traditions.

The college freshman or sophomore who joins a fraternity must submit to a set of initiation ceremonies, that is, to ritual. The ritualistic ceremonies, partly formal and partly informal, are sometimes arranged so as to humiliate the individual and to make him feel as weak as possible. At an appointed time the more formal ritual begins which magnifies the ideals and standards and glories of the group as much as possible. The

[1] Dewey and Tufts, *Social Ethics* (Henry Holt and Company, New York, 1908), p. 56. Several interesting comparisons may be made by the analytical student between this volume and a current one by James H. Tufts entitled *American Social Morality* (Henry Holt and Company, New York, 1933).

contrast is exaggerated, for the weakened individual is set over against the glorified group. In the name of group ritual many irrational jokes are perpetrated upon innocent blindfolded initiates, and thus a worthy social institution is sometimes debased by its well-meaning but stupid members.

To a surprising degree people live according to custom-control. If they live up to the level of the generally accepted group standards they feel at ease. If one's group endorses automobile speeding, cheating in examinations, midnight carousals, or lying to the assessor, the guilty person feels no pangs of conscience but may even boast of his anti-social actions. If drinking liquor is considered "smart" in a given group, then the members boast of getting "drunk"; if drinking is considered assinine by the group, the member who gets intoxicated later feels ashamed.

Group control is often found in what is called "the rules of the game," unwritten to be sure, but powerful. If the rules do not seem fair to a person he may grumble and comply, openly challenge them, or keep still and try "to get by" without observing them. These are the three major types of unfavorable reaction to group control.

Custom control may be entirely irrational; it may be injurious but maintained by an unscrupulous or intolerant leader or minority. The merely trivial may become the group standard and demand obeisance from the many. The truly worthwhile may be submerged among group values. Group control may crush worth-while personal initiative.

For his own sake as well as for the sake of the group a person cannot always accept group control uncritically. It is fortunate for any group that some members keep their minds open to the defects of existing customs and traditions, and that they are courageous enough to speak out against the group. A democracy encourages such criticism, but in an autocracy woe to the critic of the *status quo*.

Certain types of group control are useful for the age in which they originated, but normally are carried over to a succeeding age, where they are no longer sufficient because new group and personal needs have arisen. The socially more alert members recognize the inefficiency of ancient controls and strive to change them for better controls.

CONTROL BY LAW

Law is organized group control. It is composed of the laws on the statute books and of the attitudes of the people toward these laws. It is the attitudes that count the more.

Laws are not designed for the persons who have lawful attitudes. They are needed for those whose behavior is against group welfare. The exercise by the state of restraint of individuals becomes increasingly necessary in an increasingly complex collective life. When people travelled in ox carts, traffic ordinances, for example, were not necessary, but in an age of automobiles laws restricting persons must be made and enforced for two reasons: first, to protect the lawful against the reckless; and second, to keep each person from getting in the way of other persons.

The coercive character of law is justified by the need to control behavior in behalf of group standards. If everyone honestly behaved in behalf of group safety and development, few coercive laws would be needed. The law aims to maintain minimum standards of behavior as determined by group needs.

Law has been called the most specialized and highly finished engine of control employed by society. E. A. Ross has presented the twofold function of law as follows: law treats persons repressively because of certain of their aggressive acts; and persons compulsively because of their neglect with regard to other phases of life. It is generally easier to prevent individuals from aggressiveness than to secure positive coöperation.[1]

Law secures respect for itself through a system of punishments. It commonly uses both physical and financial punishment. Either it incarcerates a convicted person or else takes money from him. The more serious the offense the more likely is physical punishment to be meted out.

[1] *Social Control* (The Macmillan Company, New York, 1901). Ch. XI.

The civil and criminal law are the main pillars which sustain the social structure in any national group. Since these are the main structural props of group order, it is the lawyer's function to help preserve the social order and to secure justice. In theory the legal profession has been pronounced as much a social welfare profession as teaching or the ministry. If this view is correct then the commercialized conception of a profession, namely, of having personal services to sell to persons and to corporations who can pay is false. Those lawyers who are out to win for their clients irrespective of where justice lies are betraying their high calling. The best members of the profession consider themselves as social servants, guardians of order and justice rather than hired servants of people who can pay and who want "to get around the law" at any cost.

Laws originated in a need for justice and for order. In primitive groups a body of customs and traditions grew into rules and laws. A main source of the growth of these laws was the power of the chieftain to decide new cases. His decisions were accepted as absolute authority. Later a more adequate method of legal procedure developed in the form of courts of justice, presided over by persons specially selected for adjudicative work. Until recent decades the adjudication of new and particular cases was the chief source of additions to law; while today nearly all new expressions of law have their origins in legislative bodies, which have been created for the purpose of making laws. Unfortunately, under democracy where the people make laws, many persons feel themselves superior to the laws which they help make and hence violate them freely. Moreover, there is no end to the making of laws with the result that unscrupulous lawyers can defeat justice by playing laws and interpretations of laws and legal technicalities of law against justice. Still further, law-making bodies are often subject to endless discussion and to the influence of pernicious lobbies. In most highly complex societies built on individualism, people are not yet ready or trained for law-making, and hence the expert is developing. Early in 1933 the Congress of the United

States turned over temporarily to the Chief Executive wide discretionary powers that ordinarily are held as the prerogative of Congress only. The President thus became for a time a benevolent dictator.

Law has been based on some theory of human society.[1] Earliest Roman law, for instance, assumed the religious view of group organization inherent in ancestor worship. Later Roman law considered that the group was a matter of "contract" between independent individuals.[2] Through the influence of the church during the Middle Ages, the conception of law as a divine command dominated. Today the foundation of law is proclaimed as being the welfare of the people! There is as a rule less blind adherence than formerly to precedents often antiquated or ill-founded and more consideration of human welfare.

CONTROL THROUGH PUBLIC OPINION

Public opinion is the source of law; it is the force upon which law depends for its support. When crystallized, public opinion becomes law, either written or unwritten. Long before there were any written laws group opinion operated. On the other hand if group opinion ceases to support a law, the latter becomes a dead letter. Public opinion is seen as a main agent of social control and as the undefined force that gives group organization its content.

Public opinion is a term used in various ways. First, there is *preponderant* or *general* opinion.[3] It is an expression of the mores. It is developed partly in the conditioning processes of childhood and adolescence. It comes through indirect suggestion. It contains many elements which have never reached the level of discussion. In a scientific sense it is not public opinion at all, but it is often popularly referred to as public opinion.

[1] Charles A. Ellwood, *Methods in Sociology* (Duke University Press, Durham, North Carolina, 1933), p. 151.

[2] *Loc. cit.*

[3] W. Brooke Graves, *Readings in Public Opinion* (D. Appleton and Company, New York, 1928), p. xxvi.

Public opinion is ordinarily used in the sense of *majority opinion*. It implies that debate and discussion and a decision of some sort have occurred. As a result a majority and a minority opinion are recorded. Often there is a majority opinion and several minority opinions. Occasionally, as in Germany in the years immediately preceding the appointment of Hitler as chancellor there were several minority opinions but no majority opinion or party on political matters. When we say that public opinion favors or opposes a given procedure we usually mean that we have reason to believe that a majority of the group concerned favor or oppose.

Public opinion (majority opinion) acts more quickly than does law. It is a less expensive means of group control. As E. A. Ross has well pointed out, public opinion is less mechanical than law, and penetrates the hidden regions of life; it passes judgments upon purely private acts. It is an inexpensive means of control. The inexpensiveness of praise or blame is marvellous.[1] Human behavior is continually conditioned by the fact that public opinion will be ruthlessly expressed.

Public opinion (majority opinion) has its defects. It is not clear, or precise, or codified. It has "a short wrath and a poor memory."[2] It is rarely unanimous; an offender against society can escape the condemnation of public opinion by taking refuge among a group of friends where his fault is condoned or even praised. If responsibility can be shifted, for example, when a corporation has committed an offense, public opinion is confused. Public opinion is primitive in its methods, driven by emotional discharges, and passionate.

A bare majority on an issue fraught with emotion is rarely sufficient. The negative 49 per cent are likely to multiply their strength through organization. They may resist vigorously and surreptitiously. The 51 per cent are likely "to let down." Their attention may be diverted in many directions. They break up and each goes his own way on the assumption that the cause has been won. Hence on all social questions where deep-seated

[1] E. A. Ross, *Social Control*, p. 95.   [2] *Ibid.*, p. 96.

feelings are involved at least a two-thirds majority in each community is necessary in order that enforcement may not be defeated.

Public opinion may be *consensus opinion*, that is, it may be reached not by partisan discussion but by scientific investigation. No one wants to win for his side or to promote or defeat a cause, but everyone strives to win for the truth. Each seeks to make a correct diagnosis and contributes whatever facts he has at his command, irrespective of what the findings will show. A consensus of opinion results from a pooling of data; the product may be a new idea.[1]

Group opinion sometimes takes strange turns. The group may constrain a person to act below his own sense of values, as in the case of physicians, already mentioned in an earlier chapter, who must keep wholly silent concerning venereal diseases even though such silence subjects some women to certain contagion. A traveller may find himself entertained in a group whose standards are lower than his own, and he must decide whether to offend his hosts or to stand by his own ideals.

Propaganda is a powerful agent in public opinion. Propaganda is the process of spreading a part of the truth as though it were the whole truth or the main truth. It is partial misrepresentation. It appears in newspapers in the form of news coloration. It bobs up at election times in downright misrepresentation. It is practiced by advocates in court and by salesmen in business. Nearly all large institutions have publicity agents whose business it is to put their institution before the public in the best possible light. It hinders individual thinking and blinds public opinion.

In these days of propaganda and canned thinking vast multitudes move at the flashing lights of some invisible but colossal traffic director who flashes the lights to the copy room and then out over the country. He flashes red and the mob responds in a tremor of

[1] A. D. Sheffield, *Joining in Public Discussion* (George H. Doran Company, New York, 1922), Introduction. Also see Harrison S. Elliott, *The Process of Group Thinking* (Association Press, New York, 1928).

abhorrence at bolshevism. He flashes white and the mob moves on with a reassured delight in 100 per cent Americanism as per schedule. . . .

There will hardly be a thought all day which has not been carefully prepared by others. The problem of what they shall wear on their bodies has been decided for them by the twin gods of manufacturing and advertising. And what they shall wear on their minds has also been decided by the same twin powers. What they shall laugh at was decided six months before by the deities of Hollywood, California; while the magazine . . . newspaper designed for "the nine-year-old mind" stamp them like a giant steam roller, leaving men and women almost as much alike and as animated as a row of celluloid dolls.[1]

Art is a highly significant form of social control. The response of a group to art controls indicates the nature of the values it holds dear and the values to which appeals may be made effectively.

Art finds its expression in the order, rhythm, and symmetry upon which the universe is organized. It is natural that persons should be susceptible to "the influence of that which pervades and rules in the heavens and the earth, and in the mind and body." [2] Celestial bodies move orderly and rhythmically. Sight would not be possible if it were not for the rhythmical vibrations of "ether" and sound would be unknown were it not for the rhythmical vibrations of air. The heart beats orderly and rhythmically. It is not surprising, therefore, that human beings respond to that which is orderly and symmetrical.

Art influences and controls people through the pattern forms which it produces. These patterns give a setting to life, personal and group. They shape attitudes. They set both static and dynamic patterns.[3] The static type is represented by personal decoration, ornamentation, painting, architecture, sculpture. The dynamic arts include the dance, song, poetry, music, public speech.[4] In all these fields art creates an ideal world and

[1] Halford E. Luccock, "From Cook's Tours," *Christian Century*, January 26, 1922, p. 109.

[2] Walter D. Scott, *The Psychology of Public Speaking* (Pearson Brothers, Chicago, 1906), pp. 122, 123.

[3] Ernst Grosse, *The Beginnings of Art* (D. Appleton and Company, New York, 1897), p. 51.

[4] *Loc. cit.*

possesses a peculiar drawing power. Its appeal comes partly from the pleasing atmosphere which it creates and partly by stimulating a sense of rhythm.

Art is a strong social control because of its indirect suggestion. Its appeal is not made to reason but to the imagination. Art does not moralize; it presents beauty. Unfortunately bad people and destructive ideas sometimes don artistic forms, while good people and constructive ideas sometimes ignore the beautiful and the pleasing.

Decoration of the body is an original form of art control.[1] In his daily life the primitive Australian is satisfied with "a few spots on his cheeks and shoulders," but on festive occasions he extends painting over his body. Since bodily decorations by painting is transitory, permanence is secured either by scarification for dark-skinned peoples, or by tattooing for fair-skinned races.[2]

Civilized groups have not succeeded in freeing themselves from the decorative controls which appealed to primitive groups. The development of decoration has increased the range of materials used and refined the techniques but civilized groups have not contributed an important new form of personal decoration, according to Ernst Grosse.[3] Their originality has been almost negligible. They have lost themselves in recurrent waves of fashion imitation.

Painting, supplementing the art of drawing, may be a significant social control. It may deliver "the whole force of a historic event" or of a life-long biography in a moment of time. It may give the observer at a glance an interpretation of vast currents of affection and emotion "as they surge on in full volume."[4] The power and force of painting lie in the method

[1] Ernst Grosse, *op. cit.*, Ch. V.

[2] The feather has "maintained its original place in decoration," throughout the ages and during all the stages of culture. "It waves on the helmet of the civilized as well as on the headband of the primitive warrior." Among both primitive and civilized peoples birds have borne the chief expense of headdress; even the Bushman's fashion of wearing birds' heads, or even whole birds are perennially raised into group honor among civilized people. (Ernst Grosse, *op. cit.*, p. 105.)

[3] *Loc. cit.*

[4] John Bascom, *Aesthetics* (G. P. Putnam's Sons, New York, 1908), p. 279.

of presenting fundamental truth, current and historical, so as to influence social conditions or countless human beings. In recent years some painters, such as Herman Heyenbrock, have presented social and industrial conditions in a way that brings important principles home to people who would otherwise be unaffected. The mural paintings of Diego Rivera are credited with revealing to the world "the profound dignity of the Mexican people."

Architecture exercises a peculiar force on mankind through its pattern forms. These are: (1) structures for protection; (2) structures for transit (bridges, aqueducts, tunnels); and (3) structures for memorial purposes (for the commemoration of departed persons and of historic events).

The chief architectural form is the human dwelling. For commercial purposes there is the store, the factory, the warehouse, the bank; for education, there is the schoolhouse, college hall, library, auditorium; for government, the legislative hall, courthouse, prison, fort; for religion, the church, the cathedral, the temple; for medicine, the hospital; for the professions, the office building. Chief of all, however, is the dwelling house.

> [It is] the orb of childhood, the nest, the nursery, and the school of the human callow: it is the home of manhood, its center of exertion and enjoyment, its points of departure and return: it is the repose of age; thither weary and spent, man turns to lay down his burden.[1]

Sculpture is at one and the same time the most laborious and imperishable of art forms. Man himself is the chief subject of sculpture. The human face has been called "the citadel of sculpture." [2] Sculpture gives expression to the most prized personality traits; it puts them into forms more permanent than paintings, prose, poetry, or music. When "the solemn vital elements" of human life are presented in silent sculptural patterns, they influence people of all times, races, languages. No one can study the "Winged Victory," "Venus de Milo," Michelangelo's "Moses," his "David," or his un-

---

[1] John Bascom, *op. cit.*, p. 185.   [2] *Loc. cit.*

finished statues in the Academy of Fine Arts in Florence, and not catch something of a superhuman spirit that words cannot express.[1]

The *dance* has always had wide social significance. The dances of primitive peoples were usually mass dances, executed ordinarily by the men, with the women sometimes furnishing the musical accompaniment. The dance was used to celebrate group victories or to arouse the courage of the group preceding any serious undertaking, especially a battle. The dancing group felt and acted as a single organism. The event accustomed men who in their precarious conditions of life were driven hither and thither by different individual needs to act together with united feelings for a single object; it was a powerful element of control.

As the size of primitive tribes grew, the members became too numerous to join in the mass dance. Hence the dance lost its power to create group morale. It shifted to those forms which had a sex appeal. The square dances are socially stimulating but unfortunately have lost their popularity of decades ago. The folk dances while subject to abuses are historically attractive. The ballet dance has excellent possibilities but often degenerates into "distorted perversions of nature," arousing vulgar curiosity. The round dance has one leading social function in that it facilitates the mutual approach of the sexes, although it perennially fosters degrading patterns such as the "shimmy" or the "black bottom."

Music through its influence over the feelings is a gigantic social control. It is a language which speaks to all mankind; it leaps all racial and national boundaries. The spontaneous singing together of a group of people unites them. Choral singing, especially of the non-professional type, is effective in pro-

[1] The bronze group entitled "The Mother of the Dead," by G. S. Pietro, illustrates well the social force of sculpture. The sculptor has caught "the lonely, vacant stare" of the mother of the dead soldier and "the groping pathos" of the little grandchild in her arms, immortalized them in bronze, and set them before the world in imperishable form. The World War was followed by almost countless war memorials in all the belligerent countries, with each of them possessing all the force of powerful "collective representations."

moting a sense of brotherhood. It is one of the most influential forms of group communication. In a religious group music promotes a common spirit of worship; in military life nothing is more stirring than the martial music of a hundred piece band. National songs bring millions to their feet in enthusiastic and united acclaim.

Poetry expresses the feelings as tempered by intelligence. A single great poet or epic poem has helped to shape the configuration of a generation. Through a single work poetry has tended to give "a specific stamp to a national group." Poetry unites people whom the interests of life separate, for it invokes "the same feelings in all." Through constantly repeating its patterns, it produces a lasting mood. Poetry not only unites people, but it may also elevate them by awakening in them a more refined and a richer emotional life than that growing out of harsh, daily experiences. Many groups such as organized labor and church groups are now utilizing social poetry. By setting an industrial or social need to poetry and to music and using it in song, whole groups develop a common thrill and undertake tremendous tasks.

Social hymns combine the force of art and religion in behalf of an improved group life and socialized behavior. Religious spirit and social idealism when combined are powerful. While social hymns now represent only a fraction of all hymns they may be expected to increase in number and influence.

Social drama and *fiction* carry significant concepts to multitudes because of the wide reading and hearing which drama and fiction receive. Because of the principle of indirect suggestion upon which they are based, they may yet become leading forces in social control.

Public speaking as a form of social control is important because of its persuasiveness. To speak to an assembly of people of various callings, views, and prejudices, and "unite them in common action"—therein lies the social power of public speaking. "To make truth and justice, wisdom and virtue, patriotism and religion, holier and more socially useful than men have ever dreamed them to be before,"[1] this is public speaking at its best as a control factor.

Art as an agent of social control has changed its course many times. Among primitive peoples, ornamentation preëminently promoted technical skill. Poetry, the dance, and music arose partly because they inflamed and inspired the warriors, who were the bulwark of the group against hostile attacks. The most powerful social influence among primitives was vested in the dance.[2]

To the Greeks sculpture incorporated social ideals at their best. In the Middle Ages architecture united bodies and souls in the halls of magnificent cathedrals. During the Renaissance painting spoke a language that was heeded by all the cultivated peoples of Europe. More recently poetry and music have predominated.[3] Still more recently it would seem that the newspaper and the "movies" and "talkies" in forms many of which are far from esthetic have been taking the place of the older art controls.

Today art joins with science in determining the spirit of social organization. As science through formal and informal educational processes enlarges the intellectual outlook, so art enriches the emotional life. Among primitives art exercised its control through group unification. For many civilized persons art has overcome the humdrum of everyday life. By being accepted as a part of the mores, the customs, and the rituals, and by setting pleasing behavior patterns, art becomes a deeply influential and often unsuspected form of social control.

From a social point of view, as contrasted with art for art's sake, the problem of art, like that of religion and recreation, turns today on its service to man in his inner adjustment to an environment which shifts and changes with unexampled rapidity. It appears to be one of the three great forces which stand between man and his breakdown. Each serves in its own way to bring him comfort, serenity,

[1] William Matthews, *Oratory and Oratory* (Griggs and Company, Chicago, 1896), p. 407.
[2] Ernst Grosse, *The Beginnings of Art*, p. 313.
[3] *Ibid.*, p. 314.

and joy. It is conceivable, but by no means proved, that the development of these forces in American life would reduce the terrible decimations made by mental disorders.[1]

Group controls are as numerous as social stimuli. They operate directly as in the form of laws and indirectly as in the arts. A look, a gesture, a tune, a picture, all may be group controls. The other side of the story are the ways in which group members are conditioned to respond to direct and indirect controls. The controls and the responses to them determine the course of group change.

PROBLEMS

1. What is group control?
2. What are group controls?
3. What is a custom? Name one.
4. What is a tradition? Illustrate.
5. Why are customs and traditions so powerful in social life?
6. What is a taboo? Name a current taboo.
7. How is ritual a form of social control?
8. What is law?
9. What are the different types of public opinion?
10. Is law a basis of public opinion or public opinion of law?
11. Why was sculpture more effective among the Greeks than earlier or since?
12. Why did architecture reach the zenith of its power in the Middle Ages?
13. Why did painting exert a greater force in the Renaissance than at any other time?
14. Why has art been so generally depreciated in the United States?
15. Do you see any signs of an increasing appreciation of art in the United States?
16. Why is art a powerful element in social control?
17. What is the nature of the basic conflict between an individual and society?
18. What is the relation of personal ethics to social control?

[1] From *The Arts in American Life*, by Frederick P. Keppell and R. L. Duffus, one of a series of monographs published under the direction of the President's Research Committee on Social Trends; by permission of the publishers, McGraw-Hill Book Company, Inc. (New York, 1933), p. 207.

READINGS

BASCOM, JOHN, *Aesthetics* (G. P. Putnam's Sons, New York, 1908).

CASE, CLARENCE M., *Non-Violent Coercion* (The Century Company, New York, 1923).

COYLE, GRACE L., *Social Process in Organized Groups* (Richard R. Smith, Inc., New York, 1930), Ch. IV.

GROSSE, ERNST, *The Beginnings of Art* (D. Appleton and Company, New York, 1897).

HILLER, E. T., *Principles of Sociology* (Harper and Brothers, New York, 1933), Ch. XXXVIII.

LUMLEY, F. E., *Means of Social Control* (The Century Company, New York, 1925).

OSBORN, LORAN D., and MARTIN H. NEUMEYER, *The Community and Society* (American Book Company, New York, 1933), Ch. XXII.

ROSS, E. A., *Social Control* (The Macmillan Company, New York, 1901).

Social Control (Publications of the American Sociological Society, University of Chicago, 1912), Vol. XII.

CHAPTER XIII

GROUP DISORGANIZATION

Group disorganization is the breakdown of any of the established processes of group life. A certain amount, therefore, of disorganization is at times necessary in order to provide for a new and needed group change. Group organization may become so well fixed that it does not provide for changed conditions. A breakdown in it allows for the development of more appropriate processes.

On the whole, however, group disorganization is harmful. A well regulated group strives continually to reorganize itself wherever disorganization occurs. It seeks out the factors which bring about disorganization in order to meet the situation adequately.

Group organization may break down because of too much or too little control. If group organization is too hard and fast, adverse reactions occur, and sooner or later break out in revolutionary behavior. If organization is too free and easy, individuals prey upon each other.

In Italy under fascism, in Germany under nazi-ism, and in Russia under communism, group organization is everything and the individual is nothing if he gets in the way of the group. In the United States which has carried the individualistic philosophy of pioneer days into the complicated social life of today a situation has developed in recent decades where everybody is accused of having a "racket" and where many shrewd persons including gangsters in both the upper and the lower classes of society have thrived upon honest hard-working people.

Group disorganization may follow inadequate distribution of income and anti-social behavior of persons in high or low position. Economic injustice and social misbehavior are often interchangeable terms in the story of group disorganization.

POVERTY AND UNEMPLOYMENT

Inefficient distribution of income from labor is a far-reaching factor in group disorganization. Some occupations pay too low wages, judged by the contributions their members make to group welfare; others are paid several times what they are socially worth. There is at present little scientific relation between income and occupation. Moreover, within occupations incomes are distributed unjustly, for workers are paid on the basis of what they are financially worth to their employers instead of according to what they are socially worth to human society.

It is not surprising therefore that we find some people very wealthy and others very poor with no good reason to be found for such a wide chasm. A small percentage of people own a large percentage of the wealth; a large percentage possess little property in addition to furniture, clothes, and personal belongings plus a few dollars. Between are the upper middle class many of whom are unhappily engaged in aping the wealthy; and the lower middle class who are keenly sensitive to the injustices suffered by the poor.[1]

The causes of poverty are many. They may be given (1) as *poor heredity*, which involves the inheritance of subnormal physical or mental traits or both. It means that many individuals are hardly capable of being trained to be self-supporting. (2) A second set of causes is found in poor habits or in *attitudes*. Shiftlessness or the "I should worry" spirit (meaning "I shouldn't worry") are sometimes to blame. Poor attitudes toward one's work may explain a great deal. Poor judgment in spending is a real problem, when the stimuli to spend are numerous and powerful. The gambling spirit destroys one's earnings. Intemperance wastes economic resources. Sexual vice creates illness and inefficiency.

---

[1] A splendid analysis of the extremes of wealth and poverty in the United States two decades ago may be found in Willford I. King, *The Wealth and Income of the People of the United States* (The Macmillan Company, New York, 1915).

(3) A third set of causes of poverty is composed of changes in methods of work, new inventions, competition among business houses. Illness cuts off the pay check and runs up the expenses. The concentration of wealth in the hands of a few prevents many persons from being paid adequately for their labor, and hence is a cause of poverty. When someone without working at all receives large sums of money, and other persons of equal ability who work for long hours receive less than living wages the economic system is an accomplice of poverty.

Unemployment for long or short periods of time leads to poverty. There are two classes of the unemployed: those who would work but cannot find it; and those who have no desire to work. The fluctuations in the demand for economic goods, the changes in the seasons, the dull seasons, throw many persons out of employment annually.[1]

A permanent unemployed class is coming to be the rule in civilized countries. In the depression year of 1932 people began to talk of a permanently unemployed class in the United States for the first time in its history. It is a bad state of affairs when any nation has within its worthy citizen group a million or five million who want work but who cannot find it.

Then there are the persons who do not want work regularly or who do not want to work at all. Many of these are largely responsible for such attitudes; others only partly so. Many men start out in life with a keen desire to work and earn money, but become temporarily unemployed, begin to live from hand to mouth, and then acquire habits of idleness.

The unemployed or part-time employed person sometimes becomes a hobo, a tramp, or a bum. Dr. Ben L. Reitman of Chicago says: "The hobo works and wanders, the tramp dreams and wanders and the bum drinks and wanders."[2] St. John

[1] In many industries there are rush and slack seasons. During the latter, many workers are laid off for several weeks at a time. In the mining industry, for example, the mines are often closed more than one-fifth of the time because of accidents, breaking of machinery, and the dull season. Trade union statistics show that skilled workers are unemployed sometimes as high as 30 per cent of a given year.

[2] Quoted by Nels Anderson, *The Hobo* (University of Chicago Press, 1923), p. 87.

Tucker, one time president of the "Hobo College" in Chicago gives a somewhat similar explanation: "A hobo is a migratory worker. A tramp is a migratory non-worker. A bum is a stationary non-worker." [1]

A permanent unemployed class is a national calamity. It calls for national action, a national program, a national employment commission. Governments are giving special attention to large national construction projects in times of widespread depression. When states, counties, and cities do likewise a portion of unemployment is alleviated. Since every month of the year has its busy seasons for some industries and its dull seasons for others, a rotation might be devised in certain communities for shifting employees in the dull seasons of certain industries to industries which are experiencing rush orders. A large degree of public control is needed not only in times of depression but in normal times so as to avoid depressions and periods of widespread unemployment.

Another group of the unemployed are the idle rich. These have sometimes been called a nation's biggest social problem. Many of the idle rich feel themselves superior to the man who works for a living; they comprise an aristocracy of snobs and spendthrifts. They set wasteful examples to the less wealthy. They arouse the spirit of communism in the minds of those who work but who cannot afford the luxuries that these idle rich parade before the public. They often set questionable standards of conduct for the less fortunate to follow. They often defy law, feeling themselves above the rules and regulations that are needed, as they say, to govern the rabble. Their position at one pole of conditions of extreme economic inequality makes them partly responsible for the poverty of those at the other pole. There is less social disorganization in a society without extremes in wealth and poverty than in one characterized by a wide range of class levels.

[1] *Loc. cit.*

CRIME

Crime is another evidence of group disorganization. It is anti-group conduct as judged either by general opinion or law or by both.

To some degree crime has existed in all social groups since the beginning of the race. Today it is as common as ever, being especially prevalent in large cities. It is so extensive in the United States at the present time that it constitutes a serious blot upon our national status. An important question is: What accounts for crime?

The casual factors in anti-group conduct are exceedingly complex. They are found (1) in the physical environment, (2) in the social environment, and (3) in the individual's reactions to his social and physical environment. (1) The physical environment affects a person through climate, seasons, temperature, food. A hot climate produces an unusually high per cent of offenses against the person; and a cold climate an undue proportion of offenses against property. The winter season results in more suffering from cold and hunger than does summer and ranks high in thefts. Spring and summer are noted for an undue proportion of sex offenses.

(2) The social environment collects its toll of anti-social behavior. A higher ratio of criminality is found among the unmarried and divorced than among those living a normal family life. This fact may be explained by the greater temptations of the homeless, or to another fact, namely, that the temper and habits which render a man unfavorable to the requirements of marriage are the tendencies which manifest themselves in crime.

Concentration of population in a large city is frequently accompanied by a proportional increase in anti-social behavior. The large city is the hiding place of people with a dark record. It flaunts the allurements of wealth and luxury in the face of poverty; it excites envy; and it harbors the solicitors of vice. It allows delinquency areas to flourish.

Customs such as the public whipping of offenders, torture, lynching, night-riding tend to provoke criminal impulses. Public executions do not always repress crime but increase it by the example which the state sets in taking life. Some newspapers publish melodramatic descriptions of crime, and human life loses its sacredness.

Poverty may be a cause of crime. There are many who are constrained to steal as was Jean Valjean, rather than see the members of their own families starve and die. In a day of ostentatious display of wealth the poor man who is diligent and honest but whose family cannot obtain all the necessities of life, sometimes concludes that "property is robbery." He sees the wealthy man enjoying leisure hours with pay, and the wife of the wealthy man riding about in a limousine without doing any work at all for a living; and he concludes that "the system is all wrong."

There is a conviction honestly held by multitudes that many of the wealthy have obtained their wealth at the expense of the poor and without contributing much of value to the community. The workingman pinched by need feels no special sense of wrong in "taking" a small portion of what he considers "immorally acquired wealth." The sense of having been wronged combined with underprivileged conditions urge a person to justify anti-social acts. When big business men and financiers make millions out of speculation or gambling, when their high finance causes thousands to lose hard-earned savings, and when some men of wealth run away from their country in order to escape trial and punishment because of questionable methods of acquiring wealth, the average man is likely to feel that such examples justify him in almost any anti-social conduct. The slogan which developed in the United States a few years ago, "You cannot convict a million dollars" represented a belief that law is not to be obeyed by the rich, and hence need not be respected by anyone.

The corruption of partisan politics favors the increase of crime. "When the unscrupulous agents of city railways, railroads, and other powerful corporations," says one authority, "control the elections of aldermen in their own interest and against the public, crime is fostered through the very institutions of justice and law."

Certain suggestions stimulate anti-social behavior. Pictures and dramatic descriptions of prize fights set boys to fighting in alleys and back yards. A film showing a spectacular robbery suggests similar behavior to youthful spectators. Sensational accounts of burglaries and of trials in the newspapers and pictures in the "police gazettes" that "pollute" pool halls and similar "hang-outs" of many men arouse anti-social impulses. Gangs of boys are frequently led into crime by the "dare" of some reckless leader.

Occupations may promote anti-social conduct. Employment in dishonest kinds of business, in gambling dens, in "liquor joints," in "houses of ill fame" furthers evil deeds. Promotors of all types are now and then drawn into fraud, embezzlement, and forgery. Even some public officials find the temptations placed before them too strong and they betray the public trust in them.

(3) A person's reactions to all these and other environmental factors actually place a portion of the responsibility for his behavior directly upon himself. Of course some individuals are moral imbeciles by birth, and are never able to distinguish between right and wrong. Others are born mentally defective so that by the time they reach the age of eighteen, for example, they have the mental development and the inhibitions of children of six, ten, or twelve years of age. Since they possess the feelings, emotions, and passions of an eighteen-year-old, but perhaps the self-control of a ten-year-old child they easily become delinquent in an environment filled with high-powered temptations.

Unregulated sex impulses result in anti-social activities. There have been far more male offenders than female offenders in sex relations. As women become emancipated, however, their behavior record approximates that of men. Moreover, when women once succumb to sexual offenses they are not so easily restored to normal life as are men, partly because of the breaking down of a more sensitive organism, and of a greater despair which comes over them, and because many of the gates to respectable life are closed to them although not to men who are similar offenders.

A person's control over his behavior varies with his age. In his earliest years he may not be held accountable for his acts. Young children are easily conditioned by the attitudes of their peers or their elders to behave in all sorts of ways. In adolescence strong surges of energy may lead a youth into conflict with his environment. Sex impulses easily draw the individual into trouble. Ambition to succeed and to win, likewise carry persons beyond the bounds of fair play. The bulk of offenses against society seems to come between the ages of eighteen and forty, with crimes of cold calculation, fraud, bankruptcy, and political intrigue coming chiefly in the middle and later years. Anti-social behavior results when the individual resists the social codes of behavior. When the individual is lacking in social responsibility or when the social codes are too rigid or inadequate, anti-social conduct may be expected.

Insofar as alcoholism lessens self-control and dulls a sense of social responsibility, it is a cause of crime. It easily leads to breakdowns of personal control, to vice, and to crime. Alcohol weakens "the inhibitory power of the higher nerve centers, confuses the intellect, dulls the conscience, and sets anger and lust free without rein or bridle." Alcoholism has led to brutal treatment of wives and children, has broken down woman's finest controls, and debauched otherwise competent persons. Persons under the influence of liquor may play the rôle of idiots. In high-powered automobiles they drive recklessly; with firearms they shoot those whom they love.

In order that people may protect themselves against the anti-social behavior of other people, a special agency has been set up known as the *police*. It is the function of the police to be on the watch for overt forms of anti-social conduct and to apprehend the offender as soon as possible. Often they have been physical giants and have tended to use their physical strength to browbeat. In the United States they, as a class, have been relatively uneducated. In England, however, they represent a higher type of person. The traffic squad performs the interesting function of helping citizens from getting in each other's way. In the United States they are more courteous than the regular police and have not acquired an offensive manner. In England they are known as "Bobbies" and carry neither clubs nor guns but exercise control through their superior personal qualities; they are well-informed and intelligent.[1]

It is the function of every policeman to be an extremely valuable public servant, according to Joseph Fels. The police may be thought of as a group of social workers, knowing personally every home and all the inhabitants in their respective districts. They might be neighborhood guardians, aiding case workers, and helping to make personal adjustments wherever needed. They might inspect street cleaning, the collection of garbage, act as deputies of the assessor, and as representatives of the schools in maintaining attendance.

The *policewoman* is another factor in preventing disorganization. She supervises conditions at public dance halls, vaudeville theaters, and cheap motion picture shows, and attempts to safeguard girls and women from demoralization. The procedure has resulted in an increasing freedom with which girls and women appeal to the police department for advice and protection, in the better handling of those situations where a woman's sympathetic understanding may be more effective than a man's power, and in the care of girls and women who are brought to police stations.

Anti-social behavior and the resultant social disorganization have made necessary the *public prosecutor*, or district attorney, whose business it is to see that persons guilty of anti-social behavior are punished. He needs not only legal backgrounds

[1] The term, "Bobby," comes from the name of Sir Robert Peel who originated the system. For a time the police of this system were called "Peelers."

but also training in criminology and sociology in order that he may know the requirements of social defense.

Corresponding to public prosecution there is developing *public defense*, or more accurately, defense of offenders.   If offenders have wealth they are able to defend themselves often to the point of defeating law and justice; they defeat the just efforts of public prosecutors, and go free.   On the other hand if the offender is without money he is often helpless in a trial where he faces an an organized legal staff of trained prosecutors.   Defendants with ample means are able to employ such shrewd counsel that public prosecution is blocked, that a trial is prolonged over months and even years, and that group disorganization is increased.

Public defense, thus, has led to the creation of the office of a public defender and of legal aid societies composed of citizens interested in seeing that justice is guaranteed to the poor.   The public defender and the legal aid society are supplementary, for the office of the former is created by the county to provide legal service at public expense for the poor, and the latter comprises citizens banded together voluntarily to assist persons who are in legal difficulty but are financially unable to defend themselves.   The legal aid society usually develops first and serves until an adequate public defender's office is established.

The *jury system* is a device to safeguard the interests of the common man when charged with anti-social behavior.   If he can be tried by his peers, that is, by other common people, it is thought that justice will be more certain.   These peers however are subject to prejudices, biases, and intolerant attitudes. Moreover, their feelings are continually being played upon by unscrupulous lawyers.   Hence trial by judges rather than by juries is being advocated, because many lawyers resort to "grandstand" plays or emotional appeals when arguing directly before a jury.   On the other hand the judge is only one person. Perhaps it would be better to have a joint system, with offenders being tried, for example, before three persons, one of whom is a judge, and the other two, private citizens, with each of the three having an equal vote.

Delinquency

A large percentage of adult offenders and of social disorganization begins in childhood and adolescence. If children and adolescents can be conditioned constructively, if their feelings and emotions can be conditioned into attitudes of social responsibility, then delinquency, crime, and disorganization would be largely prevented.

Until a few decades ago in the United States, child offenders were arrested and if unable to furnish bail were placed in the regular cells of police stations. If convicted they were fined, and then sent to the city jail or prison to "pay out" their fine at a rate for example, of fifty cents a day. They were isolated as individuals.

About 1900 there came a turning point in the treatment of youthful offenders.[1] Many changes have been inaugurated, and new attitudes developed. (1) The juvenile offender is treated as a ward of the court, and not as an accused or convicted criminal.[2] (2) Separate courts have been established for children's cases; they are unlike the regular court chambers; they resemble a private conference room. Women acting as referees or judges in girls' cases have been markedly successful. It has been urged that a large percentage of juvenile court cases do not represent children's guilt so much as parental neglect and guilt. Hence not the child but the parents in certain cases are being brought into the domestic relations court which handles a considerable percentage of the cases that formerly went to the juvenile court.[3]

(3) The self-government idea that has developed in institutions for the reform of youthful offenders is meritorious. To as great extent as possible it puts youth in institutions on their own responsibility. They hold their own court and mete out

[1] Judge Ben Lindsey was one of the leading originators of this new procedure.
[2] The system of fines has been abolished.
[3] T. D. Eliot in his *Juvenile Court and the Community* (The Macmillan Company, New York, 1918) discusses clearly the strong and weak points of the juvenile court.

punishment, chiefly in terms of deprivation of privileges. Those who live according to the rules have special opportunities, which constitute stimuli to all to act in socially responsible ways. They learn social self-control through personal experiences in wholesome group life.[1]

(4) Better than institutions is *juvenile probation* under wholesome circumstances. The first offender and others who have committed minor offenses are returned to their homes or to the care of other responsible persons, and kept there under the supervision of probation officers. Youth thus is not treated as an isolated unit or as an institutional inmate but as a member of family and neighborhood groups.

It sometimes has become the rule to place on probation adolescents who have become "repeaters," that is, who are offenders for two, three, or four times. This practice constitutes undue leniency, and is taken advantage of by youth. Moreover, the police lose interest in arresting young culprits who steal automobiles or burglarize houses. The police report that it does no good to apprehend such offenders, for in a few days they are at liberty again, ready to commit new offenses. In reply, the probation officers point out that at present the alternative is the dubious proceeding of sending adolescent boys into city jails to companion idly with mature and hardened criminals, and to come out more dangerous to society than when they entered. A partial solution to the problem might come from increasing sufficiently the number and pay of thoroughly trained and competent probation officers.

(5) It is evident that the public schools are in a position to segregate all mentally defective adolescents and keep them under institutional supervision. Such a procedure would be better than to allow them to be released from school supervision at fifteen or sixteen years of age and to drift into delinquency. If the public schools would keep the mentally deficient and all

[1] For an initial account of the self-government principle in operation, see W. R. George, *The Junior Republic* (D. Appleton and Company, New York, 1910).

behavior problem youths under proper supervision until such time as they show themselves capable of social self-control, delinquency and crime could be cut down. Thus the school might take care of a percentage of cases that now find their way into the juvenile courts.

The public schools are expected to train children who come under their supervision in the practice of social self-control. If a child does not maintain a pro-social behavior standard, the schools are not justified in releasing him from its care. What does it profit a boy if he acquires knowledge but fails to develop pro-social behavior? Moreover, such a procedure plays directly into the hands of group disorganization.

(6) Rapid strides have been made since 1925 by *child guidance clinics*. They receive "problem children" and give them medical, psychological, psychiatric, and social case work attention. It has been found that a high percentage of "problem children" have "problem parents," that is, the parents have been failing to meet the needs of their children. "Treatment" has to be prescribed for the parents to the end that they change their ways in their relationships with their children. Since the child guidance clinic gives a thorough diagnosis of behavior problems in their early stages much value must be attached to it.

(7) The unfit or broken home and inadequate parents are receiving increasing attention. The inadequate home may be classified under several headings: (a) the home broken by death; (b) the home rent asunder by divorce, separation, or desertion; (c) the home entered by chronic poverty; (d) the home in which wealth and luxury have made the children irresponsible puppets; (e) the home in which the parents are too busy with business or bridge and tea parties to give adequate attention to the welfare of their children; (f) the home in which parents are anti-social and vice-ridden; (g) the home in which the parents are shiftless; (h) the immigrant home in which the parents in trying to become adjusted to modern complex life lose control over their children; and (i) the home in which the parents, otherwise fine

people, have had no training in parenthood and in the scientific principles of child guidance.

The last mentioned type of inadequate home is widespread. Every child, even of the most respectable parents, needs to be conditioned in pro-social directions. He needs to be trained, controlled, and conditioned into ways of social coöperation. Even the children of refined, generous, sacrificial parents may become intensely self-centered. Even "the noblest youths" must sooner or later gain control over their emotions and passions and develop new and better types of pro-social attitudes if they are to become worth-while citizens.

(8) Public neglect and indifference is a causal factor in social disorganization. The presence of harmful amusements operated for profit is an illustration in point. The social injustice which permits the extremes of poverty and wealth is another causal element. Public ignorance of delinquency areas is unfortunate. The practice of releasing youth from the public schools and allowing them to drift during the years of later adolescence is fraught with danger.

(9) The absence of pro-social attitudes leads to delinquency. Attitudes which give a balanced self-control, a wholesome religious outlook, a coöperative family life, and a pro-social configuration to personality are powerful antidotes to delinquency.

Social Treatment

Constructive treatment of group offenders is needed first for the sake of the offenders themselves and second as protection for the group. The offender presumably is an individual whose personality is an important desideratum. The state also has much at stake for it cannot afford to suffer too much disorganization.

Retaliation, repression, and reformation have been called "the three r's" in treating offenders. *Retaliation* gives an equivalent for what has been received. If you are to return benefits, why should you not return injuries upon the same basis of give-and-take? The impulse to "get even" is one of the oldest in human nature. An eye for an eye and a tooth for a tooth, is the motto of retaliation. Retaliation is common among primitive people and children; it is also resorted to by most civilized adults under great provocation.

Repression uses fear. To intimidate and to torture is the procedure of repression. Kings and autocrats have been prone to try to suppress crime by measures designed to intimidate and to torture. This method "held humanity in its grasp for thousands of years." [1]

Reformation as a technique for treating anti-social behavior first received serious consideration when Beccaria, an Italian, published his *Crimes and Punishment* in Milan, 1764. His book was "the sensation of the day." It openly challenged repression and with equal frankness championed reformation. The book was widely translated, and the author lived to see his ideas extensively adopted.

Another successful early advocate of reformation was John Howard of England. In 1773, he was made sheriff of Bedford and placed in charge of the jail in which one hundred years previously John Bunyan had written *Pilgrim's Progress*. During the sixteen years of his public service, almost all at private expense, he visited nearly every country accessible to European travellers. In describing his journeying in behalf of prison reform the poet has said:

> Onward he moves; disease and retire;
> While murmuring demons hate they still admire. [2]

On John Howard's tomb are these words: "He took an open but unfrequented path to immortality." Giving his life for the unfortunates of society was his sacrificial achievement.

The ideas of Beccaria and John Howard concerning reformation have been carried out in part in both Europe and America.

[1] See F. H. Wines, *Punishment and Reformation* (Thomas Y. Crowell Company, New York, 1919), for a splendid historical analysis.

[2] Quoted from Frederick H. Wines, *Punishment and Reformation* (Thomas Y. Crowell Company, New York, 1919), p. 128.

William Penn, who had been jailed in England, was one of the first persons in America to show an interest in reforming criminals. As a result of his influence the Philadelphia Society for Relieving Distressed Prisoners was organized in 1776. It became the parent of prison associations in the United States.[1]

The penitentiary in Philadelphia that was ordered in 1817 has served "as a model which has been copied in all parts of the world, with variations."[2] It has radiating wings, with cells next the outer wall and the corridor in the center, an arrangement which gives light in all cells and some sunshine in most of them. The confining of prisoners in individual cells, isolated from each other, was a reaction against the method of allowing prisoners of all degrees of criminality to associate together.

The Auburn State Prison, established about 1816 in New York, was designed to separate prisoners at night only. The convicts were employed during the day in large workshops. While at labor the prisoners had to observe the rule of absolute silence, which was enforced with exacting sternness. Silence in itself constituted a separation of prisoners and a fundamental isolation.[3]

The Elmira Reformatory in New York received its first prisoners in 1876, with Z. R. Brockway as its first superintendent. Under Brockway's direction the following principles of dealing with persons convicted of anti-social behavior were put into operation with marked success. (1) The prisoner can be reformed. (2) Reformation is the need of the individual and the duty of the state. (3) The prisoner's reformation is facilitated by his own coöperation. (4) The supreme agency for securing this desirable coöperation is power lodged in the administration

[1] In 1776, the Walnut Street Jail in Philadelphia was a place of intimidation. The first time that a clergyman attempted to conduct religious services in the yard, the jailer as a precaution against riot and to insure the preacher's personal safety, had a cannon brought into the yard and had stationed beside it a man with a lighted match (Wines, *op. cit.*, pp. 147, 148).

[2] Frederick H. Wines, *Punishment and Reformation*, p. 153.

[3] In 1825, a state prison at Sing Sing was built with convict labor following the Auburn rules; the achievement surprised the world, for it had not been considered possible to use criminals in constructing a large public building (Frederick H. Wines, *op. cit.*).

of the prison to lengthen or shorten the duration of the offender's term of imprisonment. (5) Very important is the principle that reformation must be educational. (6) Trade training is a basic need of prisoners. The aim of Elmira was to send no man out who was not prepared to do something well enough to be independent of the temptation to lie or to steal. (7) The treatment of every prisoner must be individualized and care must be given him which he needs in order to reorganize his personality. If the question is asked: Where does the punishment enter in, the answer is: In the disciplinary control which is unremitting and exacting.[1]

A new development was inaugurated when T. M. Osborne was warden of Sing Sing. He undertook, among other things, to encourage the prisoners to assume responsibility for their own behavior. Under his supervision the prisoners formed a welfare league among and for themselves. Within limits they were allowed to make their own rules of conduct and to punish violators. The plan worked well among those types of offenders who at heart were pro-social rather than anti-social. It stimulated prisoners to develop the social and self-governing spirit that is needed in ordinary group life.[2]

Special problems in the reformation of offenders will now be considered. (1) The indeterminate sentence provides that an offender may be sentenced, for example, for not less than one year or more than ten years. Until recently it was the policy to prescribe a definite period of punishment for each crime committed. The indeterminate sentence indicates that the object of imprisonment is not for punishment primarily but for the reformation of the offender and for his return to normal society as soon as he is able to lead a socially responsible life. To give this principle a fair chance to operate, it is necessary that prisons be so administered that the offenders have an opportunity to demonstrate their fitness "to work out their salva-

---

[1] Frederick H. Wines, *Punishment and Reformation*, p. 231.

[2] See T. M. Osborne, *Prisons and Common Sense* (J. B. Lippincott Company, Philadelphia. 1924).

tion under reformative conditions." Individualization of treatment is the current scientific method,[1] and a real indeterminate sentence is one in which the offender is kept under reformatory conditions until he develops socially responsible attitudes, a full occupational training, and an abiding sense of self-respect.[2]

(2) Prison labor was first introduced as "an aid to religious administrations," although it does not necessarily produce penitence. It may prove more of a boon than a punishment. Its basic value is that of reconditioning prisoners not simply physically but in their mental and social outlook on life.

The prison farm affords the discipline of hard work, the advantages of outdoor employment, of contacts with nature, of a wholesome relief from oppressive urban conditions, and the stimuli that come from working with living things. Although it lacks in not being able to train persons for urban positions, it offers other advantages vastly superior to life in jails and penitentiaries; moreover, it can be combined with any advantages in occupational training that reformatories may afford. It may also be largely self-supporting and in some instances it can afford a small allowance for the family of the offender in pay for his work.[3]

(3) The parole system recognizes the fact that prisons do not afford a good opportunity for developing a normal group life. Parole combined with the indeterminate sentence gives an offender a chance "to make good" in normal society under supervision. Doctor E. W. Burgess has shown how by studying about twenty factors concerning the life of the offenders and the conditions of offense it is possible to judge what percentage of paroled persons will make good, and what any particular person's probabilities will be of making good under parole.[4]

[1] See William Healy, *The Individual Delinquent* (Little, Brown, and Company, Boston, 1915), for an early elaboration of this method.
[2] See B. G. Lewis, *The Offender* (Harper and Brothers, New York, 1917), for further materials on the treatment of offenders.
[3] An excellent basis for a comparative study of prison systems will be found in John L. Gillin, *Taming the Criminal* (The Macmillan Company, New York, 1931).
[4] E. W. Burgess, "Factors Determining Success or Failure on Parole," in *Parole and the Indeterminate Sentence* (Parole Board of Illinois, Chicago, 1928).

(4) Adult probation is a system "not for letting people off, but of providing correctional treatment outside of prison walls." In many cases imprisonment carries with it unwholesome contacts with "toughs"; it also involves life-long disgrace, loss of status, and discouragement. Adult probation is intended for first offenders, for those not truly anti-social, for those who have broken minor regulations. The person on probation makes monthly reports, pays the fine against him in installments, and makes restitution in whole or in part to the person or persons injured by him. If he can "learn his lesson" in this way why punish him further?

(5) The county jail system such as has existed widely in the United States has been characterized as "a relic of barbarism." Its chief advocates are those who are dependent upon it for salaries or fees, or those who are unthinking regarding the proper treatment of anti-social behavior.

It causes or furthers physical deterioration. It is a sad sight to behold strong men herded in a county jail like cattle in stalls, or walking the narrow confines of a county jail "to relieve cramping limbs." Jails ordinarily do not have even a crude gymnasium in which trustworthy prisoners can exercise weakening muscles. The physical condition of prisoners is also undermined by unsanitary factors such as impure air, dirty bedding, and dark cells. Darkness, dampness, and dirt often combine to make the strong weak, and the weak still weaker.

Nerve energy is wasted. Barring a few exceptions there is little offered in the way of systematic education. With little to occupy the mind but reflections on the past, many prisoners leave jail more disorganized than when they entered. They are not reformed. The county jail is blind to its responsibility to society of making offenders into better men and women while serving their sentences. Presumably merely a place for the confinement of offenders it turns out to be "a school for crime."

First offenders and hardened offenders are thrown together. Exchange of anti-social experiences is a major diversion. The wise and experienced in crime teach the beginner "the tricks of the art" of crime. The narratives of "the tough jail-bird" impress the plastic minds of youthful offenders, and tempt them to new acts of crime upon release. The "criminal atmosphere" in a jail is very serious because so many of the prisoners are comparatively young; the jail tears down rather than builds up ethical character. It does not compare with the state or county farm for offenders as a means of securing personal reorganization.[1]

In most of the states of our country two or four state farms of at least 500 acres each, located in different sections of each state, represent a minimum need. If such farms are objected to because of the cost, the answer is that the state farm can be operated at a less actual cost than can county jails.

The problem of group disorganization raises the question of how much control shall the group exercise over its members. If too much control, personality growth will be stifled and repressed and persons be stimulated to start revolutionary movements. If too little control is exercised, some persons will take advantage of their fellows, and group morale be broken down. If the control is too direct it arouses adverse reactions and disloyalty. The question arising ever and anon is this: How shall the group control its members so that each shall have the fullest opportunity for development, and so that at the same time the group may maintain the soundest possible degree of morale and organization.

Group disorganization is due partly to the fact that material inventions and technological controls have outrun spiritual and ethical controls. Man has built gigantic industries and concocted powerful engines of war but has neglected training in group responsibility and social values. As a result powerful self-centered persons disrupt groups, and self-centered groups disrupt the larger groups of which they are parts.

---

[1] The county jail reacts sometimes as a greater punishment upon the wife and children of the offender than upon the latter himself. While the prisoner is idling away a sentence of thirty days in jail and being fed and clothed at public expense, his wife and children are deprived of a possible income from the wage-earner and perhaps are suffering for lack of the necessities of life.

All groups which have acquired power before the anti-social and unsocial attitudes of their members have been controlled and conditioned to the larger social welfare, have experienced disorganization. The need is urgent for the development of socialized attitudes on the part of all group members as an antidote against group disorganization.

PROBLEMS

1. Does it ever pay to be anti-social?
2. Which is more difficult: to be pro-social or anti-social?
3. Explain the statement: "Societies have the criminals they deserve."
4. What is group disorganization?
5. Do groups sometimes become disorganized when the individual members maintain well-organized personalities?
6. Does the presence of a large number of anti-social members always mean a degree of group disorganization?
7. What is criminology?
8. Are there "born criminals"?
9. Write out five questions for a civil service examination for policemen.
10. Explain: Labor has a reformatory influence.
11. Why is time usually necessary for the reformatory process to take place?
12. Distinguish between probation and parole.
13. Why does the jail system despite its serious weakness exist so extensively?
14. Is group disorganization ever desirable?
15. What are the marks of a healthy group organization?

READINGS

ANDERSON, NELS, *The Hobo* (University of Chicago Press, 1927).

ASCHAFFENBURG, G., *Crime and Its Repression* (Little, Brown, and Company, Boston, 1913).

BURT, CYRIL, *The Young Delinquent* (D. Appleton and Company, New York, 1929).

ELIOT, T. D., *The Juvenile Court and the Community* (The Macmillan Company, New York, 1914).

GEORGE, W. R., *The Junior Republic* (D. Appleton and Company, New York, 1910).

GILLIN, JOHN L., *Criminology and Penology* (The Century Company, New York, 1926).

——, *Poverty and Dependency* (The Century Company, New York, 1926).

——, *Social Pathology* (The Century Company, New York, 1933).

GLUECK, S., and E., *500 Criminal Careers* (Alfred A. Knopf, New York, 1930).

HAMILTON, MARY E., *The Policewoman* (Frederick A. Stokes Company, New York, 1924).

HAYNER, F. E., *Criminology* (McGraw-Hill Book Company, Inc., New York, 1930).

HEALY, WILLIAM, *The Individual Delinquent* (Little, Brown, and Company, Boston, 1915).

HEALY, W., and A. F. BRONNER, *Criminals and Delinquents* (The Macmillan Company, New York, 1926).

HEALY, BRONNER, TAYLOR, and MURPHY, *Reconstructing Behavior in Youth* (Alfred A. Knopf, New York, 1929).

LOU, H. H., *Juvenile Courts in the United States* (University of North Carolina Press, Chapel Hill, 1927).

OSBORNE, T. M., *Prisons and Common Sense* (J. B. Lippincott Company, Philadelphia, 1924).

——, *Society and Prisons* (Yale University Press, 1916).

QUEEN, S. A., and A. M. MANN, *Social Pathology* (Thomas Y. Crowell Company, New York, 1925).

ROSS, E. A., *Sin and Society* (Houghton Mifflin Company, Boston, 1907).

SHAW, C. R., *The Natural History of a Delinquent Career* (University of Chicago Press, 1931).

SHAW, C. R., et al., *Delinquency Areas* (University of Chicago Press, 1929).

SUTHERLAND, E. H., *Criminology* (J. B. Lippincott Company, Philadelphia, 1924).

THRASHER, F. M., *The Gang* (University of Chicago Press, 1927).

VAN WATERS, MIRIAM, *Youth in Conflict* (New Republic, Inc., New York, 1925).

WELLS, G. R., *Individuality and Social Restraint* (D. Appleton and Company, New York, 1929).

WINES, F. H., *Punishment and Reformation* (Thomas Y. Crowell Company, New York, 1919).

CHAPTER XIV

GROUP CHANGE

Group conditions, group controls, even group organization, are continually subject to change. Germany shifted within a score of years from monarchy to democracy and then to fascism. In 1919, the United States adopted the Eighteenth Amendment and in 1933 repudiated it. The Allies borrowed money from the United States in 1918 and in 1932 publicly defaulted.

Changes in groups are entirely natural. Students come and go but Harvard University goes on for centuries. The Bowes' family changes but Bowes and Bowes' Book Store of Cambridge, England, continues through several generations. Popes live and die but the Roman Catholic Church spans the millennia.

On the other hand some groups are temporary. A college class lasts but a few months. A swimming party is even more fleeting. A crowd on a street corner is still more evanescent. Long-lived and short-lived groups alike may serve useful functions; alike they are needed in a changing society.

More important still, the culture traits, the prevailing ways of doing and thinking, are being modified, slowly in some groups, rapidly in others. Highly significant is the fact that change takes place more rapidly in certain phases of group life than at other points. As a result group equilibrium is thrown out of balance. If the change is widespread in one whole section of a group and not elsewhere, the group may topple over, seeking a social equilibrium on a new and different basis.

Social Evolution

Evolution is a process of gradual change. It is a descriptive term. It does not give causes, but describes the ways by which nature and man and God work in the material and social and

346

spiritual world. Ordinarily change takes place slowly, gradually, minutely. The plant evolves from the seed and the man from the infant so slowly that daily growth is not detected. The process is minute.

There is *cosmic* evolution or the development of the universe according to a process of origin, development, and decay. Planets and suns undergo transitions and pass away.

A phase of cosmic evolution is *organic* evolution with its cycle of birth, maturation, and death. All life goes through this process. There is no escape. The baffling processes of organic evolution are accompanied by an infinite number of changes and modifications. Struggle for existence and survival of the fittest are terms which explains how animals and even human beings have developed.

In its more primitive expressions organic evolution is harsh and rigorous. By tooth and claw the prizes of life have often been seized by the physically strongest and the psychically shrewdest. Although these primitive techniques operate today and although nature is reckless in the development of the human population, eugenic and scientific control is slowly but surely making headway.

In all organic life coöperation as well as conflict is a rule of nature. Coöperation increases as animal life grows more complex. It must increase or a large group would go to pieces. Among higher animals those who coöperate best have the best chance of survival.[1] Hence coöperation to produce a superior race is in line with natural tendencies even though such procedure means a large degree of social control.

As the general setting of life becomes more coöperative and less competitive, the fittest to survive become those who coöperate best, instead of those who are the most ruthless. On the least desirable planes, groups contend with one another in self-centered and destructive ways. They rely on shrewdness and

[1] A comprehensive treatment of this theme was given by P. Kropotkin, *Mutual Aid*, a factor in evolution (Doubleday, Page and Company, New York, 1902).

deceit. They lie in ambush for each other; on occasion they openly rush at each other with murder in their heads and hands. On a more constructive level, groups learn to coöperate, to respect each other's virtues, and to heed an authority higher than each. Far-sighted national leaders today are struggling toward the establishment of a higher world authority, of laws of arbitration, and of a world community spirit.

In turn organic evolution has its most important expression in *mental* evolution, or the growth, functioning, and breakdown of thinking, feeling, and behaving. It is not at all clear that any mental evolution has occurred since Cro-Magnon days. All the present mental characteristics seem to have been possessed by primitive man. No advance in inhibition, perception, reasoning seems to have occurred. The intellectual possibilities of Cro-Magnon man were perhaps equal to those of modern man.

On the basis of mental evolution *social* and *group* evolution have developed. Associations of persons have no life cycle. One group may perish quickly and a similar group live on for a thousand years. A family group in China may continue practically without end; in the United States divorce may rend marriage asunder in a few months. There is no standard cycle. A nation may become disorganized and perish, or it may make the necessary adjustments and maintain a high level of activity indefinitely.

What is the main characteristic of social or group evolution? Perhaps it is an *unfolding*. Perhaps it is having a *direction*. There seems to be an increasing degree of complexity (up to a certain point) and a goal toward which social change is headed. As the word evolution implies there is an evolving out of something into something else. Moreover evolution has another key word and that is, *slowly*. Evolution is gradual, slow, step by step. A plant evolves slowly from a seed; a nation is not built in a day.

Then there is *cultural* evolution, or the development of culture patterns from crude artifacts and a simple language of signs and cries to the complex inventions of a technological age and to the literatures of current civilizations.

Culture patterns do not possess standard life cycles. They may be passed on from generation to generation. They may find themselves antiquated and change their meanings or their forms to suit the new conditions. Some are inflexible while others are supple, but their survival depends neither on their inflexibility nor their suppleness but on their ability to meet both the changeless and the changing human needs.

The thesis is that the various parts of modern culture are not changing at the same rate, that some parts are changing much more rapidly than others; and that since there is a correlation and interdependence of parts, a rapid change in one part of our culture requires readjustments through other changes in the various correlated parts of culture.[1]

Wherever some changes are made and other needed changes are belated, group maladjustment and disorganization results. Within recent centuries change usually occurs first in material culture. New inventions are made and changes in one phase of group life promptly take place. Those phases which adjust themselves first are called adaptive, and the rest, non-adaptive. Non-adaptive culture always lags behind the adaptive. Religion and law are outstanding phases of non-adaptive culture.[2] Since science makes more changes than does religion, the more scientific members of a religious group or denomination or sect change more rapidly in their ideas about religion than do the other members, and hence religious controversies arise on the basis of modernism and fundamentalism. The industrially unsuccessful, the unemployed, the free thinkers change more rapidly than the economically successful, the wealthy, and the comfortably situated in their ideas concerning economic systems. If the latter groups sit "on the lid" too long, an explosion and a revolution are likely to occur.

[1] See W. F. Ogburn, *Social Change* (B. W. Huebsch, Inc., New York, 1922), pp. 200ff.
[2] *Loc. cit.*

Of course it may be well that some elements in a culture system are more adaptive than others, in order that complete change may not come suddenly. A real difficulty occurs when the distance between the adaptive and the non-adaptive culture traits becomes so excessive that adjustments cannot be made. Another serious problem arises when material and psychical inventions develop faster than do inventions for their social control. As a result of this lag nations today possess more powerful weapons for destroying each other than they possess constructive social techniques for settling disputes amicably or for building each other up.

In studying life in *Middletown* the Lynds found that different groups of activities changed at different speeds. The order is: first, technological factors; second, uses of leisure; third, educational methods; fourth, community activities; fifth, homemaking; and sixth, formal religion. Studies in other communities are needed for comparative purposes.

Among the six major groups of activities a rough hierarchy of rates of change is apparent. Getting a living seemingly exhibits the most pervasive change, particularly in its technological and mechanical aspects; leisure time, again most markedly in material developments such as the automobile and motion picture, is almost as mobile; training the young in schools, community activities, and making a home would come third, fourth and fifth in varying order, depending upon which traits are scrutinized; while, finally, on the whole exhibiting least change, come the formal religious activities.[1]

SOCIAL REVOLUTION

Social revolution is an extensive or complete change that takes place suddenly. Revolutions, however, are a long time in coming about. Most revolutions create a powerful upheaval, uprooting both good and bad values, taking place at the price of ill will and bloodshed, and calling for extensive social reorganization.

Social revolution results from a failure of evolution. If the

[1] Robert S. and Helen M. Lynd, *Middletown* (Harcourt, Brace and Company, New York, 1929), p. 497.

latter is persistently blocked by special interests, then like a stream that is dammed up, there will be a breaking out at some weak spot above the dam with destruction immediately following and with reconstruction being imperative.

The main cause of revolution is lack of adequate reforms. Autocracy, vested interests, and intolerant leaders hold social change back unduly. They fight to remain in power by denying needed changes. Sooner or later the lid blows off and the established régime goes with it.

The leaders of a successful revolution are likely to be as ruthless when they come into power as the persons were whom they overthrew. They ride roughshod over their erstwhile opponents. They organize campaigns of suppression and of extermination. They go to as unreasonable lengths in putting their views into operation as did the persons whom they overthrew. Moreover the rank and file of revolutionists when they come into power want quick results. They are usually impatient and unwilling to wait for evolutionary developments. A real right-about-face is required when revolutionists come into power, for they must change their methods and build by slow evolutionary steps.

Incipient revolution [1] is the process by which a revolution begins and comes to a head or reaches the actual point of occurrence. When we say that the Russian Revolution occurred in March, 1917, we mean that the dramatic climax of a long-drawn-out conflict occurred on that day. For decades the storm had been brewing. The autocratic methods of those in power had created opposition. Repression had been resorted to but no change in undemocratic methods had occurred. No redress was given the people. Their grievances were ignored until a widespread and subtle organization of opposing forces was able under the strain of war circumstances to topple the Czar and his régime from power. Whether the actual toppling occurred in one year or another is of small moment. The sig-

[1] A term developed by B. V. Morkovin in a dissertation on that subject, 1930, University of Southern California.

nificant thing is the long brewing period, during which those who felt the pressure of injustice were slowly gaining organized power.

Incipient revolution has both preliminary and advanced symptoms, as pointed out by L. P. Edwards.[1] Among the premonitory signs are a general restlessness, an increase in crime, "balked dispositions," *rapport* among the repressed. Advanced symptoms are "transfer of the allegiance of the intellectuals," gradual concentration of dissatisfaction against some particular institution or class, a division among the repressors.

The actual outbreak of a revolution constitutes "a reign of terror." Uncertainty prevails everywhere. Fear lurks around every corner. Sometimes a quick *coup d'état*, as in certain revolutions in South American Republics, may occur and the reign of terror be over in a few days.

The after effects involve a number of problems such as jealousies among the revolutionists. It is easier to stand together when opposing a common enemy than when dividing up the spoils after the enemy has been overthrown. There is the inexperience of the revolutionists in large-scale constructive government.[2] They discover that many of their ideas will not work. There is danger of insurrection at home among those who have been overthrown. There is the possibility of attack from aggressive neighbors who may not favor the new régime and who may decide that the time of disorganization after a reign of terror is the hour for them to strike.

SOCIAL MOVEMENTS AND MOBILITY

A social movement is a well-defined gradual change in human affairs. It may arise out of ecological factors and inventions and thus originate as an unplanned phenomenon, or more likely it may represent a definitely planned series of adjustments extending over a period of time and possessing stages and phases.

[1] *The Natural History of Revolution* (University of Chicago Press, 1927), Chs. III, IV.
[2] *Ibid.*, p. 156.

The woman's suffrage movement in the United States is a good example of a fairly typical social movement of the planned variety. The education of women caused them to develop a sense of political injustice. They felt that they were as entitled to vote as were men, but their suggestions to this end were repulsed. Thereupon certain women set out to organize a definite movement to secure the vote for the women of the country. Various self-centered political and economic interests governed by men feared the results if women acquired suffrage and hence they set up a counter movement. The movement for woman suffrage gained adherents and suffered setbacks. It started in 1848 but did not reach its goal until 1920, or 72 years later. Nearly all the main originators had passed away but their cause had been taken up by younger women.

A movement, then, as the concept is employed in this report, is a series of events involving adjustments to a social situation; connected by a cause and effect relation; possessing an extension in time and space, and disclosing stages, transitions, tendencies, that are correlative with a changing concept of its function and indicative of its evolution.[1]

A social movement may be transformed in time into a social institution, or it may die out because its purpose has been accomplished, or because the social situation has changed and no longer requires it.[2] The play movement, for instance, was begun several decades ago in the provision of a few sand boxes and is forwarded today by public and private institutions for recreation in many countries.

Social mobility is any change in social position, such as occupational changes where persons move up or down the occupational scale, or election to office whereby a follower becomes a leader, or a leap from a low economic class to a high one, or *vice versa*. In a caste society where there is not much change in social position mobility is far less than in a democratic society

---

[1] C. E. Rainwater, *The Play Movement in the United States* (University of Chicago Press, 1922), p. 4.

[2] *Ibid.*, p. 3.

comprised of independent units free to climb high socially or to move about at will on a large social plane.

Mobility is not movement but *change* of movement.[1] Movement may be doing the same things over and over every day; it may be meeting the same persons in the same relationships; it may be almost entirely routine. Mobility is change of movement which brings new social contacts and hence new stimuli, which in turn calls forth new responses and changes in personality.

No social mobility means no new experiences and stagnation in personality. On the other hand much social mobility may mean too much personality change or instability. Equally bad is social mobility when it creates an appetite for more stimulation, irrespective of what it does to personality. In this case the result is likely to be personality degeneration or disintegration.

The effects of social mobility depend on how subject to change of attitudes one is, that is, how far he responds readily to new stimuli. It also depends on the number and force of the new stimuli to which one is subjected.[2] These are two highly significant variables.

Social mobility is either horizontal or vertical.[3] Horizontal mobility is the process of making changes on the same status level, while vertical mobility is the process of changing from one status to another, either to a higher or to a lower level. If you withdraw from one literary society and join another of equal status, you have illustrated horizontal mobility. If you cannot change from one fraternity to another you have experienced how horizontal mobility may be restricted. When you are elected president of your college class you have experienced vertical mobility of the upward variety, but if you are recalled from that office you will suffer vertical mobility downward.

[1] E. W. Burgess, in Park and Burgess, *The City* (University of Chicago Press, 1925), p. 58.
[2] *Ibid.*, p. 60.
[3] P. A. Sorokin, *Social Mobility* (Harper and Brothers, New York, 1927).

TELIC CHANGE

Some changes occur without human attention, while others are the product of human direction. The first is natural; the second is telic.

Telic change is promoted by man in order to secure progress. Sociology is interested in telic change, that is, in what can be done to improve social relationships. While sociology maintains the scientific viewpoint of endeavoring to understand what is taking place and why changes occur, it also has an interest in what may take place under direction.

Several basic questions are raised by the concept of telic change: Is there such a phenomenon as progress? If not why study sociology? If so, what are the evidences or criteria of it? How shall we know when social change is synonymous with progress? Is all evolution progressive or will it end in catastrophe? What procedures may be followed in order to promote constructive change?

A number of years ago a fivefold objective test of progress was set up by A. J. Todd. He suggested that increases in the wealth, the health, the population, the order and stability, and the opportunities of a group are evidences of its progress.[1]

By wealth is meant "real community wealth," that is, wealth used in a way to eliminate all poverty and to provide the necessities and an increasing number of the amenities or comforts of life for all. By health is meant more than a declining infant mortality rate and an increasing average length of life, but also the life that is more abundant, that is more friendly and more useful. To increase life that is mere human trash is retrogression.

By population augmentation is not meant increases in persons merely to be shot down in wars or to be ground up in machinery, but an increase in productive citizens. By order and stability is not meant stagnation, but that degree of system and organization essential for the development and conservation of new ideas. By opportunity is not meant new occasions to do evil or to be anti-social, but to do many constructive things:

[1] A. J. Todd, *The Scientific Spirit and Social Work* (The Macmillan Company, New York, 1919), 196ff.

By opportunity, I mean the chance to be well born, to be decently cared for in childhood, to be decently educated, to play; a chance to develop one's productive skill; a chance of getting into the place where one's abilities, native and acquired, can express themselves to their highest; access to all the great heritage of culture that the ages have compounded and sent down to us; and the chance to participate in every normal activity for which we are fitted.[1]

A somewhat similar list of objective tests of progress was worked out a number of years ago by E. T. Devine.[2] The present writer has modified this analysis considerably. The revised test is thirteenfold.

(1) The conservation of natural resources and the increasing utilization of these for the benefit of all, not for the gain of a shrewd few. (2) An increasing degree of sound, physical and mental heredity, and a decreasing percentage of degenerate children born of feeble-minded or alcoholic parents. (3) An environment increasingly favorable to health and a decreasing percentage of poor housing, inadequate sanitation, and contagious diseases. (4) An increasing degree of wholesome recreation and a decreasing percentage of disintegrating amusements and a lessening of the nerve-wrecking pace of urban life. (5) An increasing percentage of wholesome families and of well-trained children, and a decreasing percentage of children who are neglected by poor or by wealthy parents; a decreasing percentage of children exploited in industry. (6) More opportunities for creative effort for more people; an increasing percentage of people who find their greatest enjoyment in their work and who do not look forward to the end of the day so that they may begin to enjoy life; a decreasing percentage of workers worn out and thrown upon the scrap heap in middle life. (7) An increasing democritization of industry and business with labor, capital, and the public all having a voice in the control of industry and business, and an increasing percentage of both workers and employers who act first in behalf of the common

[1] *Ibid.*, p. 197.
[2] *Misery and Its Causes* (The Macmillan Company, New York, 1909), Ch. VI.

weal and second for themselves. (8) An increasing degree of social insurance against accidents, sickness, old age, death, and unemployment, as guarantees to the honest and hard-working but lesser privileged workers against dependency and pauperism. (9) A developing standard of living for an increasing percentage of people, involving proper nourishment, refreshing recreation, creative opportunities. (10) A decreasing emphasis on What can I get out of the government? and an increasing emphasis on What can I do for the government? (11) A spreading of the finer appreciation of music, painting, poetry, sculpture, and the other arts, as well as of rhythm, harmony, balance, order, and movement. (12) The expansion of vocational, avocational, and public welfare education. (13) The development of the more deeply spiritual and religious phases of human nature of increasing numbers of people.

In these standards a wide variety of objective and subjective phases of life are catalogued and set up as moving goals to be sought. They imply something of a balance between the material and the spiritual, between social regulation and individual initiative.

Three subprocesses of social progress have been suggested by Clarence M. Case. He calls these utilization, equalization, and appreciation.[1] By *utilization* is meant making use of the resources of nature. It is making use of one's physical environment. It includes inventions and techniques whereby man may live more and more healthily with less and less routine. It means building a material civilization in a way to leave people increasingly free for the development of spiritual values.

Equalization is the distribution of economic and material goods and also of social values such as knowledge, art, wholesome human relationships. It involves "a fair distribution of the duties, opportunities, enjoyments, and honors coincident to the processes of production." [2]

---

[1] "What Is Social Progress?" *Journal of Applied Sociology,* X: 114–19.
[2] *Ibid.,* p. 116.

Appreciation means "to estimate things in terms of worth or value, to apprehend experience from the standpoint of excellence, preciousness, and relative significance." [1] It refers to having and using values discriminately. Appreciation obtains its highest satisfaction from creative work, from overcoming defeat with victory, from stimulating others to become socially useful personalities.

These tests of progress have been modified and stated by the writer as (1) invention, (2) distribution, (3) evaluation, and (4) personalization. Invention is the development of new tools, symbols, and relationships; distribution is spreading the use of these tools and concepts to all persons competent to use them; evaluation is rating tools and concepts according to their social worth; and personalization is the growth of well-rounded, mutually responsible members of groups and society.

Telic change is *planned*. Social telesis is the process whereby groups accelerate their own development through first working out careful plans and then of carrying these out in an orderly way. [2] Upon the basis of adequate and of correctly interpreted facts any group which is sufficiently interested to do so may enter upon a definite program of directing its own activities toward constructive goals.

Telic progress involves (1) securing data such as social facts and life histories of both persons and groups, (2) accurately interpreting the facts and their meanings in terms of group and personal needs, (3) carefully developing a set of desirable goals, and (4) going ahead to achieve and to modify these goals in the achieving.

Telic change has been very sporadic. If you accept the premises of fascism, you would say that Italy in 1922 set out upon a telic era. If you accept communism then you would cite Russia's Five Year Plan inaugurated in 1928 as a large-scale example of telic change. If technocracy as proclaimed in the United States

---

[1] *Ibid.*, p. 117 .

[2] Social telesis is a term coined by the dean of American sociologists, Lester F. Ward, *Pure Sociology* (The Macmillan Company, New York, 1914), p. 463.

in the fall of 1932 were to be given an opportunity it would place the United States upon a telic basis. Democracy that has been chiefly a label for individualism in the United States has been unable to develop a real telic program. It has made attempts that have been sporadic and to a certain extent short-lived. In 1933 President Roosevelt inaugurated a telic procedure for the United States through the NRA.

Social reform is telic change in action. It is planned mass procedure. It uses a tool, such as legislation, for changing the standards and values of an entire city, state, or nation. It ordinarily uses objective, compulsory methods. It also depends upon public opinion, for only when it is supported by a strong public opinion does it accomplish much.

Social reform is generally in a hurry. It seeks short cuts. It stirs up group opinion in its favor, but often forgets that such opinion is fickle. It neglects to maintain a thoroughgoing system of education. After the Eighteenth Amendment went into effect in 1918, its advocates rested their case chiefly on enforcement, forgetting to an extent to educate the rising generation of children in its support, and failing to reëducate adult immigrants and others whose culture patterns for past generations had included the drinking of wine and beer.[1]

Social reform is general, unmindful of individuals except as the latter defy the reform. By seeing the larger needs of groups social reformers develop wholesale schemes, big ideas, and are motivated to quick action. They are impatient with evolutionary change and the slow conditioning processes.

The reformer is an inadequate investigator. He thinks he sees so clearly what he wants to reform that he is often blind to many of the facts. He is in such a hurry that he does not reflect deeply. He is so subject to wishful thinking that he overlooks major data. Sociology is not social reform; neither is it averse to social reform; but it can furnish sound bases for reform.[2]

[1] Constantine Panunzio, "Reactions of the Foreign Born to Prohibition," *Sociology and Social Research*, XVIII: 223–28.

[2] See Donald O. Wagner, editor, *Social Reformers* (The Macmillan Company, New York, 1934).

Social work is a way of adjusting personal conflicts and disorganization in society, and thus of promoting constructive and evolutionary social change. Social work as a profession is emerging from its period of youth, a period similar to that of the legal profession when ambitious young men "read law" in offices and passed the bar examinations without attending a law school. Schools for training social workers have developed in recent years until now there are training schools in many of the larger universities, although a few operate independently. Standards are being formulated for admission to the profession of social work.

Social work may be divided into group work, case work, and administrative work. *Social group work* is conducting or directing clubs and classes in social settlements, recreation centers, orphans' homes and children's hospitals, and churches. Social group work is largely composed of leadership activities for small groups. Wholesome programs are developed for the leisure time of underprivileged youth. The supervision of recreation and play is an important phase of social group work.

The person who acts as a leader of a group of lively settlement boys or girls must understand both the psychology of adolescence and of leadership, and also the sociology of natural areas in city and country. After the group leader has established rapport with the group members he is in a position to analyze their mental and social conflicts. He can help them in dissolving their mental conflicts and in settling their conflicts with other persons. Through the group members he can make pathfinder community surveys and bring about community advances.

Social case work is the assisting of persons and families to make adjustments to life problems. Too often it has had to do with economic rehabilitation only. Where economic depression rules and the case load is high the case worker has been limited largely to meeting food and rent needs. Many families through an adverse turn of circumstances, the desertion of the wage-earner or his death, or through divorce, are thrown upon the community for aid. In such an event the case worker renders temporary financial help and endeavors to put the individual or family upon a self-sustaining basis. One of the chief activities of the social worker is to mend broken lives and disorganized family groups, assisting them to make personal and social adjustments so that they may again take their places in the community as respectable and respected persons.[1]

In order to understand the problems of persons in need, the case worker must know the social groups and the group traditions of those in need. He must also understand human nature and personality. Upon these bases he assists disorganized persons and families to become reorganized.[2]

Social work administration requires first the administrative ability and training which the head of any organization must have. In addition it includes scientific case work and group work training, a broad background of human welfare experience, and a keen insight into special and concrete personality problems. Its specific qualifications vary according to the type of social institution under consideration. Its function is that of promoting constructive social change through stimulating programs of rehabilitation.

Since case work is individualistic, particularistic, and minute, the worker is likely to neglect the larger sociological aspects of his calling. Since the case worker knows life in its individual phases he is however a type of authority whom the sociologist

[1] Social case work makes diagnoses of personality problems pretty much as a physician diagnoses sickness. In general needy persons have been classified under three main headings: the physically handicapped, such as the blind, crippled, and physically sick; the mentally handicapped, such as the mentally defective or unbalanced, and neurasthenics; and the socially handicapped, the largest group of all, including the fatherless family, the neglected or dependent child, the behavior problem child, the homeless aged, the alcoholic or the drug addict, the unadjusted immigrant.

[2] Classroom discussion in sociology sometimes becomes removed from real life, but when it is conducted with reference to actual situations and problems it takes on the reality of life itself. Training courses in social work afford a happy combination of social work practice and classroom discussion which is stimulating and thoughtful. Moreover, the upper division or graduate student in sociology who supplements his classroom work by social field work places himself in a strategic position to analyze social situations accurately and to understand societary problems.

and also the reformer needs to consult frequently. Moreover, case work affords warm human contacts. The case worker has his eyes bent on the present, on today's particular needs and opportunities; the social reformer and the group worker lift their eyes more to the future. The case worker at his best is the investigator, the reorganizer of persons and families, and the collector of social data from which sociological principles may be drawn. The social reformer at her best is putting into group operation the principles which have stood sociological tests. Both are engaged in social reorganization. Both are interpreting life in terms of higher social values. Together, hand in hand, each may supply what the other lacks, and direct group change to new and more wholesome social ends.

PROBLEMS

1. What is social change?
2. Do groups traverse the same life cycles as do persons? Why?
3. What is the relation of social evolution to cultural evolution?
4. What causes cultural lag?
5. When is social revolution necessary?
6. What is the chief weakness of revolution?
7. What hinders normal social evolution most?
8. What is incipient revolution?
9. What brings about a social movement?
10. Are social movements and social reforms the same?
11. What is social mobility?
12. Distinguish between horizontal and vertical mobility by illustrations.
13. What is social telesis?
14. When is social telesis most successful?
15. How may a reformer know when a reform is needed?
16. What criteria of progress would you personally suggest?
17. How does the social case worker contribute to social change?
18. In his NRA program is President Roosevelt a social reformer?
19. Would a combined case work, group work, and reform work procedure provide adequately for social progress?

READINGS

CANNON, MARY A., and PHILIP KLEIN, editors, *Social Case Work* (Columbia University Press, New York, 1933).

COOLEY, C. H., *Social Process* (Charles Scribner's Sons, New York, 1918).

COYLE, GRACE L., *Social Process in Organized Groups* (Richard R. Smith, Inc., New York, 1930).

EDWARDS, L. P., *The Sociology of Revolution* (University of Chicago Press, 1927).

ELLWOOD, C. A., *Cultural Evolution* (The Century Company, New York, 1927).

FOLSOM, J. K., *Culture and Social Progress* (Longmans, Green and Company, New York, 1928).

HERTZLER, J. O., *Social Progress* (The Century Company, New York, 1928).

HILLER, E. T., *Principles of Sociology* (Harper and Brothers, New York, 1933), Chs. XXI, XXV, XXVI.

MACIVER, R. M. *Society: Its Structure and Changes* (Ray Long and Richard R. Smith, Inc., 1931), Part IV.

ODENCRANTZ, LOUISE C., *The Social Worker in Family, Medical and Psychiatric Social Work* (Harper and Brothers, New York, 1929).

OGBURN, W. F., *Social Change* (B. W. Huebsch, Inc., New York, 1922).

TODD, A. J., *Theories of Social Progress* (The Macmillan Company, New York, 1918).

WAGNER, DONALD O., *Social Reformers* (The Macmillan Company, New York, 1934).

WEATHERLY, U. G., *Social Progress* (J. B. Lippincott Company, Philadelphia, 1926).

WILLIAMSON, MARGARETTA, *The Social Worker in Group Work* (Harper and Brothers, New York, 1929).

CHAPTER XV

GROUP LEADERSHIP

Leadership is the process of influencing large numbers of people in important ways. It is the process of changing the attitudes and values of many persons. It is solving problems for a group. It is directing the activities of many individuals in significant particulars.

Leadership may ably defend the traditions and customs of a group, or it may successfully challenge intrenched but outworn folkways and mores. It may be the complement of followership. It may be direct or indirect; it may be partisan or scientific. It may be mental, social, or executive; it may be autocratic, paternalistic, or democratic. Leadership may be radical, liberal, compromising, conservative, or reactionary.

Leadership may originate in energy, intelligence, or in character, or in combinations of all three. Sometimes it is due to the focalization of ordinary ability, and again it is the expression of margins of uniqueness and innate superior ability. It may be due to personal magnetism; it may come from flashes of insight. It may originate in defeats. It may be accounted for by a balanced integration of many traits. It may occur at the conjuncture of ability, crisis, and opportunity.

TYPES OF LEADERS

Leadership is direct or indirect. *Direct* leadership operates in person. It is represented by the individual who directs by word of mouth the activities of other persons. *Indirect* leadership relates to making inventions which by their adoption indicate the large-scale influence of one person over the many. The former deals directly with persons; the latter with persons through intermediary objects.

364

Leadership is social, mental, and executive. While no sharp dividing line can be made, yet distinguishing characteristics are common. Social leadership is direct performance in the presence of groups. It calls for extrovertive qualities more than for introvertive ones. Personal magnetism is a powerful asset.

Mental leadership rules more definitely by ideas. It is likely to be indirect. It exercises control through the products of reason. It produces new ideas, works of art, ideals, patterns, which ultimately may be widely accepted. An Edison, a Shakespeare, a Raphael illustrate some of the different types of mental leadership.

Executive leadership is a combination of both the social and the mental. It must know people; it manipulates people; it organizes them. On the other hand, it develops new plans, ideas, schemes, organizations. It rarely appears before large groups, choosing rather a small group of lieutenants to do its bidding. It spends much time in reflection. It is more highly paid than are the other types. Its activities and responsibilities are strenuous and energy-consuming.

Leadership is autocratic, paternalistic, and democratic. *Autocratic* leadership is largely its own boss. It dominates and it drives. It is a law unto itself. Autocratic leadership today, however, has limitations, for it cannot go beyond certain points in its arbitrariness. It must be continually on guard because of the enemies which it naturally makes. The autocrat must protect himself against both personal attack and group revolution.

Paternalistic leadership is a cross between autocratic and democratic procedure. It is its own boss but it consults. It takes the needs and wishes of others into consideration, but it reserves the final decision to itself. It feels that by its superior position and experience it knows best.

Democratic leadership directs but only after a consensus of opinion has been attained and only as a spokesman of this consensus. It manifests limitless patience. It brings out initiative and responsibility in the many. In times of crises, however, it is likely to break down if people are untrained in societary matters.

In modern society democratic leadership has been giving way to dictatorship. Kings were overthrown and democratic governments were set up too suddenly, that is, before people were trained in democratic life. Democracy in practice has been synonymous with individualism, with most persons looking for private gain or advantage. Democracy has often existed chiefly in name, and hence, a recrudescence has been natural. Dictatorships of the fascist or communist variety naturally follow the breakdown of too much individualism. When the common people are educated to the point of putting habitually the welfare of the public ahead of their own personal advantage, then democratic leadership will come into its own for the first time on a large scale.

Leadership is either partisan or scientific. *Partisan* leadership takes sides. It is for or against. It favors or opposes a cause. It is on the firing line. It is represented by the debater, the lawyer, the legislator, the politician. It sees one side larger than the other and therefore is propagandistic.

Scientific leadership is impartial. It does not take sides. It looks for truth no matter which side it may be on. It favors no cause except the cause of truth. It is calm, deliberate, reasoned. It represents that phase of mental leadership which is unhurried, unprejudiced, uncommitted. It does not seek to prove or disprove, but to find out. It investigates and leads the way against the powers of ignorance and intolerance.

ORIGINS OF LEADERSHIP

A person may become a leader by *good fortune*. He may accidentally walk across the stage of life into the spotlight. If he has stamina and common sense, he may lead well. Calvin Coolidge came into the presidency of the United States accidentally but received recognition for being "silent Cal" and for not allowing himself to be stampeded out of the beaten paths.

Another person of undeveloped abilities may walk into the spotlight not in the time of calm but of crisis. The crisis stimulates him to measure up to a great need. He leaps out of his former average self into superiority. In responding to the urgent call of the hour he may surprise not only his friends but himself. There are undoubtedly countless persons who would measure up to important group responsibilities, providing an emergency should make its demands upon them.

A person may become a leader by *defending* conventional group control. He may courageously defend the established faith. He tries to keep time-honored institutions intact and to uphold venerated customs that are under attack. His ultimate place in history will depend upon whether the values he is defending are outworn and no longer useful or whether they are vital and eternal.

One may reach leadership by *challenging* the established order, especially in its moth-eaten aspects. He may organize a movement to establish a new order. He favors change. He pioneers, and leads into the unknown. He may be called a rebel or a heretic. His future rating depends upon whether his new venture was sound, timely, well executed, and successful.

Leaders thus are thrown against each other, with the defenders and revolutionists organizing their followers into hostile camps. A group which is dominated by leaders of traditional ideas tends to fall behind in the march of progress, while a movement in which the leaders favoring change are untrained, self-centered, or temperamental is likely to disintegrate.

Followership is a source of leadership. There can be no leaders without followers. To be a good leader one must know his followers. He must also know the secret of following well. To follow well and to lead well one must possess control over self. The Wisdom writer long ago said that he who ruleth his spirit is greater than he who taketh a city. Ruling one's own impulses is essential to ruling the impulses of others. Nothing inspires followers more than a courageous well-controlled person unless it be sympathetic understanding of followers. Self-control leads to control of followers.

Energy goes a long ways in creating leadership. (1) Energy expended in thoroughness affords a quality of work that sooner or later attracts attention to itself and wins recognition. (2) Energy expressed in endurance keeps a person in a contest or at the front longer than his associates are able to continue, and gives him a leadership rank. (3) Energy translated into determination and persistence likewise keeps one going while others are dropping out. Persistence wins over ordinary efforts. (4) Energy that spells courage leads the way when danger is imminent. By its very nature courage commands that respect and admiration which creates followers. (5) Energy that is used in standing by one's convictions arouses widespread support. It is synonymous with that independence which proceeds undaunted when most persons would falter and quail. If one's convictions further social welfare, then sooner or later a leadership rank will be attained. (6) Sometimes energy spreads itself out into successful versatility. A person who can do several things better than others can do them is in especial demand. Versatility may be either tandem or simultaneous, correlate or uncorrelate. *Tandem* versatility is specialization which pursues one line for a term of years and then turns to another line. *Simultaneous* versatility is specialization in two or more types of activity at once, as in the case of a Theodore Roosevelt. *Correlate* versatility is specialization in two or more related fields as illustrated by Michelangelo's achievements in painting, sculpture, and design. *Uncorrelate* versatility is specialization in unrelated fields, as in the case of Leonardo da Vinci's ability in painting, his invention of an "ox shovel," and his anticipation of the Copernican theory.

Intelligence plays a large rôle in leadership. Intelligence is energy at work solving problems, and problem-solving is perhaps two-thirds of leadership. It involves several important factors such as: (1) observation which signifies a careful noticing of both details and underlying tendencies. (2) Questioning enlarges one's store of information; it gives insight; it makes one better informed than are other persons. It indicates an inquiring mind and leads to scientific achievements. (3) Intelligence often means prevision or looking ahead. It affords the best known basis for prediction. He who can see further ahead than his fellows or who can make more accurate predictions than his fellows is in a strategic position to lead them. (4) Intelligence may mean either an intensive command of knowledge or a wide mental range. In either case it gives a person a distinct advantage over others less intelligent.

Character is vital to leadership. First, there is strength of character or sheer integration of personality traits. Second, there is ethical character, or an organization of personality traits toward what is judged to be the good. In the first sense character is either strong or weak; in the second, it is either good or bad. It is the strong character, or the good character well integrated, that often accounts for leadership. Character refers to the ends toward which energy and intelligence are directed.

Sincerity and *dependability* are the essence of character. These traits must be present or all the energy and intelligence in the world sooner or later will go into the discard. Personal integrity is a minimum essential to long-term, large-scale leadership. Anything less may "get by" for a time but not for long. "Honest Abe" is a cognomen that carries a far-reaching lesson for leaders everywhere.

Sympathy is important in social leadership, for it enables one to put himself in the place of his fellows and to understand them. Without this understanding of one's fellows, social leadership can hardly get under way. Disciplined sympathy enables a leader to keep in touch with his followers and their needs and at the same time prevents him from being victimized. It keeps one from becoming "hard-boiled." It leads a person to identify himself rationally with human welfare.

Character involves a *faith* that is necessary to leadership. Pessimism, cynicism, and hopelessness do not inspire followers. Faith in one's own powers, faith in associates, faith in humanity, faith in a cause, faith in the future, faith in the universe—all these help to give personality a leadership mien.

THEORIES OF LEADERSHIP

1. The theory of *balance* in leadership means that one personality trait highly developed by itself is not sufficient to guarantee leadership. For example, aggressiveness would need to be tempered by inhibition. Although energy and action are essential to social leadership, they might produce an unbearable obtrusiveness that would defeat leadership. They would need to be held back at times not only to keep a person from becoming a social pest but also to enable him to conserve seemingly unlimited energies. There is a limit to human strength; even the strongest are not immune to wearing themselves out by tireless activities.

Another needed balance is represented by versatility and specialization. Versatility is a prized characteristic in most social groups. It puts a person in an enviable position in one situation after another. Versatility by itself may run riot; it may spread itself out so far that it grows thin and superficial. Capable versatility transforms a person into a multiple-burdened Atlas. It needs to be balanced by concentration on a few things and by a specialization that will guarantee thoroughness. Specialization by itself, on the other hand, may mean intolerance, but when coupled with versatility gives a balance of personality that spells leadership.

A balance of optimism and pessimism is a personality combination basic to leadership. By itself optimism does not inspire prolonged followership. He who is always optimistic about everything is partially blind or stupid. He is led by an unsafe guide, namely, wishful thinking. On the other hand, the pessimistic person fails to inspire confidence. He doubts too much. When integrated, optimism and pessimism give a person a controlled forward look. They push one ahead but not with undue rapidity. They undertake difficult but not foolhardy tasks. They grin and bear obstacles. They keep a person's face pointing skyward and his feet on the ground.

Balance in leadership is complex, for it includes more than a happy combination of two personality traits. It means an organization of many different traits, supporting now one, and now another, but giving to all a super-strength which comes from unity. Balance does not mean a deadlocking or a warring of opposite traits, but a moving equilibrium of such traits, integrated and invincible as a working unit.

2. The *focalization of psychic energy* theory of leadership means that a person with standard abilities may concentrate his efforts so as to create superior results and become a leader. A person with average ability may by concentrated hard work and persistence attain the heights. He drives ahead in season and out, overcoming handicaps and defeating obstacles. He may be born in poverty and followed in his early years by discouragement, but he grimly sets his face in a given direction and never turns back. He is what Lester F. Ward has called the "genius" by hard work. He accomplishes the seemingly impossible by dogged determination. By "focalization of psychic energy" he develops superior results, and masters a part of the unknown. He is admired because he has come up from the ranks largely through his own sheer efforts.

The focalization of psychic energy theory has several phases. (1) There is spare moments' focalization whereby a person by devoting a few minutes daily to a specific activity may perfect himself and surpass and lead his fellows in that field. (2) There is intensive focalization for a short period, as in the case of the football star, the winner of an endurance contest, or of the person who rises to superhuman heights in a serious crisis of life. (3) Partial life focalization refers to devoting one's self in some particular to acquiring a special skill, so that in one field he leads all competitors while in other connections he makes a creditable but not a superior record. (4) Whole life focalization means the dedication of most of one's energies to a given program over a long span of years. One's life is so thoroughly devoted to a special activity that he attains an outstanding pinnacle of recognition. (5) Dual life focalization is the joint concentration of efforts as in the case of Pierre and Marie Curie, husband and wife, with the husband setting many of the problems and the wife carrying on experiments until radium is discovered. Doctors William and Charles Mayo, famous surgeons of Rochester, Minnesota, give each other all the credit for the success of their well-known clinic. Wilbur and Orville Wright worked together so closely that it is difficult to say who deserves the greater credit in developing the airplane.

3. The *marginal uniqueness* theory of leadership means that some persons are able to lead by their unique traits and abilities. There are different degrees of uniqueness, such as differences in aptitudes, that is, in the inheritance of artistic, mathematical, mechanical, remembering or reasoning, sympathetic response abilities. Superior uniqueness is talent or genius and makes special leadership possible.

Of course the highly talented person is likely to rest on his inherited ability and not train himself sufficiently. He may fail to conserve his precious talents, allowing his popularity "to run him ragged." He may become a "crank" and never develop a balanced, well-rounded personality. He may cut off his efficiency by becoming conceited and cock-sure.

The brilliant leader owes much to superior inherited ability. Every person possesses some unique characteristics but not to a sufficient degree to make him a leader. It is estimated that the total population of the world would have to be multiplied forty times before the lines on the tips of the forefinger of the right hands of two persons would be identical. Every individual by birth is unique; also by cultural background he is unique; and likewise by his daily experiences. This threefold uniqueness is the stuff out of which great achievements are often made.

Personal magnetism is a special form of marginal uniqueness. It sets one person off from his fellows by its unusual appeal, and enhances whatever other leadership abilities he may have. By itself it may count for little in a leadership way, but it magnifies other abilities manyfold.

Enthusiasm is often a large part of magnetism. Enthusiasm gives that sparkle to the human eye which is captivating.

Enthusiasm is "catching"; it puts a new spring into tired steps, and arouses lethargic souls. It is forward-looking; it is sunny.

Since magnetism and enthusiasm are youthful traits, they are attractive. They are exuberant, overflowing with energy. They are dangerous because they may lead astray by their very freedom from restraint, but this freedom makes them enticing. Hence while they are not leadership traits *per se*, they make almost any other personality trait a leadership trait.

4. The *flashes of insight* theory of leadership means that a person suddenly sees the connection between two previously disconnected ideas, or sees the necessary solution to a problem, and thereby is enabled to direct his associates wisely. A person who possesses deeper insight than his fellows regarding a social problem is in a position to point the way to solving that problem and to become a leader. Either insight before others attain it or deeper insight than others possess is essential to directive or creative leadership.

Insight comes in flashes. Whether one be a poet awakening at three in the morning and jotting down fast fleeting verses or a plodding scientist working away laboriously in the laboratory day after day, insight comes by leaps. In fact it appears that learning is largely a process of patient studying enlightened by sudden apprehension of connections between the known and the unknown.

Insight may be "wholesight." It may be seeing a situation in all of its aspects instead of in one of them only. Insight often comes when major relationships are understood. Most persons see only that part of a situation which is visible from their own narrow slant on life. It is the person who encompasses a situation, who walks clear around it, who gets out of his shell and sees life from the shells of other people who often has the most insight and hence is in the best position to lead.

Insight comes out of experience and knowledge. The inventor has usually built up a large storehouse of information through experimentation, so that his flashes of insight occur in a well-cultivated field. Likewise the flashes of insight of the poet are products of numerous deep-seated experiences. If we knew all we would be able to explain most flashes of insight, but without adequate data many of them are mysterious, intuitive, or accidental.

5. The *ability in disability* theory of leadership originates in Alfred Adler's discussion of compensation. In the first place special ability, talent, and genius are the result of nature's efforts to compensate for weakness and inferiority. She goes to an extreme and endows certain individuals with special ability as a compensation for certain weaknesses in them and they become known as geniuses.

We may modify this initial statement in terms of the conflict between the human organism at birth and the environment. In its earliest contacts with its environment the infant sooner or later meets with opposition. It is blocked. The environment is old, tough, and powerful. The child may recoil and resist, and in so doing develop unusual ability, even to the point of becoming superior to his peers.

Where achievement is easy, no special strength is developed. Where one succumbs weakly to obstacles and defeats, his ability remains undeveloped. Where one falls into brooding over defeats, inferiority complexes develop and personal deterioration sets in.

However, there are two other ways of meeting defeats. Both represent highways to leadership. One of these highways may be reached by reorganizing one's forces after failing to overcome an obstacle and by coming back with redoubled force and skill at the very point of previous defeat. In overcoming obstacles in this way one builds up special ability out of which leadership may emerge. Thus, in disability to meet certain situations, a person may find the very stimuli for achievement and leadership.

A classic illustration is that of Demosthenes and his boyhood stuttering. An ordinary reaction would have been to accept defeat. Not so with Demosthenes, for it is reported that he went down to the seashore, filled his mouth with pebbles and talked to the waves until he could enunciate clearly. In making such efforts he moved on beyond merely overcoming a handicap, and achieved such public speaking ability that today he is widely recognized as having been the world's greatest orator.

Further, a person may tackle a hard task and fail with no possibility of ever overcoming the specific obstacle. The defeat is final, but leadership may be around the corner. How? A person may turn his balked energy into larger channels, that is, sublimate it. A person defeated in love may dedicate his life to a public cause and achieve leadership. Balked in his North Polar expeditions Amundsen turned in the opposite direction and became the discoverer of the South Pole. A defeat on one level may be turned into a victory on a higher level, and outstanding achievements be substituted for what might have been a mediocre outcome. Hence far-reaching leadership foundations may be laid.

6. The conjuncture theory of leadership means that various factors occur simultaneously.[1] The first factor to be mentioned is personal ability, either inherited or ordinary ability that is concentrated. The next factor is a problem or a crisis of some kind. The third element is opportunity for special ability to solve the problem or meet the crisis. Sometimes one of the factors or even two are present, but unless all three come together there is no leadership. In the words of Dr. Case "the present hypothesis is that the conjuncture, or falling together, of personality traits, social situation, and event determines leadership from hour to hour in the relations of obscure persons, and from time to time in the affairs of the world." [2]

EVALUATION OF LEADERSHIP

If a person's special abilities are not appreciated or if evaluated low his leadership chances are slight. In other words a person who shows ordinary ability in a field that is appreciated by a

[1] Suggested by my colleague, Dr. Clarence M. Case.
[2] "Leadership and Conjuncture, a Sociological Hypothesis," *Sociology and Social Research*, XVI: 510–13.

group has much greater chances of leadership than does he who has unlimited ability in a direction which the group disapproves.

If ability is expressed in ways that the group favors then several gradations of leadership may be noted. (1) In the long run the leader who is appreciated least of all is he who uses his superior abilities for purely individual glorification. He may seek to dominate for his own gain. He may lead merely for the exultation of exercising power. Such forms of leadership, however, are usually short-lived or else they ultimately come to a disastrous end. To the degree that Napoleon was vain-glorious his exile was explainable and justifiable.

(2) Another type of leader who is evaluated favorably, even highly by some persons, but rather low by many, is he who leads in behalf of vested interests, of the outworn past, or of blind prejudices. Such persons as defenders of the established order deserve credit, although they often hinder the coming of needed innovations.

(3) The leader who acts as a compromisor is often praised highly as a savior and criticized severely as being two-faced, or as one who "straddles the fence." He pleases neither party to the controversy, although he may make progress possible.

(4) The judge and adjudicator often is accorded a great deal of prestige, especially if his ability and training are superior and if his decisions are noted for their fairness.

(5) Then there is the progressive leader, the one who appreciates the values originating in the past but who leads in behalf of rationalized and needed changes, who courageously faces the future even though importuned to defend the past.

(6) A person may use his superior ability to solve a highly problematic situation in behalf of a group. He may give his life to secure needed group changes. He may exercise control for no narrow purpose, spending his energy, affection, and life freely that other persons may have larger opportunities to live and to be useful. He may ask nothing for himself or for his special friends.

The most appreciated leader appears to be the person who promotes the welfare of his fellows the most freely and sincerely. Possessing views which are humanity-wide, he is one with the common people. His moral courage knows no bounds. He combines in himself the endurance of the trained soldier, the sagacity of the captain of industry, indomitable energy, and pro-social attitudes guided by vision and reason. The greatest problem-solvers become the world's greatest leaders.

PROBLEMS

1. What is leadership?
2. How is leadership related to followership?
3. Why do many able persons fail as leaders?
4. In what ways is an executive leader a social leader and in what ways a mental one?
5. When is autocratic leadership at a premium?
6. When does democratic leadership succeed best?
7. Why are there more partisan than scientific leaders?
8. Are partisan or scientific leaders needed the more today and why?
9. When is leadership easy?
10. When does energy fail to become a leadership trait?
11. How may intelligence hinder one's leadership?
12. In what way is character more important than energy or intelligence as a leadership trait?
13. What is the chief significance of the focalization of psychic energy theory of leadership?
14. What was the marginal uniqueness of Woodrow Wilson, of Gandhi, of Beethoven, of Jane Addams?
15. Can personal magnetism be developed?
16. Who may have flashes of insight?
17. How is a disability such as a physical handicap a leadership factor?
18. Why is one outstanding personality trait by itself rarely enough?
19. Cite an illustration of the conjuncture theory of leadership that you have observed.
20. Select a person whose leadership you personally appreciate most and indicate his leadership traits.

READINGS

BOGARDUS, EMORY S., *Fundamentals of Social Psychology* (The Century Company, New York, 1931), Chs. XII–XV.

BURR, WALTER, *Community Leadership* (Prentice-Hall, Inc., New York, 1929).

DURANT, WILL, *Adventures in Genius* (Simon and Schuster, New York, 1931).

GOWIN, E. B., *The Executive and His Control of Men* (The Macmillan Company, New York, 1915).

KNOWLSON, T. S., *Originality* (T. Werner Laurie, Ltd., London, 1918).

MUMFORD, EBEN, "Origins of Leadership," *American Journal of Sociology*, XII: 216–40, 367–97, 500–31.

PITKIN, WALTER B., *The Psychology of Achievement* (Simon and Schuster, New York, 1931).

TERMAN, LOUIS N., "The Psychology and Pedagogy of Leadership," *Pedagogical Seminary*, XI: 113–51.

VAN BUSKIRK, W. R., *The Saviors of Mankind* (The Macmillan Company, New York, 1929).

ZINK, HAROLD, *City Bosses in the United States* (Duke University Press, Durham, N. C., 1930).

CHAPTER XVI

GROUP RESEARCH

Sociology as the study of group life and processes is intensely interested in group research. By research it lives and develops. Research is a scientific inquiry into the nature of phenomena and of the laws governing them; group research is the investigation of the underlying processes operative in the lives of persons associated together.

There has been and is a great deal of superficial speculation regarding the nature of human society and its problems. In fact every person indulges at times in common sense observations about social life. Something more is needed, namely, data that are scientifically derived, classified, analyzed, and interpreted. To meet this need social surveys and statistics have developed; social case analysis is in process of developing. Sociological research uses both statistical analysis and case analysis.

Social Surveys

A social survey is the collecting of data concerning the living and working conditions, broadly speaking, of the people in a given community. Social surveys had their origin centuries ago. Piece-meal and isolated work in collecting social data may be found as early perhaps as 3,000 B.C., when according to Herodotus, data were collected concerning the population and wealth of Egypt. William the Conqueror in England in the middle of the eleventh century prepared the *Domesday Book*, which mentions the names of landlords, treats of the customs of the realm, describes the towns and cities, lists the occupations, and gives a census of the people together with references to their economic and social conditions.

More recently Frederick William I of Prussia instituted a
systematic collection of facts relating to population, occupations, and the like. The technique was developed further by
Frederick the Great, who was instrumental in developing a
system for the gathering of facts about nationality, age, deaths,
agriculture, and manufacture. In 1790, the United States
originated the modern census, which through the succeeding
decades has steadily grown in extent and importance.

More intensive social studies were begun with the work of
Captain John Graunt of London, who made the first recorded
analysis of vital statistics, that is, of birth rates, death rates,
marriage rates, and so on. Quetelet, a Belgian astronomer and
statistician, included in his investigations social, moral, and
physical characteristics of man, and arrived at conclusions
which indicated that all types of human acts, especially crime,
suicides, and accidents occur with significant regularity.

Frederic Le Play in the middle of the eighteenth century
became the originator of the modern social survey. He began
with the family as a definite unit for sociological study, and
analyzed income and outlay. He made the family budget the
center of his study, holding that the income and outgo factors
would explain a great deal about the nature of specific families.
If you would know a family ask to see its budget and the interests
of its members will be revealed. In his best known treatise [1] he
presents monographic studies of thirty-six families and gives
data on property, religion, family organization, occupations; he
also contributes to the methodology of the social survey.

Ernst Engel, using some of Le Play's materials and other
data, applied quantitative methods still further and evolved
laws concerning the income and expenditures of workingmen's
families. He supplemented the social survey with basic interpretations of survey data. His main induction was that as the
income of a workingman increases there is about the same increase in expenditures for clothing, rent, fuel, and light; an
excess increase in expenditures for education, recreation, and

[1] *Ouvriers européens* (Paris, 1864).

health; and a lesser increase in expenditures for food. He made other generalizations, for example, that the higher the ratio of expenditures for food the lower the status of the family. Engel applied statistics to social facts and founded one of the first seminars in social statistics.[1]

In England in the latter part of the nineteenth century Charles Booth produced his monumental survey in ten volumes of the living and laboring conditions of working people in East London.[2] In these volumes he gave to the world "a veritable storehouse" of social and economic facts. They show "the numerical relation which poverty, misery, and depravity bear to regular earnings and comparative comfort, and describe the general conditions under which each class lives." Booth's treatise is also a study in cartography, being noteworthy for its colored maps showing the variations in poverty, street by street.

In the United States the "Pittsburgh Survey" which was made in 1907-1908 under the direction of the Russell Sage Foundation, inaugurated the social survey movement in this country. It appeared in six volumes and covered nearly all the main phases of social and economic life. It was followed by surveys of many cities. It represents what is known as the general survey, which includes data concerning housing, health, amusements and recreation, industry, immigrants, schools, churches, welfare institutions, delinquency and crime.

In contrast with the general survey there is the special social survey, which is usually confined to some one special problem, such as housing, health, or welfare agencies. It is possible for a group of citizens to conduct a special survey to good advantage at a small cost, whereas such a group would be unable to complete a general survey. In either case there are four major problems: (1) To secure adequate finances, (2) to obtain the proper investigation for the given community, (3) to conduct

[1] In Berlin, 1852.
[2] *Life and Labor of the People in London* (Macmillan and Company, Ltd., London, 1902-1903).

the survey in a scientific, fearless way without antagonizing weak agencies or anti-social persons to the point where defeat is invited, and (4) to put into effect the findings of the survey.

A survey is made for the same purpose that a business house takes an inventory at stated intervals. In the case of the inventory the factors leading to losses can be discovered and prevented and factors leading to gains can be noted and emphasized. In much the same way a community can discover its disintegrating factors and work out plans of prevention and of increasing the efficiency and number of its constructive elements. More important, upon the basis of extensive social data, sound and far-reaching principles of social advance can be determined.[1]

A wise community will plan to inventory itself not once, but at stated intervals, perhaps every five years. By so doing, a community can determine its wholesome tendencies and the nature of its underlying processes.

The literature on social surveys is twofold: (1) manuals, explaining how to conduct surveys, and (2) reports giving the results of actual surveys. The latter type of documents has become extensive in scope and volume. It furnishes quantities of information for sociological analysis as well as for public distribution and consideration.

Social Statistics

Sociology is interested in quantitative measurement and requires at least an elementary knowledge of social statistics. August Comte, the founder of sociology, insisted at the outset upon a mathematical foundation for sociology. Sociology can go as far as the tools of social research will carry it, particularly those of social statistics and of social case analysis based on the life history applied to human facts.

Social statistics is mathematics applied to human facts. Statistical methods call for objective data that can be counted

[1] For an account of how to conduct a community survey inexpensively see James A. Hodgson, "A Low-Cost Community Survey," *Sociology and Social Research*, March–April, 1934.

or measured in some way. Statistics means that facts when measured by different observers using the same methods will always yield the same results. Social statistics ranges from simple formulae to an understanding of the theories by which these formulae are derived. It includes comprehension of the strong and weak points of various formulae for handling particular types of data.

Social statistics as a basis of sociological research begins with a knowledge of *means*, such as the arithmetic means, or ordinary average, and the weighted means designed to give different values to different units in a series.

There is the *mode*, or prevailing fashion or type; and the *median* or middle item in a series. The *range* is the spread of the items in a series, and the frequency is the number of items that appears in each class of items in a series. Quartiles refer to dividing all the items into four equal sections, and quintiles into five equal parts.

Any series of social items may be *discrete* or *continuous*, according to the data that are being measured. Money in the form of dollars and cents represents a discrete series; the height of persons represents a continuous series. Wages paid employees, the population of a community, the birth rate, and the like, furnish discrete series of data. In each case the base is a definite unit. On the other hand the heights or weights of a number of persons can never be given with complete accuracy in exact units. The base is continuous.

Measures of *dispersion* are important for they show how much the units deviate from the mean, the mode, or the medium. There is the mean variation or deviation which shows what the average deviation of all the items is, for example, from the mean. The standard deviation is a refinement of the mean deviation; it gives greater weight to extreme deviations from the norm.

The *normal frequency curve* [1] depicts the balanced way in which a large number of correlated items ordinarily group themselves.

[1] Sometimes called the biological curve.

At either side the curve drops down to the horizontal base line indicating that at either extreme of a group of data the number of items is very few. In the middle the curve rises to a rounded height, depicting the average and the items nearest the average as being most numerous.

Skewness is the degree that a group of items vary from a normal frequency curve. A frequency curve may be skewed either to the right or to the left, showing not only that the number of items on one side of the mode, for instance, are more numerous than on the other side, but also the degree to which the abnormality takes place.

Correlation is the comparison of two groups of data. One group is measured in terms of the other. If they vary together in the same direction, positive correlation exists. If the price of wheat and of potatoes vary in opposite directions step by step a negative correlation exists. If one varies without similar or an opposite variation in the other then no correlation exists. Perfect correlation is represented by 1.00, while positive or negative correlation is indicated by a plus or a minus number respectively; both are less than 1.00 and both may approach 0. These numbers are known as the coefficients of correlation. The variable that is used as a measure is called the standard variable and the other the relative variable. If variables vary together either in the same or opposite directions it is often assumed that a causal relationship exists between them but this is sometimes a debatable issue.

The *probable error* means that in sampling data some error is bound to occur. If one could measure all the items of a large series such as the total population of the earth, there would be no probable error. If one could measure three-fourths of the population a small error would probably occur, but if one measured only every fifth person, the probable error would be greater. The probable error, therefore, refers to the difference in measurement found between the results for a sample and the results that would occur if a complete canvas were made. It is expressed in terms of both plus and minus, denoting both a plus and minus variation from the ascertained norm. It makes unnecessary the measurement of all the items in a given series.

Sampling is the selecting of a certain percentage of a group of items according to a predetermined plan. The common statistical procedure is called random sampling, that is, choosing not according to personal interest or convenience but impersonally at random. Choosing every fifth item, for example, is random sampling.

Index numbers are base numbers against which to measure changes. The index number serves as a basis for giving at a glance a story of relative values. Wages and prices are often treated in terms of index numbers.

A *questionnaire* is a list of questions given to a number of persons for them to answer. It secures standardized results that can be tabulated and treated statistically. A questionnaire must be worded very carefully, otherwise different persons will interpret it differently and give answers that are not comparable or classifiable. The number of questions on a questionnaire must be kept small, for many people have been "questionnaired to death." The questionnaire is a useful device for gathering considerable data quickly.

A *schedule* is a form of abbreviated questions which the investigator usually keeps himself and fills out as he proceeds with his inquiry. A great deal of classifiable data can be collected on schedules. It is one of the best known techniques for gathering data.

A *scale* is a standard against which to measure unmeasured factors. It is composed "of specimens being measured" that have been arranged in an ascending or descending order. The distance between these specimens is equally spaced as determined by a considerable number of competent judges.[1] The items measured are given values according to the items of the standard against which they are measured.

---

[1] See "The Social Distance Scale" by the writer, *Sociology and Social Research*, XVII: 265–71. This brief article demonstrates how a simple scale may be made.

A *test*, such as the well-known intelligence test, is a quantitative rather than a qualitative measure. The question is: How many problems can a person solve correctly in a given time period? A test must be so difficult that no one can solve all the problems in the allotted time, and yet easy enough so that each person can solve some of the problems. One purpose of a test is to compare the ability of different persons; another, is to measure one person's ability at successive intervals in order to determine whether or not any improvement has occurred.

SOCIAL CASE ANALYSIS

Sociology is seeking new tools of research. Social surveys have not penetrated social problems deeply enough; and social statistics have remained too coldly aloof. Sociology seeks to know attitudes and values, the favorable and unfavorable feeling responses, the nature of social situations, of social conflicts, of assimilation, of adjustments and of reorganization both of personalities and of groups. It investigates subjective materials and tries to make them objective so that they may be scientifically interpreted. It begins with personal experiences and ends in social processes.

Sociology is more interested in the *meanings* of social facts than in social facts themselves. It traces all social data back to human experiences and the reactions to these. It seeks out meanings in order to understand the reasons for social conflicts, the nature of personality, and sound ways of securing personal and social reorganization.

Sociology has a special interest in problems such as these: Why is it that one person reacts in one way to a certain event and another person in the opposite way to the same event? Why is an experience defined or interpreted in one way by one person and reacted to in an entirely different fashion by another person? If these contradictory results are due to differences in the configurations of personalities, then what factors account for the differences in personality configurations? These are but a sample of the problems with which sociology is concerning itself today.

Sociology as a science is developing a real body of concepts. If there can be no science without tools and if concepts are tools then it is important that sociology pay close attention to concepts. Sociological concepts already mount upward into the hundreds.[1] While many of these are of minor importance all lend themselves to the following classification:[2]

1. Ecological (position, natural area, invasion, segregation, succession);
2. Cultural (mores, diffusion, acculturation);
3. Societal (group, community, social situation);
4. Personality (attitudes, values, status);
5. Processual (conflict, accommodation, socialization);
6. Organizational (organization, disorganization, reorganization);
7. Change (mobility, evolution, revolution, progress);
8. Methodological (social statistics, participant observation, interview, life history, social case analysis).

Sociology begins its research by choosing its problems carefully. It tackles these with as few prejudices and biases as possible; it endeavors to eliminate all wishful thinking. At the outset it enters upon a period of exploration, that is, of seeking the best sources of data. The student confers with as many persons as possible who might have had interesting experiences regarding some phase of the specific problem. He inhibits the popular desire to get results quickly, knowing that such a plan will bring superficial findings, and that someone else will be obliged later to do his work all over again. He resists the temptation to go straightway in the most promising direction. In sociological research a period of exploration is required during which the student holds in abeyance the logical procedure and turns aside from beaten paths. He treks about as if he were seeking for hidden clues, inquiring of chance individuals as well as of selected persons, seeking openings to pertinent materials. Exploration thus is both irregular and systematic,

[1] See E. E. Eubank, *The Concepts of Sociology* (D. C. Heath and Company, Boston, 1932).
[2] See the writer's *Contemporary Sociology* (University of Southern California Press, Los Angeles, Second Printing, 1932).

traversing unbeaten paths and uncharted regions as well as the usual channels.

After the preliminary exploration for data is made, the real search begins, and interesting personal experiences are pursued skillfully. Personal experiences are emphasized above all else, for it is experience which gives meaning to anything that we understand or know. Experiences are more than events; they include reactions to events. Experiences determine attitudes of life, and give configuration or shape to personality. They help to determine what a person's reactions will be to all succeeding experiences. They explain why personal disorganization occurs, and how personal reorganization may take place. They make clear why social conflicts arise and continue; they elucidate the processes of social coöperation. They tell the story of how a person defines or interprets any social situation, and why one person defines a situation in one way and another person in an entirely different fashion. To get at the experiences, however, which lie "in the back of people's heads," and to get them out "upon the table" where they can be studied objectively is not easy.

The sociology student may make a survey of a portion of some community or area in which he is interested and treat the results statistically, or he may plough deeper and examine a social situation where conflict or coöperation or both occur, learning the origins and nature of the underlying social processes. If he chooses the latter method he develops the interviewing and life history techniques as tools.[1]

The research student adds the *interview* method to his repertoire, and secures *life histories* and similar materials. These are then treated by the *social case analysis* method. The sociologist uses this interview, life history, and case-analysis technique after he has exhausted the research possibilities of the

[1] At the University of Chicago considerable success has been attained from giving students in sociology beginning with the sophomore level a variety of field study projects. The methods that have been used and the valuable teaching materials that have been developed are ably presented by Vivien M. Palmer in her *Field Studies in Sociology* (University of Chicago Press, 1928).

survey-statistical method. He views the latter as a means of securing as accurate a statement of his problem as possible, and then searches after the meanings of his statistical findings by interviews, life histories, case-analyses. He views statistical analysis and social case analysis as complementary. One is an essential aid to the other. The statistical procedure helps him to locate representative items or units for case-analysis purposes.

The student learns to interview by interviewing, as well as by studying the ways of the research interview. He may also learn much from other types of interviewers, such as the doctor, the lawyer, the detective, the psychiatrist, the social worker, and the newspaper reporter. He takes time, and he moves painstakingly. He does not ask the interviewee for causal explanations but seeks as many antecedent happenings and experiences as possible. The interviewee's explanations are often significant because of the biases and prejudices which they disclose. Sequences and coexistences of experiences are sought first, and interpretations are worked out later.

Experiences are usual or unusual. Of the usual a few representative ones [1] are sufficient. They throw light on what is standard and generally understood. The unusual experiences are often very significant, for they may represent new trends, origins, explanations of different reactions to a given social situation, the bases of misunderstandings, and the like. All unusual experiences should be sought out so long as they throw new light on the problem being studied.

The *life history* is a full account of a person's significant experiences and of his reactions to them in terms of attitudes, given by the person himself. It is a complete document freely stated. Though it be inaccurate at points or warped by faulty remembering it is still valuable, providing it be a bona fide document. The way that a person remembers an experience even though he recalls it inaccurately is highly significant, for his distorted remembrance rather than the event as it actually

[1] Whether they are representative or not may be determined by statistical criteria.

happened explains his present reactions. Not many persons give their life histories accurately, but nearly everyone can be trained.

Letters are often valuable research documents. In the letter to a close friend one is likely to pour out his experiences and his feelings. He is more likely to say what he thinks than when he fills out a questionnaire. He may not make the reservations that he does when being interviewed.[1]

It is important to distinguish between the *opinions* and the *attitudes* of an interviewee. Opinions are less reliable than attitudes, for a person ordinarily expresses opinions freely, but under a test he will act differently and reveal unexpected attitudes. His sequences of acts disclose his attitudes and the processes of their operation, which are the goals that a research person seeks.

Classification and the *forming of new categories* are important sequels to social case analysis. In sociological research one takes each important datum and classifies it, that is, he fits it in at the proper place with the classified knowledge already in stock. He pigeonholes it at the appropriate spot. If, however, a datum does not lend itself to such classification, then it is set aside by itself. If other unique data of the same type of uniqueness are found, a new category of knowledge may be instituted. By classifying a datum it becomes understood; and likewise by building a new category of data it in turn develops a meaning.

Participant observation is a special method of gathering data.[2] According to it the research student takes part in a specific situation or he lives and functions in a given community. In this way he gets the feel of what is going on. He becomes an insider and is admitted to the secrets of the community life.[3] He then retires from the situation and writes out his observations as

[1] E. S. Bogardus, *The New Social Research* (Jesse Ray Miller, Los Angeles, 1926), Ch. VIII.
[2] See E. C. Lindeman, *Social Discovery* (Republic Publishing Company, Inc., New York, 1924), Ch. VII.
[3] See R. S. and H. M. Lynd, *Middletown* (Harcourt, Brace and Company, New York, 1929).

objectively as possible. There are of course varying degrees of participant observation.

There is also *non-participant observation*. The non-participant observant remains aloof, and describes the behavior by time intervals of the observees.[1] The behavior of children has been treated in this way to good advantage. In observing a group of children some are seen to play day after day by themselves, some always seek the company of others, some regularly dominate, others regularly follow, and so on. After a period of observation of this type it is possible to give a significant picture of the attitudes of the observees.[2]

RISE OF SOCIOLOGY

Sociology as the science that has given more attention to group research than has any other has had a fascinating development. During the first half of the nineteenth century scholars began to consider individuals as members of social groups. August Comte, a Frenchman, led the way, developing what he called a positive philosophy,[3] and coining the term sociology about 1838. The second half of the past century saw more activity of a sociological nature. Herbert Spencer in England developed a set of principles of sociology and German and Austrian writers made pioneering contributions of a social philosophical nature. Lester F. Ward, an American paleontologist, wrote his *Dynamic Sociology* (1883)[4] and as a result achieved the title of dean of American sociologists. According to him sociology is the last and highest landing on the staircase of knowledge, or the cap sheaf and crown of any true organization of the sciences.[5]

[1] Dorothy S. Thomas and Associates, *Some New Techniques for Studying Social Behavior* (Teachers College, Columbia University, New York, 1929).

[2] For a current critique of methods of social research see Charles A. Ellwood, *Methods in Sociology* (Duke University Press, Durham, North Carolina, 1933).

[3] See A. Comte, *Positive Philosophy* (tr. by Martineau. Bell and Sons, London, 1913).

[4] D. Appleton and Company, New York, 1911.

[5] L. F. Ward, *Outlines of Sociology* (The Macmillan Company, New York, 1898), p. 20.

The closing decade of the nineteenth century witnessed the introduction of courses in sociology into American universities. Franklin H. Giddings at Columbia University, Albion W. Small at the University of Chicago, and Frank W. Blackmar at the University of Kansas were among the first to inaugurate university courses in sociology.[1]

Sociology is one of several social sciences, and holds a relation to the others paralleling that of psychology. As psychology analyzes mental processes, so sociology analyzes social processes. All the special social sciences rest on an understanding of both mental and of social processes, hence upon both psychology and sociology.

Sociology thus has its own territory of research. As psychology in its study of mental-behavior processes contributes to all the specific social sciences, so sociology in its study of social processes likewise contributes to all social sciences.

Current sociological development is taking a fivefold trend. (1) There is the ecological approach, according to which spatial position and relationships are considered of great importance. Changes in spatial positions and relationships of persons are even more significant.

(2) The cultural approach is also enjoying widespread attention. The culture elements in group life are basic to any other phase of life. They often explain attitudes and conflicts between attitudes. They account for the slowness of real social change; they are the essence of group organization.

(3) The psycho-social phases of group life are perhaps the heart of sociology. They are composed on one hand of personality factors such as attitudes and values, and on the other hand, of group factors, such as social processes and organization. Because of their subjective phases they are especially difficult to study objectively.

(4) Social technology takes sociological data and deductions and works out programs of social reorganization. It originated

---

[1] Dr. Small deserves special mention because of his distinction as the founder and the editor for many years of the *American Journal of Sociology*.

years ago in charitable and philanthropic work which had been based on common sense rather than on scientific sense. It began with ancient and simple methods of helping one's neighbor, and extends today to current scientific efforts to solve human problems. It includes modern social work, social reform, and social amelioration.

(5) Then there is sociological research which is concerned with better methods for securing and interpreting data. It seeks sharper tools for diagnosing personal experiences and social conflicts. It demands a more thoroughgoing technique for analyzing social processes.

(6) Social philosophy, the first phase of sociology to develop, consists of far-swung interpretations of personality and society on the basis of scientifically derived data about these phenomena. It is supported by those sociologists who insist that sociology is more than a mere science, and who are quite dissatisfied with the analytical and piece-meal findings of sociology.

Current sociology is the product of these six lines of development which are now being merged and which are creating a new, distinctive morale along the whole sociological front. Sociology is becoming a tangible, dynamic, scientific study of personal experiences, group phenomena, and social processes.

Sociology is growing more scientific. It is moving away from metaphysics on one hand and from social reform on the other, and concentrating on concrete studies and better methods of research. It is now taking hold of concrete sections of human relationships and analyzing their meanings. It is growing weary of the dogmatism of rationalization and skeptical of that reform which does not first have an adequate comprehension of underlying social processes. There are hundreds of persons ready to turn their hands to reform to one who is able to analyze the deep-seated social processes.

Outstanding in the development of sociology is its growth in the last twenty-five years as *a teaching subject*. It is being accorded an important place in the curriculum of colleges and universities. The teaching of sociology is becoming highly diversified.

(1) The teaching of sociology began in the advanced field of post-graduate university work. It originated in courses in social philosophy and general sociology for mature students. It dealt with theory. It had little unity, for each teacher developed his own system.

(2) In recent years the number of specialized undergraduate courses in sociology, such as those dealing with poverty, delinquency, the family, eugenics, has increased with amazing rapidity. The college is rare indeed which has no course in sociology, some offering ten or twenty, even fifty or sixty courses in those institutions where sociology has been developed extensively. The organization of departments of sociology either as separate units or as a part of a large social science division has gone ahead widely in the United States.

(3) The teaching of the introductory course in college sociology has been developed further than has any other course in the field. More textbooks for this course have been written than for several others combined. Until recently there has not been a great deal of uniformity in these, but now a concensus of treatment is developing.[1]

(4) The high school is slowly being recognized as a field for teaching sociology although not necessarily under that name. An already overcrowded curriculum has opposed the introduction of sociology courses, but sooner or later the need of high school students for sociology whether they go on to college or not will be recognized. Being at an age when individuality asserts itself and when group readjustments are many, high school students especially need to study group life.[2]

(5) Sociology in teachers' colleges is developing belatedly. The teacher needs not only to know subject matter, her pupils as individuals, but also the group life of which her pupils are a product, and also the nature of the group life for which she is fitting her pupils. Primarily the teacher does not simply teach

[1] An excellent symposium of ten articles dealing with the introductory course in sociology will be found in the *Journal of Educational Sociology*, VII: 1–82.
[2] See Read Bain, "High School Sociology," *The High School Teacher*, VII: 134–37, 153–55.

a child a certain subject; she teaches pupils subjects so that they may succeed in group life, not in self-centered ways but for the good of other persons and of groups, and thus for their own highest personality development. Teaching is a process of fitting pupils to become socialized group members in their vocations and in their daily social relationships.

(6) Social studies are being introduced in the grades, especially in the upper grades. The need for them in the lower grades is also great. The teaching of them in the grades is no more difficult than the teaching of elementary mathematics or any other subject. The presentation of social ideas and the development of group responsibility normally begun in the home during the first year of the child's life may well be continued in an organized way by the school when it is entered by the child at the age of five or six years.

By teaching sociology the leaven of socialized thinking can work out into and through all group life. In consequence socialized behavior may develop; social planning can be furthered and a new social order be evolved. Individualized thinking and behaving by itself will ruin society; they need to be balanced by socialized procedures.

Sociology has much of value to offer the student.

(1) Sociology suggests permanently significant concepts regarding human life. It deals with concepts that are the largest dependable terms known to mankind, that pertain to the deepest elements of human nature; and that explain the diversified activities of human beings.

(2) Sociology presents a point of view which is both comprehensive and penetrating. The sociological attitude is that of viewing every social problem objectively and without bias. It seeks neither to prove nor to disprove, but to find out. It is the scientific attitude applied to personal and social problems.

The sociological attitude gives unbiased attention to all sides of any social problem. To meet this standard is not easy even when a person is simply an impartial spectator and has no personal interests involved in the situation; but when one's attitudes and welfare are located on one side or the other of the struggle, it is exceedingly difficult to view all phases of the situation impartially.

(3) Sociology points the way to socialized personalities. It defines both a rich and balanced personality and a dynamic and wholesome group life. It defines standards for a socialized society. It explains the essence of a genuine democracy where a person rules others not primarily for his own gain but for the common weal. Sociology indicates the necessity of overcoming narrow personal prejudices, egoistic ambitions, and class hatreds. Its findings stimulate every person to render a full measure of service to every other person and to the common good.

(4) Sociology balances the age-long emphasis on self-development with concepts of social development; it balances self-culture with social culture. Self-development and -culture are essential but without the controlling influence of socialized attitudes civilization wobbles. Sociology gives to troubled persons as effective a key to the problems of personal and associative life as has yet been made. It lays bare personal chicanery and group trickery; at the same time it depicts the constructive elements of wholesome living.

The development of sociology as a science is reflected in the history of the American Sociological Society.[1] In 1930, this organization rounded out a remarkable quarter-century of history. A study of the annual reports of the Society shows that during its first quarter of century (1) it turned from subjective generalizations toward objective, concrete studies. (2) It has seen general philosophizing give way to specific inquiry. (3) It has shifted from reform to research; and (4) from emphases on applied sociology to ecological, cultural, and psycho-social approaches. (5) It has penetrated beneath social pathology to social process. (6) It has discarded crude tools, such as analogies, for the sharp instruments of statistical pre-

[1] While sociology originated in Europe, and has made progress in China, India, Argentina, Canada, and other parts of the world, its greatest advancement has occurred in the United States.

cision, and for meaningful case-analyses. Altogether, the results have been worthy of sturdy pioneers.[1]

Sociology today is engaged chiefly in the study of social processes. It is making concrete studies of significant social situations and analyzing the changes that are taking place in human relationships. It is discovering the modes of these changes, that is, processes. It searches for the processes that bring about organization, disorganization, and reorganization of both persons and groups.

Sociology is working industriously at the problem of predicting human behavior. The studies that show how behavior can be predicted not only in the mass but even with reference to individual persons are making headway. After all the measure of any science is the degree to which it can predict what is going to happen in its field of research, and the measure of sociology depends upon how far sociology can predict human behavior under given conditions.

PROBLEMS

1. What is the difference between a census and a social survey?
2. How would you go about starting a social survey?
3. Contrast a social survey and a community case history.
4. What is the strength of social statistics?
5. Why is social statistics inadequate?
6. What are the distinctive characteristics of sociological research?
7. Why do personal experience materials have research value?
8. What is an interview guide?
9. How does the interview guide differ from the questionnaire?
10. How does a questionnaire differ from a schedule?
11. What are the merits of a life history?
12. In what ways is sociology a science, and in what ways not?
13. Why has sociology been one of the latest sciences to develop?

[1] Adapted from a " Note " by the author in the *Publication of the American Sociological Society*, XXV: 1, 2 (February, 1931). For an interesting statement of the changes taking place in sociology, see C. H. Cooley, " Now and Then," *Journal of Applied Sociology*, VIII: 259–63. Also see Edward A. Ross, "Watchman, What of the Night? " *Sociology and Social Research*, XVIII:110–14 (November–December, 1933).

14. Why has sociology developed so rapidly as a college study?
15. Why should social science studies have a place in the grades?
16. What is the sociological attitude?
17. What is a socialized attitude?
18. What is a socialized personality?
19. Why is there a need today for sociology?

READINGS

BINGHAM, W., and B. V. MOORE, *How to Interview* (Harper and Brothers, New York, 1931).

BOGARDUS, E. S., *The New Social Research* (Jesse Ray Miller, Los Angeles, 1926).

BURGESS, E. W., "Trend of Sociological Research," *Journal of Applied Sociology*, VIII: 131–40.

DITTMER, C. G., *An Introduction to Social Statistics* (A. W. Shaw Company, Chicago, 1926).

ELLWOOD, CHARLES A., *Methods in Sociology* (Duke University Press, Durham, North Carolina, 1933).

ELMER, M. C., *The Technique of Social Surveys* (Jesse Ray Miller, Los Angeles, 1927).

LUNDBERG, GEORGE A., *Social Research* (Longmans, Green and Company, New York, 1929).

ODUM, H. W., and K. JOCHER, *An Introduction to Social Research* (Henry Holt and Company, New York, 1928).

PALMER, VIVIEN M., *Field Studies in Sociology* (University of Chicago Press, 1928).

RICE, STUART A., editor, *Statistics in Social Studies* (University of Pennsylvania Press, Philadelphia, 1930).

WHITE, R. CLYDE, *Social Statistics* (Harper and Brothers, New York, 1933).

A SOCIOLOGICAL REFERENCE LIBRARY

ANDERSON, NELS, and E. C. LINDEMAN, *Urban Sociology* (Alfred A. Knopf, New York, 1928).

BERNARD, L. L., editor, *The Fields and Methods of Sociology* (Henry Holt and Company, New York, 1934).

BOGARDUS, E. S., *Contemporary Sociology* (University of Southern California Press, Los Angeles, 1931).

——, *A History of Social Thought* (University of Southern California Press, 1929).

CARPENTER, NILES, *The Sociology of City Life* (Longmans, Green and Company, New York, 1931).

CASE, CLARENCE M., *Outlines of Introductory Sociology* (Harcourt, Brace and Company, New York, 1924).

CHAPIN, F. STUART, *Cultural Change* (The Century Company, New York, 1928).

COOLEY, C. H., *Human Nature and the Social Order* (Charles Scribner's Sons, New York, 1922).

——, *Social Process* (Charles Scribner's Sons, New York, 1918).

——, *Social Organization* (Charles Scribner's Sons, New York, 1909).

DAVIE, MAURICE R., *Problems of City Life* (John Wiley and Sons, Inc., New York, 1932).

DAVIS, JEROME, *Contemporary Social Movements* (The Century Company, New York, 1930).

DAWSON, C. A., and A. E. GETTYS, *An Introduction to Sociology* (Ronald Press, Chicago, 1929).

ELLIOTT, MABEL A., and FRANCIS E. MERRILL, *Social Disorganization* (Harper and Brothers, New York, 1934).

ELLWOOD, CHARLES A., *Methods in Sociology* (Duke University Press, Durham, North Carolina, 1933).

——, *Cultural Evolution* (The Century Company, New York, 1927).

——, *The Psychology of Human Society* (D. Appleton and Company, New York, 1925).

GILLETTE, J. M., *Rural Sociology* (The Macmillan Company, New York, 1928).

GILLIN, DITTMER, and COLBERT, *Social Problems* (The Century Company, New York, 1928).

GILLIN, JOHN L., *Social Pathology* (The Century Company, New York, 1933).

——, *Poverty and Dependency* (The Century Company, New York, 1926).

——, *Criminology and Penology* (The Century Company, New York, 1926).

GILLIN, J. L., and F. W. BLACKMAR, *Outlines of Sociology* (The Macmillan Company, New York, 1930).

GOODSELL, WILLYSTINE, *Problems of the Family* (The Century Company, New York, 1928).

GROVES, ERNEST R., *An Introduction to Sociology* (Longmans, Green and Company, New York, 1932, New Revised Edition).

HANKINS, FRANK H., *An Introduction to the Study of Society* (The Macmillan Company, New York, 1928).

HART, HORNELL, *Science of Social Relations* (Henry Holt and Company, New York, 1927).

HAWTHORNE, H. B., *The Sociology of Rural Life* (The Century Company, New York, 1926).

HAYES, E. C., *Sociology* (D. Appleton and Company, New York, 1930).

HAYNES, FRED E., *Criminology* (McGraw-Hill Book Company, Inc., New York, 1930).

HILLER, E. T., *Principles of Sociology* (Harper and Brothers, New York, 1933).

HOUSE, FLOYD N., *The Range of Social Theory* (Henry Holt and Company, New York, 1929).

LUMLEY, FREDERICK E., *Principles of Sociology* (McGraw-Hill Book Company, New York, 1928).

LUNDBERG, BAIN, and ANDERSON, *Trends in American Sociology* (Harper and Brothers, New York, 1929).

MACIVER, R. M., *Society* (Ray Long and Richard R. Smith, Inc., New York, 1931).

MANGOLD, GEORGE B., *Social Pathology* (The Macmillan Company, New York, 1932).

ODUM, H. W., *Man's Quest for Social Guidance* (Henry Holt and Company, New York, 1927).

OSBORN, L. D., and M. H. NEUMEYER, *The Community and Society* (American Book Company, New York, 1933).

PALMER, VIVIEN M., *Field Studies in Sociology* (University of Chicago Press, 1928).

PARK, R. E., and E. W. BURGESS, *Introduction to the Science of Sociology* (University of Chicago Press, 1921).

REINHARDT, JAMES M., and GEORGE R. DAVIES, *Principles and Methods of Sociology* (Prentice-Hall, Inc., New York, 1932).

ROSS, E. A., *Principles of Sociology* (The Century Company, New York, 1930).

SOROKIN, P. A., *Social Mobility* (Harper and Brothers, New York, 1927).

SUTHERLAND, E. H., *Criminology* (J. B. Lippincott Company, Philadelphia, 1924).

TAYLOR, CARL C., *Rural Sociology* (Harper and Brothers, New York, 1933, Revised Edition).

THOMPSON, WARREN S., *Population Problems* (McGraw-Hill Book Company, Inc., New York, 1930).

TODD, A. J., *Theories of Social Progress* (The Macmillan Company, New York, 1918).

WALLIS, WILSON D., *Culture and Progress* (Whittlesey House, McGraw-Hill Book Company, Inc., New York, 1930).

WALLIS, W. D., and M. WILLEY, *Readings in Sociology* (Alfred A. Knopf, New York, 1930).

WISSLER, CLARK, *An Introduction to Social Anthropology* (Henry Holt and Company, New York, 1929).

——, *Man and Culture* (Thomas Y. Crowell Company, New York, 1923).

WOOD, ARTHUR E., *Community Problems* (The Century Company, New York, 1928).

YOUNG, KIMBALL, editor, *Social Attitudes* (Henry Holt and Company, New York, 1931).

INDEX TO PROPER NAMES

INDEX TO TOPICS